How to Do *Everything* with Your

Treo™ 600

How to Do
Everything
with Your

Treo™ 600

Derek Ball
Dayton Foster

McGraw-Hill/Osborne

New York   Chicago   San Francisco   Lisbon
London   Madrid   Mexico City   Milan   New Delhi
San Juan   Seoul   Singapore   Sydney   Toronto

McGraw-Hill/Osborne
2100 Powell Street, 10th Floor
Emeryville, California 94608
U.S.A.

To arrange bulk purchase discounts for sales promotions, premiums, or fund-raisers, please contact **McGraw-Hill**/Osborne at the above address. For information on translations or book distributors outside the U.S.A., please see the International Contact Information page immediately following the index of this book.

How to Do Everything with Your Treo™ 600

1234567890 CUS CUS 01987654

ISBN 0-07-225581-1

Publisher	Brandon A. Nordin
Vice President &	
Associate Publisher	Scott Rogers
Acquisitions Editor	Megg Morin
Project Manager	Betsy Manini
Project Editor	Emily Rader
Acquisitions Coordinator	Agatha Kim
Technical Editor	Michelle White
Copy Editors	Mike McGee
	Judy Wilson
	Emily Rader
Proofreaders	Paul Medoff
	Judy Wilson
Indexer	Jack Lewis
Composition	International Typesetting and Composition
Illustrator	International Typesetting and Composition
Series Design	Mickey Galicia
Cover Series Design	Dodie Shoemaker

This book was composed with Corel VENTURA™ Publisher.

Dedication

For Devon, the newest of my muses. May your life be full
of wonder, amazement, and happiness. Love, Dad.

—Derek

For my wife Kate, and for Derek—your friendship, support,
and guidance over the years mean more to me than you know.

—Dayton

About the Authors

Derek Ball is President and CEO of Sonic Mobility, Inc. (www.sonicmobility.com), a company focused on delivering solutions for handheld wireless devices such as the Treo 600. Derek has published ten other books on technology topics and has traveled the world speaking at conferences and seminars on emerging technology. In between trips, Derek lives in Calgary, Alberta with his wife, Lesley; daughters Jamie, Carly, and Devon; and golden retriever, Casey.

Dayton Foster is VP of R & D for Sonic Mobility, Inc. Dayton has extensive experience with all aspects of mobile devices including the Treo 600. He currently lives in Calgary, Alberta with his wife, Kate.

About the Technical Reviewer

Michelle White is a Senior Product Manager at palmOne and was the lead Product Manager for the Treo 600. She has spent nearly half her career in the handheld and smartphone industry and was responsible for the IBM WorkPad line of handhelds at Palm Inc., Handspring Visor, Visor Platinum, Visor Edge, Treo 90, and most recently the Treo 600.

Contents at a Glance

Part IV   Appendixes

Contents

Foreword

I am delighted to be able to introduce you to *How to Do Everything with Your Treo 600*. I had the pleasure and privilege to witness up close the development by Handspring of the devices leading up to the 600 and then, ultimately, the launch and phenomenal success of the Treo 600. As I write this foreword, a leading analyst has just raised the rating of palmOne stock based on the great demand for this leading-edge product. This book will help you understand what all the fuss is about and help you make full use of this incredible product and all of its capability.

I served on the Board of Directors of Handspring from the early days of the company. The founders of Handspring—Donna Dubinsky, Jeff Hawkins, and Ed Colligan—were also the team that developed and launched the original PalmPilot. Handspring's founding innovation was a Palm OS–based handheld computer, the Visor, which included the Springboard expansion slot. One of the breakthrough expansion products designed for the Visor was called VisorPhone. The exciting part of VisorPhone was the software developed by Handspring to provide the telephone functionality and, even more importantly, to integrate the phone functions with the personal information management software—the Contacts list, for example. The ability to dial directly from the Contacts with a minimum of keystrokes and to see the name of any of those contacts on an incoming call were real breakthroughs that hadn't been seen before.

Although VisorPhone was a real innovation, its form factor was just too unwieldy. But the enthusiastic response of users inspired Jeff Hawkins and the Handspring design team to create an entirely new product—a handheld organizer where the phone was designed into the hardware and software from the start. The first product in the new design was the Treo 180, a unit with a clamshell cover and, for the first time in the "smartphone" world, a keyboard. The 180 was not only an organizer and mobile phone, it was also a data communications device with software that enabled the user to send and receive e-mail and connect to personal and corporate e-mail systems. At the time of the 180 launch, I was carrying three devices—a Blackberry for e-mail, a mobile phone, and a Visor PDA. I was able to discard all three devices and carry only the Treo that did everything! The 180 was certainly another breakthrough, but it took the next models, the Treo 270 and 300, to really take off.

I still remember going to Board meetings and seeing Jeff and Donna and Ed present mock-up designs of a device that would do everything the earlier Treos did, but in a form factor that was no larger than a regular cell phone. We were all skeptical that it could be done, but sure enough the Treo 600 began to take shape steadily. I still remember the excitement we all felt when we got to hold the first preproduction models. The screen was the brightest and most readable we'd ever seen. The device somehow had been sculpted to fit perfectly into the hand. It looked great and felt perfect. It had once seemed impossible to fit a useable keyboard into a handheld shaped like a phone, but somehow the team had done it. At last, the Treo 600 had arrived. It was greeted with rave reviews, and even now no other product has been able to top it. Demand exceeds supply, and you see the 600s everywhere in the hands of the "cool" crowd.

So, what's up with this book? From my personal experience and talking to other regular Treo 600 owners, we are all still finding capabilities of this amazing product that we hadn't known about before. There are all kinds of cool shortcuts to make the 600 do amazing things. Because the Treo 600 is a Palm OS–based device, there are thousands of programs available to enhance the core functions of the 600 or to run other kinds of applications, games, or communications programs. There are web sites optimized for the Treo and everything from e-mail to instant messaging programs. Until now, getting to learn all of this world of information has been a hit-or-miss process of exploration. The user manual covers the basics but can't begin to scratch the surface of everything you can do. There are several web sites that provide information and discussion groups, but you have to really hunt to find what you need. What the Treo 600 world has needed is an expert guide that would lead directly to what we needed to know.

This, then, is the book you hold in your hands. Not only was I around for the development of the Treo 600, I've known the coauthor of this book, Derek Ball, for a long time. I was the founder and CEO of a company called Powersoft in the early 90s, and we had a very successful development tool for Windows called PowerBuilder. Derek Ball was the author of several very successful, definitive books that helped thousands of programmers make the most of PowerBuilder. He's not just really smart, he has the knack of explaining subjects that are sometimes complicated and making them easily understood by all. Dayton Foster adds tremendous enthusiasm and knowledge to the project also, and that combination of know-how and enthusiasm make a great team.

I know when you're through with this book, Derek and Dayton will have you as enthusiastic about your Treo 600 as I've been. In fact, I'm looking forward to learning some new things from them myself. Enjoy the book and the Treo 600!

Mitchell Kertzman
Partner
Hummer Winblad Venture Partners

Acknowledgments

Writers are a strange lot. Technical writers perhaps even more so. We have had the tremendous opportunity (curse?) to embark upon several book projects in the past. However, as is typical with "selective memory," we often forget what a monumental effort it actually takes to complete a book, not only on the part of the authors, but of all the other people who are involved in the project and without whom a book would ever see the light of the sun through the bookstore window.

First of all, we want to thank you, the reader. We hope that with this book we can deliver to you information which will help enhance your mobile lifestyle!

There are a great many people we would like to thank who have contributed to this book, but thanks hardly seem to be enough. Megg Morin at McGraw-Hill/Osborne has worked on three of our books with us and has consistently been amazing. From the initial book proposal through the writing, editing, and delivering of all the elements of the book, Megg had to deal with our ins and outs and ups and downs. Megg, you are great to work with and have added an incredible amount of value to this book, as well as all of our previous efforts. We look forward to future projects together!

Special thanks also need to be extended to Agatha Kim for acquisitions coordination; Emily Rader for project management; and Mike McGee, Judy Wilson, and Emily Rader for copy editing this book with skill and finesse. Thank you!

Our technical editor, Michelle White, has been invaluable in making sure our information is as accurate and up-to-date as possible. Thank you, Michelle, for helping to ensure the quality of this book, and for all of your suggestions and recommendations, which have greatly improved the value of this book for the reader.

There are many other individuals behind the scenes involved in the production of the book whose names we may not know but whose contribution to delivering this book into the reader's hands is no less significant. Your efforts are also appreciated.

And finally, to our wives, and kids (for Derek), who have put up with late nights and family activities we couldn't go to, for encouraging and supporting us through this process. Your love and support made all of this possible. Our deepest gratitude and love.

Introduction

When U.S. Robotics introduced the first PalmPilot to the world, it began a revolution that would see millions of mobile computing devices in the hands of everyday people. The latest in that extended family, the Treo 600, has extended that to new extremes.

This remarkable device contains so much power that mobile individuals can now do things never before possible with a PDA. Beyond simple contact and calendar management, now people can send and receive e-mail, write documents, build spreadsheets, make presentations, surf the Internet, and so much more, all from a device that easily slips into a pocket.

The recent merger of Palm Inc. with Handspring to create palmOne promises a future of even more powerful, flexible, and portable devices. The future of the Treo continues to grow more and more interesting as the power and battery life of these devices grow, and yet they become smaller and more portable—and with the introduction of integrated wireless technology, more connected! More and more people are adopting this device and integrating it into their mobile lifestyles.

Who Should Read This Book

This book is intended for all Treo 600 owners. If you're a new Treo 600 owner, this book will help you understand how to get started using your new Treo properly. For the owner who has had a Treo for a while, this book will help you understand how to get more out of your investment.

Whatever your level of experience with the Treo, you will find relevant information in this book to do things with your Treo that you haven't done before.

You can follow along with the information in this book as it walks you through using built-in applications such as Word To Go and Sheet To Go. In other sections of the book, you will find opportunities to read about the potential of the Treo and future devices, and perhaps you will choose to integrate Global Positioning System (GPS) or wireless connectivity into your mobility.

How This Book Is Organized

We have organized this book in sections to enable you to jump right into the area that is most relevant to you. Part I, "Meet Your Treo 600," introduces you to the basic setup of your Treo and also explains how to use the powerful built-in software that comes with it. You will learn how to get connected with voice, messaging, e-mail, and the Internet.

Part II, "Maximize the Capabilities of Your Treo," switches the focus to more advanced topics such as device security, performing mobile presentations, working with documents and spreadsheets, and using Global Positioning Systems for personal navigation. Part III, "Select Essential Hardware Accessories and Software for Your Treo," shows you what kind of external devices you can use to expand the functionality of your Treo and how to use the myriad third-party products designed to increase the storage of your Treo 600, turn your Treo 600 into a navigational tool, and more. The appendixes of the book are there to help you troubleshoot some common problems with the Treo 600, as well as point you to other resources that you might want to investigate for more information on your device.

As you read through the text, you'll see we've included sidebars for points of specific interest, so watch for the sections labeled "How To" and "Did You Know?," as well as Cautions, Notes, and Tips for special information about the section you are currently reading.

We hope that you will find this book helpful as you learn to live the mobile Treo lifestyle! We use our Treos on a daily basis, and they have almost become extensions of our arms. Our most critical information is never more than a moment away, and we can consolidate many disparate information sources into one location. Your Treo 600 can become as important a productivity tool for you as it is for us. We use it to find our way around foreign cities when we travel, give presentations while on the road, wirelessly stay connected to the office to manage our infrastructure and data, send and receive e-mail, and so much more!

If you would like to contact the authors or have questions about your Treo 600, please contact us by e-mail at treo600@telus.net.

Part I

Meet Your Treo 600

Chapter 1

The Treo 600… Not Just Another Palm!

How to...

- ■ Live the mobile lifestyle
- ■ Live with less paper

Ever since we human beings learned to store information somewhere other than in our heads, we have been working on ways not only to make permanent records of our information but also to take those records with us, wherever we go. Over many millennia, this pursuit has taken us from crude paintings on cave walls, to hieroglyphics on stone tablets, to papyrus, to the printing press, to the day planner, and now to the personal digital assistant (PDA).

No longer are we are satisfied to simply carry our information with us. We are pushing for a new era of portable information. We want our PDAs to do more than was even hinted at by early science fiction writers and television shows like "Star Trek." More than ever, we want our devices to become an extension of ourselves, to function as a personal secretary, travel agent, guide, doctor, communicator, and entertainment device.

Palm has been, by far, the most successful in selling PDAs. In fact, Palm PDAs have been so successful that many people refer to any handheld computer as a "Palm," much the same way people use the brand name Kleenex to refer to facial tissue and Xerox to refer to a photocopy.

Recently, many people have been interested in the idea of a device that would merge their cell phone and PDA into a single unit. In response to this market, companies have developed a variety of devices running a variety of operating systems; however, most of these devices have met with limited success. In general, manufacturers took one of two approaches in the endeavor to create a combined cell phone–PDA device. The first approach was to take their existing PDA platform and essentially glue a cellular phone to it. This was less than successful, as evidenced by the low adoption rates of the dozen or so products that took this approach. The second approach was to take a compact cell phone and give it a tiny screen as well as the ability to hold some contacts and do e-mail (as if you could ever truly do e-mail on a keyboard with only nine buttons!).

These two approaches left users very dissatisfied. The end results were too bulky, had poor battery life, inadequate screens, or lacked the necessary input capability to be truly useful.

Leaping into the raging river of this opportunity is the Treo 600. It is actually the fourth in the series of Treo devices from Handspring (recently merged with Palm,

Inc. to form palmOne), but it is the first to truly meet the needs of the end user and deliver mass market appeal and functionality. With its sleek compact styling, powerful Texas Instruments OMAP processor, abundant memory, and ultra bright and clear touch screen, this device sports an adoption rate unlike any Palm device in recent history. It is a convenient size, so average cell phone users who switch to the Treo 600 don't feel like they are carrying around and speaking into a brick, yet Handspring didn't make the mistake of making it too small. There is an ample full-color screen and a full QWERTY keyboard for thumb typing.

The Treo 600 proved to be so popular that currently it is hard to find the unit on store shelves, although increased production as a result of the Palm merger with Handspring should remedy this problem by the time this book hits the shelves.

The Treo comes in many flavors, supporting both CDMA (Code Division Multiple Access) and GSM (Global System for Mobile Communications) wireless networks, and is often customized as part of the deal with the carrier, or wireless service provider, that is offering the device to its subscribers. For example, both Sprint and Orange offer versions of the Treo 600 that have been customized from the standard model, as you can see in Figure 1-1.

FIGURE 1-1   The Treo 600 is available in slightly different configurations from many different vendors.

It used to be that a PDA was more of a status symbol than a truly practical tool, but that is changing as the PDA converges with the mobile cellular phone. The latest release of the Palm OS, the operating system that powers the Treo 600, is well suited to performing not only the job of a PDA but also that of a true communications tool—handling e-mail, phone calls, voice mail, and Short Message Service (SMS) and Multimedia Message Service (MMS) communication.

The History of Palm and the Palm OS

The lineage that precedes the Treo 600 is long and interesting. Without going into too much depth, it can be useful to understand the quantity and quality of engineering that lead up to the leading-edge device you now hold in your hands.

The first successfully commercialized version of what has now commonly become known as the PDA was developed not by Palm, but by Apple. This device was called the Newton, and it featured a touch screen with built-in, space-age handwriting recognition. Unfortunately for Apple, the device was a total flop. Technologists and venture capitalists alike described the PDA market as not being viable.

Luckily for us, Jeff Hawkins didn't agree with them. He first had the idea for his portable computing platform about the same time that the Apple Newton was breaking up on the rocks. He shopped his idea around but was unable to find anyone who would back it. Finally, some risk-taking visionaries at U.S. Robotics got behind Hawkins' project, and the first U.S. Robotics PalmPilot was born. The device had limited functionality, particularly in comparison to today's mobile powerhouses, but it struck a cord with both the technology early adopters and also the all-important executive crowd. The PalmPilot took root and flourished.

U.S. Robotics was acquired by 3COM, which later spun off Palm as its own company. By this time, although there were a few other players, none were achieving the market success of Palm. Microsoft's first entry into the mobile computing space, Windows CE 1.0, was a complete disaster and was generally rejected by consumers. This would not be Microsoft's final challenge to Palm, as the future would show.

By this time Palm had achieved a tremendous milestone. Independent software developers who had been diligently working and deploying software for this mobile miracle had now produced, in aggregate, over 10,000 software applications for the Palm platform. This was very important because no one buys a computer that doesn't have software. With software galore to choose from, Palm owners could count on finding software to help them manage their wine cellars, fly their airplanes, record home inspection data, or just about any hobby or occupation.

Then Palm hit some challenging times. The future vision that Jeff Hawkins had for the Palm line differed from that of the Palm management team. Jeff Hawkins left

Palm to found Handspring, a new mobile hardware platform that would license and use the Palm Operating System (Palm OS).

With its expandability, the Handspring Visor was a leap away from the current Palm hardware. It featured a "Springboard" slot that allowed the user to plug in external expansion modules to turn the Visor into a pager, a bar code scanner, and much more. In fact, this Springboard expansion module was where Handspring first cut its teeth with a GSM phone expansion called the VisorPhone, shown in Figure 1-2. Hawkins' vision extended beyond just plug-in expansion slots. He saw the day when the PDA would merge with your mobile phone to allow you to carry one device instead of two. This was radically different from the vision at Palm, which was to deliver more powerful, but not connected, PDA devices.

Handspring's next-generation devices were called Treo. The first Treos were, as many groundbreaking devices are, not warmly embraced by the targeted end buyers of the devices. The devices were bulky, with a flip-top cover that was inconvenient for answering calls. Consumers told Handspring that they liked the idea, but the implementation was not up to their expectations. Handspring went back to the drawing board and in late 2003 produced the Treo 600 device. This device took all of the feedback from the earlier generations of devices and delivered it in a single, well engineered, full-featured package.

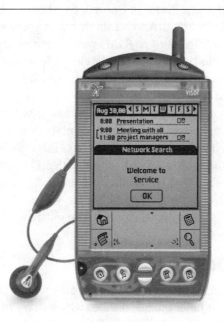

FIGURE 1-2   Handspring's first attempt at delivering a telephone on its platform was the VisorPhone.

You might think this is the end of our story (or at least so far), but it isn't. Back at Palm, the company was struggling. The world had told Palm that the market for PDAs that weren't "connected" and able to get data in real time was shrinking. Palm attempted to respond with a new generation of devices, which contained local wireless networking (802.11, or Wi-Fi), and the Tungsten W, a Palm PDA that with a plug-in ear bud could work as a phone. While Handspring was busy hitting the target with their second shot, Palm was shooting wide and missing the target completely with the Tungsten W.

Next came the big surprise. Palm was going to acquire Handspring and bring back into the fold the talent and vision that previously it had lost. Palm spun its operating system division out as a new company called PalmSource and merged Handspring and Palm together into a new company called palmOne. Suddenly Palm's future seemed very bright, with the best-selling PDA platform and the market's hottest converged *smartphone* (the name for a combined cellular phone and PDA device) back under one roof all running the Palm OS.

As Palm was getting well positioned for the future, Palm's rivals were not sitting still. Microsoft had been very busy revising and improving its Windows CE product into a more viable platform. The latest release, called Windows Mobile 2003, is now center stage in high-quality mobile products produced by HP, Toshiba, Dell, and many others. Microsoft has also introduced its competing platform for smartphones, called Microsoft Smartphone 2003. In Europe, Symbian took a commanding lead in the connected-device market. And while this was going on, a small Canadian company called Research In Motion (RIM) was becoming the dominant vendor in selling wireless connected e-mail mobile devices ("connected" meaning devices that continually send and receive e-mail through the wireless connection without having to be synced) to large corporate buyers.

As the future becomes the present, these four vendors will battle for market share. For a very long time, there will be a variety of platforms to choose from, which, for the consumer, will help to keep prices low and innovation high. Palm has the largest foundation of the four vendors to work with and has a tremendous base of loyal customers. The Treo 600 is, without a doubt, one of the leading converged devices on the market today. As a Treo 600 owner, you can be comfortable that you have a well-developed piece of hardware with an outstanding pedigree.

Treo vs. Other Devices

Now that you are a proud owner of a shiny Treo 600, you might find yourself being approached by owners of other mobile devices who will try to engage you in debate about your device vs. their own. To compare one mobile device to another is to tread into the arena of religion for many PDA users and can be dangerous territory for any author. That being said, we offer a brief comparison here of some of the devices.

Treo 600 vs. Other Palms

Palm is not the only company that uses the Palm OS. In addition to the variety of devices in the Palm lineup, there are many third-party licensees, including Sony, Symbol, IBM, Samsung, and Kyocera. The key differentiator between the Treo 600 and other Palm-based devices is the Treo's focus on being a phone and communications tool. High-end Palm devices like the Tungsten T2, from Palm, and the CLIÉ, from Sony, feature much more advanced screens and more powerful processors than the Treo and thus can perform more intensive number crunching and multimedia capabilities. However, as communications tools, they pale in comparison to the Treo, whose phone and data connectivity is a core component of the system.

There are other mobile phones that feature a Palm OS, such as those offered by Kyocera and Samsung, but they are literally cell phones "glued" onto a Palm handheld with very little integration between the phone and the PDA. They tend to be bulky and to be poor communications tools.

Treo 600 vs. the Microsoft Pocket PC Phone Edition

The closest offerings to the Treo from the Microsoft side of the fence include the Pocket PC Phone Edition (sold by various vendors under different names, including XDA, MDA, and Siemens SX56), and integrated phone–MS Pocket PC offerings from Audiovox, Toshiba, Samsung, and others. (Newer versions of the Pocket PC platform software are called Windows Mobile 2003.)

These units are, in general, more bulky than the Treo and have a shorter battery life. They often feature more powerful processors and higher screen resolutions, which can improve software that is processor intensive (like video) or requires more display area (like spreadsheets), but this rarely impacts the core usability of the device and has a negative impact on the battery life.

The Pocket PC units generally have more available user memory than the Treo 600; however, the availability of the Secure Digital (SD) expansion slots on both devices makes extra memory easily available if you find that you require more.

You may find some Pocket PC enthusiasts talking up the multitasking capabilities of their units. The ability for the processor to work on more than one task at a time is an important feature of the mobile environment. Current versions of the Palm OS support only limited multitasking, and this can place some limits on using the tools as connected devices, particularly if you need to connect to your office network using a virtual private network (VPN). The VPN software must run in the background while you are doing other tasks. This has been addressed partially on the Treo, which runs Palm OS 5.2. You can successfully run software, such as a VPN, on these units, as well as have some programs run in the background (for example, e-mail syncing and MP3 players). PalmSource has promised a new operating system, called Palm OS 6.0, which will fully support multitasking. Future devices in the Treo family will likely run this upgraded operating system when it is available, but the current devices should meet your needs, as they can successfully handle the essential tasks such as VPN connectivity and e-mail syncing.

Multitasking, the ability for the PDA to actually be running two or more programs at the same time, can become an extremely valuable feature as you learn to expand your PDA experience beyond the basic built-in applications. For example, with multitasking, you can connect to your wireless provider and download your e-mail in the background while surfing the Web and pasting information from a web site into your mobile word processing application. This complex activity isn't possible on the majority of the Palms currently in circulation. PalmSource's latest OS 5.2 release is technically capable of multitasking, but the company licensed the technology from a third party and is expressly forbidden as part of the agreement from exposing the multitasking capabilities to developers.

Applications

There are two categories of applications for Treo: those that come with your device and those that are provided by third parties. A number of applications come bundled with your device, including contact management, e-mail, notes, To Do lists, and calendaring software. Whether you prefer these built-in applications or third-party products will usually depend on what you used before you turned to your smartphone device.

The Treo 600 also comes standard with many other applications, including a read-only version of Documents To Go for viewing Microsoft Word and Excel documents. There is also software for viewing PowerPoint files on your smartphone, but that is not included as part of the standard offering and must be purchased separately. At a minimum, these applications allow easy access to your existing files or to file attachments that arrive in your e-mail Inbox. Also, depending on which carrier you purchased your Treo 600 from, you may find some other software goodies preinstalled on your device or on its companion CD. For example, the Treo 600 available in Italy comes with QuickOffice Premier software for working with Microsoft Office files created on your desktop with Word and Excel.

Where the Palm platform really shines is in the variety of software designed for it; more than 10,000 third-party applications are currently available for the Palm. In contrast, there are less than half that many applications currently available for the Pocket PC platform. The large number of Palm applications is a direct result of Palm's early ability to grab market share and, concomitantly, Windows CE's previous inability to achieve significant market penetration. This advantage of Palm is slowly decreasing, however, as other platforms such as Microsoft and Symbian are making inroads into Palm-dominated territory.

Expandability

It is important with any mobile computing platform to be able to make it do more than it does out of the box. Expandability of such a device can come through a variety of physical or wireless connections to storage devices or peripherals.

The Treo 600 can currently be expanded through one of two standards. The most common expansion technique is through Secure Digital (SD) cards. The SD card is a very economical and efficient expansion option weighing in at the size of a postage stamp. The Treo 600 sports an SD expansion slot on the top of the device. The small card in the slot when you receive the Treo is a "blank" and doesn't serve any purpose except to keep the dust out of the slot when there is no card inserted.

The second expandability option for the Treo 600 is through the sync/charge port at the bottom of the device. This port is a serial port that can be used to connect your Treo to a variety of devices such as Global Positioning System (GPS) navigation units (discussed in detail in Chapter 14).

This is very comparable to the expandability options of other devices, with one notable exception. Many of the higher-end devices from non-Palm manufacturers feature built-in support for Bluetooth wireless connectivity. What Bluetooth does is allow you to connect wirelessly over a very short distance (usually less than 30 feet) to accessories. The most common uses for Bluetooth are for wireless headsets for speaking on the phone or listening to music and also for connecting to GPS receivers for navigation. Although the current models of Treo do not support Bluetooth, you will soon be able to add it through an SD card; however, this is very limiting because you cannot have two SD cards inserted at the same time. This makes Bluetooth GPS impractical on the Treo because there is no external storage for your GPS maps. Hopefully, future versions of Treo will include Bluetooth support.

The Bottom Line

The Treo 600 device is an ideal blend of portability and power. Its compact size, combined with a large, full-color screen and quality voice telephone, has made this one of the hottest smartphones on the market today. The devices are flying off the shelves at an unprecedented rate. The fact that Palm OS drives the Treo 600 means you can run many of the over 10,000 software titles currently available for the Palm platform, giving you immediate access to an amazing portfolio of applications.

With the Treo 600, you can now perform functions that were literally the realm of "Star Trek" until recently—real-time communication (including voice, e-mail, and instant messaging) and digital photography. The Treo 600 offers one of the first truly usable "converged" devices.

The Treo Family

This book is focused specifically on the Treo 600 smartphone device from palmOne. However, there are other devices produced by Handspring prior to the palmOne merger that also carry the Treo moniker. Here is a short pedigree of the roots of the Treo 600.

Treo 180

Handspring's first converged PDA cell phone was the Treo 180. This wasn't the first Handspring phone—the VisorPhone was, but it was the first one that had the cell phone integrated, which is where we will begin. It featured the Palm OS version 3.5, and the address book was conveniently renamed the Phone Book. It featured an integrated flip-top cover, as shown in Figure 1-3.

When the flip-top cover was opened, the Treo 180 would automatically turn the PDA on and open the phone book for you to select a contact to call.

This unit could only pick up e-mail or perform data functions by dialing the Internet like a modem and could manage only minimal data speeds. As such, it was more like the Kyocera and Samsung combined PDA and cell phones. This device was actually produced in two formats. The first format had a standard Graffiti handwriting recognition area and no keyboard. The second format had a small built-in keyboard without the Graffiti entry area. The latter was the winner, and it became the standard for future Treo devices. Even with that, the sales volumes of the Treo were only a shadow of what the Treo 600 is achieving currently.

FIGURE 1-3   The Treo 180 was the first Handspring device to feature an integrated mobile phone.

Treo 270

Just like successive generations of the Wright brothers' first airplane, which soared only a short distance, time and engineering effort has allowed successive generations of Treo devices to grow into much more. The Treo 270 featured a full-color screen and was the first Treo to take advantage of General Packet Radio Service (GPRS) to provide continuous data connectivity (often referred to as "always-on" connectivity) and therefore constant access to e-mail. For the first time, you really could treat the Treo as a universal communicator. In reviews, it was often compared to the communicator that Captain Kirk used on "Star Trek." The flip-top cover seemed to be an obvious effort to replicate that space-age device. It was still, however, a larger device than what the general consumer wanted to carry around, and, although it was adopted by technology innovators, it never successfully penetrated the main stream.

Treo 300

Next came the Treo 300, which ran on the Sprint PCS network. It was very similar to the Treo 270, but the advanced PCS (Personal Communications Services) network allowed for even tighter integration of data functions. It was virtually feature-identical to the Treo 270, with 2.5 hours of talk time and over 150 hours of standby time—a convenient feature, depending on how much you used the functions of the Palm organizer.

All of these devices had a common complaint: they were too big to be carried as your every day cell phone. The idea was solid, but the mass market of cell phone buyers weren't buying them, and it was a little early for business executives to be seeking mobile e-mail and web browsing. But the stage was set, and the next model, the Treo 600, hit the market right at the leading edge of demand for mobile connected wireless devices.

Adopt the Mobile Lifestyle with Your Treo 600

As PDAs have become more popular, many people seem to be carrying them around in their briefcases or pockets, and yet it is amazing that many people also still carry around paper-based day planners and business card files or keep that trusty paper phone book by the telephone (although it always seems to have been moved by someone when you need it most).

In order to get the most out of your smartphone device, it is important to adopt habits that will centralize all of your information in your device. For example, you will never make effective use of your smartphone if you keep some of your appointments in a paper calendar and some in your Treo.

The fact that the Treo 600 is also your cell phone makes it a little easier to have it with you all the time. Many people are already conditioned to carry their cell phones with them everywhere they go, so substituting the Treo 600 for your cell phone is the easiest habit to adopt.

Tips for Adopting the Mobile Lifestyle

Here are some suggestions to help you integrate your smartphone device into your life:

■ Pick one point in the day, usually at the very beginning or very end of the day, entering any business cards that you have picked up into your Outlook Contacts folder or Palm Desktop. This will keep your Treo 600 business contacts completely up-to-date through the HotSync process. (See Chapter 3 for more on HotSync.) Then you can discard the business cards, or, if you feel compelled to keep them, you can place them in a binder to be kept in your office. (Being an old-world guy who has trouble parting with the attractive cards, I keep mine in binders in my office, but I reference them electronically.)

■ Whenever someone gives you personal contact information such as a phone number, resist the urge to scribble it on a piece of paper and stuff it in your pocket or briefcase. We all have drawers of unidentifiable scribbled phone numbers that aren't of much use. These scraps of paper also don't tend to be in your hand when you need to call that person back. Instead, take the extra 45 seconds to put that person's information into your Treo 600. Then it will be permanently preserved and available to you any time you need it. Also, this information will be backed up on your computer the next time you HotSync your Treo.

■ When you book an appointment or plan an event, even in the distant future, always enter the event into your smartphone calendar immediately. If you do this consistently, you will learn to trust the calendar in your Treo 600. If you aren't consistent, you will find yourself missing appointments or double-booking as you try to organize yourself with both a paper system (or worse, your memory) and a Treo 600.

■ If you use your Treo for expense management, use the same diligent technique of entering all your receipts or financial information into your financial management system once a day. You will find more information on useful financial software in Chapter 12.

■ Whenever you think of something you need to do, be it personal or professional, instead of "making a mental note," put it into your Tasks application on your Treo 600. You can categorize it, prioritize it, and assign a date to it.

■ Every morning when you get up, look at your calendar and To Do list. If there is something that you know is happening that day that isn't in your calendar, enter it. If there is something you need to get done that day, put it on your task list. Not only does this help to keep track of your tasks and appointments, it helps you to feel that you've accomplished something when you look back on your day. Instead of that "where did the day go, and did I actually get anything done?" feeling that sometimes comes at the end of the day, you will be able to look at your list and see at a glance all the activities and tasks that you knocked off.

■ When a special event occurs, such as a birthday or anniversary, record it in your calendar as a recurring event. That way your Treo will become a true personal assistant by reminding you to make a dinner appointment or pick up a gift well in advance of the date!

■ Try to find things that you are already doing that you might be able to do better with the Treo 600. For example, I work out at the gym regularly and am an avid runner. I use third-party software to help me track my workouts and fitness goals. If you are watching what you eat, check out the diet and nutrition software that is available for the Treo. And if you are an avid wine connoisseur, you can load up databases of different wines, and so on. The amount of software available for the Treo is truly impressive.

Keep Your Treo with You

Making the best use of your Treo also means that you need to keep it with you as you live out your mobile life. The Treo, although small and lightweight, isn't quite small enough to slip into your shirt pocket or the back pocket of your pants like a wallet. It also isn't as small as the tiny mobile cellular phones that are popular these days. However, if you are accustomed to carrying your mobile phone clipped to your belt or in you briefcase, then establishing the habit of keeping your Treo with you shouldn't be difficult.

Your Treo weighs less than a conventional portable CD player and is as easy to carry with you. In fact, you will probably find your Treo works as well or better than your CD player while you run, work out, or perform any such activities. What's more, with MP3 (a popular audio file format) files, you will never again experience that annoying skipping that even the very best "skip-free" CD players are prone to.

For casual walking around, cargo pants with the side pockets can be very useful places for storing your Treo. For more of a business casual appearance, Dockers has released a line of casual pants called "Mobile Pants," which contain a special pocket for holding your Treo. This idea is a good one; unfortunately, Dockers' execution wasn't great. The pocket is a little small. It is possible to squeeze in the Treo, but it can be a little hard to retrieve in a hurry when your phone rings (or vibrates, which presents a whole new social problem). Unless you are standing at just the right angle, the bulge of the Treo is still obvious, and don't you dare sit down! Dockers has the right idea; hopefully, other clothing manufacturers will actually try putting a Treo into the pocket and using it before they tout their clothing as "Mobile" wear! For the business executive, the Treo fits extremely well into the pocket of a suit or sports coat.

One popular method for carrying the Treo is to use the supplied hip holster or to get a third-party case with a belt clip. In Chapter 16, we reference case vendors that provide high-quality cases for your Treo 600.

There are other carrying methods as well, such as the secret agent–style under-the-jacket holster or the multipocketed vest. One of the vests specifically targeted to the PDA owner is the SCOTTeVest (www.scottevest.com). It is a lightweight water-repellent vest that looks rather like a safari vest. It is loaded with pockets for all your wireless toys and has a unique feature: Velcro-enclosed conduits to hold all the wires that connect your devices together and keep the cords tucked safely away. They call this a personal area network, or PAN. The vest isn't something that you could wear to a business function; and for personal recreational wear, the $160 price tag is rather steep. For those of you who like leather, SCOTTeVest has also introduced a leather jacket with the same integrated pockets and PAN features.

Another consideration for the mobile worker who often has to travel with the Treo, and a laptop, are the plethora of cables and chargers needed to carry with them. You can significantly cut down on the number of cables with some third-party products. For example, the iGo Juice product (www.igo.com), shown in Figure 1-4, is a universal charger that can charge your laptop and your Treo from a wall outlet, car power outlet, or the armrest outlet on some airplanes.

Personally, I find I need to give a lot of PowerPoint presentations on the road, and that is one reason why I have had to carry both my laptop and my Treo. Now you can do presentations right from your Treo with products like the Pitch Solo

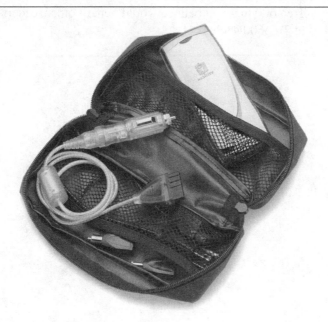

FIGURE 1-4   The iGo Juice makes it easy to travel with multiple devices because you only need one charger.

from iGo, the same vendor that sells the Juice product mentioned above. The Pitch Solo connects to any VGA monitor or projector and allows you to show full PowerPoint presentations right from your Treo! More details on this are provided in Chapter 11.

The sync cable and charger that come with your Treo are bulky to travel with, but there are many third-party cables that are much smaller and easier to travel with. One of these is BoxWave's Mini-Sync charging cable (www.boxwave.com), which is intended to charge your Treo from the USB port on your computer. It also allows you to HotSync your Treo.

Wrap It Up

The Treo 600 is a compact and powerful communication, business, and entertainment tool. It is highly versatile, and there are so many different things that you can do with this "Swiss Army knife" of smartphones that it is difficult to cover absolutely everything in this book; however, we will explore many topics in the chapters to help you get the most out of your Treo, though, from our experience, we cannot cover every way in which you will use your Treo 600. If you come up with an interesting way to use your Treo 600 that you believe would benefit other readers of this book, please e-mail us at Treo600@telus.net.

Chapter 2

Get Started with Your Treo 600

How to…

- Unpack your Treo

- Turn on your Treo for the first time

- Navigate your Treo using the touchscreen and five-way navigation control

- Set up your Treo preferences

- Use the Applications Launcher

- Use the preinstalled Treo applications

- Upgrade from previous versions of Palm

- Synchronize data from your old Palm device to your Treo 600

- Beam your business card and other useful information

You just purchased a new Treo 600—or perhaps you've had it for a while—and now you want to find out how to get the most out of this great device. In this book, you will find entire chapters dedicated to specific functionalities like using the phone, camera, and e-mail. This chapter addresses the features and configurations that you will likely need to set up and understand sooner, rather than later. This book is written as a reference book, so you can read it start to finish or jump around from chapter to chapter, depending on what you want to do with your Treo. Let's get started!

Unpack Your Treo and See What's in the Box

When you open the box and take out the contents, you'll notice that your Treo 600 smartphone comes with the following items:

- **AC charger cable**   The cable you plug into the wall to charge your Treo.

- **USB HotSync cable**   The cable you use to HotSync data between your Treo and your PC.

NOTE   *If your PC doesn't have a USB port, you can purchase a serial synchronization cable from palmOne. For more information, refer to Chapter 16.*

■ **Hands-free headset**   A headset useful for situations where you need your hands or where you want to use your Treo (to take notes, for example) while on a call.

■ **Case**   A case that will protect your Treo from damage. You can learn more about what case options are available for your Treo in Chapters 9 and 16.

■ **User guide**   Documentation for your Treo 600.

■ **Synchronization software CD-ROM (Windows and Macintosh)**   Software for synchronizing your Treo and PC data. This CD includes a PDF version of the user guide.

First Steps to Getting Started with Your Treo

After you have unpacked your new Treo and pulled all the included gadgets and connectors out of the box, you will likely want to begin getting familiar with the Treo layout and functionality.

Charge Your Treo Battery

Before you can get started using your Treo, you will need to charge the battery. Handspring recommends at least three full hours of charging, or charging the Treo until the LED is solid green. At this point, you only need to connect your Treo to a power outlet using the charger/sync cable included with your Treo. You don't have to connect the Treo to your PC in order to charge it. It is important, however, to be sure you charge your Treo fully the first time you charge it. This will help ensure you get the maximum life out of your battery.

Information about Your Treo Battery

Your Treo has a nonremovable rechargeable lithium ion battery, and your battery life depends on the type of Treo you have:

■ **GSM/GPRS**   A GSM/GPRS Treo allow up to six hours of talk time and up to ten days of standby time.

■ **CDMA**   A CDMA Treo allows up to four hours of talk time and up to ten days of standby time.

The Treo 600 battery recharges very quickly, and a car charger or add-on battery pack will help extend your battery life and increase your mobility. The Treo also has features, like auto-off, that well help you get the maximum battery time.

Get Oriented with Your Treo Hardware

You will quickly be able to get the most out of your Treo by becoming familiar with the buttons, switches, and general layout of your Treo before you get started. This section provides an overview of the parts.

On the top of your Treo are the following components, which are shown on both a GSM/GPRS Treo and a CDMA Treo in Figures 2-1 and 2-2, respectively:

- **The ringer switch**   This switch allows you to toggle easily between silent and active modes. For example, if you are going into a movie theatre and don't want to turn the phone off, you may want to turn your Treo to Sound Mode Off to avoid bothering other people during the show.

- **Wireless Mode button**   You can use the Palm OS features of your Treo independently of the wireless features and applications, because both the screen and Wireless Mode have been designed so that they can be turned on and off separately.

NOTE   *You have to hold this button down for a few seconds when turning Wireless Mode on and off.*

- **Antenna**   The antenna is used to send and receive wireless data.

- **Stylus**   The stylus is used for navigation using the touchscreen and also doubles as a Reset tool available by unscrewing the pointer of the stylus.

- **Infrared (IR) port**   The IR port allows you to wirelessly beam records between Treo 600s and other Palm-powered devices.

FIGURE 2-1   Components on the top of your Treo (GSM/GPRS system)

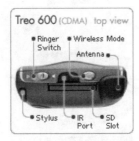

FIGURE 2-2   Components on the top of your Treo (CDMA system)

■ **SD slot**   An expansion slot to add memory, software applications, and content.

■ **SIM tray**   This is where your SIM card is. (See Chapter 5 for more information about SIM cards and wireless connectivity.)

On the left side of your Treo are the volume controls, shown in Figure 2-3, which allow you to adjust the volume level of the phone. Intuitively, the top button turns the volume up, and the bottom button turns the volume down.

The back of your Treo contains the following components, shown in Figure 2-4:

■ **Camera lens**   Taking digital photographs with your Treo is covered in Chapter 7.

■ **Speaker**   The speaker allows you to hear system sounds and ringtones.

■ **Reset button**   The reset button allows you to perform a reset on your Treo.

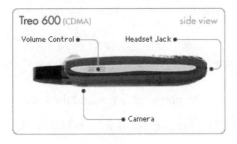

FIGURE 2-3   Volume controls (on the left side of your Treo)

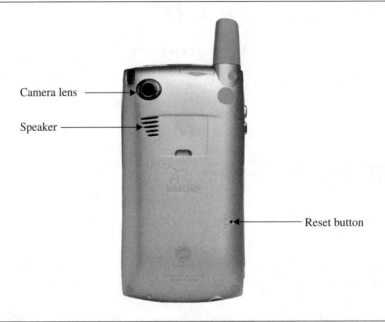

Camera lens

Speaker

Reset button

FIGURE 2-4 Components on the back of your Treo

The bottom of your Treo contains three items, shown in Figure 2-5:

■ **Headset jack** A 2.5 mm jack

 You will need a 2.5 to 3.5 mm adapter to use stereo headphones in this jack.

■ **Connector** This connector is used for HotSyncing and power supply.

■ **Microphone** The microphone picks up your voice when you are talking on the phone.

The front of your Treo sports the following features, shown in Figure 2-6:

■ **Phone speaker** The phone speaker is at the top, above the screen.

■ **Touchscreen** The Treo screen is a 160×160 bright-color, touch-sensitive screen.

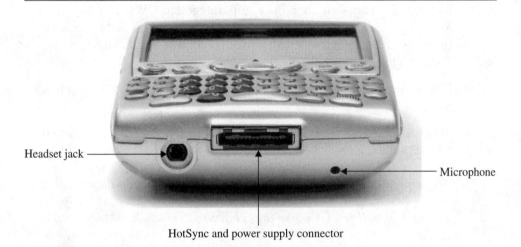

Headset jack

Microphone

HotSync and power supply connector

FIGURE 2-5   Components on the bottom of your Treo

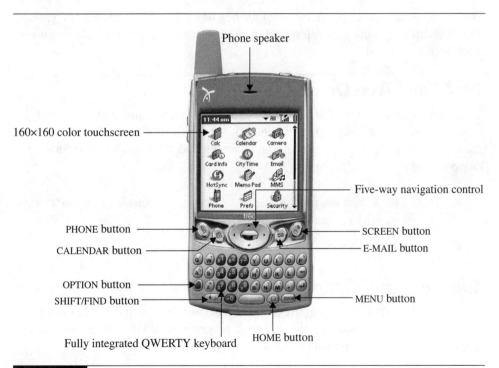

Phone speaker

160×160 color touchscreen

Five-way navigation control

PHONE button

SCREEN button

CALENDAR button

E-MAIL button

OPTION button

SHIFT/FIND button

MENU button

Fully integrated QWERTY keyboard

HOME button

FIGURE 2-6   The front of your Treo

■ **Keyboard** The Treo contains a fully integrated QWERTY keyboard including a backlight so you can see the keyboard in low-light conditions. Here you'll also find the OPTION, SHIFT/FIND, HOME, and MENU buttons, discussed later in this chapter.

■ **Five-way navigation control** This convenient disc allows for one-handed navigation.

■ **Shortcut buttons** These are quick-access buttons—PHONE, CALENDAR, E-MAIL, and SCREEN.

 When we instruct you to press one of the buttons shown in Figure 2-6 (or the UP, DOWN, LEFT, RIGHT, and CENTER buttons on the five-way navigation control) we will say simply to press PHONE, CALENDAR, OPTION, SHIFT, and so on.

Turn Your Treo on for the First Time

Turning on your Treo is, of course, only the beginning of a series of steps in getting your Treo up and running. Some other initial steps are covered next, including using the Welcome Wizard.

Turn Your Treo On and Off

Your Treo is designed so that you can use the traditional Palm features, like the Address Book or Calendar, independently of the wireless features. For this reason, there are separate controls for turning the screen and Wireless Mode off and on independently.

■ To turn the screen on, press the SCREEN button, the outside button to the right of the five-way navigation control.

■ To turn the screen off, press the SCREEN button again.

The Welcome Wizard

The first time you power up your Treo, you will be prompted with the initial Welcome process. Press SCREEN to begin the Welcome program, which then steps you through defining your location and calibrating the touchscreen.

You can launch the Welcome program at any time by selecting the Welcome icon from the Applications Launcher.

Learn How to Navigate the Treo Screen

Navigating the Treo screen is similar to navigating your PC screen. There are two ways to do it. You can either use the five-way navigation control or the touchscreen and stylus.

TIP *Unlike Windows and other desktop operating systems, the Palm OS is designed so that many of the screens and applications don't have a menu item that allows you to close the application or get back to the Applications Launcher. Press HOME, located to the right of the SPACEBAR, to get back to the Applications Launcher.*

Get to Know Your Treo Buttons

There are a few buttons on your Treo that you will want to become familiar with because they allow you to launch the most common functionalities quickly. The appearance of the buttons makes the functionality obvious.

- **PHONE** This button allows you to access your phone, camera, contacts, and favorites easily.

- **CALENDAR** This button functions as the shortcut for launching your calendar.

- **E-MAIL** This button allows you to access your e-mail quickly.

- **SCREEN** Your Treo automatically turns the screen off to save your battery, and you can use this button to turn your screen on and off.

- **OPTION** This button is used in combination with other keys and is conceptually similar to the SHIFT key on your PC keyboard for typing secondary characters on the keyboard. For example, to type the @ symbol, press OPTION and then the letter I.

Customize Your Shortcut Buttons

You can customize what actions each of these main shortcut buttons does. For example, if you find that you use the Documents application more than you use the Calendar, you can modify your preferences to launch Documents when the CALENDAR shortcut button is pressed. To customize the buttons, do the following:

1. Go to the Applications Launcher by pressing HOME (the button displaying a house icon, to the right of the SPACEBAR).

2. Find and select Prefs from the Applications Launcher.

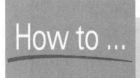 **Avoid Demagnetization**

Demagnetization is not a word that you use every day, but it is one that you should be familiar with. Your Treo contains a speaker; and like most other speakers, it includes a large magnet. This is important to know because when you place a magnet near a credit card or other magnetized items, it can become demagnetized—sometimes making it completely unusable. The types of cards that can be erased if you store them too close to your Treo include credit cards, automated bank machine cards, your driver's license, library cards, and so on. So, either keep your cards separate from your Treo or use a case that appropriately divides the two.

3. Select the menu at the top right-hand corner of the screen, and then find and select the Buttons item. You will see the screen shown in Figure 2-7, which shows the buttons on the left half of the screen—the PHONE, CALENDAR, E-MAIL, and SCREEN buttons, and next to each button icon, the application that is launched when you press that button.

4. To change what application a particular button is linked to, select the menu to the immediate right of the button name and choose a new application to associate with that button.

If you are still getting used to your Treo, you may want to leave the default setting in place until you better understand how to get the most out of your Treo.

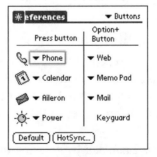

FIGURE 2-7 Changing button properties

2

Use the Five-Way Navigation Control

Your Treo is equipped with a five-way navigation control, shown in Figure 2-8, which is an exceptional navigation feature that allows you to navigate menu options, onscreen commands, links for web pages, messages, and so on, using only one hand. The five-way navigation control allows you to move between fields and screens. You can do this by pressing the direction arrows on the control to move around. Selected fields and objects will be highlighted or will appear to have a halo around them. To select an item that is highlighted, press CENTER (the button in the center of the control). It works in much the same way as clicking a mouse button.

Use the Stylus and Touchscreen

In addition to the five-way navigation control, your Treo also is equipped with the latest touchscreen technology, allowing you to navigate around the interface by selecting menus and tapping on objects and fields with the stylus. The stylus can be found at the top right-hand corner of your Treo, as shown earlier in Figure 2-1.

TIP *Make a habit of putting the stylus back when you are finished with it. It is very easy to misplace. In fact, you can buy three-packs of styli (yes, oddly enough the plural of* stylus *is* styli*) for your Treo just in case you are unlucky enough to lose them as often as some of us do.*

Use the Keyboard

The Treo is equipped with an integrated keyboard. Most people use the keyboard by holding the Treo in both hands and using their thumbs to type. If you are not used to using this type of keyboard, it will likely be awkward at first, but you should become proficient with it quickly. Following are a few pointers to get you going.

Use the Keyboard Backlight

The Treo 600 keyboard is backlit so that the numbers, letters, and symbols on the keyboard can be read in low-light conditions. The backlight is automatically activated

FIGURE 2-8   The five-way navigation control

for the first few seconds of use within the phone application and can be manually activated by pressing any button on the keyboard.

■ To turn on the backlight, press OPTION (analogous to the SHIFT key), and then the letter P.

■ The backlight will turn off if the keyboard is not in use.

Use Keyboard Menu Shortcuts

On any screen, you can view a menu of possible actions by pressing MENU on the keyboard. You can also choose any of the menu items by pressing the shortcut button that corresponds to the item in the menu.

For example, Figure 2-9 displays a menu that is available within the Calendar application. To delete the selected Calendar event, simply press D on the keyboard. This shortcut functionality helps minimize how often you have to alternate between using the keyboard and using the touchscreen.

Enter Lowercase and Uppercase Letters

The following are a few tips on entering upper- and lowercase letters.

■ To type a lowercase letter, press the desired button.

■ To type an uppercase letter, press SHIFT, and then press a letter button. You don't need to hold down SHIFT while typing a letter.

■ To turn Caps Lock on, press SHIFT twice. To turn it off, press SHIFT again. When Caps Lock is on, a symbol appears in the lower-right corner of the screen.

FIGURE 2-9   Using menu shortcuts

Enter Numbers, Punctuation, and Symbols that Appear above the Letters on the Keys

The OPTION button functions like the SHIFT key on a standard PC keyboard. Press OPTION, and then press the button with the desired character shown above the letter. You don't need to hold down OPTION while pressing the second letter button.

To turn Option Lock on, press OPTION twice. To turn it off, press OPTION again. When Option Lock is on, the Option symbol appears in the lower-right corner of the screen.

Type Special Characters—Symbols and Accented Characters

As you begin to use the keyboard to type text, you will undoubtedly encounter moments of frustration as you scan the keyboard to type a specific character and can't find it. An example of such a character is an underscore (_). In order to deal with the challenges of the diminutive Treo keyboard, palmOne has had to invent some new ways to allow you to type the full character set. The ALT button, to the left of the SPACEBAR on the keyboard, allows you to scroll through related characters until you find the one you are looking for.

Each keyboard character button has an associated set of related characters. For example, you use the A button to type any of these characters: Á À Ä Â Ã Å Æ.

Follow these steps to type an underscore.

1. Launch Memo Pad and choose the New button—or any other application that allows you to input text.

2. Press OPTION and then S.

3. A dash will appear on the screen.

4. Press ALT, to the immediate left of the SPACEBAR.

5. You will see a list of available characters to choose from, as shown in Figure 2-10.

6. The underscore is the second character in the list; select it, and your dash becomes an underscore.

The fastest way to find alternate characters is to go to the keyboard help within each application. The keyboard help lists all of the alternate characters and their corresponding keys. There is also a table in the Treo user guide called "Symbols and Accented Characters" that shows which buttons relate to which special characters.

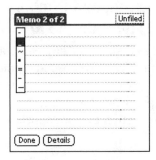

FIGURE 2-10   Typing special characters

Cut, Copy, and Paste Text

When you are typing text, especially repetitive text, it is useful to be able to cut, copy, and paste text between fields and screens. On any screen where you are working with text, you can cut, copy, or paste text by highlighting the text (to select text, drag the stylus across the words you want to cut or copy) and pressing MENU. Depending on the screen you are on, the cut, copy, and paste commands, as well as a few others, should appear under the Edit menu, as in Figure 2-11.

Use Menus to Navigate

There is a MENU button on the bottom right-hand section of the keyboard. Selecting this button on any screen will bring up a menu related to that screen. An alternate way to view the menu is to tap the application name in the top left-hand portion of the screen.

FIGURE 2-11   Cut, copy, and paste text

Several manufacturers sell external keyboards that attach to your Treo and allow you to enter and edit text using a more traditional PC keyboard. Accessories are covered in more detail in Chapter 16.

Lock Your Phone and Data

Chapter 13 covers security, but we'll also mention it a bit here since it's an important topic. One of the first things you should consider doing is protecting your Treo and data from unauthorized use. The convenience and power of the Treo 600 can be offset by some of the risks associated with such a small device capable of storing a significant amount of information. Your Treo can be easily lost or stolen, and it is more likely to be left unprotected on a desk or lent to an acquaintance to make a phone call than a larger device might be. If your phone or data (Contacts list, e-mails and attachments, photos, memos, and so on) get into the wrong hands, the consequences could be significant for you and your company.

The good news is that Handspring has built some powerful security features into your Treo to help minimize these risks. Your Treo includes several features that help you protect your phone from careless or malicious users and keep both it and your data private. Handspring has thought this out well; your Treo can still be used to make emergency calls even if the handset is locked.

Configure Security for Your Treo

The Security settings can be accessed from the Applications Launcher by selecting Security. This is where you can set your Security preferences. Specific fields are explained next, and an image of the Security screen is shown in Figure 2-12.

FIGURE 2-12   Configure your Security settings

Password

The Security application on your Treo allows you to configure the Treo's security level. On the Security screen, you can define a password to unlock the device and files. You can also set a Hint question to help remind you of your password in case you forget it. This comes in handy since some of us have a tough time choosing and remembering passwords for all of our hardware, network, and Internet accounts.

Auto Lock Your Treo

The Auto Lock setting allows you to configure the conditions that automatically lock your Treo. Once locked, you will have to enter a password to unlock, and use, your Treo. Following are your Auto Lock options:

- **Never** Your Treo will not lock at any time.

- **On Power Off** Your Treo will lock when you turn the power off.

- **At a Preset Time** Your Treo will lock at a specific time—for example, at 10 P.M. every day.

- **After a Preset Delay** This is likely the most secure choice. For instance, you can set it to lock if it's not used for five minutes.

Current Privacy

The Current Privacy setting allows you to define protection for your records. What this means is that you can flag records as Private so they are either masked or don't appear in your Contacts list at all, until you change the Current Privacy setting to Show Records. For example, if you lend your phone to someone and they select Contacts, they will be unable to view Private records. Your Current Privacy options include the following:

- **Show Records** Does not hide records flagged as Private.

- **Mask Records** Private records will appear in the list as grayed-out lines. To view a Private, grayed-out, record, tap it and enter your password.

- **Hide Records** Private records will not appear in the record list at all. To show Private records when this setting is enabled, either return to the Security screen or within the Contacts screen press MENU, press OPTION, select Security, change the setting to Show Records, and enter your password.

Flag a Record as Private

You can flag a contact record as private by following these steps:

1. Press PHONE.

2. Press DOWN on the five-way navigation control.

3. Select a contact that you would like to flag as private.

4. Choose Edit, and then select Details.

5. Select the Private check box and click OK, as shown in Figure 2-13.

Set Up User Preferences

You may customize your Treo to suit your specific needs and preferences by selecting Prefs from the Applications Launcher. You have control over many of your Treo attributes, including the following:

- ■ **Buttons** This is where you choose which applications are associated with the buttons on your Treo.

- ■ **Connection** This is where you can select and edit the connection options for your Treo.

- ■ **Date & Time** This is where you define your date, time, and time zone preferences.

FIGURE 2-13   Flag a contact record as private

- **Default Apps**   Sometimes one application looks for another application to handle data. For example, a mail application might launch a browser when you choose a link in an e-mail message. This is where you define these associations.

- **Display**   You can determine your screen contrast and brightness here.

- **Formats**   This is where you can define how data is formatted. You can use regional default settings or define each data type separately.

- **General**   Here is where you can define Auto-off, sounds, and display colors.

- **Keyguard**   This screen allows you to define the events that trigger the Auto-Keyguard and helps minimize unintentional keyboard button presses.

- **Network**   This is where you configure your wireless connection and also the screen that you will use to connect to, and disconnect from, the network.

- **Owner**   This is where you define your personal contact information.

- **Shortcuts**   Shortcuts are abbreviations for commonly used words. You can use shortcuts to minimize typing. One of the default examples is "me" as the abbreviation for "meeting." After you have defined shortcuts, you can use them when typing by first pressing the Function key and then typing in the shortcut abbreviation.

- **Sound**   This screen allows you to define volume levels and the sounds that your Treo will make when specific events occur.

- **Touchscreen**   This is a screen that is also part of the Welcome wizard and allows you to calibrate your touchscreen to ensure that your Treo correctly recognizes where you tap the screen.

Your user guide does a good job of describing what each of these options does, so we will only focus on the ones you are most likely to need set right away. Your preferences are accessed from the Applications Launcher by selecting Prefs and tapping the menu in the top right-hand corner of the screen, or by pressing MENU.

NOTE   *There is an entire cottage industry dedicated to allowing you to personalize your Treo. For example, you can apply custom "skins" to make your Treo more accurately reflect your personality (or quirks ☺). Interface "skins" are covered in Chapter 4.*

Safeguard Your Personal Info Using Owner Preferences

The Owner Preferences is where you record information such as your name, company name, phone number, e-mail address, and so on.

If you lock your keyboard, the Owner Preferences information appears on the screen that requests your password to unlock it, and you must also enter your password to change the Owner Preferences information.

1. Press HOME to open the Applications Launcher.

2. Choose the pick list in the upper-right corner, and then select All.

3. Choose the Prefs icon.

4. Choose the pick list in the upper-right corner and select Owner.

5. If you assigned a password with the Security application, choose Unlock, enter your password, and then choose OK to continue.

6. Type the text that you want to appear in the Owner Preferences screen.

Date & Time

When you set up the Welcome wizard, you set up some of this information, so ideally it should already be correctly set. We mention it here again only because it is important to ensure that your Treo is set up properly and that you know where to go to change your settings. This also ensures that other applications that depend on your Prefs, like the CityTime application, work properly.

The Sprint Treo 600 (CDMA) supports the ability to use network time instead of requiring you to set the date and time manually. On the Sprint Treo, there is a Date & Time dialog box with a "Use Network Time" check box. To set your Sprint Treo 600 to use the network time, follow these steps:

1. Start the Applications Launcher by pressing HOME.

2. Choose the pick list in the upper-right corner, and then select All.

3. Choose the Prefs icon.

4. Choose the menu in the upper-right corner and select the Date & Time option.

5. Check the Use Network Time check box.

The CityTime application has a slick graphical interface that allows you to choose four different cities around the world so you can see the current time in those locations whenever you like. You can also tap on the world map to see the current time in other locations.

Configure Your Wireless Connection Information Using Network Preferences

The Network Preferences screen is where your network settings are configured. These settings allow you to connect to your service provider's wireless network. Usually, your Treo 600 ships with your network settings already configured, so you shouldn't have to configure them. (Wireless connectivity is covered in more detail in Chapter 5.)

Once your network settings have been correctly configured, the Network screen is where you will connect and disconnect from the wireless network depending on what you need to do.

Define More of Your Preferences Using General Preferences

The General Preferences screen is a catchall for settings that do not warrant their own categories. Here you can set the auto shutoff interval, the beam receive feature, and define the sounds and screen colors for your Treo. To get to the General Prefs, follow these steps:

1. Start the Applications Launcher by pressing HOME.

2. Choose the pick list in the upper-right corner, and then select All.

3. Choose the Prefs icon.

4. Choose the menu in the upper-right corner and select General.

The General settings that you can change to suit your preferences include the following:

■ **Auto-Off After** The time that elapses before your screen automatically turns off. Setting this to a relatively short time will help preserve your battery life.

■ **System Sound** The volume for system beeps and alerts.

- **Game Sound**   The volume for game sounds.

- **Beam Receive**   The setting for whether you want your Treo to receive beamed information.

- **Colors**   This allows you to change the interface colors by selecting from a set of predefined color schemes.

Sound

Sound Preferences is where you can define the sounds that your Treo makes and when they are made. This is a handy feature. I wish my home phone had this capability—especially because one ring for everything seems pretty inadequate after the Treo 600. For example, you can set up your Treo to make different sounds depending on whether an incoming phone call is from a known caller or an unknown one.

> **TIP**   *Your Treo 600 ships with many different sound files from which you can pick and choose for various functions. Many Treo users enjoy downloading and using additional tones as well as the default sounds. There are many places on the Web that allow you to download and install new ringtones—and any MIDI file will work with your Treo. One of the many sites that offer MIDI sound files you can download for your Treo's ringtones is http://mididb.com.*

Keyguard

The Keyguard Prefs screen allows you to define the events that trigger the Auto-Keyguard and disable the touchscreen. This helps minimize unintentional key and touchscreen input when you are using your Treo as a phone.

- **Auto-Keyguard**   You can set the Auto-Keyguard to automatically disable the keyboard within a specific time period after the power is turned off.

- **Disable Touchscreen When**   You may set your Treo to disable the touchscreen when you are on a call or when an incoming call is received.

Launch Applications on Your Treo

The Applications Launcher is a graphical view for browsing and launching your applications and settings and looks like the screen in Figure 2-14. It is always available

FIGURE 2-14   The Applications Launcher

by pressing HOME on the bottom of the keyboard. The installed applications are separated into default categories. As you add or remove applications, you can group them in ways that make them easy to find. You can view the application categories by selecting the menu at the top of the screen or by scrolling through the categories by repeatedly pressing HOME.

Perform Common Treo Tasks

This section briefly covers some of the most common tasks you will use your Treo for, including managing your contacts, defining your business card, and setting up your favorites.

Manage Your Contacts

Your Contacts can be found under the Phone menu. If you are familiar with Palm-powered devices, Contacts is the new name for what was previously called the Address Book. You can store a lot of information about a contact there, and you can phone or e-mail the contact directly from the contact record. This is covered in more detail in Chapter 10.

Add a Contact

You can create a new contact on the fly using your Treo, which is great for storing contact information for people you have just met. If you have several contacts to enter,

2

it may be a tad tedious to enter them on the Treo. Unless you are an adept thumb-typist, it is likely most efficient to enter new contacts into the Palm Desktop software or into Microsoft Outlook on your computer and then synchronize the contact data between the Treo and your computer. Synchronizing your Treo with your PC is covered in detail in Chapter 3. Here are the steps for adding a contact on your Treo:

1. Press the PHONE button to the left of the five-way navigation control.

2. Use the five-way navigation control to select the Contacts list.

3. Choose New Contact.

4. Use the five-way navigation control to move between fields and enter information.

5. Optionally, you can place the entry in a category or mark it private. To do this, choose Details.

6. You can also add a note to a contact entry by choosing Note.

7. After you enter all the information, choose Done to save the record.

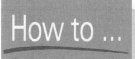

How to ...   Recover Your Treo if You Lose It

A great idea to help you recover your Treo 600 in the event that it is lost is to store an "If found call..." contact so that the person who finds your Treo can easily discover who it belongs to and return it. A handy trick is to create a new contact consisting of your contact information that will always show up first in your Contacts list, and will therefore be obvious. To do this: create a new contact, and in the Last Name field enter **If found call...,** and then in the Home field type in your home phone number. If you type two dashes in front of the "if found" text, this contact will show up higher in the list than any legitimate contact that begins with a letter. This will increase the odds of recovering your Treo if you lose it.

Quickly Find a Contact

When you are looking for a specific contact, scrolling through the list can be very slow, especially if you have a lot of contacts. Fortunately, your Treo has a feature commonly known as type-ahead functionality. You can quickly locate a contact by opening your Contacts list and beginning to type the contact's name. There are three ways to find a contact using the type-ahead functionality:

- Type the first initial and last name.

- Type the first name.

- Type the last name.

After you have typed a few letters, the Contacts list will jump to the contacts that match what you have typed. Once you are in the correct range, you can also navigate the list using the UP and DOWN buttons on the five-way navigation control.

View or Change Contact Information

Once you have located the contact that you want to view or modify, and it is highlighted on the screen, select it by tapping it on the screen or pressing the CENTER button of the five-way navigation control. This will show the contact details and allow you to select the Edit button to make changes to the contact.

Define Your Business Card

Your business card is a contact record containing your personal contact information that you would like to share with others. Once you have defined your business card, you can "beam" it to other Treo and Palm users. The steps for creating your business card are listed next:

1. Go to your Contacts list by pressing PHONE to the left of the five-way navigation control and then selecting Contacts.

2. Create a new contact by pressing MENU and selecting New Contact.

3. In this new record, enter your own information.

4. While still in Contact Edit view, press MENU.

5. From the Record menu, choose Select Business Card.

6. Your business card is now saved.

Now you can beam your business card to other Palm OS devices. Beaming information is covered in more detail in the section "Beam Data Using Your Treo's Infrared Capability" at the end of this chapter.

Define Favorites

What are Treo Favorites? You are probably familiar with using favorites in your web browser. The Treo extends the concept of favorites even further. In order to make your Treo even easier to use, you may define up to 50 Favorites that can be quickly accessed using a menu or a keyboard shortcut. The types of actions that can be stored as a Favorite are as follows:

- **Dial a phone number**   Essentially the same as putting someone on a speed-dial list

- **Launch an application**   A shortcut to allow you to quickly launch applications

- **Access a web page**   Conceptually the same as storing your Favorites in your PC web browser

- **Address a text message**   Similar to adding someone to a speed-dial list to allow you to quickly send SMS text messages to your friends and family

- **Access your voicemail**   A shortcut that dials your voicemail

Your wireless service provider has likely already preprogrammed some of the items in your Favorites list, such as its support number and your voicemail.

Access Your Favorites

You can trigger your Favorites in a couple of different ways:

- **Using the Favorite buttons**   You can see your Favorite buttons by pressing the PHONE shortcut button and selecting Favorites with the five-way navigation control. To scroll through your Favorites, use the number bar at the bottom right-hand corner of the screen.

- **Using the keyboard**   When you are in the phone's Main, Favorites, or Dial Pad view, you can press and hold a Quick Key to launch the Favorite associated with that keyboard button. You can define Quick Keys for each of your Favorites (Quick Keys are optional). Quick Keys can only be letters and are not case-sensitive.

Explore the Applications Installed on Your Treo

In addition to the configuration and preferences utilities installed on your Treo, there are several applications included. Software titles may differ slightly depending on where and when you purchased your Treo. Some of the commonly installed applications are listed and described in the following sections.

Calc

This built-in calculator application comes in handy and has much more power than I can use. You can choose the type of calculation you need to perform by selecting among several options, including statistics, finance, and weight/temperature. Calculator includes a basic calculator, plus an advanced calculator with scientific, financial, and conversion functions.

Switch Between Basic and Advanced Calculator Modes

To change the type of calculator you want to use, follow these steps:

1. While pressing MENU on the keyboard, press the OPTION button and then select the Toggle Mode menu item. (Toggle Mode allows you to toggle between the basic calculator and the advanced calculator.) This will put you in the Advanced Calculator mode.

2. In the Advanced mode, choose the menu near the upper-left part of the screen and select which Advanced Calculator function you would like to use. Your options include the following:

   - **Math**   This option allows you to perform advanced mathematical functions such as exponents, roots, and logarithms.

   - **Trig**   This option allows you to select trigonometric functions such as sine, cosine, tangent, and variants.

   - **Finance**   This option allows you to perform financial calculator functions such as APR and amortization.

   - **Logic**   This option allows you to perform hexadecimal characters in keypad, as well as logic functions such as and, not, or, and xor.

   - **Statistics**   This option allows you to perform statistical functions such as sum, factorial, and random number generator.

- **Weight/Temp**   This option allows you to perform weight and temperature conversions for both the metric and English measurement systems.

- **Length**   This option allows you to perform length conversions for both metric and English values.

- **Area**   This option allows you to perform area conversions for both the metric and English measurement systems.

- **Volume**   This option allows you to perform volume conversions for both the metric and English measurement systems.

- **Eng(x) (Engineering Notation)**   This option allows you to define an integer for the number of decimal places to display, and then select Eng(c) to round calculations to that decimal place using engineering notation. You can also choose the menu located in the upper-right corner of the screen to select whether you want to display numbers in degrees, radians, or grads.

Calendar

The calendar offers several ways to view your schedule information and allows you to view and edit appointments and schedule new appointments. The calendar will remind you of scheduled events, and when you have HotSync installed and configured, you can synchronize your Outlook or Palm Desktop calendar to make sure you don't forget a thing.

Display Your Calendar

To view your calendar and schedule meetings or events, follow these steps:

1. Press CALENDAR (the button to the left of the five-way navigation control) repeatedly to cycle through the various active views.

2. Use the five-way navigation control to move to another day, week, or month.

3. Choose Go or press MENU. From the Options menu, choose Go to Day and choose a date from the calendar.

The Calendar is covered in more detail in Chapter 10, but here are a few of the things that you can do with it:

- Schedule a new event

- Add an alarm reminder to a scheduled event

- Schedule an untimed event (an event that does not occur at a particular time, only on a specific day—such as a birthday or anniversary)

- Edit or delete a scheduled event

- Schedule a repeating event (a recurring event such as a mortgage payment or weekly sales meeting)

Customize the General Preferences for Your Calendar

You can define how your calendar should behave by setting your calendar general preferences, which include the following:

- **Start Time and End Time**   The times that your day typically begins and ends. For example, some people may begin work at 6:00 A.M. and end at 4:00 P.M. while others may have a more traditional 9:00 to 5:00 workday.

- **Event Duration**   This is the typical default event duration, which you can change when you schedule a meeting.

- **Week Start**   The day of the week that your workweek typically begins. For many of us it is Monday, but you can change it to be whatever you like.

- **Initial View**   This allows you to define how your Calendar screen looks when you initially launch the Calendar.

- **Button Views**   This allows you to define which Calendar screens appear when you press the CALENDAR button repeatedly.

- By default, you see Day and Month Views, but you can also see other views.

To set your calendar preferences, follow these steps:

1. Press CALENDAR, and then press MENU.

2. From the Options menu, choose Preferences.

3. Set your preferences for each item.

CityTime

The CityTime application has a slick graphical interface, shown in Figure 2-15, that allows you to choose four different cities around the world so you can see the current time in those locations whenever you like. You can also tap on the world map to see the current time in other locations. For this application to function correctly, your home city and time must be correctly configured.

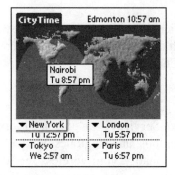

FIGURE 2-15   CityTime

Documents—Docs To Go and Sheets To Go

Documents To Go allows you to view Microsoft Word e-mail attachments, and Sheets To Go allows you to view Microsoft Excel e-mail attachments. The preinstalled versions are limited to read-only functionalities. You can purchase a product upgrade that allows you to use your Word, Excel, and PowerPoint files on your Treo, including the ability to modify and create new documents. More detail on this topic is included in Chapter 11.

Mail

Mail is the built-in e-mail application on your Treo that provides wireless access to an existing POP3 e-mail account. Mail allows you to:

- Send and receive messages

- Attach items to outbound e-mail messages

More information about setting up and using e-mail on your Treo is included in Chapter 6.

Memo Pad

The Memo Pad allows you to create and store notes on your Treo (for example, directions to your niece's interpretive dance recital). Memo Pad is covered in more detail in Chapter 10.

SMS

SMS (Short Message Service) messages are brief notes, up to 160 characters long, that you can exchange with other mobile phones that have SMS capability. SMS is covered in more detail in Chapter 5.

MMS

MMS (Multimedia Message Service) is an enhanced form of SMS messaging that lets you send photos, animations, and ringtones wirelessly with your Treo. In order to use this Treo MMS functionality, your wireless service provider must support MMS, and MMS must be enabled on your account. MMS functionality is covered in more detail in Chapter 5.

 *MMS is not available by default on Sprint Treo 600s, but an MMS alternative called "Picture Mail" is available. See Chapter 5 for more on MMS.*

SplashID

SplashID is a personal identification organizer that allows you to securely store your personal identification information, including usernames, passwords, credit cards, calling cards, bank accounts, PINs, and other information. The data is stored in a secure, encrypted format, which is accessible on your Treo. A product upgrade is available that also allows you to synchronize and access data on your PC. SplashID is covered in more detail in Chapter 10.

SplashMoney

SplashMoney is a personal finance application that helps you manage and track your finances on your Treo, including budgeting and reporting, scheduled transactions with reminders, secure password protection, and other handy features. A product upgrade is available that allows you to synchronize and access your data on your PC. SplashMoney is discussed in more detail in Chapter 12.

SplashShopper

SplashShopper is a shopping list application that allows you to keep grocery lists, movies to see, CDs to buy, books to read, and any other lists you might want to track and store on your Treo. A product upgrade is available that allows you to synchronize and access your shopping list data on your PC. SplashShopper is discussed in more detail in Chapter 10.

To Do List

Many of us rely on our To Do lists to help us remember what we have to accomplish today, this week, or this year. The To Do List application allows you to keep a list of tasks and keep a record of completed tasks. This application is covered in detail in Chapter 10.

Blazer Browser

You can browse the Internet in full color on your Treo using the preinstalled Blazer Web Browser. The Blazer Browser allows you to store bookmarks (conceptually the same as Favorites on most PC web browsers), save web pages for offline viewing, and copy text from a web page. It even gives you the ability to view web pages in Optimized mode. Optimized mode reformats web pages into one column so information is easier to view on your Treo screen. Web browsing is covered in more detail in Chapter 5.

Games

You may not have based your decision to purchase your Treo 600 solely on its gaming capability, but be warned—the Treo 600 has converted more than a few of us to closet gamers. The bright color screen and sound capability make playing games on the Treo 600 a surprisingly satisfying experience. The Palm operating system is a very popular platform for game engineers, so there is a seemingly perpetual stream of new games arriving on the market, many of which are freeware (free software) or shareware (software that can be tried out and then purchased for a nominal fee). The games that are listed in this chapter are limited to the ones that come already installed on your Treo 600, but games are covered in more detail in Chapter 8.

Zap!2016

This game is a variation of the classic "shoot all of the spaceships that drop down from the top of the screen without getting shot or crashed into" game. It comes complete with color and sounds, and if that wasn't enough, you also get weapons and power-ups, over 50 different aliens, seven deadly boss enemies, and seven levels with scrolling backgrounds. You navigate your spaceship using the five-way navigation control and fire your weapon using the SCREEN button. The developer of the game has several different games that run on the Palm OS, all of which can be found at www.astraware.com.

Klondike 22

What useful time-saving handheld device would be complete without a game of Solitaire? Klondike allows you to play the commonest variation of Solitaire in full color on your Treo.

Upgrade from a Previous Palm OS Device

If you are already a seasoned user of Palm or Handspring handhelds, you may be interested in upgrading your data and applications from your previous Palm-powered handheld to your Treo 600. This section discusses some differences that you should be aware of and also covers the steps to upgrade smoothly.

Transfer Applications and Data from Your Old Palm

If you are upgrading to the Treo 600 from another Palm device and want to transfer compatible applications and data from your previous device to your new Treo, there are a few steps that you need to perform:

1. HotSync your old device with your old desktop software to ensure that your data is backed up.

2. Install the Palm Desktop synchronization software on your PC—more detailed information is covered later in this chapter. The "Palm Desktop and HotSync Manager for Treo 600" software for both Windows and Mac is on the CD that shipped with your Treo and is available for download from palmOne.

   a. During the installation process, perform a HotSync operation with your Treo 600.

   b. Amidst the operation, you will be prompted to enter a username for your Treo 600. Be sure to use the same username you used on your old device.

 If any of the applications you were running on your old device are not compatible with your Treo 600, the HotSync Manager may quarantine and not install them.

If you plan on continuing to use your old Palm device, you will need to perform a hard reset to delete the username in order to avoid conflicts because that username is now associated with your Treo 600. Each device you synchronize with your PC must have a unique name, so the next time you synchronize your old device, be sure to assign it a new username.

What Is New and Different on the Treo 600?

If you are upgrading from a previous Palm device, you are likely an expert on using the interface and functionality of the old device. Just the same, there are a few changes you should know about when it comes to your Treo 600:

- **Address Book**   This application is now called Contacts.

- **Date Book+**   This application is now called Calendar.

- **Applications Launcher**   This was likely called the Home screen on your older Palm.

- **Find**   This is the global search engine. You may be used to launching this functionality by tapping the Magnifying Glass icon in the Graffiti area. On your Treo, you can access Find by pressing OPTION and SHIFT together.

- **Menu commands**   You can now access system menus by pressing the MENU button.

- **Backlight**   Your Treo 600 includes a keyboard backlight for use in low-light conditions. To turn the backlight on—with the screen on, press OPTION, and then press P.

- **CENTER button**   If you are used to a previous Treo phone, you may be accustomed to using the SPACEBAR to activate commands or dial numbers. Navigation on your Treo 600 is slightly different and uses a combination of buttons, touchscreen taps, and the five-way navigation control. Don't worry, you'll get used to navigating your Treo 600 quickly.

- **SCREEN button**   The fourth button on the right is used to turn the screen off and on. It's not an application button, by default, but if you like, you can remap this button to an application by changing your preferences.

- **Internet connection**   Your Treo 600 was designed so that your network settings were automatically configured for you.

- **Five-way navigation compatibility**   Some Palm OS 5 applications are optimized for five-way navigation on devices other than your Treo, so you may notice inconsistencies when using software that is not designed specifically for your Treo 600.

- **Palm Desktop**   Your Treo 600 ships with Palm Desktop 4.1 for Windows and Macintosh.

Beam Data Using Your Treo's Infrared Capability

Your Treo includes an IR (infrared) port that lets you wirelessly beam information to another Palm-powered device that also has an IR port. You can beam contact records, your business card, and applications to other IR-capable handhelds. The IR port is located on the top of your Treo, between the Wireless Mode button and the ringer switch, behind the small dark shield.

What Is the Range of Infrared on the Treo 600?

According to palmOne, the maximum infrared beam distance with your Palm handheld may vary from 24 inches (61 cm) to 39 inches (1 m). The beam distance variation is dependent on the age and condition of the power supply in your Treo, as well as the power supply in the receiving handheld. For best results, point your IR port directly at the IR port of the receiving unit, while maintaining a beam distance between 3 inches (7.6 cm) and 24 inches (61 cm). In the authors' experience, attempting to beam a contact record between two brand-new, fully charged Treo 600s failed if the Treos were placed much more than 24 inches apart.

Beam Your Business Card to Another Palm-Powered Device

Instead of scrambling to find a pen and paper to give someone your contact information, an easy way to share your contact information is to beam it to the person's Palm device from your Treo 600. The steps for beaming your business card are shown here:

1. Press PHONE, and then press MENU.

2. From the Record menu, choose Beam Business Card.

3. When the Beam Status dialog box appears, point the IR port on your Treo directly at the IR port of the receiving device.

4. Wait for the Beam Status dialog box to indicate that the transfer is complete.

Beam a Contact Record

In addition to beaming your business card, you can beam any contact record or category. This can significantly reduce the time to get contact information. To beam records, follow these steps.

1. Press PHONE, and then choose Contacts.

2. Choose a record that you want to beam, and press MENU.

3. From the Record menu, choose one of the following:

   ■ **Beam**   Sends an individual record

   ■ **Beam Category**   Sends all records in the current category

4. When the Beam Status dialog box appears, point the IR port on your Treo directly at the IR port of the receiving device. The device receiving the beamed information needs to be on and in range—18 inches at most—and the user of the receiving device will have to accept the data before transmission proceeds.

5. Wait for the Beam Status dialog box to indicate that the transfer is complete before you move your Treo. Once the transfer is complete, the user of the device that received the data can either accept or discard the beamed information.

Beam an Application

There are many software developers that program applications specifically for Palm-powered devices like your Treo 600. Now Palm users can beam their favorite applications and games to other Palm users. It is a lot less work than searching the Web for a download site. Not all applications can be beamed. If an application cannot be beamed, a lock icon appears on the Beam screen next to the application's name.

So, just how long does it take to beam an application? Well, for reference, one of the authors beamed a larger-than-average 338K application to another Treo 600, and the process took 50 seconds.

To beam an application, follow these steps:

1. Start the Applications Launcher by pressing HOME.

2. Press MENU.

3. From the App menu, choose Beam.

4. Choose Beam from the menu and select whether the application you want to beam is located on your Treo or on an expansion card. (There's more about using expansion cards in Chapter 15.)

5. Choose the application to transfer.

6. Choose Beam.

7. When the Beam Status dialog box appears, point the IR port on your Treo directly at the IR port of the receiving device.

8. Wait for the Beam Status dialog box to indicate that the transfer is complete before moving your Treo.

Receive Beamed Information

To receive beamed information on your Treo, including business cards, applications, and data, you need to actively accept the data before the download process can begin by following these steps:

1. Turn on your screen.

2. Point the IR port on your Treo directly at the IR port of the transmitting device to open the Beam Status dialog box.

3. When the Beam Status dialog box appears, you can choose a category for the entry to be placed into. The default categories are Business, Personal, Quick List, and Unfiled.

4. On the five-way navigation control, press UP to receive the beam or DOWN to refuse it.

Wrap It Up

Congratulations! If you made it through this chapter, you are well on your way to being able to tell your friends and colleagues that you are a bona fide Treo 600 expert. We covered a lot of ground here, and much of the chapter discussed your Treo from the perspective of the out-of-the-box capabilities utilizing the built-in hardware and software. Hopefully, you are discovering additional uses for your Treo 600 that exceed the reasons why you purchased it in the first place. Many of the topics presented here, and many others, are expanded later in the book. Now that you're warmed up, let's move on to the next chapters, which discuss synchronizing your Treo with your PC, using your Treo phone, and getting connected in the world of wireless data.

Chapter 3

Synchronize Your Treo with Your PC

How to...

■ Install and configure the Palm Desktop synchronization software

■ Synchronize contacts and other data between your Treo and your PC

■ Use Palm Desktop applications

■ Use Chapura PocketMirror to synchronize your Treo with Outlook

■ Use other personal information manager applications with your Treo

■ Use HotSync conduits with third-party applications

This chapter discusses topics about the synchronization of your Treo data with your personal desktop computer and includes benefits, technical alternatives, and steps for getting set up.

What's on the Treo Companion CD

Your Treo 600 ships with a CD that contains some useful documentation and software. The most important item on the CD pertaining to this chapter is the HotSync software that runs on your PC and allows you to HotSync your Treo 600 with your PC. The CD contains the following items:

■ **Palm Desktop synchronization software**   The HotSync software allows you to synchronize data between your PC and your Treo, as well as install applications and files using your HotSync cable.

■ **User Guide (PDF)**   This document includes general user information about using your Treo 600.

■ **Acrobat Reader**   This software allows you to read the User Guide.

■ **Applications**   These consist of the default applications, including productivity tools such as the Date Book and Address Book applications, as well as games such as Solitaire.

Connect Your Treo to Your PC

Your Treo works together with your PC to allow you to easily manage data and applications on your Treo. The process of synchronization allows you to enter information on your computer and then efficiently transfer that information to your

Treo. Of course, the process works the other way as well: changes that you make on your Treo can be transferred to your PC during the synchronization process. The actual synchronization process is configurable and is covered in more detail later in this chapter in the section "Configure HotSync Manager."

Do You Need a PC to Make the Most of Your Treo 600?

Actually, you don't need a PC to use your Treo. You can use your Treo as a stand-alone unit without ever connecting it to a PC. That said, there are many benefits associated with using a PC with your Treo. It is a good idea to set up your PC to sync with your Treo. Even if you only use your PC to load applications and back up your Treo data, it is a powerful combination that can save you a lot of time.

Before you can synchronize, you need to install the Palm Desktop synchronization software on your computer. Even if you already own a Palm-powered device and have installed a previous version, you must install the software that comes on the CD with your Treo.

HotSync Synchronization

The term *synchronization* can be a little bit misleading when we are talking about the way palmOne uses the term. If you look up "synchronize" in the dictionary, you will likely find something such as what is found on www.dictionary.com:

- ■ To occur at the same time; be simultaneous

- ■ To operate in unison

Synchronized swimming, for example, involves two or more swimmers moving in exactly the same way at exactly the same time. But when we are talking about synchronizing your Treo data between your Treo 600 and your personal desktop computer, it does *not* mean that the two are doing the same things at the same time. There is a time lag involved. What we are talking about is roughly as follows: at the time you synchronize, called a *HotSync operation,* your Treo data on both your Treo and on your PC is the same. The data remains in synchronization until you change information on either your Treo 600 or your PC. When you change information on one or the other, the two become out of sync until the next time you perform a HotSync operation, at which time your Treo data on your Treo and your Treo data on your PC are synchronized once again.

To perform this synchronization of Treo data between your Treo 600 and your PC, palmOne provides software called HotSync. When you have installed the HotSync software, along with the Palm Desktop software, you use the HotSync software and HotSync charger cable to connect your Treo to your PC. You begin the HotSync process by pressing the HotSync button on the HotSync cable. This is all covered in detail in this chapter.

Treo-to-PC Connection Options

There are several different ways that you can connect your Treo to your PC:

- **Local connection options**   The first time you perform a HotSync operation you must use one of these methods to establish a username:

  - **Cradle/cable**   This is the most common method. Here, your Treo is physically connected to your PC using a USB or serial port sync cable.

  - **Infrared**   This method allows you to HotSync wirelessly with your PC and requires that your PC have an infrared port.

- **Direct network connection**   This method allows you to HotSync your Treo using another PC connected to the same local area network (LAN) or wide area network (WAN) as your PC. The PC that you connect your Treo to must be running HotSync manager software, and your Treo must be connected to it using a cradle, cable, or infrared communication.

- **Remote connection options**   It's possible to synchronize your Treo remotely using a wireless connection through your wireless service provider. Some extra hardware and setup effort is required to get this to work properly, however. You'll need both a modem attached to your PC and a phone line for the exclusive use of your desktop computer. If you'll be dialing in to a corporate remote access server (RAS), you'll have to configure the RAS to accept connections between your Treo and your PC.

Considerations When HotSyncing with a Modem

If you are away from your PC for extended periods of time and cannot HotSync your Treo directly with your PC using the HotSync cable, you may need an alternate way to HotSync. One of your options is to perform a HotSync operation remotely using the wireless connectivity on your Treo and a phone-line modem connected to your PC. This method of performing a HotSync operation requires that you have a modem connected to your PC, and here are a few points to consider when evaluating this option:

- Wireless networks tend to be much slower than wired connections, so if you are syncing a lot of data, the process will be slow.

- Depending on the service agreement you have with your wireless service provider, you will need to be conscious of how much data you are sending through the wireless network. Data coverage charges can be substantial if you use more than what is specified in your contract.

What Is the Palm Desktop Synchronization Software?

The Palm Desktop synchronization software that comes with your Treo is a suite of applications that allows you to manage data on your PC and synchronize data between your PC and your Treo. The software components include the following:

- **HotSync**   HotSync is the process of synchronizing data between your Treo and your PC. HotSync is initiated from your Treo by pressing the HotSync button on the sync cable. The HotSync button is located on the end section of the HotSync cable that connects to your Treo. The HotSync software must be installed and running on the PC that you are synchronizing data with.

- **Palm Desktop**   The Palm Desktop software includes the following applications and is essentially the tool that you will use if you do not use Outlook:

  - **Date Book**   Allows you to schedule and set alarms for single and recurring events, as well as view your calendar information.

  - **Address Book**   Allows you to track your business and personal contacts, including addresses and phone numbers.

TIP   *Some of the terminology between the Palm Desktop applications and your Treo phone functions can be a little confusing, so here are a few clarifications. The Palm Desktop Date Book = the Treo 600 Calendar, and the Palm Desktop Address Book = the Treo 600 Contacts. The data is essentially the same between the corresponding applications, but the naming conventions are slightly different.*

■ **To Do List**   Allows you to view and manage your tasks, including the ability to set priorities and due dates for each task. You can also save a record of complete tasks.

■ **Memo Pad**   Allows you to save notes for meetings or other events not associated with the Date Book, Address Book, or To Do list.

■ **Install tool**   Allows you to manage the applications that are installed on your Treo. Selected applications will be installed automatically on your handheld the next time you HotSync.

■ **Treo Pictures**   Allows you to automatically download to your PC the digital photos that you take with your Treo.

■ **Chapura PocketMirror**   Required if you are an Outlook user, this software serves as the synchronization conduit between your Treo and Microsoft Outlook and allows you to maintain your data—contacts, calendar information, tasks, and notes—on both your Treo and in Outlook.

Add Functionality to Your Palm Desktop

The Palm Desktop functionality may be expanded through Palm Desktop Extensions. This set of add-on features, such as expense management, is available from palmOne and other third-party software vendors.

Install Palm Desktop Synchronization Software on Your PC

You need to install the Palm Desktop synchronization software on your PC before you can synchronize your PC and your Treo. If you are upgrading from another Palm-powered device and have installed a previous version of the Palm Desktop, you must upgrade to the Palm Desktop software version that comes on the CD with your Treo.

System Requirements

The Palm Desktop is designed for the most common desktop platforms, including Windows and Macintosh. The minimum system requirements are given in the lists that follow. If you are unsure of your PC configuration, the most important thing to know is what operating system is running on your PC.

3

> **TIP** *On a Windows PC, you can find out what operating system is installed by right-clicking the My Computer icon on the Desktop, and selecting Properties.*

For Windows 98SE, ME, 2000, or XP*:

- 32MB of memory
- 30MB of free hard disk space
- CD-ROM drive
- An available USB port
- USB HotSync cable (included with your Treo)

*Later versions may also be supported.

For Windows NT 4:

- 32MB of memory
- 30MB of free hard disk space
- CD-ROM drive
- An available serial port
- Serial HotSync cable (sold separately)

For Macintosh OS 10.1–10.2.*x**:

- 32MB of memory
- 25MB of free hard disk space
- CD-ROM drive
- USB port
- USB HotSync cable (included with your Treo)

*Later versions may also be supported.

The Installation Process

The installation process is straightforward and involves repeatedly clicking OK or ENTER, but there are a few screens that you will want to pay more attention to. These will be discussed shortly.

Before you begin the installation process, your Treo must be connected to your PC with the synchronization cable. If your PC does not have a USB port, you will need to purchase a serial cable before you can get started.

To begin the installation process, insert and run the companion CD that came with your Treo on your PC. (If you don't have the CD, the software can be downloaded from www.palmone.com.) The installation process is relatively straightforward and intuitive, with a series of "Next" selections. (There are two screens you will want to pay close attention to, however, and they are discussed next.) If you get stuck on any of the screens, click the Help button.

The Outlook Detected and Conduit Selection Screens

If you use Microsoft Outlook, the installation program will detect whether or not Microsoft Outlook is installed. If Outlook is detected, you will see the screen shown in Figure 3-1.

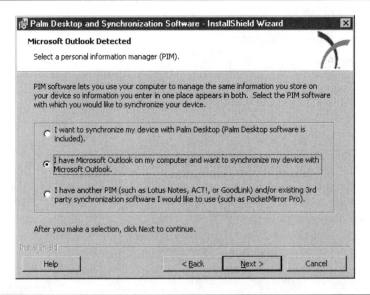

FIGURE 3-1   Outlook has been detected.

If you would like to synchronize your Outlook data with your Treo on an ongoing basis, ensure that the Outlook option is selected and click Next. If for any reason you do not want to synchronize with Outlook on an ongoing basis, you may choose to use the Palm Desktop or a different PIM (personal information manager) such as ACT!, GoldMine, or Lotus. Afterward, choose the third option and click Next.

If Outlook is not detected, you will see the screen shown in Figure 3-2. If you are not an Outlook user and you don't currently use a PIM, then the Palm Desktop applications offer a great way to manage your contacts, calendar information, tasks, and notes. If you use another PIM application, then there may be third-party software that allows you to synchronize your Treo with the software you use. More information is available toward the end of this chapter in the section titled "What if I Don't Use Outlook?"

Select User Screen

Your username is the key that allows the Treo synchronization software to know which device goes with which set of personal information on your desktop computer. Every Treo has a username associated with it. The username uniquely identifies your device when you synchronize with your PC. The Select User screen looks like that shown in Figure 3-3. To create a new user, click the Create New User button and enter your username, which can be anything you like.

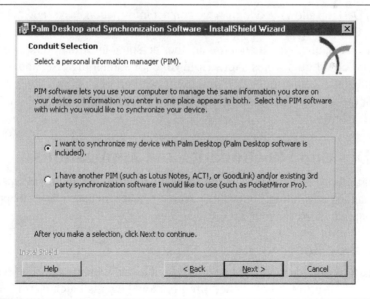

FIGURE 3-2   Outlook has not been detected.

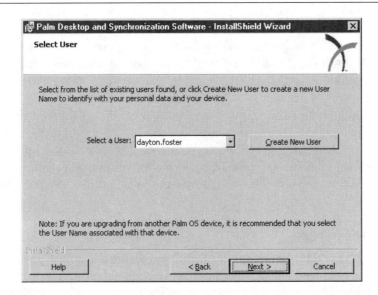

FIGURE 3-3   The Select User screen

Learn the Palm Desktop

The Palm Desktop allows you to manage contact information, tasks, and appointments on your PC and synchronize your data with your Treo. The Palm Desktop is particularly valuable if you do not use another personal information manager (PIM) such as Outlook, Lotus Notes, Act!, GoldMine, or something else, and some of the functionality will be useful even if you don't need all of it. If you don't currently use one of these other PIM applications, then you will likely find the Palm Desktop extremely useful.

Palm Desktop Functionality and Applications

The Palm Desktop consists of several useful subapplications, including applications for calendar and scheduling, contact management, a task manager, and an application to install applications on your Treo.

Use the Date Book

The Date Book application allows you to schedule and manage calendar events. This is particularly useful for both scheduling personal events (such as reminders for birthdays and anniversaries) and for storing meetings and events. A useful feature

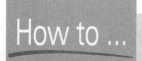

Upgrade from a Previous Version of Palm

If you are upgrading from an older Handspring or other Palm OS device and you used the PC you are using now to HotSync, you will already have a username associated with the older device, and it will show up in the drop-down list. If you want to synchronize your new device with your existing data, you should choose your old username from the Select a User drop-down list. Your data will be transferred to your new device when you synchronize during the installation process.

is the ability to set an alarm that will serve as a reminder for a future event. For each Date Book event, you can define the following:

- **Event Title**   A name for the event that will make sense to you when you are alerted.

- **Event Time and Duration**   The time of day that the event will take place and how long it will take. If an event is not time-specific, such as a birthday, select the No Time radio button.

- **Event Date**   The calendar day on which the event occurs.

- **Alarm**   You can set the Event Alarm to remind you how many minutes, hours, or days there are before the Event occurs. For example, you may want to set an alarm of several days to remind yourself to prepare a report for the Board of Directors, while you may only need a 15-minute alert to remind you of a lunch meeting.

- **Repeat**   You can define an event to repeat. This is useful for an event such as a mortgage payment or monthly sales meeting, and the event can be set to repeat daily, weekly, monthly, or yearly.

- **Note**   The Note tab allows you to store more information about a particular event, such as directions to the meeting.

Use the Address Book

The Address Book allows you to manage names, addresses, phone numbers, and other information for your personal contacts. For each contact in your address book, you can store phone numbers, e-mail addresses, mailing addresses, and notes. You can also flag a contact as private and categorize each contact as personal, business, or something else. Changes you make to your contacts, in either the Palm Desktop or on your Treo, will be synchronized the next time you HotSync.

Use the To Do List

The To Do List is simply a digital version of the traditional paper-based task lists that many of us use to help us get organized. The To Do List allows you to manage tasks, set priorities for each, associate items with categories, and mark confidential items as private. You can view your tasks by due date, priority, and category. Your To Do items show up in the Date Book Today view so you can see what you have to do today. You can also designate a To Do item as Complete so that you have a running record of how much you have accomplished.

Use the Memo Pad

The Memo Pad application is a nice place to record and store information that doesn't fit logically into the Date Book, To Do List, or Address Book applications. You can create memos that are up to 800 words, import larger files, and view your memos in alphabetical order or in the order in which they are displayed on your Treo. Memos can also be categorized and flagged as private.

Use Treo Pictures

The Treo Pictures function is not an application—it serves as a shortcut to the directory where HotSync stores your Treo pictures on your PC. By default, the photos that are transferred to your PC when you HotSync are stored in the Treo Pictures folder in the Handspring directory, C:\Program Files\Handspring\Treo Pictures\ *username,* where *username* is your Treo username.

Use the Install Tool

The Install tool allows you to select applications or files—such as databases or network configuration files—that you want to install on your Treo the next time you HotSync. With the Install tool, you can install applications or files both on your handheld and on an expansion card. (Expansion cards are discussed in Chapter 15.) The types of files that can be installed on your Treo, or expansion card, include standard Palm file types, such as PRC, PDB, PNC, SPC, and others. Note that the Treo 600 does not support the file type PQA. Also, nonstandard file types such as JPG, HLP, DOC, and so on, can be installed on your Treo only on an expansion card and only if your handheld or expansion card contains an application that can read or open that file type.

CAUTION *Your Treo is designed so that any applications or files you install, other than those that were preinstalled when you purchased your Treo, run in RAM (random access memory) and are not stored on the disk drive. This is only important if you need to hard-reset your handheld, because if you do hard-reset, your installed applications will be deleted. They will be reinstalled the next time you HotSync, however, as long as you have them selected in the Install tool. Any applications or files that are installed on an expansion card will be stored on the card until you remove them—that is, they are not deleted if you hard-reset your Treo, provided you installed the applications using the Palm Desktop Install tool. Applications that were beamed (beaming is covered in Chapter 2) or downloaded directly onto your Treo from the Internet using the Browser may be lost when you perform a hard-reset on your Treo.*

Install Applications and Files on Your Treo with the Palm Desktop

Applications for your Treo are generally single files with a filename ending in .prc. This makes installing new applications on your Treo easier than installing software on a PC or server. The Palm Desktop software allows you to select applications or files that are stored on your PC to be installed or copied to your Treo the next time you HotSync.

Install Applications or Files on Your Treo

The Install tool in the Palm Desktop allows you to select the applications or files that will be installed on your Treo the next time you HotSync.

1. In the Install Tool dialog box, if you have more than one Palm username associated with your PC, make sure your username is selected, and then click Add.

2. In the Open dialog box, browse to select the applications or files to install.

3. Click OK, and then click Done.

The application or file that you have added will be loaded onto your Treo the next time you HotSync.

Install Applications or Files onto an SD (Secure Digital) Card on Your Treo

If you have an SD card, or cards, you can install and run applications on it. There are a couple of reasons you may want to install and run applications on an SD card. The first is that it allows you to maximize the memory on your Treo, and the second is that if you have more than one SD card, you can swap applications as you need them without taking up unnecessary memory space on your Treo. The steps to install an application on an SD card are as follows:

1. In the Install Tool dialog box, if you have more than one Palm username associated with your PC, make sure that the username you want is selected; then click Add.

2. In the Open dialog box, browse to select the applications or files to install and click OK.

3. Click the Change Destination button.

4. Choose the drop-down menu entitled Install To and select SD Card.

5. If you would like to move an item from one list to the other, click the item and then click the arrow pointing to the other list.

6. On the Change Destination screen, click OK.

7. On the Install Tool screen, click Done.

Remove Applications or Files from Your Treo

There are several reasons why you may want to uninstall applications or delete files. Perhaps you no longer need a particular application, or an application doesn't do what you want, or you need to free up memory on your Treo. Applications are removed directly from your Treo and not through the Palm Desktop. The steps to uninstall an application or file are as follows:

1. On your Treo, go to the Applications Launcher by pressing the HOME button on the keyboard.

2. Press the MENU button.

3. Select Delete.

4. A screen that looks like the following will appear. Select the file or application you would like to remove or delete.

5. Select Delete.

At the top of the screen there is a graphical indicator showing how much available memory you have left on your Treo. If the bar stretches across the entire screen, you'll want to remove some data or applications.

Special Cases to Consider When Removing Applications and Files

Some scenarios warrant discussing a few caveats in regard to removing applications from your Treo. The preceding steps applied to the simplest scenario, where you are removing third-party applications and nonsystem data. Other scenarios you may encounter include the following:

- You want to remove an application that was preinstalled on your Treo when you received it but that doesn't appear in the Delete list.

- You want to delete files that don't show up in the Applications Launcher.

- You uninstalled an application, but it shows up again when you HotSync.

You Cannot Uninstall Built-In Applications   Some of the applications on your Treo cannot be removed, thus they do not show up in the Delete list. These built-in applications do not affect your memory since they are loaded permanently in the read-only memory (ROM).

Uninstall Hidden Files   Use the following information with caution. It is only mentioned here to let you know it is possible. If a file doesn't show up in the Delete list, it may be a "hidden" file. Hidden files can be deleted but only with a third-party application, such as FileZ or zCatalog. The use of these applications is not recommended because removing system files or data may cause your Treo to become unstable and may negatively affect the HotSync process.

Why Do Deleted Applications Come Back?   Some of the applications loaded on your Treo may be backed up on your desktop. If an application that you deleted from your Treo is backed up on your desktop, it will be reinstalled the next time you HotSync. This is extremely helpful in the event that you have to perform a hard-reset on your Treo, because it means that you will only lose the data that has changed since the previous HotSync. If you are intentionally trying to delete an application that was backed up, then you will have to remove the application from your PC as well as from your Treo.

To remove the application from the backup folder on your PC, follow these steps:

1. Navigate to the Backup folder in your Palm application folder.

   ■ The Backup folder is usually found in the Handspring or Palm folder. For example, on my Windows PC, it's in C:\Program Files\Handspring\dayton\Backup.

   ■ If your PC is a Macintosh, you can locate the Backup folder using the Find function under the File menu.

2. Find the file or program you would like to delete—it will likely end with either a .prc (a Palm application file) or .pdb (a Palm database file) extension—and select File | Delete.

Import and Export Data in the Palm Desktop

One of the strengths of the Palm Desktop is its ability to import and export data. This makes it relatively easy to move data between the Palm Desktop, other applications, and the personal information manager software. There are even Palm-only proprietary formats called "archives"—including Date Book Archive (*.dba), Address Book Archive (*.aba), To Do Archive (*.tda), and Memo Pad Archive (*.mpa)—that allow you to easily swap data between Palm Desktop users or offer an easy way to back up your Palm Desktop data.

Note that CSV (Comma Separated Value) files can be used if none of the other platforms are supported.

Supported Palm Desktop Import and Export File Formats

Your Treo is capable of importing and exporting several file formats. The supported
Palm Desktop import and export file formats according to palmOne are listed here:

- Date Book formats
  - Date Book Archive (*.dba)—Palm proprietary
  - vCal files (*.vcs)
- Address Book formats
  - Address Book Archive (*.aba)—Palm proprietary
  - Comma delimited (*.csv, *.txt)
  - Tab separated values (*.tab, *.tsv, *.txt)
  - vCard files (*.vcf)
  - CSV files (Lotus Organizer 2.*x*/97 mapping)
- To Do List formats, To Do Archive (*.tda)—Palm proprietary
- Memo Pad
  - Memo Pad Archive (*.mpa)—Palm proprietary
  - Comma separated (*.csv, *.txt)
  - Tab separated values (*.tab, *.tsv, *.txt)
  - Text (*.txt), vCal

Import Data into the Palm Desktop

To import data into the Palm Desktop, ensure that the data you want to import matches
one of the supported formats from the preceding list and then follow these steps:

1. In the Palm Desktop application, select the File menu.
2. Select Import.
3. A dialog box similar to that shown in Figure 3-4 will open.
4. Select the appropriate choice from the Files of Type drop-down list.

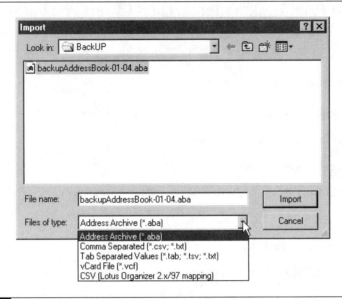

FIGURE 3-4 Importing data

5. Browse to the file you would like to import.

6. Select Import.

It is always a good idea to test an import by importing a small part of the data first, especially if you are about to import a large amount of data. If imported data doesn't import exactly as intended, it could prove a time-consuming task to manually clean up or delete data.

Import Data that Is Not Already in a Supported File Type

If you would like to import data that is not already in an acceptable import format, you may still be able to import the data, but it may take a little "massaging." Most applications can export data into a CSV (Comma Separated Value) format, which can then be imported into the Palm Desktop. But, before you import thousands of records in this manner, try exporting a small amount of data from the source application and import it into the Palm Desktop to make sure that the data is translated correctly and that you don't end up with phone numbers in the name fields, for example. Another option, although a potentially slow one, is to cut and paste data from one application to the other.

Export Data from the Palm Desktop

To export data from the Palm Desktop, follow these steps:

1. Select the Palm Desktop application you would like to export data from (Date Book, Address Book, To Do, or Memo).

2. Select File | Export to open a dialog box like the one shown in Figure 3-5.

3. Browse to the file location where you want to save the exported data.

4. Enter a filename and select the export format type.

5. Select the range, either All or Currently Selected Records.

6. Click Export.

> **TIP**   *Remember that if you export data in any of the Palm proprietary "archive" types (.dba, .aba, .tba, or .mpa) you will only be able to use the data within a Palm Desktop application, whereas if you export data in a nonproprietary format (.csv or .txt), you will be able to use the data in other applications as well.*

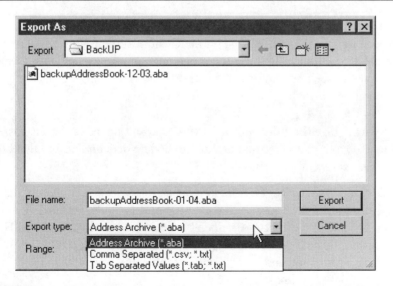

FIGURE 3-5   Exporting data

Configure HotSync Manager

The HotSync Manager allows you to modify your synchronization settings. Even though you may never need to change the default settings, there are situations where you may want to modify them temporarily. Therefore, it's valuable to be aware of these settings.

The HotSync Manager Custom screen can be accessed from the HotSync menu in the Palm Desktop, and it looks like this:

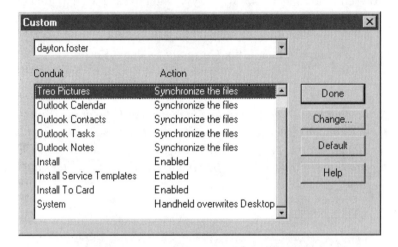

For each item in the conduit list on the Custom screen, you can change how you want HotSync to deal with data. For example, if you select Contacts and click Change, you will see a screen similar to the one shown in Figure 3-6. Here you have four different options:

- **Synchronize the Files** This is the default setting. Here, data is passed both to and from your Treo and desktop to update data and ensure that both have the most recent version.

- **Desktop Overwrites Handheld** When this selection is chosen, the desktop always overwrites your Treo data. This means that if you update a record on your Treo, it will be overwritten by the desktop the next time you HotSync. This would be a good choice if on your Treo you only read your Address Book information and never modify records. It also results in faster HotSync operations if you have a lot of data.

3

■ **Handheld Overwrites Desktop**   When this selection is chosen, your Treo always overwrites your desktop data. This means that if you update a record on your desktop, it will be overwritten the next time you HotSync. This is a good choice if on your desktop you only read your Address Book information and only modify records on your Treo. It also results in faster HotSync operations if you have a lot of data.

■ **Do Nothing**   When this option is selected, no data will be synchronized between your Treo and your desktop, and each will have its own data. This option defeats the core benefits of synchronization but it does have its uses. For example, perhaps you don't have time to HotSync all of your Address Book data because you have been on the road for a month and have added thousands of records, and you're only interested in moving your digital photographs to your PC during the HotSync. In this scenario, you could change all of the HotSync Custom conduit actions to move nothing except Treo Pictures.

Add Functionality to Your Palm Desktop

Another advantage of the Palm Desktop is a side effect of palmOne's dominant position in the mobile device and software marketplace. PalmOne and other application developers perpetually release new and updated software both for Palm-powered devices and the Palm Desktop. This means that there are software

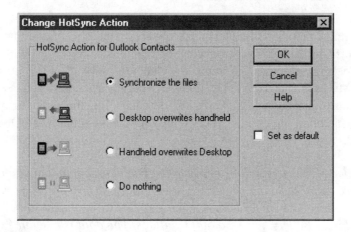

FIGURE 3-6   The Change HotSync Action screen

add-ons for the Palm Desktop that allow you to do even more with it. Ways to add functionality to your Palm Desktop include extensions and add-ins.

Palm Desktop Extensions

Palm Desktop extensions are applications that you can install individually and use within the Palm Desktop window to add more functionality. For example, a particular extension might allow you to record and track your expenses. Buttons for extensions appear on the Launch bar. Each extension runs within the Palm Desktop and may add new buttons or menu items to the interface. Extensions can be downloaded from palmOne and other third-party software vendors. Check www.palmone.com for information about new extensions.

Palm Desktop Add-Ins

Palm Desktop add-ins are different from extensions because they add functionality to the built-in Palm Desktop applications. For example, an add-in called Delete Duplicates checks for and removes duplicate records in the Palm Desktop software applications.

Add-ins are available from Palm and other third-party software vendors. Check www.palmone.com for information about new add-ins.

Use PocketMirror to Synchronize Your Treo with Outlook

If you use Microsoft Outlook as your personal information manager, you will be pleased to know that the Palm Desktop software includes a conduit that allows you to synchronize the data on your Treo with your Outlook data. This conduit application is called PocketMirror and is produced by Chapura (www.chapura.com).

PocketMirror is an application that runs on your PC and allows you to synchronize data between your Treo and Microsoft Outlook, including the ability to sync Outlook Contacts, Calendar, Tasks, and Notes with your Treo Contacts, To Do List, and Memo Pad.

> **TIP** *Some of the terminology between the Palm Desktop applications and your Treo phone functions can be a little confusing, so here are a few clarifications. The Palm Desktop Date Book = the Treo 600 Calendar, and the Palm Desktop Address Book = the Treo 600 Contacts. The data is essentially the same between the corresponding applications, but the naming conventions are slightly different.*

Once installed, the PocketMirror user interface is accessible within the Microsoft Outlook application. You'll notice two specific additions to the Outlook interface:

- **PocketMirror folder**   In the folders view, you should see a folder called PocketMirror, as shown in Figure 3-7. The PocketMirror folder contains two subfolders:

  - **Archive**   PocketMirror creates a special archive folder in Outlook to store archived handheld items. This means that if you delete a handheld item *and* select the Save Archive Copy on PC option, PocketMirror will move that item out of the Outlook folder it was in and put it into your archive folder.

  - **Conflicts**   Any time the HotSync process encounters data conflicts, it will back up the conflicting data in the Conflicts folder. This means you'll have a backup if a record is inadvertently overwritten during a HotSync operation.

- **Chapura Settings menu**   Shown in Figure 3-8, the Chapura Settings screen lets you manage your Treo user accounts, as well as modify how PocketMirror synchronizes your data.

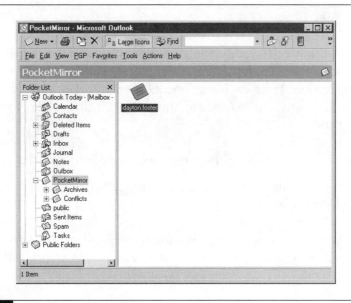

FIGURE 3-7   The PocketMirror folders

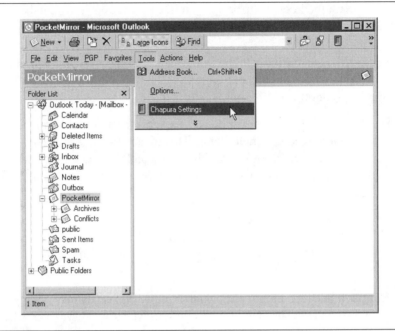

FIGURE 3-8 The Chapura Settings menu

Change Chapura Synchronization Preferences

The synchronization settings in the Chapura Settings screen control the way PocketMirror conducts the synchronization process, and can be defined separately for each application. The four Treo applications that PocketMirror synchronizes are Contacts, Calendar, To Do List, and Memo Pad. To change the synchronization settings for a user:

1. Launch Chapura Settings from the Tools menu and select the user.

2. Click the Settings button to open the Change Synchronization Preferences screen.

You can modify the synchronization settings independently for each application (Outlook Calendar, Outlook Contacts, Outlook Tasks, and Outlook Notes) and also define your preferences for System and Install syncing.

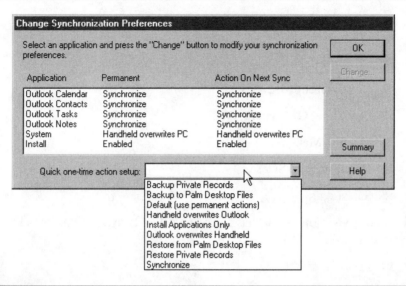

FIGURE 3-9   The Change Synchronization Preferences screen showing one-time actions menu

One-Time Synchronization Options

In addition to configuring your HotSync settings to have them used on a permanent basis, you can use the Change Synchronization Preferences screen to run one-time processes. One-time options are available by clicking the Quick One-Time Action Setup drop-down menu shown in Figure 3-9. This allows you to perform one-time actions without affecting your permanent settings, including the ability to perform actions like Back Up Private Records, Install Applications Only, and Restore from Palm Desktop Files.

What if I Don't Use Outlook?

Your Treo ships with the Palm Desktop and the PocketMirror conduit for Outlook. If you use another personal information manager application, there may be third-party software that allows you to synchronize. Following are some examples:

- PumaTech (www.pumatech.com) offers conduits for

  - Microsoft Outlook
  - Outlook Express

- ACT!
- Lotus Notes
- Schedule+
- Novell Groupwise
- Day Timer Organizer
- Meeting Maker
- Oracle Mobile Sales
- SalesLogix
- Lotus (www.lotus.com) has a product called EasySync Pro that allows you to sync with
  - Lotus Notes
  - Lotus Organizer
- CompanionLink (www.companionlink.com) offers conduits for
  - ACT!
  - GoldMine
  - Lotus Organizer
  - Outlook
  - Schedule+
  - TeleMagic

Use the HotSync Conduit with Third-Party Applications

When you install an application on your Treo that uses or stores files and data, it will likely use a "conduit" application to transfer the data between your Treo and your PC. You can modify your conduit settings for this through the HotSync manager. Each conduit will have different application-specific items that allow you to define how you would like the synchronization to occur.

NOTE   *The term* conduit *refers to software that allows data to be transferred to and from both your PC and your Treo during a HotSync operation. Many third-party applications install a conduit when you install software on your Treo.*

To help explain third-party conduits, it may be helpful to use an example. One third-party application that has its own conduit is the application we used to take screenshots of Treo 600 screens for this book. The software is called ScreenShot5 and is produced by LinkeSoft (www.linkesoft.com).

After installing the application using the Treo 600 Install tool, the conduit appears in the HotSync Custom settings list. You can get to the Custom settings by launching HotSync on your PC (not on your Treo). You can then browse to the HotSync Custom settings by clicking the HotSync icon in your toolbar and selecting the Custom menu item. You can also browse to the HotSync Custom settings in the Palm Desktop by selecting the HotSync menu at the top and choosing Custom. The Custom settings screen looks like this:

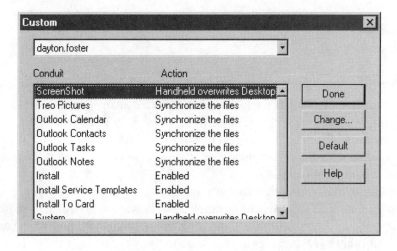

The ScreenShot-specific conduit appears at the top of the list. To view and change the settings, click Change. Figure 3-10 shows the conduit-specific synchronization items that you can change. For this particular application, you can choose where you would like the screenshot images to be stored when you HotSync and what format you would like the images saved as. Again, the types of things that you can modify are specific to each application conduit.

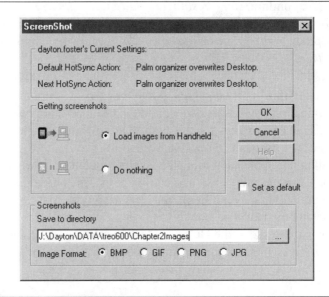

FIGURE 3-10   Conduit-specific synchronization items

Wrap It Up

The combination of a Treo 600 and a desktop PC offers many benefits, and, ultimately, performing routine HotSync operations can make your life easier. This chapter covered some of the benefits and also reasons why it is a good idea to synchronize your Treo data with your PC regularly, not the least of which is that it offers a great way to back up your Treo data.

In addition to ensuring that your personal information is the same on both your desktop PC and your Treo, synchronization also allows you to copy music, pictures, applications, and information back and forth between your PC and your Treo. This is especially valuable when files are too large to transfer quickly to your Treo using a wireless data connection or when data entry is too time consuming using the Treo keyboard. Once you are set up to HotSync, your Treo and your PC make a great combination to help you get the most out of your Treo 600.

Chapter 4

Make Calls with Your Treo

How to...

■ Dial a number from your Contacts

■ Configure your phone display and sounds

■ Use speed-dial for one-button calling

■ Set up custom ringtones and pictures for specific callers

■ Prevent accidental calling with the Keyguard

The Treo is a very high-quality telephone and communication tool. As a new Treo owner, I am sure that one of the first things you did was make a phone call. One of the strengths of the Treo is that you are able to pull it out, turn it on, and make your first call without the need to consult the manual or read a book. This is the hallmark of user-friendly technology. Some parts of the Treo are just that simple, but some of the other things you may choose to do are not quite as obvious.

The Treo is capable of much more advanced calling features, and in this section of the book we will help you make better use of the more advanced phone capabilities of your Treo including custom ringtones, picture display, conference calls, speakerphone, speed dial, hands-free calling for safer driving, and much more. If you are already comfortable with all the basic calling functions of your Treo, skip the following "Use the Basic Phone" section and go right to the advanced calling.

NOTE *I want to make sure with this book that we aren't rewriting the Treo 600 instruction manual. I will spend very little time on the basic functions of the Treo, assuming that you have read the manual and what I will present here will only be refreshers. If you have lost your Treo manual, you can download it from the palmOne site at http://support.handspring.com/. With the merger between Palm and Handspring, the web site will likely go through some changes over the next year. If the link listed here fails, go to the www.palmone.com web site and select Support to get to the user manual downloads.*

Use the Basic Phone

As long as you have wireless service where you are, using the Treo as a telephone is very straightforward. This section will familiarize you briefly with the basic controls to use while you are on a call.

Dial a Call

Often, the initial comment we hear when people first look at our Treo 600s is about how small the keyboard is. Then follows the question, "How do you make a phone call on that?" There are actually seven different ways you can dial a call on a Treo 600.

Keyboard

You can use the number buttons on the keyboard to dial a number when you are in phone mode (pressing the leftmost hard button beside the navigation control). The number pad is embedded within the standard keys on the keyboard. In order to make them stand out for easy dialing, they are highlighted in a blue or black color. In phone mode, you don't have to press ALT (which is blue or black in color depending on the Treo model you have) to access the numbers, you can just type them directly, and then press RETURN to dial the number.

The Dial Pad

Luckily for those of us with big fingers, in addition to the hard keyboard, the Treo 600 features a "soft" keyboard right on the screen that you can easily tap out a number on with your fingers. It's shown in Figure 4-1.

In phone mode, the soft Dial Pad will automatically appear when you press the leftmost button beside the navigation control (this button has a small picture of a telephone on it).

NOTE   *If you are using the Orange version of the Treo 600, pressing the left button will not bring up the Dial Pad. Instead, it will open a bitmap explaining how to dial your phone from the hard keyboard. You will also find some additional differences on an Orange Treo, such as that the default configuration for the navigation control is slightly different than what is mentioned in these chapters.*

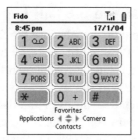

FIGURE 4-1   The Treo 600 features both a hard and soft keyboard.

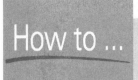 **Look Up a Number on the Fly**

Have you ever wished you could look up a number for someone on the fly? There are many web sites now that will provide directory assistance in your local area. In your web browser, you can go to www.anywho.com to look up a person or business in the U.S. AnyWho also has a link to other lookup services online for many other countries around the world at www.anywho.com/international. Once you find who you are looking for, the person's number will show up as a hyperlink (underlined). Tap the link with the stylus, or select it with the five-way navigation control and press the CENTER button.

In addition to the browser-based service, there is a free utility called Directory Assistant that you can load on your Treo for looking up U.S. phone numbers. You can download a free copy of Directory Assistant at http://home.triad.rr.com/rlwhitt/palm/#da.

Residential Query	16 Result(s)	Get Directions
Last Name whitt	First Citizens Bank	From: Clear Addr Book
First Name rick	First Citizens Bank	Address
City or Zip clemmons	Lowe's	City
State ▼ North Carolina	Lowe's Food No 144	State Zip
Results ▼ 25	Lowes Food Stores	To: Clear Addr Book
☐ Add to existing results	Lowes Food Stores	Address 5901 University Pkwy
☑ Disconnect after search	Lowes Food Stores	City WINSTON SALEM
Search Lookup Close	Lowe's Food No 144 200 Summit Square Blvd WINSTON SALEM, NC 27105 (336) 377-9525	State NC Zip 27105 Get Directions Lookup Close

You can then type in your number and press the Dial soft button to initiate the call.

The Recently Called List and the Call Log

When you are in phone mode, you can also use the five-way navigation control to perform a variety of actions. Pressing the CENTER button will open up the list of numbers that you most recently dialed, as shown in Figure 4-2.

The first entry on the menu will simply return you back to the Dial Pad to place your call manually. The bottom ten entries on the list will be the names or numbers of the last ten telephone numbers you called. If the number is in your contact list, then the name of the person or company you called will be displayed followed by a letter in parentheses to show if you called them at home, work, on their mobile,

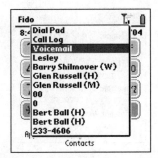

FIGURE 4-2   The list of most recently dialed numbers makes it easy for you to connect to a number that you called recently.

or another way. Highlighting the number with the five-way navigation control or tapping it with the stylus will cause that number to be dialed.

The second entry on the list will open up your Call Log. The Call Log displays a chronologically sorted list of all of your calls, starting from the most recent, as shown in Figure 4-3.

Each entry will show you who the call was with (by name if the number you called is in the Contacts list, or by number if it is not), if it was incoming or outgoing by the direction and color of the small arrow to the left of the name, and the date of the call. You can select any number on this list and press the Dial soft button to make an immediate call to that person. If the person isn't already in your contact list, you also will see a soft button labeled Add Contact, which will take you to the new contact window, discussed in detail in Chapter 2.

When a call is highlighted in the Call Log, you can press the Details soft button to see a detailed accounting of the call, as shown in Figure 4-4.

FIGURE 4-3   The Call Log will show you a list of all of your calls, allowing you to dial any number you've communicated with or see the details of a specific call.

FIGURE 4-4   You can view the detailed information from any call that is still in your Call Log.

The information you can see includes the duration of the call, and if you were roaming at the time or not.

This call log can get quite large if you use your Treo frequently, so it is useful to empty it from time to time. You can delete a particular entry out of the call log by selecting it and then opening the menu and choosing Delete Record. You can clear the entire log at once by selecting the Purge menu item.

> TIP   *Push-To-Talk (or "walkie-talkie" style) communication between mobile phones has recently become very popular. The current models of Treo 600 that are on the market today do not support this feature; however, some carriers such as Orange in the UK have announced that they will be releasing a version of the Treo 600 that has Push-To-Talk functionality. Keep your eyes open for this device later in 2004.*

Dial from Contacts

You can also dial any phone number that is in your Contacts application. From within the phone application, you can launch the Contacts application by pressing the five-way navigation control in the appropriate direction. Then you can type in the first few letters of a person's name (first or last) or just type the person's initials, so if you wanted to dial "Michelle White", you could type in "mich" or "mw" or "white." All of these would pare down your Contacts list and probably find Michelle quickly. Because this feature is so compelling and useful, there is a preference setting under the Options menu called Display Preferences where you can switch the mode by which the phone begins to dial when in the Phone application main view. Out of the box, the Treo is configured to "Typing dials phone number" so people can get used to just dialing with the keyboard. However, many people change this setting to "Typing starts Contacts search" since most people have all of the numbers they want to dial in their Contacts list.

The Contacts application is covered in more detail in Chapter 10.

Speed Dial from Favorites

You can also dial using the Favorites application, which is discussed in the "Use Advanced Calling Features" section of this chapter.

Dial Through Hyperlinks

If someone sends you an e-mail with a phone number, or if one shows up in a web page, SMS, or MMS message, it will appear with an underline beneath it. This indicates it is hyperlinked and if you tap it, or select it with the five-way navigation control and press the CENTER button, your Treo will automatically dial the number for you!

Use "On Call" Controls

When you are actively engaged in a call, the controls that appear on the Treo will be different, as shown in Figure 4-5.

FIGURE 4-5   The options available to you when you are in the middle of a call include Hang Up, Speakerphone, Hold, Mute, and show the Dial Pad.

Some of the things you can control during a call include the following:

- **Volume** The volume up and down buttons on the side of your Treo allow you to change the volume of the speaker or earbud while in the middle of the call. Note that these are not soft buttons but hard controls on the left side of your Treo 600. This is very useful if you find you are having trouble hearing the person you are speaking with, or if the call is too loud, making it uncomfortable for your ear.

- **Hang Up** This self-explanatory button will disconnect the current call.

- **Speakerphone** This button will turn your Treo into a speakerphone by increasing the volume of the speaker significantly so it can be heard by everyone in the immediate proximity. The microphone sensitivity will also be turned up to enable everyone who hears the call to speak and participate. Pressing this same soft button again will return you to regular phone mode, allowing you to hold the Treo up to your ear to continue the call in private.

- **Hold** This button will put a caller on hold, permitting you to take or place a second call (if your plan with your wireless service provider, the company who provides your phone service, supports this). Once a call is on hold and you have a second call, you can actually conference the two (or more) calls together. Again, this is a feature that must be supported by your carrier and your calling plan.

- **Mute** The button with the picture of a microphone allows you to mute your call so that the other party on the call cannot hear what you are saying. You will know the call is muted because the microphone will show a red X through it. Pressing this button again will unmute your call and allow the other party to hear you.

- **Dial Pad** The small button that looks like a little telephone dial pad will open up the full Dial Pad screen, allowing you to enter keystrokes. This is important for voicemail systems and Interactive Voice Response systems that require you to press numbers on your phone to initiate actions.

While in the middle of a call, you can continue to use your Treo as a regular PDA to make notes, look at documents, and perform other functions. To return to the call in progress, simply press the PHONE hard button to the far left of the five-way navigation control.

FIGURE 4-6 Ringer volume can be set with the physical buttons on the side or through the Sound Preferences in the options menu.

Change Volume and Vibrate Settings

The volume of the Treo ringer can be controlled either from the hard controls or from the preferences for the phone. The hard controls are the volume controls on the left side of the Treo. Pressing the UP or DOWN button will increase or decrease the volume of the ringer as appropriate (as long as you are not on an active call, in which case they will not change the ringer volume; they will change the speaker volume for the call). On the screen, you will see a graph showing the current setting for the ringer.

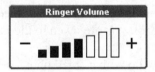

Alternatively, you can also set the ringer volume by selecting Sound Preferences from the Options menu on the main telephone window, as shown in Figure 4-6.

Use Advanced Calling Features

Learning to use your Treo to make and receive calls is quite intuitive; however, once you have mastered that, it is time to start learning how to do some of the more advanced functions that can really make the most out of your Treo investment!

Speed Dial a Favorite Number

The Treo 600 has a very useful feature called Favorites. In addition to being able to define shortcuts to your most frequently used applications and web sites, it also is where you can set up specific contacts as speed-dial numbers. With the touch of a single button you can instantly be connected to up to 50 of your most frequently called numbers.

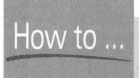 **Disable the "Special Keys"**

The engineers at Handspring created the Treo so that when the phone rings, you can press special keys on the hard keyboard to take a certain action. Pressing the SPACEBAR or RETURN will answer the call, and pressing BACKSPACE will ignore the call. While this seems like a good idea, this has actually created a number of problems. If you carry your Treo in your pocket, purse, or any kind of case, a small amount of pressure may continually be placed on the SPACEBAR. That means you may miss a call because your phone never rang at all, but immediately auto-answered the incoming call. This happens even if the Keyguard is on.

Handspring is not currently offering any way to fix this problem with the phone, so an enterprising Treo 600 user has created a "patch" for the phone that disables these special keys. As this software does not come from Handspring, you must assume responsibility for using it; however, if you are experiencing the "special key" problem, this may be the solution you are looking for. You can learn more about it and download the patch for free from www.tvbilly.com/DAAK/.

Favorites are accessed from the phone Dial Pad screen. When you press the TOP button of the navigation control, you are taken to the Favorites screen, as shown in Figure 4-7.

Speed-dial favorites show up with a small phone beside them and a name. On the right side of each favorite button, you will also see a letter or number representing a key on the keyboard. To speed dial a number, you can press and hold the key on the keyboard from the Phone screen to immediately begin dialing that number.

FIGURE 4-7   The Favorites feature of the Treo allows you to create one-button access to your favorite phone numbers, messaging numbers, applications, and web pages.

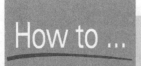 **See All the Numbers for a Contact in My Favorites**

When the focus is on a specific speed-dial Favorite, you can press the SPACEBAR and the Treo will display all the phone numbers associated with the contact in your Contacts list. This means that instead of just having one number for the speed dial, you can access all the numbers. In order to enable this feature, the speed-dial Favorite must have been set up using the "lookup" feature.

4

You can also press the soft button on the interface of the Favorites screen to do the same. The Favorites screen only shows you ten of your favorites at a time, but at the bottom-right of the screen you will see five boxes numbered 1 through 5. Each of these boxes represents a different page of favorites. The page you are currently on is highlighted. You can move from page to page by tapping any page number with your stylus, or you can use the navigation control to move left or right through the pages.

To create a new speed-dial number, you can tap on any empty speed-dial button. This will open the Add Favorite screen, as shown in Figure 4-8.

The Type drop-down is where you will select the type of Favorite you are creating. This will default to be a speed-dial, but you can change this to create a link to an application, web page, or messaging number.

The Label field is the label that you want to appear on the favorite soft button so you can recognize it on the Favorite screen. There is a button labeled Lookup that will let you select a contact from your list of Treo contacts to fill in the label and number.

The Number field is the field that you want to speed dial when this favorite is selected.

FIGURE 4-8   The Add Favorite screen is where you will create your new speed-dial number.

The Quick Key field is where you will select a single key from the keyboard that you want to define as the Quick Key for this favorite. This means that when the phone interface is up, if you press and hold this key on the keyboard, it will automatically speed dial that number. For example, in Figure 4-7, you can see a speed dial defined as "Lesley" with a Quick Key of "L." Pressing and holding L when the Treo is turned on will initiate the speed dial of a call to Lesley.

The More button on the bottom-right opens up a screen of extremely useful features, as shown in Figure 4-9.

The extra digits option is a feature that is extremely valuable for many uses. It allows you to choose specific digits that you want dialed in after the number is called. Two examples of how this might be used include the following:

- **Entering a password**   Some numbers when you call them require you to enter a password. For example, when you call your voicemail account, you might be prompted to enter your pass code and then press #. You can define a set of extra digits to perform this automatically. If your pass code was 7124, you could define extra digits of 7124# and then select the Dial Extra Digits Automatically check box to automatically authenticate with your voicemail system when you speed dial the number.

- **Routing a call through an automated attendant**   Many organizations now use an automated attendant to answer calls. This is when the organization's telephone automatically picks up your call and tells you to press a specific button to connect to a department, or to dial the extension of the person you are trying to reach. If you wanted to speed dial someone at an office number with an automated attendant, you could use the extra digits to dial their extension. For example, if you wanted to call someone at 555-6134 and then connect to extension 214, you would define extra digits of ",,214". The two commas are there to create a delay to allow the automated attendant to answer and get ready for the extension. Each comma creates a one-second pause before dialing the next digit.

The Ringtone and Image boxes allow you to define custom ringtones or picture IDs for calls from this number, as discussed in the following sections.

Two final things to be aware of for speed dialing are how to edit a defined speed-dial number and how to organize your Favorite numbers. To edit a favorite, use the five-way navigation control to highlight the button, and then use the stylus, or the MENU button, to open the menu and select the Edit Favorites Button menu item.

4

FIGURE 4-9   The More Options screen allows you to define dialing of extra digits as part of the speed dial, as well as define custom ringtones and a picture ID for this phone number.

On the same menu, you will also see the Edit Favorites Pages menu item. Selecting this item will open the Edit Favorites Pages screen, as shown in Figure 4-10.

To move a defined Favorite button, tap and hold your stylus on the button. Then, without lifting the stylus from the screen, drag the button to the space where you want that button to appear. If that space is already occupied, your Treo will bump the existing button one button down. If the space you wish to move your Favorite to is on another page, then you can drag and hold your button on the icon at the bottom of the screen representing another page and wait. The Treo will then open that Favorites page and allow you to drop your button into any space on that page.

Tap the Done button when you are finished organizing your Favorites.

Manage, Set, and Download Ringtones

One of the fun and useful things about the Treo is the ability to set different ringtones for different types of callers. The advantage of this is that you can tell from the sound whether the person calling is your spouse, your boss, or someone else you know.

FIGURE 4-10   The Edit Favorites Pages screen allows you to reorganize your Favorites buttons into whatever order you like.

Then you can choose whether to take your phone out of the case and answer, or not! You can also choose from a vast library of free ringtones to further personalize your Treo.

The standard format for ringtones is called MIDI, which is an acronym for Musical Instrument Digital Interface. The MIDI standard is convenient and compact, but sounds mechanical on the Treo in comparison with popular sound formats such as MP3. With third-party software (discussed later in the section "Download New Ringtones"), you can use other sound formats for your ringtones, such as the popular MP3 format and .WAV files.

Set Ringtone Preferences

Ringtones are managed through Sound Preferences. You can navigate to Sound Preferences in two different ways. The first is by opening the menu and selecting Sound Preferences under Options. The keyboard shortcut for this is to press MENU and then W. This opens up the Sound Preferences window, as shown in Figure 4-11.

The second way to get to this interface is to choose the Preferences icon from the Application Launcher and then choose Sound from the drop-down menu in the top-right corner of the screen.

The Application drop-down box must have Phone selected to see the options for the phone; otherwise you will be setting sound preferences for other Treo applications. To manage your ringtones, select the Tones box directly beneath the Application drop-down. The Sound Preferences screen will appear, displaying various ringtone options, as shown in Figure 4-12.

The Sound Preferences (ringtone options) screen lets you set a different ringtone for the following notification types:

- **Known Callers**   These are callers who are in your Contacts list on your Treo.

- **Unknown Callers**   For callers who aren't in your contact database.

FIGURE 4-11   The Sound Preferences window lets you change the audible tones for the phone, including the volume, vibration, and ringtones.

FIGURE 4-12   This screen lets you select custom ringtones for different categories of callers.

■ **Roaming Calls**   For calls that come in while you are roaming.

■ **Voicemail**   The tone that gets played when a new voicemail is received.

■ **Service**   This tone sounds when your Treo successfully connects to your service provider for your phone service.

Manage Ringtones

On the bottom-right corner of the Sound Preferences (ringtone options) screen, you will see a button labeled Manage. Tapping this button will open the Manage Sound screen, as shown in Figure 4-13.

This is the entire list of MIDI ringtones stored on your Treo 600. Tapping the Play button will play the tone that you currently have selected in the list. The Send button will allow you to send the currently selected ringtone to another user either by beaming it, or through MMS.

FIGURE 4-13   The Manage Sound screen lets you listen to, rename, delete, or send a tone.

The Edit button will open a window where you can change the name of the tone or choose to delete the tone.

Set Caller-Specific Ringtones

In addition to setting a ringtone for a specific type of caller, you can set a different ringtone for when someone calls that you would like to know immediately who it is. You might set it to play "Hard to Say I'm Sorry" by Chicago when your spouse calls, "Take this Job and Shove It" by Johnny Paycheck when your boss calls, or whatever makes you happy!

To do this with your Treo 600 is rather nonintuitive. Instead of assigning a custom ringtone in the Contacts application, you have to do it in your speed-dial favorites. Thus, you are limited to a maximum of 50 numbers (the maximum number of speed-dial numbers you can define) for which you can define custom rings.

As discussed earlier, you will need to be on the Edit or Add Favorite screen to change to a custom ring for the specified number. Once on that screen, you can press the More button to open the More Options screen that was shown to you earlier in Figure 4-9. On this screen, the Ringtone drop-down allows you to select a custom MIDI ringtone to play when a call comes in from this number.

Download New Ringtones

You can easily download new ringtones to your Treo from third-party web sites. One popular web site for free MIDI ringtones is www.mididb.com. You can navigate to this web site using the built-in Blazer Web Browser, as discussed in Chapter 5. At this web site, you can select from a number of categories of music to find your favorite ringtone. Once you have the song picked out, simply click the link in the web browser to begin downloading the song to your Treo. You will then be able to see the details of the file and confirm the download, as shown in Figure 4-14.

Associate a Picture with a Specific Caller

Another fun feature of the Treo 600 is its capability to have a picture of a caller (or any other image that will jog your memory) show up in your screen when that person calls you. It can be a photo you've taken with the Treo, or you can sync pictures from your desktop over to the Treo to use. For example, when my coauthor Dayton calls me, on the screen a picture pops up of Dilbert talking on the phone.

| FIGURE 4-14 | New ringtones can easily be downloaded to your Treo through the web browser. |

You can set up this picture ID function in the Favorites area the same way you set up a ringtone. In the same More Options window shown earlier in Figure 4-9, you can select the check box to tell the Treo you want it to display a picture for this phone number. A button will appear labeled Select Image. When you tap the button, you will be able to select an image from the images taken by the camera. After selecting the image you want, a "thumbnail" (smaller version) of the image will appear next to the Image check box on the More Options screen. Tapping this image will allow you to select a different image.

If you want to use a picture other than the one taken with the camera, you can do this by moving the image on your PC to the Treo Pictures folder. When you installed the Treo software on your PC to enable syncing, you should have had a shortcut placed on your desktop automatically to Treo Pictures. If it isn't there, navigate to the folder in the hierarchy. By default, it will be in your C:\Program Files\Handspring\Treo Pictures\ folder. Inside this folder will be a folder with your Treo User ID. Inside that folder is a folder called Transfer. Putting an image in this folder will cause the image to be uploaded to your Treo on the next HotSync. Once on your Treo, you will be able to select it as a picture ID image.

TIP
When you place a figure into the Treo Pictures Transfer folder, it should be uploaded to your Treo on the next HotSync. If it doesn't appear, check the Treo Pictures conduit settings in the HotSync manager to ensure it is set to Synchronize. For more information on setting custom conduits, refer to Chapter 3.

Prevent Unauthorized Calls with Call Barring

Call Barring is a feature from your wireless service provider that allows you to set restrictions on what kinds of calls you are allowed to make and receive. This service is not available from all service providers, so you will need to check with the carrier that you specifically connect with. The purpose of call barring is to allow you to stop unauthorized calls from reaching your Treo.

The types of calls you have control over will vary, depending on how your wireless service provider has decided to configure the service. Call-barring options are divided into two categories: outgoing and incoming. Some of the commonest call-barring options include the following:

- Outgoing

    - **None**   No outgoing calls are barred. Anyone using the phone can call anywhere in the world.

    - **All**   No outgoing calls are allowed. The Treo cannot make any outgoing calls, even local.

    - **International**   You cannot make calls to international numbers.

    - **International Except Calls Home**   You cannot make calls to international numbers except for the number on record with the carrier as your home number.

- Incoming

    - **None**   No incoming calls are barred. Anyone can call this Treo.

    - **All**   You will not be able to receive any incoming calls on this Treo.

    - **Only When Roaming**   You can receive calls when you are on your home network, but not when you are roaming on another service provider's network. For example, if your service provider is AT&T, you can only receive calls when your Treo is connected to the AT&T network. When you are roaming on the Cingular network you will not be able to receive any calls.

In addition to these standards, various carriers will have different call-barring options. For example, if you purchased your Treo from Orange in the UK, your phone will come preconfigured to bar calls outside the UK or from Premium Numbers.

Call-barring options are set at the service provider and are usually protected by a password that has been set up by your carrier. If you do not know what that password is, you will need to call your carrier to get the password in order to make any changes to your Call Barring preferences.

To access your Call Barring preferences, from the main phone screen navigate to the menu. From the menu, under the Options menu item you will see an option called Call Barring. Selecting Call Barring will open the Call Barring screen, as shown in Figure 4-15.

From this screen you can select the changes you want to make to your call-barring options. The first time you enter this screen, your Treo will contact your service provider automatically to download what your service provider's call-barring options and settings are. On subsequent visits to this screen, it will not. If your service provider has made changes in their call-barring settings that aren't reflected on your phone, you can select the Get Status button to update the cached information on your Treo. The Password button allows you to enter your carrier-provided password to authorize the call-barring changes you are making.

Prevent Accidental Calls with Keyguard

Have you ever had your phone ring, and picked it up, only to hear some background noise, maybe a car driving, and someone talking in the distance? I have had many of these calls. Someone sits on their phone, which causes some buttons to be pushed, and suddenly they are placing a call to someone and they don't even know it. In addition to being annoying to the person being called, this is costly to the caller as this eats through your airtime minutes and runs down your battery.

To prevent this, the Treo 600 has a Keyguard feature. What the Keyguard does is prevent accidental dialing of your Treo. If you push any buttons on your Treo, you will see a small message that appears in the bottom of the screen.

FIGURE 4-15   The Call Barring preferences allow you to restrict what kinds of calls can be made or received on your Treo in order to prevent unauthorized use of the device.

This message tells you that the Keyguard is active and you must push the CENTER button in the middle of the navigation control in order to unlock the phone. The Keyguard will activate automatically after the phone has been off for 30 seconds. You can turn the Keyguard off or change its settings in the Preferences application under the Keyguard option, as shown in Figure 4-16.

On this same screen, you can also disable the screen of the Treo so you can't accidentally tap the screen and disconnect your call.

If you want to manually turn Keyguard on and power off the screen, you can do so by pressing the OPTION button (the blue button on the bottom-left of the keyboard) and the SCREEN button (the button to the far right of the five-way navigation control) at the same time.

One step beyond Keyguard is to implement a Power On password, which will challenge you to enter your password when your Treo is started up. This feature is covered in detail in Chapter 13.

Forward Your Calls

Call forwarding is a fairly standard phone feature from most wireless service providers, yet making it work has often been extremely difficult on mobile phone handsets.

FIGURE 4-16   The Keyguard preferences will let you adjust the behavior of the Keyguard feature.

Often, this feature is never utilized by mobile phone users because of the challenge of having to remember obscure codes to begin or end forwarding, and advanced call-forwarding features, such as "transfer only when busy" or "transfer on no answer," are even more cryptic.

Luckily, the Treo 600 makes this process remarkably easy to accomplish. If you want to set a call-forwarding number, you can do so on the Call Preferences screen, which is shown in Figure 4-17.

The Call Preferences screen is opened by navigating to Call Preferences under the Options menu in the main phone interface. The first time you open this screen, your Treo will connect to your carrier to determine how your call-forwarding information is currently set. Very likely, your phone will be set to only call forward when busy, or when there's no answer or no service. The number that you will see it call forwarding to is for your voicemail on your phone (if your service plan includes a voice-mail option, that is; otherwise these options will likely be set to "Don't Forward Calls").

The first drop-down selection field on the screen is labeled Forward All Calls. There are three options in this list, the first of which is Don't Forward Calls. When this option is selected, calls come to your Treo 600. The second thing you will see in the list are phone numbers. These are phone numbers that your Treo is aware of that you might want to forward all your calls to. Often, one of them is your voicemail number. Selecting that option means that no calls will come to your Treo; instead, they will all go directly to voicemail. This is useful if you are in a meeting and don't want your Treo vibrating or ringing and distracting you. I have added to my list my home phone and my office main phone line, allowing me to direct calls to those two locations when I choose. The final option in your list is Edit Numbers. When you select that option, the Edit Number dialog box will open.

FIGURE 4-17   Forwarding calls is an easy feature to implement on the Treo 600.

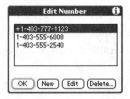

This dialog box will display the entire list of numbers that you have entered as possible call-forwarding numbers. You can select any number in the list and edit it, or delete it. You can also add new possible call-forwarding numbers to the list by pressing the New button and filling in the number. All numbers you enter in this list will appear in the drop-down selection boxes in the Call Preferences screen as numbers that you can call forward to.

In addition to the Forward All Calls option, you can select settings for what you would like to have happen with your call if your phone is busy, you don't answer it when it rings, or your Treo is off or not in a wireless service area. You can set different options for all three if you choose.

Manage Two Calls

Call Waiting is a feature that you may, or may not, have on your calling plan with your service provider. If you are already on a call when another call comes in, you will hear an audible sound (if your ringer switch isn't set to vibrate) and a visual alert will show up on the screen of your Treo, as shown in Figure 4-18.

When the second call comes in, you can choose to answer it or ignore it with the buttons on your screen. If you ignore it, the call will either ring until the caller hangs up, or will transfer to whatever number you specified for your Call Forwarding

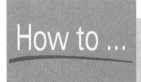 **Block Your Outgoing Caller ID**

If you don't want the people you are calling to be able to see your phone number on their phones when calling them, you can block your outgoing caller ID on the Call Preferences screen by checking the Block Outgoing Caller ID check box. This feature must be supported by your service provider in order for you to be able to do this. Some service providers charge a fee for this service.

FIGURE 4-18   The Call Waiting feature issues a visual and audible alert to let you know a second call is coming in while you're on another call.

When Not Answered option (discussed earlier). If you answer it, you will see on your screen both of the calls that you are currently connected to, as shown in Figure 4-19.

The call you are currently speaking with is shown as Active while the other call is shown as On Hold. The Active call will have a color phone icon next to it, while the On Hold call will have its icon grayed out.

There is a row of buttons on the bottom that will allow you to disconnect the Active call (or calls), switch to speakerphone mode, swap calls (puts the Active call On Hold and makes the previous On Hold call Active), or conference the calls (makes both calls active so all three parties can hear and speak with each other).

TIP   *Remember that when you have two calls going, your wireless carrier will be charging you for the airtime for both calls, even if one of the calls is on hold!*

If you do not want to have Call Waiting as a feature on your Treo, you can disable the feature in the Call Preferences screen, as shown earlier in Figure 4-17, by checking the Disable Call Waiting check box.

FIGURE 4-19   When you are connected to two calls, you will see both calls on the screen of your Treo.

Customize the Look of Your Phone

One thing that almost every user likes to do with their phone is find some way to make it distinctively their own. In addition to custom ringtones, you can use third-party software to change the appearance of the phone dialer and Favorites screen.

One such third-party application is called Skinner from 79b Media (www. 79bmedia.com). The Skinner application comes with three free "skins" to change the appearance of your phone.

You can also create your own skins with the Desktop Skinner application, and many free skins can be downloaded directly from the 79b Media web site.

Use External Headsets

Sometimes you may not want to hold your Treo up to the side of your head to make a call, and you don't want to use the speakerphone due to privacy concerns or background noise. In these situations, you can use an external headset. Another advantage of the external headset is that you can use your Treo to play games, take notes, or do other things, while in the middle of a call.

The Treo comes with an earbud-style headset that you can use right away. Since it's not the highest-quality headset, you may want to consider upgrading it to a better one if you use it frequently.

To use an external headset, simply plug it into the bottom headset jack of your Treo. The external speaker will automatically turn off and all sound will now come through your headset. The microphone on the standard headset is built into the cord and will hang at the side of your face when the earbud is in your ear. On the microphone, there is also a small button that you can push to answer an incoming call or disconnect the call you are on.

Fortunately, the Treo 600 uses the most common standard headset jack, a 2.5 mm headphone plug. This is a big advantage because you can buy headsets from a very large number of vendors. (Some of the vendor headsets that we tested for this book are detailed in Chapter 16.)

> TIP   *One third-party headset mentioned in Chapter 16 is the retractable earbud from Zip Linq (www.ziplinq.com). Personally, I ruin three or four earbud-style headsets a year. This is because when you are not using them they seem to miraculously tie themselves into knots in the glove box of your car. Headset cables that aren't in use seem to always be in the way. The Zip Linq retractable cable automatically winds the cord around a small spring-loaded spool that conveniently tucks the cord away and reduces the headset to a very manageable size that is easy to store and carry around.*

Set Dialing Preferences

Depending on which part of the world you live in, you will have different dialing preferences options you will want to set on your Treo. These dialing preferences allow you to adapt how the Treo behaves in certain dialing conditions. These preferences are really only relevant in North America; thus the first check box on the Dial Preferences screen, as shown in Figure 4-20, is labeled North American Dialing.

In some regions in North America, you must dial the area code for your call even if it is a local call. You may have a lot of your contacts in this region with only seven-digit numbers, but due to changes from the carrier, you must dial a ten-digit number to reach them. If this is the case, you can check the second check box to add the three-digit area code for your region to the front of all seven-digit numbers. For example, if you live in Vancouver, you need to prefix all your seven-digit numbers with 604.

FIGURE 4-20   Dialing preferences can be set for North American customers to modify how numbers that are dialed out of your Contacts list are handled.

The last check box on the screen allows you to force the Treo to always dial a 1 in front of the area code. This is useful if you store the numbers in your Contacts list without the 1. The Treo will automatically add this for you. If it is a local call, most carriers are sophisticated enough to recognize this and drop the 1 (and area code, if applicable) when placing the call.

Wrap It Up

With the information in this chapter, you should now be comfortable using the advanced features of the Treo to maximize your voice communications with call forwarding, speed dialing, conference calling, and other sophisticated features. No more are you limited to just "dial" and "answer" functions!

Chapter 5 Connect Wirelessly

How to...

- Configure your Treo for wireless data
- Connect to the wireless data network
- Browse the Web
- Use Multimedia Messaging Service (MMS)
- Use Sprint Picture Mail
- Use Short Messaging Service (SMS)
- Use third-party wireless applications
- Find helpful Treo 600–specific web sites

The most useful and, arguably, the most interesting features of your Treo involve wireless connectivity. Obvious examples include using the phone, sending and receiving e-mail, and browsing the Web, but there are many other things you can do using the wireless capabilities of your Treo 600. This chapter includes topics such as configuring your Treo for wireless connectivity, and using Multimedia Messaging Service (MMS) and Short Messaging Service (SMS). It also contains a listing of other wireless options and third-party wireless applications designed for your Treo.

Wireless and Nonwireless Modes

Your Treo essentially uses two independent modes: Organizer Mode and Wireless Mode (phone, SMS, e-mail, web browsing). While the Wireless Mode is turned off, you can still use all of the functions that don't require wireless connectivity, such as the organizer, contact list, calendar, music, and so on. One reason that you may want to leave the Wireless Mode off when not using it is that it significantly improves how long you can go without recharging your Treo battery. Another advantage of being able to turn the Wireless Mode off is that you can continue to use the nonwireless features on an airplane where Wireless Mode may interfere with the airplane navigation systems.

Multitasking: Use Nonwireless Applications while Talking on the Phone

You have complete access to all of your other applications, except those that use the serial library during a call, such as another wireless application. Therefore, you

Did you know?

Your SIM Card

SIM cards are small smart cards that fit inside phones based on the GSM (Global System for Mobile Communications) technology. Your SIM card contains personalized information about you, including your network activation, phone number, and voicemail access number. Your wireless service provider uses the SIM information to register and track your Treo on the network.

If your Treo is hosted by Sprint on a CDMA (Code Division Multiple Access) wireless network, you don't need a SIM (short for Subscriber Identification Module or Subscriber Identity Module) since the settings are downloaded directly to your CDMA radio and are specific to each carrier. For instance, the same settings that work on the Sprint CDMA network will not work on the Verizon network. If your Treo 600 is a GSM/GPRS version, the SIM card may already be inserted into your Treo. In order to use the phone, e-mail, or web features of your Treo, you will need an activated SIM card. If a SIM card did not come with your Treo, you need to contact your mobile service provider to subscribe to a GPRS (General Packet Radio Service) data plan, where you will be given a SIM card.

5

can view your calendar, enter an appointment, write a note, create a To Do item, take a picture, or enter contact information in your address book, all while talking on the phone. Being able to multitask in this way is even more valuable if you are using a phone headset or are using the speakerphone functionality (covered in Chapter 3), so that you can continue talking on the phone while working on your Treo. The caveat to multitasking on your Treo is that you cannot simultaneously make voice calls and use wireless data. For example, you can't talk on the phone and browse the Internet at the same time.

NOTE
If you receive a phone call on the Treo 600 while using it to browse the Web or read your e-mail, you will receive an alert on the screen that allows you to choose between answering the call and sending it directly to voicemail. Whatever wireless functions you were using when you received the call will pause until you have finished using the phone.

Turn Wireless Mode On and Off

The state of the Wireless Mode determines whether you can connect to a mobile network to make and receive phone calls and use other wireless services like e-mail or web browsing.

To turn the Wireless Mode on, press and hold the Wireless Mode button, until you hear a series of ascending tones indicating Wireless Mode has been activated. When Wireless Mode is on, your Treo connects to a mobile network, allowing you to use the phone and Internet features (your wireless service provider must support data services, however).

Press and hold the Wireless Mode button again to turn off Wireless Mode. A series of descending tones will sound. When Wireless Mode is off, your Treo does not have a connection to any mobile network. You can still use the organizer and other Palm OS features. This is ideal for airplane flights and for maximizing battery life since leaving the connection open uses more battery power.

Get Connected

One of the most compelling reasons why many of us purchase the Treo 600 in the first place is the wireless data capability. This section covers wireless data topics such as ensuring that you have the appropriate contract with your wireless service provider (WSP), browsing the Internet, and sending MMS (Multimedia Messaging Service) and SMS (Short Messaging Service) messages using your Treo 600.

Using Wireless E-Mail, Web Browsing, and Data Applications on Your Treo

Your Treo 600 is essentially two devices in one: a cell phone and a wireless computer. The wireless computer component of your Treo requires different wireless services than the phone. It is important to understand that a wireless service provider (the company you pay to use your Treo phone) tends to view wireless voice and wireless data services as separate. Ideally, both your service contract and Treo were set up correctly when you purchased your Treo and you are immediately able to use the mobile phone and take advantage of advanced features like SMS and MMS (used for taking and sending digital photos and downloading ringtones, for example), e-mail, and the Internet. However, not all wireless service providers (WSPs) offer data services, and some WSPs, though they do offer them, do not automatically include such data services in your phone plan.

Make sure that your service contract includes data services and that they have been activated. Some providers separate data services into Internet, MMS, and SMS functions, so you should make sure each one is included in your plan in order to take advantage of all the features offered by your Treo. Some of the brand names for data services are listed in the next section.

> TIP *Your Treo does not need or utilize WAP service, so if your wireless service provider offers it as an optional charge, decline it.*

Brand Names for Wireless Data Services

5

When dealing with a wireless service provider—also known as a *carrier*—it is helpful to be aware that each has its own names associated with its wireless data services. Examples include the following:

- **AT&T** GPRS—mMode
- **Cingular**
  - **GPRS** Wireless Internet Express
  - **Dial-up** Wireless Internet
- **Fido** GPRS—GPRS Access
- **Rogers AT&T** GPRS Data Access
- **Sprint PCS** 1xRTT*—PCS Vision
- **T-Mobile**
  - **GPRS** T-Mobile Internet
  - **Dial-up** This service doesn't have a brand name, but it is enabled automatically on the T-Mobile networks.

What if My Wireless Service Provider Does Not Offer Wireless Internet Service?

Some wireless service providers offer wireless data but not wireless Internet. If your wireless service provider does not offer wireless Internet service for your Treo, you may also need an Internet service provider (ISP). Confusing? Well, the reason for this is that some wireless service providers offer data services (the ability to send/ receive data wirelessly) but do not act as a gateway to the Internet. In such cases, you may need to use a separate ISP to access the Internet with your Treo.

Another solution is to change your service contract to another wireless service provider that offers full voice, data, and Internet service. However, this may not be a realistic option if you live in an area where coverage is only offered by a wireless service provider, or if you are locked into a long-term contract, or if your Treo is "SIM-locked" and thus permanently linked to a particular wireless service provider.

How Do You Know if You Are Connected to a Wireless Network?

There are a series of icons that appear on the upper right-hand corner of your Treo screen that indicate the current state of wireless connectivity.

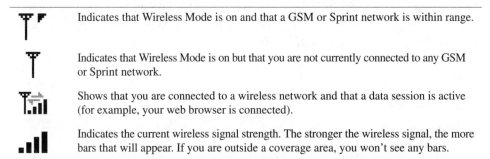

	Indicates that Wireless Mode is on and that a GSM or Sprint network is within range.
	Indicates that Wireless Mode is on but that you are not currently connected to any GSM or Sprint network.
	Shows that you are connected to a wireless network and that a data session is active (for example, your web browser is connected).
	Indicates the current wireless signal strength. The stronger the wireless signal, the more bars that will appear. If you are outside a coverage area, you won't see any bars.

Of course, the easiest way to check whether you have Internet access is to launch the Blazer Web Browser to see if you can view a web page. To launch the built-in Blazer Web Browser:

1. Open the Applications Launcher screen by pressing the HOME button to the immediate right of the SPACEBAR on the keyboard.

2. Find and launch the web icon, which is an image of the earth.

The browser is likely already set up to go to the Handspring or palmOne web site, but you can choose another web site that you know will be there by selecting the WWW button on the bottom of the screen and entering the site address (for example, www.google.com for Google).

If you are unable to connect to the Internet, there are two things to check:

■ Your wireless service contract, to ensure that you have wireless data and Internet service.

■ Your network settings, to ensure that your Treo is correctly configured for wireless data.

FIGURE 5-1 The Network Preferences screen

Configure Your Wireless Network Settings

Your network settings are specific to your wireless service provider (the company that provides your wireless connectivity, such as Sprint, Cingular, or T-Mobile). In fact, your Treo may already be configured for wireless data connectivity. To check the settings or enter new information, access the Network Preferences screen shown in Figure 5-1. To do this, follow these steps:

1. Press the HOME button to open the Applications Launcher.

2. Find and select Prefs.

3. Select the menu in the top right-hand corner of the screen.

4. From the menu list, select Network.

If the network data is blank and you don't have the information, you will have to contact your wireless service provider to get the necessary information. Many of the wireless service providers list this information on their support web sites. The network information you need includes the following:

■ **Service** You can set up several wireless network accounts. Service is a logical name that you give to this connection, but the name does not technically affect the connection.

■ **Connection** This field is a drop-down list that allows you to select what type of connection the settings are used for, as shown in Figure 5-2.

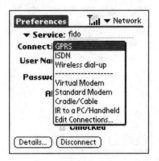

FIGURE 5-2   The network connection services list

- GPRS

- ISDN

- Wireless Dial-Up

- Virtual Modem

- Standard Modem

- Cradle/Cable

- IR to a PC/Handheld

- Edit Connections…

- **User Name**   The network username given to you by your wireless service provider.

- **Password**   The password given to you by your wireless service provider.

- **APN**   The APN is the *access point name,* which is the Internet address of your wireless service provider's wireless data acccss point. It will take the form of something like internet.orange.com, or it could be an IP address (for example, 199.71.43.254).

Browse the Web

Once you are connected to the data network and to the Internet, you can use your Treo to browse the Internet. The Internet originated in the 1960s but has only become a commonplace facet of our culture in the last 10 or 15 years, revolutionizing communication and the sharing of ideas and information. The Web has also significantly altered commerce. Many companies and retail outlets would not consider doing business without a web site and e-mail. Entire books have been written about the impact that the Internet has had on the world, so it doesn't make sense to go into it here except to say that the ability to browse the Web on a Treo can be tremendously useful.

Use the Blazer Web Browser

Your Treo was shipped with a built-in web browser called the Blazer Web Browser, which you can use to surf the Internet. Several third-party browsers are available for your Treo. A list of available browsers is shown later in this chapter. For many users, however, the Blazer browser not only provides enough functionality but has the added benefit of having the application reside in Read-Only Memory (ROM), thus preventing it from using up any user-available memory as third-party web browsers would. The section "Blazer Web Browser Supported Media Types" at the end of this chapter describes the technical, download, and media capabilities of Blazer.

Blazer Browser Basics

The Blazer Web Browser on your Treo provides an easy way to access and view web pages. The first generation of mobile web browsers was somewhat limited. Many of the first browsers designed for mobile devices required adherence to WAP (Wireless Application Protocol) and could not handle features like JavaScript or frames. This meant that many web sites were either not accessible at all, or were less than perfectly user friendly. The Treo 600 Blazer Web Browser belongs to the latest and greatest of mobile browsers. Now you can use your Treo to view all web sites, including sites with security and even advanced features like JavaScript and frames.

Use Blazer to View a Web Page

To view a web page with the Blazer Web Browser, follow these steps:

1. Ensure that Wireless Mode is turned on. This is covered earlier in this chapter in the section "Turn Wireless Mode On and Off."

2. Press the Applications Launcher, and then select the HOME button.

3. Find and select Blazer from the list of applications.

4. Your Blazer browser likely is configured to open the palmOne or Handspring web site by default, as shown in Figure 5-3. If a page doesn't load automatically, choose the Home icon at the bottom of the screen.

FIGURE 5-3   The Blazer screen

5. To view a specific web page in Blazer, select the WWW button and enter a web site URL address that you would like to view (for example, www.google.com, as shown in Figure 5-4).

6. After a few seconds, you should see the web page you requested. If these steps don't result in being able to view a web page, you may want to read the section in this chapter called "Get Connected."

View Web Pages in Wide and Optimized Modes

Most web pages are not properly formatted for the smaller screens on mobile devices. Web pages are generally designed for much larger displays—at least 800 by 600 pixels—and layouts do not take into account the idiosyncrasies of mobile devices

FIGURE 5-4   Go to Web Page screen

and the latency of wireless networks. The Blazer Web Browser, in addition to some other mobile browsers, has implemented ways to improve your wireless web browsing experience. An innovation that drastically improves wireless browsing is the Blazer Web Browser Optimized Mode.

Optimized Mode   The Blazer Web Browser uses patent-pending technology designed to optimize web pages for your Treo screen. Most web pages are formatted for viewing on a much larger PC screen than your Treo screen.

The default Blazer browser mode is called Optimized Mode, which reformats web pages into one column to make best use of your Treo screen real estate. This means that viewing web pages in Optimized Mode reduces the amount of scrolling you have to do to see information on the screen. A side effect of this feature is that web pages with rich graphical content tend to look a little like Picasso portraits.

Wide Mode   Depending on the type of web page you are viewing and how you want to interact with the page, you may also view web pages in the Blazer Wide Mode. An example of a page that you would likely want to view in Wide Mode is a page that includes an image of a map that is wider than 160 pixels. Wide Mode means that no formatting of web pages is done on your behalf and the page is presented the same way it would look on a desktop PC. But, because your Treo screen has a 160 by 160 pixel screen and web pages are generally designed for much larger screens, you will have to scroll around both vertically and horizontally to see all of the content on a particular web page.

Change Between Optimized and Wide Modes   You can choose to view a web page in either Optimized or Wide Page Mode by simply toggling between the two settings. The settings can be found under the Blazer Page menu, as shown in Figure 5-5. A visual indicator (a square) appears to the left of the menu item showing which mode is currently active. In Figure 5-5, the screen is in Optimized Mode.

FIGURE 5-5   Change between Optimized and Wide Page Modes

Navigate the Web with Blazer

Blazer functions in much the same way that a desktop web browser functions, so if you are familiar with common desktop browsers—Netscape Navigator and Microsoft Internet Explorer are the most common—this will be relatively obvious, but we recommend reading the section "Configure Your Blazer Preferences," later in this chapter, to learn about settings that are unique to the world of mobile wireless Internet browsing.

The navigation buttons at the bottom of the Blazer screen allow you to easily move around the Web. There are three ways you can use them:

- Tap the touch screen with the stylus.

- Using the keyboard, press the SPACEBAR to jump down to the browser icons, and then navigate using the five-way control.

- Press the MENU button and access the same commands through the menu using the five-way control.

The navigation buttons and their functions are listed next and are shown in Figure 5-6.

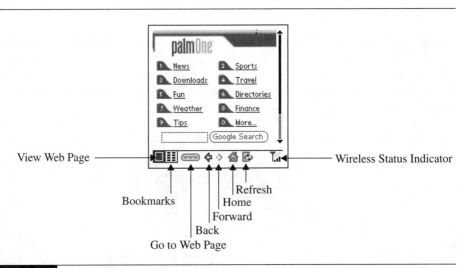

FIGURE 5-6   Blazer Navigation buttons

- **View Web Page**   You can toggle between your Bookmarks view and the web view. Selecting this button shows your web page view.

- **Bookmarks**   These permit you to store web site addresses and access pages without retyping the URL. For more information, see the upcoming "Create a Bookmark" section.

- **Go to Web Page**   This option allows you to view a specific web site. To do so, choose this menu item, enter the web site URL (for example, www.treo600.com), and select OK.

- **Back**   This option takes you to the previously viewed web page.

- **Forward**   Takes you to the next web page. This is only enabled if you have a page to go forward to.

- **Home**   This opens your default web page (you can change your default Home web site in the Blazer Preferences screen). More information can be found in this chapter under the section "Configure Your Blazer Preferences."

- **Refresh**   This option downloads the latest version of the web page you're currently viewing. Handy if the data on the page changes regularly.

- **Wireless Status Indicator**   This icon displays the current state of your wireless connection.

Move Around a Web Page with Blazer

When viewing a web page using Blazer, you can navigate the links and menus in much the same way you would using a desktop PC browser. To follow a link to another web page, you can do either of the following:

- Tap the link on the touch screen with your stylus.

- Navigate the screen with the five-way navigation control—move around until the link is highlighted and select it by pressing the center of the five-way navigation control. Using the five-way navigation control for navigation can be a challenge until you get used to how the cursor moves around the screen (use left and right instead of up and down). Once you get the hang of it, it's a great way to navigate the Web using only one hand.

Create a Bookmark

Blazer Bookmarks are similar to the favorites concept in PC-based web browsers. Bookmarks allow you to store web site addresses and quickly access pages without retyping the URL. Blazer allows you to store up to 100 Bookmarks. To create a Bookmark, follow these steps:

1. Browse to the web page you want to bookmark (for example, www.google.com).

2. Press Menu.

3. From the Page menu, choose Add Bookmark.

4. Now, whenever you want to view www.google.com, all you have to do is switch the view to Bookmarks and select the Google bookmark. This saves a lot of thumb typing, especially when dealing with long web site addresses.

Save a Web Page for Offline Viewing

Occasionally, you may want to save a web page to your Treo. For example, here are a couple of common scenarios:

- You want to capture and save the information on the web page for reference purposes (such as a symphony orchestra concert schedule).

- You don't have time to read a particular web page, and you want to save it so you can read it at a later time without having to download it again.

To save a particular web page, do the following:

1. Browse to a web page using the Blazer browser, or if you are already looking at the page you want to save, press the MENU button.

2. From the Page menu, select Save Page.

3. A dialog box like that shown in Figure 5-7 will appear, called New Saved Page Bookmark, where you can type in a Name and a Description for the page to help you identify it later. The Preview at the bottom allows you to see how the Bookmark will look after you have saved the page. Obviously, keeping the Name and the Description text short so that it is visible and helpful when later looking for the Bookmarks is beneficial.

4. After saving the page, you can access it at any time from your Bookmarks view.

View Bookmarks or Saved Pages

After you have created Bookmarks and saved web pages, you can access them both on the Bookmarks view in Blazer, as shown in Figure 5-8. You can access your

FIGURE 5-8   A new saved page Bookmark

Bookmarks view from the Blazer main screen by pressing the icon that's second from the left at the bottom of the screen, or by pressing the MENU button and selecting Bookmarks View from the Page menu.

Saved web pages, as opposed to bookmarked web pages, are indicated in the Bookmarks view by a small triangle in the upper-right corner of the bookmark.

Edit or Delete Bookmarks   You may edit or delete bookmarks as your needs change by following these steps from the Bookmarks view screen.

1. Press the MENU button.

2. From the Bookmarks menu, choose the Edit Bookmarks option.

3. Choose the bookmark you want to edit or delete.

4. Enter the desired changes to the bookmark, including Name, Description, or URL.

5. Select OK.

FIGURE 5-7   Bookmarks and Saved Pages view

Arrange Your Bookmarks and Saved Pages   Blazer allows you to store up to 100 bookmarks and saved web pages. The Bookmarks view consists of ten pages containing ten bookmarks. Because you have ten different pages of bookmarks to work with, this enables you to organize your bookmarks in any way that makes sense to you so you can find what you are looking for quickly. For example, one page may include financial web sites, one page may include weather sites, or you may put a list of Hot Dog Eating Contest web pages, and associated sites, on one bookmark page—the point is, you can arrange your bookmarks into whatever groupings makes sense to you. To arrange your bookmarks, follow these steps:

1. From the Bookmarks view, press the MENU button.

2. From the Bookmarks menu, choose the Edit Bookmarks option.

3. Type a title for this page—Hot Dog Eating Contests, for example.

4. Use your stylus to drag and drop bookmarks into different positions on the current bookmark page.

5. You can move a bookmark to a different page by dragging and dropping it on the appropriate page icon.

6. When you are finished arranging your bookmarks, select OK.

Download Files from a Web Page

The Blazer browser allows you to download files that you can use on your Treo, such as applications, images, sounds, documents, and others. Any file that is downloaded to your Treo is automatically associated with the application that can open and use the file.

To download a file from the Internet, whether an application, image, or another type, follow these steps:

1. Browse to the page that contains the link to the file you want to download.

2. Highlight the link using the five-way navigation control, or tap the screen and press CENTER on the five-way navigation control to begin the download process.

TIP   *Remember that large files may take several minutes to download over the wireless network. For large files, you may want to download them onto your PC and then load them onto your Treo using HotSync.*

Navigate Web Sites with Split Pages—Frames

There are some web sites that use a type of navigation and screen layout called frames. A web page that uses frames splits the web page content into multiple separate areas on the screen, and each area has its own set of scroll bars. Blazer allows you to "zoom in" to a specific frame on a web page to make it easier to view the content. To zoom in to one particular framed area, follow these steps:

1. Load the web page that contains frames in the Blazer browser.

2. Tap the screen inside the area frame that you want to get a better view of. (Don't tap on a link, or you'll end up jumping to wherever that link is pointed.)

3. Tap the magnifying glass icon located in the button bar on the bottom of the screen. Note that the magnifying glass icon only appears in the button bar if the current page you are viewing consists of frames.

4. After you tap the magnifying glass icon, only the selected frame will be visible. To return to the full-page view, tap the icon again.

Copy Text from a Web Page

Chapter 2 covered how to cut, copy, and paste text on your Treo in order to move and copy text between applications and documents. The same basic logic applies here as well.

1. Use your stylus to highlight the text you want to copy.

2. Press the MENU button.

3. From the Edit menu, choose the Copy option.

4. Now, browse to the application, document, e-mail, and so on where you want to paste the copied text.

5. Place the cursor where you want to paste the text.

6. Press MENU again.

7. From the Edit menu, choose the Paste option.

View Your History of Previously Viewed Web Pages

The Blazer Browser stores a record of the web pages you have visited previously. This provides an easy way to help you find pages quickly. You can even add a page

FIGURE 5-9   The History screen

in your History list to your Bookmarks by selecting the web page from the list and tapping the Bookmark button, as shown in Figure 5-9.

Send a Web Page Address to Another Person Using SMS

If you find a web page that you would like to share with a friend or business acquaintance, you have a few different options. You can copy the web page address (for example, www.webpage.com) using the steps outlined in the "Copy Text from a Web Page" section in this chapter and paste it into an e-mail, or you can send it using Short Message Service (SMS). SMS is covered in greater detail in the SMS section of this chapter. If you are not familiar with SMS, you may want to read that section before continuing with this one. Assuming that you know all about SMS, here are the steps to send a web page address to another person using SMS:

1. Using Blazer while viewing the web page you want to send to another person, press the MENU button.

2. From the Page menu, select Send Page Address.

3. Your Treo will create a new SMS message containing the web page address.

4. Enter the phone number of the person you want to send the address to, along with any text or smiley faces that you like, and select Send.

Find Text on a Web Page

Sometimes scrolling around a web page looking for a particular word or phrase, especially on a page with a large amount of text, can be a slow and tedious process, not to mention hard on the eyes. Fortunately, Blazer comes equipped with a search tool to allow you to quickly find what you are looking for. The steps to search a page are as follows:

1. In Blazer, if you haven't already, load/view the web page you want to search.

2. Press the MENU button, and from the Page menu, select Find Text on Page.

3. In the dialog box, type the word or phrase you're looking for and select Find.

> **TIP** *When searching for text in a web page, the text you enter for Blazer to find can be incomplete. For example, if you are searching for the word "Nostradamus," typing **ostra** in the Find dialog box would probably find the Nostradamus text because "ostra" is likely unique; but, in general, the more precise you are in your search, the better your chances of finding the information you want.*

Dial Your Phone Using a Phone Number on a Web Page

This handy feature leverages two unique capabilities of your Treo. It combines using information from the Web to directly dial your phone, and it does it seamlessly. Phone numbers displayed on web pages show up as underlined hyperlinks, as shown in Figure 5-10. When you select the link, a dialog box pops up, as shown in Figure 5-11; just select the Dial button on the screen, and the phone number is dialed. Isn't that a nice way to combine the wireless Web with a wireless phone?

> **TIP** *Online phone directories make this feature even more convenient. Most phone companies offer their phone directories online, so you can easily use your web-browsing capabilities to dial your phone for you. Call me lazy; it's still a great feature.*

FIGURE 5-10   Phone links in Blazer

FIGURE 5-11   Phone links in Blazer (dial)

Configure Your Blazer Preferences

The types of browser settings you can define include establishing your default home page, defining whether or not images are shown on web pages, and how you want Blazer to handle cookies and memory management. These topics, and a few others, are covered next.

Set Your Default Home Page

Your Home page is the web page that opens when you launch Blazer and when you tap the Home button in the Blazer button bar. To set your Home page, follow these steps:

1. Launch Blazer.

2. Press the MENU button on the keyboard.

3. From the Options menu, select Preferences.

4. Select the Home Page field and enter the URL for your Home page.

5. Select OK.

Set Your Default Initial Blazer View

You have two choices for your default view when you launch Blazer. You can either see the Bookmarks view or your home page. To set your default view, follow these steps:

1. Launch Blazer.

2. Press the MENU button on the keyboard.

3. From the Options menu, select Preferences.

4. Next to the Initial View text, there are two buttons, like those shown in Figure 5-12.

   ■ By selecting the button on the left (it looks like a single page), your default view will be your Home page.

   ■ By selecting the button on the right (it looks like a two-column list), your default Blazer view will be your Bookmarks view.

5. Select OK.

Set Whether You Want Blazer to Show Web Page Images by Default

This feature is directly related to the speed of wireless networks and the size of the Treo screen. If what you really want to see on a web page is the text, then why take the time to download images to your Treo before you can begin reading the page? The answer is that you don't have to. You have the option of not displaying images, by default. This means you will be able to see information from a web page on your Treo screen in less time. To set Blazer to not show images by default, follow these steps.

1. Launch Blazer.

2. Press the MENU button on the keyboard.

3. From the Options menu, select Preferences.

4. Check the box to the left of Don't Show Images.

5. Select OK.

FIGURE 5-12   Blazer Preferences screen showing Initial View buttons

Even with the Don't Show Images check box checked, you can still see a particular image by selecting the image placeholder box (the place where images would be if they were shown on the screen) on the web page.

Set a Limit on Memory for Storing Recently Viewed Pages—Cache

Blazer and every other web browser stores web page information so that when you return to a web page at a later time it doesn't need to download all of the images and text again. Blazer simply reuses the information that was stored the first time you viewed the page. This allows the pages to load faster. The place where web page files and information are stored on your Treo is called the web cache. Memory management can be an issue on resource-constrained devices such as your Treo. So, within Blazer you can decide how much memory you want to allocate to Blazer. To view and change the cache size, follow these steps:

1. Launch Blazer.

2. Press the MENU button on the keyboard.

3. From the Options menu, select Preferences.

4. Select the Advanced button. The Advanced Preferences page should appear, as shown in Figure 5-13.

5. Next to Set Limit on Memory for Storing Recently Viewed Pages (Cache), you will see the amount of memory currently set aside for the Blazer web page cache. You can change the number if you want:

   ■ If you are running out of memory on your Treo, you will want to reduce this number.

   ■ If you find that you do a lot of web browser work and memory is not a problem, you may want to increase the number.

6. Select OK.

Use Blazer Memory Management

At any time, you may free memory that is allocated to the browser cache by clearing memory used by recently viewed web pages, history, and cookies. To clear this information, follow these steps:

1. Launch Blazer.

2. Press the MENU button on the keyboard.

FIGURE 5-13 The Blazer Advanced Preferences screen

3. From the Options menu, select Preferences.

4. Select the Advanced button. The Advanced Preferences page (see Figure 5-13) will appear.

5. Select the Memory Management button.

6. On the Memory Management screen, you can see how much memory is being used. You have three Clear buttons allowing you to select which information you want to delete.

Set a Proxy Server—Advanced

Many Internet accounts require that your Treo connect to a Proxy Server. If this is the case, you can define the proxy setting by selecting the Set Proxy button. The information needed to define your proxy includes the following:

■ **Proxy Server address** Usually an IP address in the form of 10.10.10.1.

■ **Port number** The default is 80, but you may change it if necessary.

This information needs to be provided by your Internet service provider, so contact your Internet service provider or IT administrator to find out what settings to use.

Set Whether Blazer Should Accept Cookies

Selecting the Accept Cookies check box allows some web sites to store personalized information on your Treo. Some sites do not work properly unless you select this option.

If you are a savvy web user, you may already know that web cookies are files that some web sites send to your browser for storage. These files are intended to make your browsing experience better by allowing the web site to store information about you or your preferences on your Treo. Some web sites require that your browser accept cookies.

Other Web Browsers for Your Treo

Your Treo 600 ships with the Blazer Web Browser already installed. The Blazer is a great browser, and it is worth mentioning that you also have other browser options. This section lists a couple of the more common browsers and discusses the difference between online and offline browsers.

When considering third-party web browsers, it is important to pay attention to the amount of memory a particular browser application requires to install and run. Some third-party browsers use significantly more memory than others, and this means that you will have to be more conscious of memory management and that you may experience decreased performance.

Types of Web Browsers—Online and Offline

Two types of web browsers are available for your Treo. The Blazer Web Browser is what is known as an "online" browser. This means that the browser accesses the Internet in real time using the wireless network to download web pages.

The second type of web browsers are called—what else?—"offline" browsers. Offline browsers are designed to allow you to download web pages from your PC during the HotSync process and then save them on your Treo so you can view them at any time without needing to connect to the Internet. There are a couple of significant advantages to the offline variety: stored Internet pages and information are immediately available without requiring a live connection to the Internet, and viewing pages is obviously faster because they're stored locally on your Treo. For example, you can download web pages using HotSync in order to browse them later on an airplane where you can't use your wireless connection. Offline browsers are also advantageous for storing pages you need to access on a regular basis. Many online browsers also allow you to save web pages for offline viewing. Need both an online and offline browser? Nothing says you can't use both.

Some of the online browsers available include the following:

- Xiino, formerly PalmScape (www.ilinx.co.jp)

- EudoraWeb (www.eudora.com)

- PocketLink (www.mdevelop.com)

The following are a few of the offline browsers available:

■ AvantGo (www.avantgo.com)

■ Plucker (www.plkr.org)

■ HandStory (http://handstory.com)

Web Sites with Content Dedicated to the Treo 600

A comprehensive list of web sites dedicated to Palm Powered– and Treo 600–specific topics is shown in Appendix B at the end of the book. Many of these web sites include news and user forums where you can search, view, and post opinions and questions about your Treo. It can be a great way to learn how other Treo 600 owners use their Treos. Often, web sites are great places to find out about new applications and accessories for your Treo 600. Some of the most enlightening information available on these sites comes from other Treo users who describe the products they have tried. Of course, any posted opinion should be taken with a grain of salt since it is just an opinion. That said, if 200 people say a product is great and one person says it isn't, it's pretty easy to determine the level of user satisfaction.

Treo 600–Friendly Web Sites

While the majority of web sites are formatted for PC screens, many web sites have a specific set of pages designed for viewing on wireless handheld devices. The primary difference is that there is less screen content in order for it to fit more easily on the screen, as well as less graphical content (fewer pretty pictures and image buttons) to help reduce the time it takes to download a page to your Treo. The following is a short list of web sites that have been designed for your Treo and other handheld devices:

■ **Financial**   CNN Financial (www.cnnfn.com/pushthis/avantgo/channel.html)

■ **News**   USA Today (www.usatoday.com/palm/)

■ **Phone**   InfoSpace Yellow Pages (www.infospace.com/info.avant/yellow.html); InfoSpace White Pages (www.infospace.com/info.avant/index_ppl.html)

■ **Sports**   FOX Sports (www.foxsports.com/palm/)

■ **Technology**   ZDNet (www.zdnet.com/zdnn/feeds/palmpilot/pageone/)

■ **Travel**   MapQuest! (www.mapquest.com/avantgo/)

■ **Weather**   The Weather Channel (http://harvest.weather.com/3com/avantgo/)

One Stop, Plain and Simple

I have owned and operated almost every Palm OS device that has ever been released. I love technology and especially Palm gadgets. I fell in love with smartphone devices when I purchased the Kyocera Palm phone a few years ago. I loved the ability to browse the Internet, send and receive e-mails, and, of course, the phone.

Then the Handspring Treo came along. I purchased the Treo 300 in August of 2002, and it instantly replaced all of my other devices! I loved the color screen, even if it was not hi-res, and I was able to do everything on it that I needed to. I used it daily to check sports scores and e-mail, buy and sell a little on eBay, and keep in touch via the phone. In October of 2003, I became very excited when all the rumors started flying around about the Treo 600 that was to be released late in 2003. I read everything I could about it, and I was particularly intrigued by a preview on www.TreoCentral.com. In that preview was a screenshot of the Handspring Treo portal, which was designed to be Treo-friendly. I researched how to make a web site along those lines, where I could provide the Treo community with news, weather, and links to other Treo-friendly sites. I came up with a name, Treo1.com, and a slogan, "one stop, plain and simple," and set out to design my site. In a couple of months, I had made a site that I believed looked good, was easy to navigate, provided a lot of content for Treo users, and most important to me, was able to be updated easily anywhere I could connect with my new Treo 600. The best part is that I regularly update my web site right *from* my Treo 600!

—Jim Mahon, Branford, Connecticut
www.treo1.com

Eventually every popular web site will offer pages designed for wireless handheld devices, and while not every web site is at that stage now, many offer customized pages for handhelds. Often, there is a link on the main page of a web site that allows you to link to pages designed for your Treo. Keep this in mind as you browse the Web with your Treo. It can drastically improve your Treo 600 web-browsing experience.

MMS

MMS (MultiMedia Messaging Service, also known as *picture messaging*) has been gaining popularity as an easy way to share short messages consisting of images, text, and sounds. In order for MMS to work, both the sending and receiving devices must be MMS capable. The types of content you can send in an MMS message include the following:

- **Ringtones**   MIDI up to 16-voice polyphony, Standard or SP-MIDI format, and up to 64KB per sound file

- **iMelody**   Up to 64KB per sound file

- **Sound clips**   Up to 30 seconds playback time, 64KB per sound file

- **Pictures**

  - **JPEG**   Up to 640×480 pixels, 64KB-per-image files

  - **GIF**   Up to 640×480 pixels, 64KB-per-image files

Note that not all Treo 600s ship with MMS software installed. For example, Sprint Treo 600 handhelds do not ship with MMS. That said, Sprint Treos do ship with a similar service called "Picture Mail" that allows you to send MMS-type messages.

MMS vs. E-Mail

Depending on the type of e-mail account you have, you can send the same content with e-mail that you can with MMS. So why use MMS? The primary answer is that MMS is *designed for* mobile devices, while e-mail has been *adapted for* mobile devices. The result is that MMS is easier and faster to use. E-mail and MMS are based on similar technologies with the primary difference being that MMS messages are sent straight to the receiving handheld, while e-mail messages are sent to the receiving person's e-mail account. So, e-mail is not downloaded until the e-mail server either "pushes" the message to the recipient's handheld or the recipient's handheld checks the e-mail server for new messages. This means that there will be delay between when an e-mail is sent and when the recipient receives it. This is less of an issue when you use MMS to send a message.

Of course, all of this depends on both the sending handheld and the receiving handheld having MMS capability. At this point, MMS has not yet been as widely adopted as e-mail, so e-mail is still the most common way to send content-rich messages.

Get Ready to Send an MMS Message

You will have to have MMS enabled on your Treo and in your service contract with your wireless service provider before you can send an MMS message. To do this, you may have to contact your mobile service provider to add MMS to your account. Of course, there is an extra monthly service charge for MMS.

MIDI Sound Files

MIDI stands for Musical Instrument Digital Interface, a type of sound file and, more specifically, a communications protocol that allows electronic musical instruments to interact with each other. MIDI requires software to create MIDI files and client software to read and play MIDI files. Your Treo has the software to read MIDI files and can play MIDI files. Most ringtones are MIDI files are played by your Treo when you receive a phone call.

You cannot use your Treo phone and send an MMS message at the same time.

Send an MMS Message

To send an MMS message, perform the following steps:

1. Access the Applications Launcher screen. To get there, press the HOME button, and then choose the MMS icon. An MMS window should appear.

2. From the MMS list view, choose New.

3. Address the new message by either using your Contacts list or by entering the phone number or e-mail address of the recipient in the To field.

4. Press the DOWN button on the five-way navigation control.

5. Type in the message's subject text.

6. Press DOWN to highlight the image icon, and then press the CENTER button of the five-way navigation control.

7. Choose the type of file you want to add to the message.

8. Follow the onscreen steps to insert the file.

9. Select Preview to view your message as the recipient will see it.

10. Select Send.

The Treo comes equipped with preconfigured templates. Select the Inbox pull-down menu and choose the last item, Templates. Four templates will appear from which you can choose, each with animated graphics and sound.

Use Sprint Picture Mail

If your Treo 600 is hosted by Sprint, it uses the CDMA wireless network. The CDMA wireless network does not currently support MultiMedia Message Service (MMS), but Sprint has included Sprint Picture Mail, which allows you to do some of the same things you can do with MMS. As with MMS, you may have to pay additional fees for Picture Mail service. If you're not sure if your Sprint contract includes Picture Mail service, either check your contract or contact Sprint directly to find out.

Send a Picture Using Sprint Picture Mail

You can share a picture with someone who uses a Treo 600 or PCS Vision Phone, or you can send pictures to someone by e-mail. In order to use Picture Mail, you need a Picture Mail web site account. The first time you use Picture Mail, you will be prompted to set up a Picture Mail account with a password. In the Password field, enter the password of your choice, between four and eight characters long. You will receive confirmation that your account is set up, after which you may begin uploading and sharing your Treo photos.

Reduce the Size of a Photo Before You Send It Using Sprint Picture Mail

Your photos are sent, and received, in less time if you send smaller image files. Picture Mail allows you to reduce the size of your photos before you send them. To reduce the photo size prior to sending it, follow these steps.

1. Launch Picture Mail from the Applications Launcher screen.

2. Choose Pictures view and select the picture you want to send.

3. Choose Share.

4. In the To field, type the e-mail address or phone number of the recipient. (The recipient must have a Picture Mail account to receive the message.)

5. In the message area, you can type text to send with the photo or select from the Canned Message list to select an appropriate predefined phrase and save yourself some typing.

6. Select Share.

When you choose Share, your photo will be uploaded to the Picture Mail web site and sent to the recipient's Picture Mail account. The recipient can view the photo and message using any web browser by logging in to his or her user account on the Picture Mail web site.

Receive Sprint Picture Mail

You can set your Treo to download any new messages automatically or have it display an alert to notify you that a new message is available for you to download. When you receive the alert telling you of a new Picture Mail message, you can choose from the following options:

- **Go To**   This downloads the message immediately.

- **Snooze**   This closes the alert but will remind you of the message again in five minutes.

- **OK**   This closes the alert without downloading the message.

Access Your Sprint Picture Mail Inbox

You can access your Picture Mail account at any time using your Treo. The steps for accessing your account are listed here:

1. If Picture Mail is not currently running, press the MENU button on the keyboard to open the Applications Launcher, and then find and select the Picture Mail icon.

2. Once Picture Mail is running, choose the web icon. This will open your Inbox.

3. With your Inbox displayed, you can choose from several options:

   - **Share Inbox**   Enables you to share all of your photos in your Inbox.

   - **Save Inbox As**   Copies your photos in your Inbox into a new album.

   - **Move All Pictures**   Transfers the photos in your Inbox to an existing album.

   - **Back**   Returns you to the Camera application on your phone.

   - **Album List**   Displays a list of all of your photo albums in your Picture Mail account.

One of the advantages of your Picture Mail account is that you may access it any time using any web browser. This allows you to view and manage your photos from, essentially, anywhere you can access a web browser. The web site address is www.picturemail.sprintpcs.com.

Customize Your Sprint Picture Mail Settings

There are several Sprint Picture Mail configuration settings that you can change to suit your needs. The settings that can be changed are listed here:

5

- **Default Name**   The default name assigns a name to the next series of pictures that you take, such as MingsBDay001, MingsBDay002, and so on.

- **Category**   This setting allows you to set the default category of the pictures you take from now on.

- **Picture Size**   This setting lets you set the default size for the pictures you take with your Treo. There are two size options: Large (640×480 pixels) and Small (160×120 pixels).

- **Play Capture Sound**   This setting lets you determine whether or not your Treo will play a sound when you take a picture.

- **Confirm Before Deleting**   This instructs Sprint Picture Mail to ask whether you're sure you want to delete a picture before deleting it.

- **Confirm Before Saving**   With this setting, Sprint Picture Mail prompts you to confirm whether or not you want to save a picture before it is stored on your Treo.

- **Backup Settings**   This allows you to back up your Treo image database on your computer.

You may access any of these settings by following these steps:

1. If Picture Mail is not currently running, press the MENU button on the keyboard to open the Applications Launcher, and then find and select the Picture Mail icon. From any Picture Mail view, press MENU.

2. From the Options menu, select Preferences.

3. Change any of the settings and select OK.

Third-Party MMS Applications

There are some software vendors that offer MMS applications for your Treo. This is especially important if your Treo, including those sold by Sprint, does not have a built-in MMS client.

Pixer MMS

Pixer MMS allows you to send photos, animations, and picture messages to e-mail boxes and mobile phones from your Treo 600 using MMS. More information about the software is available on the Electric Pocket web site (www.electricpocket.com), and the product is available for sale from Handango (www.handango.com).

SMS

If you have not personally used SMS messaging, you may have heard about it. SMS (Short Message Service) is extremely popular in Asia and Europe and is just beginning to catch on in North America.

What Is SMS?

Short Message Service is basically a mechanism of delivery of short, text-only messages using mobile wireless networks. SMS offers a store-and-forward method of transmitting messages to and from mobile devices like your Treo. SMS messages are short messages that you exchange with other mobile phones and devices that have SMS. Messages longer than 160 characters are split into multiple messages. You should refer to your service plan for per-message costs and availability on your wireless network.

An SMS message (text-only) is sent from the sending wireless device and is stored in a central short message center, which then forwards it to the intended recipient's wireless mobile device. So, in case the recipient is not available, the short message is stored and can be sent later.

What's So Great about SMS?

So why would you use SMS? Like many technologies, there are specific functions that make SMS more valuable than its conventional competition. For example, SMS is well suited for exchanging small messages like "See you at 8:45 tonight at the theatre" because SMS is much less expensive than calling someone using your Treo phone to give them the exact same message. In fact, calling the person to give them the exact same message almost invariably takes more time and costs more.

Many SMS users think it an excellent technology for "chatting" (done using Chat View). If you have ever used instant messaging applications on your PC, the concept is very similar. With SMS, you type and send short text messages (and appropriate smiley face icons) back and forth with another SMS user while the conversation is visible on the screen in a single thread. This provides a more interactive feel to your messaging.

One of the advantages of SMS, similar to e-mail in this regard, is that all of the major wireless mobile networks support SMS, so it is becoming a universal standard that can be used across a wide variety of wireless mobile devices and networks.

What You Need to Send and Receive SMS Messages

SMS does not require a specific account like e-mail requires an e-mail account, but a few things need to be in place for SMS to work properly. The Treo 600 is SMS-capable right out of the box, but all of the following points need to be true for both your Treo and the wireless device that you will be exchanging SMS messages with. In order for SMS to work, both the sending and receiving mobile devices must:

- ■ **Be SMS-capable**   Not all of the available wireless mobile devices and cellular phones are capable of sending and receiving SMS messages.

- ■ **Be hosted on an SMS-capable wireless service provider wireless network**   Not all wireless service providers have made the necessary technical upgrades for SMS.

- ■ **Have SMS included in their service contracts**   This is not necessarily part of the default wireless contract.

The size limit of SMS is 160 characters if Latin alphabets are used (English, French, German, Spanish, and so on). If non-Latin alphabets like Chinese, Korean, or Arabic are used, the limit is shortened to 70 characters.

Send an SMS Message

You can use your Treo to easily send and receive SMS messages, as long as the items cited in the preceding section are all true. To create and send an SMS message, follow these steps:

1. Ensure that your Wireless Mode is turned on. (This was covered earlier in the chapter in the section "Turn Wireless Mode On and Off.")

2. Press the HOME button to view the Applications Launcher screen.

3. Find and select the SMS icon.

4. Your SMS Inbox will open. If you have any messages, they will be listed here.

5. Select the New button at the bottom of the screen.

6. A new SMS screen, like that shown in Figure 5-14, will open. You can then begin typing your message.

NOTE   *The "To" address information that you need to send an SMS message is the recipient's phone number or Internet e-mail account address. The phone number must be in the international format. For example, in North America, the recipient's number would take the form of 1-555-555-5555.*

7. Type the full phone number or e-mail address of the recipient or, if the intended recipient is in your Contacts list, start typing the first initial and last name (without spaces). Afterward, press the DOWN button on the five-way navigation control and choose the recipient's phone number or e-mail address from the list that appears.

8. Type your message (including any smiley icons if you feel it adds to the mood of the message).

9. Select Send.

Use QuickText and Emoticons

The SMS application on your Treo gives you a great time-saving feature called QuickText. QuickText allows you to select a message from a preexisting list of phrases. This allows you to quickly insert common text with emoticons (also called smiley face icons), as shown in Figure 5-15.

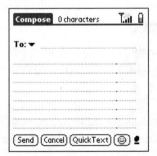

FIGURE 5-14   The new SMS screen

FIGURE 5-15   QuickText options

You can even edit your QuickText list and add new messages that you can reuse by selecting the QuickText button, and then selecting Edit QuickText from the menu. Or you can add emoticons to spice up your messages or help set the tone of a message.

Receive SMS Messages

While your phone is on and you are in an area of wireless coverage, you will automatically receive any SMS messages sent to you. You can configure your Treo to instantly notify you when new text messages arrive through a ringtone and vibration, or an onscreen alert, whichever you prefer.

- When you receive an alert notifying you of a new SMS message, choose the Go To button. Once you are viewing the message, of course, you can reply as well.

- To dismiss an alert, choose OK, and the message will be saved in your SMS Inbox.

- If you want to be reminded of the new message again in five minutes, choose Snooze.

Use Links in SMS Messages

palmOne has done a great job of allowing you to combine the various functions across applications on your Treo. For example, you may use content in SMS messages to launch other applications and utilize different functions on your Treo. When you receive an SMS message containing a telephone number, e-mail address, or web site

URL, you can dial the number, send an e-mail message, or go to the web page by tapping on the linked text. To see this in action, follow these steps:

1. Open the Applications Launcher by pressing the HOME button on the keyboard. Find and select the SMS application to launch it.

2. Select an SMS message from the list.

3. Select the e-mail address, phone number, or web site URL that appears as underlined blue text.

4. Your Treo will automatically launch the appropriate application from the selected link. In other words, if you tapped a phone number, your Treo phone will activate.

What Other Wireless Functions Can You Use Your Treo For?

This section is designed to provide a brief listing and overview of some of the ways you can use your Treo 600. One of the great things about Palm-powered devices, like your Treo 600, is that the Palm developer community is extremely active, and new products (and therefore new uses) for your Treo 600 are constantly being introduced. Chapter 1 explained why the Treo 600 is much more than just an updated PalmPilot, with its wireless capabilities putting it in an entirely different league.

Download and Install Applications Wirelessly

Many applications have a small enough file size that you can download them wirelessly and install them directly to your Treo without the HotSync installer. In fact, many software developers offer shareware and freeware applications that you can download from reseller and company web sites.

TIP   *Shareware is software you can download and use without needing to immediately pay. It is a great way to try out software before you buy it. If you decide you want to use the software on a regular basis, simply purchase a license key, usually online, with your credit card. Most shareware applications are functionally limited to encourage you to pay for the software in order to get the fully functional version.*

There are several web sites that resell applications for your Treo 600. Many of these sites allow you to pay for, download, and install applications and games to your Treo, and do it wirelessly. A prime example of a web site that lets you do this is palmOne (www.palmOne.com).

NOTE *Some applications require a conduit application that runs on your PC to facilitate application data synchronizing during HotSync. Any conduit applications need to be installed locally on your PC.*

Use Your Treo as a Wireless Modem for Your PC

Wouldn't it be great if you could use the wireless capability of your Treo to connect your PC or laptop to the Internet? Well, you can. PdaNet is an application that allows you to do exactly that.

The www.junefabrics.com web site states the following about PdaNet: "Software to drive your Treo PDA as a wireless modem for your PC, PdaNet allows your PC to go online by connecting to your Treo PDA cell phone through the HotSync USB cable. If you own a Treo 600 with the Sprint PCS Vision Plan or GPRS service (such as that from T-Mobile, Cingular, or AT&T), you can use it as a wireless modem/ISP for your computer."

It is worth mentioning again that any use of your Treo that involves sending large amounts of data over the wireless network may involve extra costs on your monthly bill, so you need to be aware of the details of your wireless data plan to prevent any surprises.

Expand Your Treo Wireless Connectivity Options

Your Treo is equipped with a Secure Digital expansion card slot to allow you to extend your phone in several great ways. Your expansion options are covered in detail in Chapter 15, but they are worth mentioning in the wireless connectivity section because you can use compatible expansion cards to increase your wireless networking options. Your Treo comes equipped right out of the box with either GSM/GPRS or Sprint/ CDMA wireless connectivity capability, and with the right expansion cards you can also use 802.11 (also known as wireless LAN or Wi-Fi) or Bluetooth connectivity. Both 802.11 and Bluetooth are short-range wireless networks—so they are only useful if you have access to the appropriate network infrastructure—but each offers a cost-effective, and often better performing, wireless connectivity. Bluetooth SD cards are not currently available, but several vendors will be releasing Bluetooth-capable

SD cards soon. Visit www.palmOne.com for more information. Vendors that currently offer Secure Digital 802.11 expansion cards include the following:

- Sychip (www.sychip.com/wlan-module.html)
- SanDisk (www.sandisk.com)

Use Your Treo to Connect to a Virtual Private Network

Remote workers and telecommuters have used virtual private network (VPN) technology with PCs for years to allow them to securely access company computer networks over long distances. You may have heard of a wide area network (WAN), which is a generic term for a computer network that is spread out over a large area—possibly over the entire world. This is really what we're talking about when we talk about VPNs. The most useful characteristic of a VPN is that it uses public networks, such as the Internet, to connect a remote user to a corporate network—and it does it securely. This is important because organizations and, increasingly, individuals are concerned about Internet security, so anything that can help minimize the risk of using the Internet is a good thing. Fortunately, there are software vendors that know that a wireless mobile device such as your Treo presents unique security challenges and have chosen to develop technology to address these problems and allow you to use your Treo on a VPN. VPN tools for your Treo are covered in more detail in Chapter 13.

Computer System and Network Management Tools

This topic is aimed directly at information technology professionals, network security people, and anyone responsible for managing computer systems and networks—even if it is just your home network. Tools for remote management of computer systems have been available for years. Technologies such as Citrix, Terminal Services, remote access servers (RAS), and many others, allow IT people to remotely access computers, servers, and networking hardware. These technologies are all designed for use while connected to traditional wired infrastructure—cable or phone lines. Now, the availability of truly next-generation wireless devices, such as the Treo 600, prompts the comment, "Would it ever be great if I could manage my servers and networks with my Treo!" Well, there have been some companies that have answered that question while overcoming the idiosyncrasies of the relatively small screen, the relatively slow wireless networks, and concerns about wireless security.

sonicadmin

Sonic Mobility (www.sonicmobility.com) has been delivering mobile systems management software for a few years now and has an impressive customer list, including a major national defense contractor, branches of the U.S. military, and several Fortune 500 companies. With its product, sonicadmin, you can use your Treo to securely connect to your back-end computer systems and network hardware to diagnose and fix problems or do routine maintenance using a wireless connection.

The software includes an embedded client that runs on your Treo and a server component that runs in your computer network. The types of things you can manage include the following:

- Integration to allow mobile management of the following third-party applications:

  - MS Exchange

  - RSA SecurID

  - NetIQ AppManager

  - OpalisRobot

  - TelAlert

- Management of Windows systems, including the following:

  - User management

  - Event logs

  - DNS management

  - Print service management

  - File Explorer functionality, and even e-mail files from a remote computer

  - Services and server processes

  - Server and device management: logoff, shutdown, or force-reboot servers

  - Power to external devices, including servers, switches, and so on

  - The command-line interface and VT100 Terminal Emulation to manage Telnet or SSH devices

Mobile TS

Mobile TS is a useful application that allows you to connect your Treo to Windows desktops and workstations using the Windows Terminal Services or Remote Desktop capabilities built into many Microsoft Windows operating systems. More information is available on the DDH Software web site at www.ddhsoftware.com.

GPS, Navigation, and Maps

Being wireless means that if you get lost you don't have the option of following your network cable to find your way back to the office, but the good news is that your Treo makes a great compass, map, and helpful navigation tool. You can convert your Treo into a stand-alone tool for GPS (Global Positioning System), covered in detail in Chapter 14, and use it to display maps and driving directions. You can even load maps of entire continents on your Treo to help you find your way around. One such application is Mapopolis Navigator for Palm OS 5.0 GPS Bundle (www.mapopolis.com). Mapopolis Navigator costs approximately $249 and makes your Treo 600 the ultimate in-car navigator. The bundle comes with a mouse-type GPS, a Y-cable, and the Navigator for Palm OS 5.0 software with U.S. maps on CD. It allows you to plot your course and have it guide you with visual and audible prompting, and you will never again have to figure out how to refold the road map!

Stock Market Applications

It isn't difficult to imagine that your Treo mobile connectivity capability offers a great way to keep you in the loop with changing information. Certain information is very time-sensitive, and the ability to receive real-time information updates can be extremely valuable. Some application vendors also provide software that keeps you abreast of changes in the stock market.

Charts

Charts, by Tawacentral, is an application for displaying price charts, retrieving delayed quotes, and viewing the fundamental financial data of stocks traded on North American and worldwide markets.

With this program, stocks can be organized into separate watch lists for easier management of your portfolio. Using Charts is as simple as entering one or more stock symbols and performing a HotSync operation, which downloads all the necessary information from the Internet and uploads it to your handheld.

Chart MA Stock

Chart MA Stock graphs share prices, volumes, and MA lines from any exchange. Download historical data when you HotSync your Treo. You can specify stocks for a period of time and graph them with moving averages. You can also reanalyze stocks using different periods, scales, and MA values.

Chart MA can be downloaded from Handango (www.handango.com), and product information can be found at the Pen Systems web site (www.pensystems.com).

TTY—Teletypewriter for the Deaf

TTY, which stands for *teletypewriter,* is a special device that lets people who are deaf, hard of hearing, or speech-impaired use the telephone to communicate by allowing them to type text messages back and forth instead of talking and listening. Many people use TTYs, not just those who are deaf. A TTY is required at both ends of the conversation in order to communicate, however. If you use a TTY device, you can use your Treo to facilitate communication between you and someone who also uses a TTY device. One company that manufactures TTY devices that you can use with your Treo is Ultratec (www.ultratec.com). TTY-specific adaptor cables to connect the TTY to your Treo are available from Hitec (www.hitec.com).

Other Wireless Topics Worth Mentioning

Wireless technology is changing rapidly and will continue to do so for quite some time. It doesn't make sense to try and learn everything about wireless just to make the most of your Treo. There are a few wireless connectivity topics you may want to be aware of with regard to your Treo.

What Is Dial-Up?

The world of wireless acronyms and terminology can be difficult to decipher, and we don't want to load you up with a bunch of meaningless terms, but some are more important than others. "Dial-up" is a term you will occasionally see relating to wireless data on your Treo. You may remember the old computer dial-up modems that allowed computers to communicate using phone lines—well, dial-up for your Treo is similar. Dial-up uses the Treo phone for data communications instead of using the data channel. It is generally a secondary mode of communication when regular wireless data connectivity is unavailable. For example, your Treo may automatically begin using dial-up mode when you're roaming and it is unable to connect to the primary means of connectivity, which is usually GPRS. Dial-up connections also allow you to access the Internet using the Treo phone.

Why "Dial-Up" May Be Important to You

There are a few reasons why dial-up mode may by important to you.

■ **Cost**   Some wireless service providers charge extra for time spent in dial-up mode. So, if your wireless service contract is held by a carrier that charges extra for dial-up mode and your Treo switches to dial-up mode when you are roaming, the difference will show up on your next bill.

■ **Your WSP does not offer wireless Internet**   Dial-up mode may be used to access the Internet by allowing your Treo to connect to an Internet service provider (ISP) account.

Roaming

Roaming is the term wireless service providers use to describe the situation where you are outside of your primary coverage area but are still connected to a wireless network. Your ability to "roam" outside your coverage area is dependent on the relationships between wireless service providers in other areas and on the details of your service contract. You can roam and use another carrier's wireless network as long as your wireless service provider has a roaming agreement with the other carrier to allow your Treo to connect to that carrier's network. There are two main reasons why roaming is important:

■ **Dollars and cents—or euros, francs, yen, and so on**   You pay your wireless service provider for your service, but if you move into an area where you are using another wireless service provider's network, someone has to pay for that service. Therefore, there must be a business agreement between the two wireless service providers so that the WSP providing your roaming can bill *your* WSP, who in turn bills you. So to cover the associated extra accounting costs, many wireless service providers charge you more when you are roaming.

■ **Performance in dollars and cents**   In areas where normal service is not available, some carriers may resort to a "backup plan" and allow you to use a dial-up connection to access the Internet. The performance of dial-up is slower, and there may be an added fee for using the service. So, if you don't want to use this dial-up option when roaming, be sure to disable any automatic Internet connections you may have set up, such as checking your e-mail.

Blazer Web Browser Supported Media Types

This section is primarily intended for individuals with prior technical knowledge about web technologies and also serves as a reference if you are experiencing difficulties viewing specific web sites. (You can view and use most web sites using the Blazer browser.) What follows is a list of what is, and is not, supported on the Blazer Web Browser version 3.0.

The following Blazer markup languages are supported:

- HTML 4.01
- XHTML 1.1
- XHTML Mobile Profile
- cHTML (iHTML)
- WML 1.3
- DHTML
- DOM

The following Blazer style sheets are supported:

- Cascading Style Sheets as called for in the WAP2 specification:
    - CSS1
    - CSS2

NOTE   *The Treo 600 web browser will show content regardless of CSS support.*

The following Blazer scripting languages are supported (WML script is not, however):

- ECMAscript (JavaScript 1.5)
- DeviceID (lets a web site store cookies effectively)

These Blazer image formats are supported:

- GIF
- Animated GIF
- JPEG
- PNG
- WBMP

NOTE *Blazer version 3.0 does not support BMP-formatted images.*

The following Blazer cookies are supported (thus the Blazer Web Browser supports cookies stored on the client):

- Session cookies are cleared 10 minutes after you exit the browser or 25 minutes after your last interaction with the application.

NOTE *Desktop PC browsers are generally configured to clear session cookies immediately when you exit a web application or web page. But, due to the unique nature of browsing the web using the Treo 600, some tweaks have been made so that usability is maximized. For example, you may need to take a phone call or check the calendar and then return to the browser. If so, it makes sense to have session cookies kept around for a longer period of time. Of course, all of this is done behind the scenes, so you don't have to worry about it.*

The following points should be noted when it comes to downloading particular file types supported by the Blazer Web Browser:

- Some download file types have a size limit. This means you won't be able to download these specific file types if they are too big. Specifically, MID/MIDI files cannot be larger than 64KB.

- You can only download files from the web browser if that file type is supported by an application on your Treo 600 (including third-party applications). For example, you can download any MIDI file less than 64KB and use it as a ringtone. You can also download any .prc (Palm OS application) or .pdb (Palm OS database) file, and it will be installed on your Treo.

- Out of the box, the web browser in Treo 600 allows you to download these file types: JFIF, JPE, JPEG, JPG, MID (less than 64KB), MIDI (less than 64KB), OPRC, PDB, PRC, TXT, and VCF.

- You can download other file types with the help of third-party software. For example, if you install Documents To Go from DataViz, you will be able to download .doc (Microsoft Word) and .xls (Microsoft Excel) files and open them directly in Documents To Go on your Treo.

Blazer can't access web pages containing any of the following elements (they're not supported):

- Java applets

- Plug-ins (Flash, Shockwave, audio, video, and so on)

- BMP

- WML script

Wrap It Up

Your Treo 600 offers powerful wireless connectivity capabilities. Network capability is no longer restricted to corporate networks and desktop PCs. As software and hardware vendors (as well as generally inventive people) continue to recognize the vast possibilities of mobile devices and networks, your options will continue to grow. So, in addition to your Treo being an excellent mobile phone, it is capable of many other valuable tasks, as diverse as playing games in real time with other Treo users, navigating the nation's highways, browsing the Web, checking your palmOne stocks, and managing your network systems from anywhere.

Chapter 6

Send and Receive E-Mail

How to...

- Select the right e-mail software for your needs

- Set up your Treo to send and receive e-mail

- Use Treo Mail

- Customize your e-mail

We decided to create a separate chapter just on Treo 600 e-mail because there are enough options and choices for setting up and using e-mail that the topic can get confusing quickly. This chapter identifies the three general types of e-mail accounts, discusses your software options, and guides you through the steps to get each up and running—or rather, get you up and e-mailing.

E-Mail—The Killer Wireless Application for Your Treo

E-mail has revolutionized the way we communicate, and in many cases e-mail has even altered the way we do business. Extending e-mail into the wireless realm has enabled us to be connected no matter where we are. Of course, not everyone thinks that this is a good thing, but for many of us it offers freedom from the constraints of the office environment while still allowing us to be involved and in touch. The Treo 600 lets you send and receive e-mail in many different ways, and perform tasks usually relegated to the desktop, such as managing contacts and viewing attachments. Regardless of how many other applications you use on your Treo, or how often you play games or listen to MP3s, you will likely use e-mail almost as much as you use your Treo phone.

Get Connected

Your wireless service provider, the company you are paying to use your Treo as a phone, classifies e-mail as data. Not all mobile phone contracts include data service by default. If you know that your contract includes data service, then great! If you are not sure, you may want to take a look at your contract to find out, or give the company a call. In order for your Treo to send and receive e-mail, you must have data service included with your Treo phone plan. This topic is covered in more detail in Chapter 5.

Understand Your E-Mail Options

Several different technologies and configurations allow you to send and receive e-mail on your Treo, so it's important that you understand the available options and what their differences are before you get started. If you already have an e-mail account, or many e-mail accounts, your options are relatively straightforward because you don't have to consider all of the available options. The four major types of e-mail accounts you can use with your Treo are POP3, corporate (Exchange and Lotus Domino), IMAP, and web-based e-mail. Each type is described in more detail later in this chapter.

Understand E-Mail Account Types

6

The type of e-mail account you have determines the type of software you will need to run, as well as how to configure your Treo to send and receive e-mail. Generally, e-mail accounts fall into one of four categories:

- **Corporate e-mail such as MS Exchange/Outlook or Lotus Domino**   If you have an e-mail account through your employer, chances are it's one of these, but this isn't always the case.

- **POP3 (Post Office Protocol 3) e-mail such as Eudora, Outlook Express, and Entourage**   If your Internet service provider (such as EarthLink, AT&T WorldNet, BellSouth, Shaw, Telus, Comcast, O2, Orange, SBC, or Verizon) hosts your e-mail account, then it is likely a POP3 account.

- **IMAP (Internet Message Access Protocol)**   This is a method of accessing electronic mail or bulletin board messages that are kept on a mail server. IMAP permits a "client" e-mail program on your Treo (or PC) to access remote e-mail message stores as if they were local. For example, e-mail stored on an IMAP server can be manipulated from a home desktop computer, a workstation at the office, or a notebook computer while traveling, without the need to transfer messages or files back and forth between these computers. Many of the corporate e-mail account types support IMAP e-mail. Some IMAP e-mail software options are listed later in this chapter in the section "IMAP E-Mail Application Options for Your Treo 600."

- **Web-based e-mail such as Hotmail, Yahoo!, Netscape, Lycos, and Excite**   You typically use these types of e-mail accounts by going to a web page and logging in to your account to send and view e-mail.

Yahoo! can be either POP3 or web-based e-mail depending on your account type. Yahoo! offers free web-based e-mail, so if you didn't pay anything to get your Yahoo! e-mail account, then it is a web-based account. But, if you paid to upgrade to Yahoo! Premium, you may use your account with POP3 software on your Treo.

Find Out Your E-Mail Account Type

You need to find out what type of e-mail account you have (POP3, corporate—Exchange or Domino—or web-based e-mail) in order to choose the correct Treo software and configure it properly so you can use e-mail.

Ask for Help

Asking for help is a lot like asking for directions. Nevertheless, asking the proper people the right questions can save you a lot of time and frustration. The fastest way to find out information about your e-mail account is to call up the Support desk of the organization that provides your e-mail. Usually, just introducing yourself, explaining why you're calling, and asking whether your e-mail account is a POP3 account will start you down the right path. If, on the other hand, the company you work for provides your e-mail, great! Go bug the e-mail or systems administrator; you may even be able to persuade her to set up your Treo for you—something well worth the price of a soy latte if you find that a little bribery is necessary.

Use Online Support Resources

If you're more of a figure-it-out-yourself type of person, many service providers have excellent online knowledge bases that can supply you with all the information you need. So, if you know the company that provides your e-mail, go to their web site and find the Support section. PalmOne also has an excellent Support and FAQ section at www.palmone.com.

Don't Already Have an E-Mail Account?

If you don't already have an existing e-mail account, your options are a little simpler because you don't have to worry about corporate e-mail solutions like Exchange or Lotus Domino. With corporate e-mail out of the picture, your remaining options are POP3 and web-based e-mail.

Set Up a New POP3 E-Mail Account

POP3 (Post Office Protocol 3) is a common e-mail standard that is widely supported, so it is relatively easy to find a service provider that offers POP3 e-mail accounts.

If You Have a Home Internet Connection   If you already have an Internet service provider that provides your home with Internet access, the company supplying your connection can likely set you up with a POP3 e-mail account. In fact, the cost is often included in your Internet fees. Contact the company to find out how to get set up, and then get the POP3 set-up information covered later in this chapter in the section "Set Up a POP3 Account."

If You Don't Have a Home Internet Connection   If you do not have a home Internet connection, there are organizations that provide free POP3 e-mail accounts. As with most things, you get what you pay for, so if you choose to use a free provider, don't expect high reliability or top-notch service. Examples include www.HotPOP.com and www.gmx.co.uk, but a quick Internet search will produce several others. The most reliable POP3 option is to purchase e-mail service from a web-hosting company. The cost of POP3 service is reasonable ($20 per year in North America) and will vary between providers, so shop around and make sure you find a provider that is both reasonably priced and that will provide quality customer service when you need it. E-mail is transported on the Internet, so the physical location of the company hosting your POP3 account is relatively unimportant. Having said this though, service may be slower if your e-mail server is located on a different continent.

Set Up a New Web-Based E-Mail Account

The fastest and simplest way to set up an e-mail account is to use web-based e-mail. To do this, just use your Treo web browser to open a web page and log on to view and send e-mail using the web page. Before you decide whether web based e-mail is right for you, take a look at the following sections which describe some of the advantages and disadvantages of using it.

Advantages of Web-Based E-Mail   There are pros and cons associated with each of your Treo 600 e-mail options. Here are some of the best features of web-based e-mail:

- **Cost-effective**   In fact, web-based e-mail is usually free.

- **Easy to set up**   Just fill out a form and you're registered.

- **Easy to use**   Web-based e-mail typically has simple user-friendly interfaces.

- **Accessible**   Web-based e-mail can be accessed easily from any device with a web browser, including your home, office, or neighbor's PC. (Note that POP3 e-mail can also be accessed from other computers and devices, but it's not nearly as easy to set up.)

Disadvantages of Web-Based E-Mail   While web-based e-mail is the easiest option to set up, there are some limitations you should be aware of:

- **Screen size**   Browsing web pages that are generally designed for a much larger screen can be trying. (Note that an increasing number of web-based e-mail providers provide specific pages that are formatted for mobile devices such as your Treo.)

- **Slow speed**   Browsing web pages on most wireless networks can be too slow for many users, so you may want to first try out web-based e-mail to make sure it's not too slow for you. Many users don't find speed to be a problem, however.

- **Having to check for e-mail**   One of the advantages of POP3 e-mail is that you can set up the client software to check for new messages at timed intervals and alert you when new messages are received. When you use web-based e-mail, you have to log into your e-mail to see if there is anything new. This means that important e-mail may go unnoticed for long periods of time until you check you account.

Some examples of organizations that offer free web-based e-mail include the following:

- Yahoo! Mobile Mail: www.yahoo.com
  (mobile site: http://mobile.yahoo.com/mail)

- Hotmail Mobile: www.hotmail.com
  (mobile site: http://mobile.msn.com/hm/folder.aspx)

Ultimately, you may need to try a few different e-mail options to find the best one for you.

Use Palm Mail for Your POP3 E-Mail Account

PalmOne includes free software called palmOne Mail that allows you to use your Treo with your POP3 e-mail account. Depending on when and where you purchased your Treo, Palm Mail may already be installed on your Treo. GSM versions come preinstalled with Mail, while Sprint CDMA Treo users can download it for free from the palmOne web site at www.palmone.com.

Configure Palm Mail

Before you can configure your e-mail account, there are several pieces of information you will need from the company that hosts your POP3 account. If the Mail application is not preinstalled, you can download it for free from the palmOne web site.

> TIP   *Several third-party software options allow you to use POP3 e-mail with your Treo 600. These options are listed later in the chapter. We focus on Palm Mail specifically because it includes features that most users need and is offered for free from palmOne.*

Set Up a POP3 Account

Whether you use the palmOne Mail application for Treo 600, or choose another POP3 solution, you'll need the following information from your e-mail service provider or support desk:

- **E-mail address**   An address such as dayton@business.com

- **E-mail username**   Your account name

- **E-mail password**   The password associated with your account

- **Incoming (POP3) server name**   A POP3 server name (such as pop3@yahoo.net)

- **Outgoing (SMTP) server name**   An SMTP server name (such as smtp@yahoo.net)

- **Is SSL required for your POP3 or SMTP connection?**   Most e-mail providers do not require SSL encryption, but it's important to know whether SSL is required for your account so you can correctly configure Palm Mail.

- **Is a separate password needed for outgoing messages?**   Some e-mail providers require the sender's username and password to send messages. This allows them to prevent unauthorized use of their e-mail servers.

Once you have the necessary POP3 information, follow these steps to configure Treo Mail. There are several screens where you will have to enter data. Be sure you have the correct information and that you don't make mistakes when inputting data. Yes, of course, this is obvious, but take it from us, being extra careful here can save you time and unnecessary frustration.

1. Go to the Applications Launcher screen, and press the HOME button.

2. Find and launch Mail. If Mail does not appear in the Application Launcher, then you will need to install it. However, if it does appear the first time you launch Mail, the application will step you through a set of screens to help you get your POP3 account set up. If Mail has been launched previously, you may access the Mail configuration screens by launching Mail, pressing the MENU button, selecting the View button, choosing New Account or Edit Accounts, and pressing the New button.

3. Select your POP3 provider from the list. If your e-mail provider does not show up in the list, choose Other and click Next.

4. There are three successive screens where you will have to enter information collected from the organization that provides your e-mail.

   ■ **The Name tab**   As shown in the screen in Figure 6-1

      ■ **Account Name**   This name is required so that the server can identify which mailbox it needs to access.

      ■ **Full Name**   Your first and last name.

      ■ **Email Address**   Your address (such as dayton@telus.net).

      ■ **User Name**   This is your logon name and may be the same as your account name or the first part of your e-mail address—meaning it can be the text before the @ sign in your e-mail address.

      ■ **Password**   Whatever password you have chosen.

FIGURE 6-1   The Name tab

FIGURE 6-2   The Server tab

- ■ **The Server tab**   As shown in Figure 6-2

  - ■ **Incoming (POP3) Server**   This is the Internet address of the server
    that your Treo will receive e-mail from—for example, pop.telus.com.

  - ■ **Outgoing (SMTP) Server**   This is the Internet address of the server
    that your Treo will send e-mail to—for instance, smtp.telus.com.

- ■ **The Advanced tab**   As shown in Figure 6-3

  - ■ **Leave Mail on Server**   Check this box by default. If you do not
    check it, any e-mail downloaded to your Treo will be deleted from
    the e-mail server. By checking this box, it ensures that e-mail will
    not be deleted on the e-mail server and you will have a backup of
    received e-mail. This is also important if you review e-mail using
    a PC or another handheld device.

FIGURE 6-3   The Advanced tab

- ■ **SSL Required for POP3**   Most mail servers don't use SSL, but it's important to know if yours does so you can configure your Treo appropriately.

- ■ **SSL Required for SMTP**   Again, most mail servers don't use SSL, but you should know whether yours does so you can configure your Treo as needed.

- ■ **For Outgoing Mail Server**   Some servers require a username and password to send e-mail. This is necessary to prevent unauthorized use of an e-mail server.

   - ■ **User Name**   Likely the same as your e-mail username

   - ■ **Password**   Likely the same as your e-mail password

Once you have entered all of the necessary information on the Name, Server, and Advanced tabs, and selected the Next button, you will see a Setup Complete! screen that allows you to test your e-mail connection by clicking the Connect button. If you get a "Server Not Found" error, you guessed it—you aren't quite finished.

If you are sure your e-mail and server information are correct and complete, and the connection test still fails, go back and double-check the information to make sure that you didn't "fat finger" and mistype it. Often, starting over is less time-consuming than trying to figure out what went wrong in the first place.

Use Palm Mail

After you have configured Palm Mail and successfully connected to the mail server, you are essentially ready to begin sending and receiving e-mail. Of course, the first thing you should do is send a test e-mail to your e-mail address to ensure you receive it and that everything is behaving as it should. See the section later in this chapter entitled "Compose and Send E-Mail—Basic."

Compose and Send E-Mail with Palm Mail

Many options are available to you when using Mail to compose and send e-mail messages. The following section describes the most basic way of composing and sending a message. There is also an advanced way of doing this (described a little further on). Advanced doesn't mean that the steps are more difficult, it just means that e-mail is covered in a lot more detail.

Compose and Send E-Mail—Basic

The easiest way to test your Treo Mail is to compose a new message and send it to yourself. These steps are the same whether you are sending an e-mail to yourself or to someone else.

1. In Mail, press the MENU button, select Message, and then New. The New Message screen looks like the one shown in Figure 6-4.

2. Enter the e-mail message.

   ■ **To** Fill in the To field with the recipient's e-mail address. The recipient will be your e-mail address if this is a test message.

   ■ **Subject** Fill in the Subject field with a short description of the e-mail.

   ■ **Body** Fill in the Body section with the message content.

3. Once all of the fields have been filled in, press the Send button.

4. Your Treo will connect to the Internet and forward the message to the e-mail server.

TIP *Another time-saving feature of your Treo is that it allows you to easily look up and populate the recipient's e-mail address by typing in the first and last initial or last name in the To field. Press RETURN on the keyboard, and a lookup screen will be displayed with any name and e-mail addresses that match your search. Scroll to the match and press the CENTER button on the five-way navigation control to add the name to the To or Cc fields.*

If you sent the message to your own e-mail account, you likely won't receive the message back at the same time you send it. Wait a few minutes and then press

FIGURE 6-4   The New Message screen

the Send button on the screen. Afterward, press the Receive button on the screen or select the appropriate menu item under Messages. You should then receive your test message.

Compose, Send, and Manage E-Mail—Advanced

Palm Mail offers flexible and powerful e-mail options for your Treo. Once you have mastered the basic e-mail capability, there is a more advanced functionality to help you customize your e-mail, such as working with e-mail attachments, customizing your e-mail, and organizing your messages.

Change the Main View

The first screen you see when you launch Mail is your Mailbox. You can change what messages you want to view by selecting the secondary menu, as illustrated in Figure 6-5. The view options include the following:

- **Inbox** All received messages will appear in this view until you delete or file them.

- **Outbox** The Outbox contains any outgoing e-mail messages that have not yet been sent.

- **Deleted** The Deleted view lists any e-mail messages that you have deleted but that have not yet been purged. The Deleted box is similar to the Recycle Bin on your PC. You can purge (permanently delete) messages by choosing the Purge option under the Message menu.

- **Filed** The Filed view contains any messages that you move from your Inbox to the Filed folder. The Filed folder is where you will move messages that you want to keep.

- **Draft** The Draft view lists any e-mails you have chosen to save as drafts. Usually you save a message as a draft if you have not finished composing it and want to send it later.

- **Sent** The Sent view lists all of the messages you have sent from your Treo.

Use the Palm Mail Application Menus

Palm Mail is a full-function e-mail client. All of the functionality of the application can be accessed from the application menus. The items that appear in the menus will vary slightly depending on the screen you are currently on and what you are doing when you view the menus.

FIGURE 6-5 Change your e-mail view.

Use the Mail Message Menu

The Message menu offers a list of actions that you can perform on one or many e-mail messages. You can access the Message menu by launching Mail and then selecting the MENU button. Your Message menu should look like that shown in Figure 6-6. The following are available actions you can take with e-mail:

- **Send and Receive** When you select the Send and Receive menu (this button is visible on some screens), your Treo will send pending e-mail and check the server for new messages. You can configure your Treo to automatically check for e-mail at regular intervals on the Options | Preferences | Delivery menu.

- **New** Select this option to create a new e-mail message.

FIGURE 6-6 The Mail Message menu

NOTE   *CC is the acronym for "carbon copy." Use CC when you would like a recipient, in addition to the person your sending the e-mail to, to also receive a copy of the message. They are not expected to reply. An example of when someone may want to CC someone could be a sales associate who CCs her boss on all e-mails sent to clients so her boss is aware of what she is doing. The recipients will see all of the people that received the e-mail.*

BCC is the acronym for "blind carbon copy." BCC is similar to CC, but the difference is that none of the people who received the e-mail will see who was BCC'd on the e-mail. This is essentially a stealthy way of ensuring that someone else, other than the main person you sent the e-mail to, also receives the message.

- **Reply**   Select this option when you want to reply to the sender(s) of a selected e-mail message. To reply to all of the e-mail recipients, including the recipients in the Cc and Bcc fields, use Reply All. You can determine whether or not your e-mail replies will include text from previous messages on the Options | Preferences | Message screen.

- **Reply All**   Select this option if you want to create a reply message that will be sent to all of the e-mail addresses in both the To and Cc fields.

- **Forward**   Select this option if you want to send an e-mail in your Inbox to another person.

- **File**   The File command allows you to store e-mails in a folder separate from the inbox.

- **Delete**   The function of this action is obvious, but it is worth noting that deleted messages are moved to the Deleted folder until you select the Purge action.

- **Purge**   The Purge action permanently deletes any messages in the Deleted folder.

- **Mark Unread**   The Mark Unread action makes messages that you have already read appear to be unread. Pretty simple. This feature is an effective way to indicate that a message needs to be revisited later—after all, it seems a natural inclination to want to read a message that looks unopened.

Find a Specific E-Mail Message with the Mail View Menu

Your View menu should look like the screen in Figure 6-7, where the menu items allow you to jump to different positions in your e-mail list and sort your e-mail. This is helpful if you have a lot of e-mail and you find that scrolling through the list to find a particular message is too time-consuming.

- **Top of List**   Lets you jump to the top of the list.

- **Bottom of List**   Lets you jump to the bottom of the list.

- **Sort by Date**   Sorts your e-mail by the date received.

- **Sort by Name**   Sorts your e-mail by the contact name.

- **Sort by Subject**   Sorts your e-mail by the e-mail subject.

- **E-mail Account**   If you have multiple accounts, shows them by name on the bottom of this screen. (In Figure 6-7, you see the account treo600.) You can switch among accounts by selecting from the list the one you want to work with.

- **New Account**   Allows you to add new accounts. Palm Mail allows you to manage up to five different POP3 e-mail accounts. To add new accounts, click this option and fill in the information. The required information was covered earlier in this chapter in the section "Set Up a POP3 Account."

- **Edit Accounts**   Lets you edit your POP3 account settings. If you are experiencing difficulty sending or receiving e-mail, this is where you will check and modify e-mail account settings.

FIGURE 6-7   The Mail View menu

Use the Mail Options Menu

Your Options menu should look like the screen in Figure 6-8 and allows you to define your Delivery, Delete, and Message preferences, among other things:

- **Font** This appears in the menu only if you are creating or editing e-mail and allows you to change the size of the font you would like to use.

- **View Brief Headers** This option appears in the menu only if you are viewing a list of messages. Selecting it will allow you to see more of the header information, so more messages fit on the screen. You can toggle between View Brief Headers and View Full Headers.

- **View Full Headers** This option appears in the menu only if you are viewing a list of messages. Selecting it will reveal more information in the e-mail headers. You can toggle between View Brief Headers and View Full Headers.

- **Preferences** The Preferences tab consists of three subtabs that let you define how you would like Mail to behave, including settings affecting e-mail delivery, e-mail deletion, and your e-mail signature.

    - **The Delivery tab** The Delivery tab, shown in Figure 6-9, allows you to set various delivery parameters, such as the following:

        - **Get Mail** This topic is covered in more detail later in this chapter in the section "Configure When You Want Your Treo to Check for New E-Mail."

FIGURE 6-8   The Mail Options menu

FIGURE 6-9   The Mail Options Preferences Delivery tab

- **For Each Message Get**   This option allows you to define how much message information your Mail application, by default, pulls down to your Treo from the e-mail server. This is valuable because it allows you to minimize the amount of unnecessary data being sent over the wireless network, and how much memory is used up by e-mail messages. By minimizing this number, less data is initially downloaded. However, if you want to see the rest of a message, you can still choose to do so.

- **Only Get Mail**   This option allows you to configure your Treo to get only a portion of your e-mail when it downloads messages from the e-mail server. This is valuable because there will be times when you don't want to pull all of your e-mail from the server. For example, if you have to do a hard-reset on your Treo, which deletes all of your data, you probably won't want to pull all of your e-mail down to your Treo, only that from the last few days. This is also a consideration because you are paying for the amount of data you send over the wireless network.

- **Delete tab**   This tab, shown in Figure 6-10, allows you to configure how Mail should deal with deleted messages.

  - **Confirm Message Deletion**   If you uncheck this option, you will not be prompted with an Are You Sure? message before the e-mail is deleted. Deleted messages are moved to the Deleted folder by default, so you can still recover mistakenly deleted messages until they are purged.

  - **Return to List View after Deleting a Message**   This simply allows you to define which screen you end up on after you delete a message.

- **Message tab**   This tab, shown in Figure 6-11, allows you to define more detailed e-mail preferences.

FIGURE 6-10   The Mail Options Preferences Delete tab

- **Include Original Text when Replying**   When this option is selected, any message that you reply to will include the text in the original message. Unchecking this option results in less over-the-air data transmission.

- **Include Attachments when Forwarding**   When this option is selected, any e-mail that you forward will include any attachment files. Unchecking this option results in less over-the-air data transmission.

- **Always Show Bcc**   This option determines whether or not the Bcc field in your e-mail messages appears on the screen by default. You may want to uncheck this box if you don't normally use the Bcc option or if you want to avoid unnecessary clutter on the small screen.

- **Always Bcc This Address**   This option is very specific and most users won't benefit from its use, but it is valuable if you want a copy of all e-mail messages to go to a specific person or to another e-mail account.

- **Alerts**   The Alerts tab is a duplication of the Sound Preferences screen that allows you to define when an alert is generated and what sound each alert should make. This is covered more fully in Chapter 2 in the section "Sound."

FIGURE 6-11   The Mail Options Preferences Message tab

- **Connection Log**   The connection log is a record of your Treo e-mail connection activity. It is a great source of information when troubleshooting e-mail connection problems. The Log stores information such as the following:

  - **Account Name**   If you have more than one POP3 account, indicates which account created the log entry.

  - **Connection Type**   Shows whether the connection was user-initiated (manual) or automatic.

  - **Start Time**   The time the connection was initiated.

  - **Status**   Whether the connection was successful or if it failed, and the possible reasons for its failure.

  - **Duration**   How long the connection was held.

- **Tips**   The Tips screen provides helpful user tips for using Mail. By launching Tips, you can browse through screens that provide information about specific functionalities.

- **About**   Most applications, including Mail, have an About screen that displays information about the software, including the version number and who created the software.

Configure When You Want Your Treo to Check for New E-Mail

The default setting is to Get Mail Manually, which means that your Treo will not check for e-mail until you press the Send and Receive button. You can also configure your Treo to automatically check the server for new e-mail. If you would like your Treo to check automatically, you can define the time interval in Mail Preferences (Figure 6-9) by clicking the MENU button, selecting the Options menu, and choosing Preferences.

Define an E-Mail Signature

Your e-mail signature is information that is added to the end of the e-mail body when you compose and send an e-mail. By default, Mail adds "Sent from my Treo" to the bottom of your e-mails, but you have the option of creating a more informative or creative signature if you like. You may edit your e-mail signature in Mail by clicking the MENU button, selecting the Options menu, choosing Preferences, selecting the Message tab, and choosing the Signature button. Change your signature text to whatever you like and then click the Done button, as shown in Figure 6-12.

FIGURE 6-12 The Signature screen

You also have the option of defining whether you want your signature to be added to New Messages Only, to All Messages, or to No Messages.

Third-Party POP3 E-Mail Application Options for Your Treo 600

If Palm Mail is not exactly what you need, there are third-party e-mail applications that allow you to use your Treo with your POP3 e-mail account. The following list outlines the various POP3 e-mail client software options for your Treo. Specific product information is available from the product web sites and an updated list of products is available on the palmOne web site at www.palmone.com.

- SnapperMail (www.snappermail.com)—also supports IMAP accounts
- Corsoft Aileron (www.aileron.com)
- Eudora for Palm OS (www.eudora.com)
- VersaMail (www.versamail.com)—also supports IMAP accounts
- Iambic Mail (www.iambic.com)—also supports IMAP accounts

IMAP E-Mail Application Options for Your Treo 600

Internet Message Access Protocol (IMAP) is a method of accessing electronic mail or bulletin board messages that are kept on a mail server. IMAP permits a "client" e-mail program on your Treo or PC to access remote e-mail message stores as if they were local. For example, e-mail stored on an IMAP server can be manipulated from a desktop computer at home, a workstation at the office, and a notebook computer while traveling, without the need to transfer messages or files back and forth between these computers. Many of the corporate e-mail account types support IMAP e-mail, such as the following:

- VersaMail (www.palmone.com/us/software/versamail)
- SnapperMail (www.snappermail.com)
- Iambic Mail (www.iambic.com)

Corporate E-Mail Options—Microsoft Exchange and Lotus Domino

If your e-mail account is hosted and managed by the company you work for, there is a high likelihood that it's either Microsoft Exchange or Lotus Domino. In order to use your Treo for e-mail in either of these environments, you need third-party software designed specifically for Exchange or Domino. Fortunately, there are several companies that offer such software for your Treo 600.

Set Up Your Treo to Use a Corporate E-Mail Account

If the organization you work for uses Microsoft Exchange or Lotus Domino, then the first thing you should do is contact your organization's e-mail administrator or Help Desk to find out whether the company already has an e-mail solution for Palm-powered devices. If you are not the first one in your company to get a shiny new Treo, then chances are your company already has the necessary software and the understanding of how to get your Treo e-mail set up. If you don't find the help you need within your Information Technology staff—or if you are the IT staff—then refer to the following sections on using Exchange and Lotus Domino e-mail on your Treo.

Push E-Mail

Traditional e-mail is non-push. But what the heck does that mean? Well, to explain it properly, we should probably explain "push" e-mail first. Push e-mail is sent to your Treo without requiring any effort from you or your Treo besides turning the wireless mode on. E-mail simply shows up when you are not looking because it is pushed to your device from the e-mail server. Non-push e-mail, on the other hand, requires you to actively request to send or receive e-mail before your Treo will connect to the e-mail server to send any pending e-mail, and to check for new e-mail. The free Palm Mail application is a non-push e-mail application. If you would prefer a push application, there are several third-party applications to consider.

 Push e-mail applications use a software component that interacts with the e-mail server.

Software that Allows You to Use Corporate E-Mail Systems

Several vendors provide third-party e-mail applications that allow you to use your Treo with your corporate e-mail account, as listed here. Specific product information is available from the product web sites, and an updated list of products can be found on the palmOne web site at www.palmone.com.

- Visto MessageXpress (www.visto.com/treo600)

- Infowave SymmetryPro (www.infowave.com)

- Basejet (www.basejet.com)

- Notify Technology NotifyLink (www.notifycorp.com)

- Seven (www.seven.com)

- Sprint PCS Business Connection (Sprint customers only; http://businessconnection.sprintpcs.com)

- GoodLink (AT&T and Sprint customers only; www.good.com/index.php/treo_600.html)

Wrap It Up

Only a few short years ago, mobile devices and networks were designed specifically to allow users to make and receive wireless phone calls. The Treo 600 offers a quantum leap forward in mobile technology. PalmOne has extended tried-and-true mobile phone technologies to allow us to send and receive e-mail from virtually anywhere. The promise of a true mobile office has never been closer.

Arguably, getting the e-mail functionality set up on your Treo 600 for the first time may be the most confusing and challenging part of configuring your Treo. But armed with the information presented in this chapter, you should be well on your way.

Chapter 7

Take and Send Photos

How to…

- Take a photo

- Send photos to others

- Move a Treo photo to your PC—Windows and Mac

- Use third-party software to edit your photos

- Personalize your Treo with wallpaper and photo caller ID

- Use third-party software to manage your photos

One of the most significant recent advances in consumer electronics, besides your fantastic Treo, has been the evolution of digital photography. And, as if your Treo doesn't let you do enough already, it also allows you to take digital snapshots, save them, and send them to others.

Technical Information about Your Treo Digital Camera

The Treo camera is not intended to capture monumental sweeping mountain landscapes to hang on your wall or to record your wedding reception for generations to enjoy. Although you certainly can do that if you like. The camera is really intended as a fun way to take snapshots anywhere and share them with friends. Your built-in Treo camera features include the following:

- Single-focus VGA lens

- Photo-taking capacity of up to 0.3 megapixels, including two optional pixel resolution sizes, 640×480 and 120×160. It is important to know that your Treo camera takes photos in 16-bit color and that the screen display on the Treo 600 only shows the photos in 11.5-bit color (3,375 colors)—this means that your photos look better when you copy them to your PC because when they are downloaded to your computer, the final image is compressed in JPEG format and saved as a 24-bit format image.

> TIP   *Your Treo screen resolution is lower than the photo resolution your Treo camera can take. This means that your resulting photos will be of a higher quality than what you see on the screen when you take the photo or when you view your photos on your Treo.*

- HotSyncing and moving your photos to and from your PC. (Synchronization of your Treo with your PC is covered in Chapter 3.)

- Sending photos to others using e-mail, MMS, or Sprint Picture Mail. (E-mail is covered in Chapter 6 and MMS and Sprint Picture Mail are covered in Chapter 5.)

- Copying images to your PC in standard JPEG format files (.jpg files). The JPEG file format is named after the Joint Photographic Experts Group and is pronounced "jay-peg." JPEG is the most popular format for digital photographic images.

> NOTE   *Your Treo does not have a flash, so you need to take this into account when taking photos in low-light conditions. Photos taken in dim light will tend to be grainy and of poor quality.*

Take Pictures with Your Treo

If you are the type of person that likes to press every button and simply play around with your new electronic toy before reading about its features and how they work, then you may already have taken some photos of your pets, office, friends, and so on. But if you haven't yet ventured into the world of Treo 600 digital photography, here's your chance to get started. To take a photo, follow these steps:

1. Choose something to be your photo subject, taking care to ensure that the object is in bright light (the more light there is, the better your result will be).

2. Press the PHONE button.

3. Press the MENU button to open the Applications Launcher, and find and select the Camera icon. (On most Treo 600s, you can also press the PHONE button and press the RIGHT button on the five-way navigation control to select the Camera application.)

4. The screen now becomes your camera view finder, and you will be able to see what the camera is "seeing"—this feature also means that you don't have to hold the camera up to your eye to see where the camera is pointing. You can hold it any way you want as long as you can see the screen

5. Point the camera at your target, which should be at least 18 inches from your Treo.

6. When your target is framed on the screen (while holding the camera as still as you can), press the CENTER button of the five-way navigation control or tap the Capture button on the screen.

After the image has been captured, it will be accompanied on the screen by three button options to choose from: Save, Don't Save, and Send.

Take a Quick Series of Photos

There may be times when you want to take a sequence of photos in a row during a relatively short period of time. For example, a sequence of a friend jumping off of a balcony holding only a Mickey Mouse umbrella in one hand and a frothy pink beverage in the other. These photos may be followed by a sequence of photos of the same friend getting his ankles adjusted at the hospital. There are a couple of Treo settings that you can change to allow you to minimize the interval between successive photos. (Translation: they let you take a bunch of photos in a row quickly.) When selected, these two settings slow down the repeated picture-taking process and interrupt the pattern of taking several pictures in a row:

- **Play Capture Sound** This setting produces a camera sound effect, and it delays the process by a second or more.

- **Confirm Before Saving** The screen containing your photo and Save, Don't Save, Send buttons that pops up by default after you take a photo is a more significant interruption than the camera sound setting because it requires an action from you that may take several seconds to complete, such as selecting the Save option and readying the camera for the next photo.

To change both of these default settings, follow these steps.

1. Launch the Camera application by doing one of the following:

  - Press the HOME button, and then find and select Camera.

  - Press the PHONE button and press the RIGHT button on the five-way navigation control.

2. From any Camera view, press MENU.

3. From the Options menu, choose Preferences.

4. Uncheck both of the following settings:

- Play Capture Sound

- Confirm Before Saving

With these two settings disabled, you can take a series of photos much more quickly than before.

Tips for Taking Photos with Your Treo 600

You probably aren't surprised that your Treo doesn't produce photographs like a Hasselblad 501 or an 8-megapixel digital SLR. But, it has been our experience, and that of many others, that there are steps you can take to help ensure you produce high-quality digital photos with your Treo. In fact, there are a few web sites where Treo users showcase their Treo photos, clearly showing that if you understand your Treo 600 camera you can take some great photos. You can find these web sites by typing **Treo 600 camera** into the Google search engine (www.google.com). Of course, if you already have a good working knowledge of photography, some of these suggestions will seem basic. Nevertheless, they are very important for maximizing the quality of your photos.

Use Good Light

Your Treo doesn't have a flash, so your subject's light source is one of the most important factors to consider when taking photos with your Treo. (Note that the term "subject" is just an artsy way of saying "that thing you're taking a picture of.") Of course, in many situations, the source and location of the light is beyond your control. For example, it usually isn't very practical to wait for the sun to move across the sky so that the daylight illuminating your squirrel subject is coming from *just* the right angle. Low lighting will be obvious on the screen because you will see little blue pixels on the screen. A couple more tips are listed next.

Ensure the Main Light Source Is Behind You, Not the Subject   Often, if you take photos of people with the sun shining behind them, your resulting photos are more like silhouettes of the people than detailed likenesses. A photo will turn out better if the sun is behind you when you take it because the sun will be facing your subject and will provide more of the light your Treo needs to capture the image.

Move the Camera Until You Don't See Washed-Out Areas   When looking at the screen in camera mode, you may notice that areas of high contrast, as well as very bright or reflective areas, will seem washed out or whiter than they should. Often, moving the camera slightly to change the angle of the shot will allow the camera to recompose the image so it more accurately reflects what the scene looks like.

Take a Picture Within Two Seconds of Launching the Camera

Some users who have taken a picture within two seconds of launching the camera (before the screen has had time to compose the image) have reported that their picture quality is improved. The success of this technique seems to depend on the user and the individual Treo 600. You may find it doesn't make much difference at all, but it's worth mentioning here as an addition to your bag of Treo tricks.

Take Multiple Pictures of the Same Subject

If you have the time, it is always a good idea to take a few photos of the same subject from different angles and distances. One of the best things about digital photography

My Advice for Taking Photos with Your Treo

My advice starts with having the right attitude about the Treo camera. Work within its capabilities, not against its limitations. It's a simple camera, so keep your pictures simple. Use one clear, unmistakable subject in the frame. Bright colors are also good, but high-quality light, preferably natural light, can really make pictures shine. Get in as close as possible to the subject and trim away distractions. I did this with the Graffiti art shots that are on my web site. Those are close-ups from much larger murals; the important thing is that I focused in on what I thought the camera could handle. In the spirit of working within its capabilities, remember that close-up shots of static, brightly lit objects suit the character of the camera. So don't expect to get Ansel Adams–quality shots out of this thing—it's just not that kind of device. Work with what it is, and you can get some great results. You can see examples of my Treo 600 photography on my web site.

—*Mark Thomas, New York, NYA*
www.sorabji.com

is that you can simply delete any photos you don't want, and it doesn't cost you a thing—unlike film photography where you have to pay for the film to be developed before you can find out whether that photograph of your thumb is worth keeping or not.

Keep the Treo Still While Taking a Picture

Keeping your Treo still while you snap your shot is another very important aspect of taking good photos. If you can, steady your arm on a table, tree, or parking meter, and your shots will improve. You will notice that even a little bit of movement will cause blurring in the photo. Of course, if you *want* a little blurring in your photos for artistic effect, that's easy enough to do.

Save a Photo on Your Treo 600

7

Once you have captured an image with your Treo, you can choose to save the image. To help you organize your photos, you can save an image to a specific file folder. Immediately after taking a photo, you will see your new photo, along with three button choices—Save, Don't Save, and Send—as shown in Figure 7-1.

Rename a New Photo Before You Save It

Your new photo is assigned a default name something like Picture009_05Feb04, which may not be very useful in identifying the photo from a list later on, without looking at it; but you have the option to rename the photo before you save it. To rename the file, simply select the text in the upper-left corner and type in a new name.

FIGURE 7-1   Saving a photo

File a New Photo

You can file your photos in folders to help better organize them. PalmOne uses the term *category* to allow you to define groups that help you organize your information. Categories are conceptually similar to files, folders, organizational units, shopping carts, and other organizational types you've run across in the past. Categorizing and renaming photos when you save them may not seem like a big deal when you only have a few photos, but later on when you have hundreds or thousands of photos, you'll be thankful you took the time to get organized now. For more information on photo naming, see the section "Define a Default Picture Name" later in this chapter.

To save the photo to a specific category, follow these steps:

1. Immediately after you have taken a photo, select the menu in the top-right corner of the screen and select the category this photo should be filed in. If you want to create a new category, simply follow these steps:

   a. Select the Edit Categories option from the menu.

   b. Type in a name for the new category.

   c. Press OK.

2. Press the Save button.

Now you will be able to easily locate your new photo later on both your PC and on your Treo.

View a Photo on Your Treo 600

You may view your saved photos on your Treo at any time by following these steps:

1. Press HOME to open the Applications Launcher screen.

2. Find and select the camera icon.

3. Choose the Pictures view icon at the bottom of the screen to see a list similar to that shown in Figure 7-2.

FIGURE 7-2   A picture list in Pictures list view

4. Scroll down until you see the photo you want to view and select it by either tapping the touchscreen or pressing the CENTER button on the five-way navigation control.

5. From Pictures view, you can browse to the previous photo in the list by selecting the Prev button or skip to the next photo by selecting the Next button.

Send a Photo to Others

When you are browsing your photos, or immediately after you have taken a photo, you can choose to send the photo to someone else using either e-mail or MMS (Multimedia Message Service, covered in Chapter 5). Whether or not you have MMS is dependent on the capabilities of your wireless service provider network and the details of your service contract, and it is often a separate service that is charged on your monthly bill.

Send a Photo Using E-Mail

Before you can send a digital photo using e-mail, you will need to have an e-mail account that is correctly configured on your Treo. (E-mail is covered in depth in Chapter 6.) Provided your e-mail is correctly configured and you are in a wireless coverage area, the steps for e-mailing a photo that you have already taken and saved on your Treo are as follows:

1. Launch the Camera application (as described in the earlier section "Take a Quick Series of Photos").

2. Press the Pictures view (the second icon on the bottom of the screen that looks like a list).

3. Select the photo that you want to send either by tapping the touchscreen or by using the five-way navigation control to highlight the photo.

4. Press the Send button on the screen.

5. A menu will appear with the choices Mail and MMS (assuming you have MMS capability on your Treo), as shown in Figure 7-3.

6. Select Mail, and then select OK.

Type in the e-mail address of the person to whom you want to send the photo. If the recipient's e-mail address is stored in your Contacts list, you can begin typing the recipient's name, and the rest of the field will fill in as your Treo finds the match in the Contacts list.

Select the Send button (or select Send Later if you are not currently connected to the wireless network and want to delay sending the message until your next connection).

Send a Photo Using MMS

If your Treo is correctly configured for MMS (Multimedia Message Service) and you are in a wireless coverage area, the steps to send one of your stored photos using MMS are as follows:

1. Launch the Camera application (as described in the earlier section "Take a Quick Series of Photos").

2. Press the Pictures view (the second icon on the bottom of the screen that looks like a list).

FIGURE 7-3   Send a photo using e-mail or MMS

3. Select the photo you want to send either by tapping the touchscreen or by using the five-way navigation control to highlight the photo.

4. Press the Send button on the screen.

5. A menu will appear with the choices Mail and MMS (assuming you have MMS capability on your Treo), as shown previously in Figure 7-3.

6. Select Mail, and then select OK.

7. Type in the phone number or e-mail address of the person to whom you want to send the photo. If the recipient's e-mail address is stored in your Contacts list, you can begin typing the recipient's name, and the rest of the field will fill in as your Treo finds the match in the Contacts list.

8. Select the Send button (or select Send Later if you are not currently connected to the wireless network and want to delay sending the message until your next connection).

Move a Photo on Your Treo 600

Once you have taken a photo, you may want to move it on your Treo to another category or to a memory expansion card. Moving photos between categories allows you to better organize your photos. Here are some of the reasons you may want to move photos to an expansion card:

- To free up memory on your Treo

- To move the images from your Treo by removing the expansion card that holds them and plugging it into to another device or PC. The topic of expansion cards is covered in Chapter 15, but to summarize, you can use removable memory cards to store images and other files without using precious Treo memory.

To move a Treo photo, follow these steps:

1. Launch the Camera application (as described in the earlier section "Take a Quick Series of Photos").

2. Press the Pictures view (the second icon on the bottom of the screen that looks like a list).

3. Select the photo you want to send either by tapping the touchscreen or by using the five-way navigation control to highlight the photo.

4. Press MENU on the keyboard.

5. From the Picture menu, choose the Move option.

6. Choose either the category or expansion card that you want to move the photo to.

7. Select Move.

Delete a Photo from Your Treo

One of the many great things about using your Treo camera is that you don't have to keep your photos or pay for film development. If you decide you want to delete a photo that is saved on your Treo, follow these steps.

1. Launch the Camera application (as described in the earlier section "Take a Quick Series of Photos").

2. Press the Pictures view (the second icon on the bottom of the screen that looks like a list).

3. Select the photo that you want to delete either by tapping the touchscreen or by using the five-way navigation control to highlight the photo.

4. Select the Delete button on the screen.

5. If you are prompted to confirm the delete, select OK.

PalmOne has designed your Treo camera to make it extremely easy to take digital photos. Some of the more advanced features of the camera and some of the things you can do with your photos are covered later in this chapter.

Configure Your Treo Camera Options

There are a few configurable options that you can change to adjust the camera for your specific needs.

Define a Default Picture Name

A default picture name on your Treo looks something like Picture009_05Feb04. This naming scheme tells you what day a photo was taken, but you may want a little more information to help you identify pictures later. One option is to name every photo immediately after you take it; option is to set the default name to something useful for a series of pictures. For example, you may want a series of photos that you will be taking at Dave's 42nd birthday party to begin with the name "DavesBDay." To change the default name, follow these steps:

1. Launch the Camera application (as described in the earlier section "Take a Quick Series of Photos").

2. From any Camera view, press MENU on the keyboard.

3. From the Options menu, choose Preferences.

4. At the top of the Preferences screen, there is a field called Default Name. In this field, you can type the name of the next series of photos that you are going to take—for example, "DavesBDay," as shown in Figure 7-4.

Now, every subsequent picture will have a name beginning with the new default name and the number of the photo. You can change the default name at any time to better reflect the name of your next series of photos.

Define the Default Category for New Photos

Your categories are conceptually similar to file folders, and they allow you to organize your Treo files, including your photos, in a way that helps you store them in logically organized groups. This helps you find things more quickly when you need to.

When you take a new photo and save it, without changing the category, it is saved into the default category. You can change the category by selecting an alternate category for the photo from the Category menu. If you like, you can also change the default category. This enables you to create a more appropriate category name than

FIGURE 7-4   The Preferences screen

"uncategorized" and speeds up the process by immediately saving your photos in the most appropriate category so that you can easily locate a particular photo later on. To change the default category, follow these steps:

1. Launch the Camera application (as described in the earlier section "Take a Quick Series of Photos").

2. From any Camera view, press MENU on the keyboard and choose the Preferences menu option.

3. Select the Category pull-down menu and choose the category that you would like to be the default category for new photos. You can add a new category by selecting the Edit Categories option from the list.

4. Select OK, and if you edited your categories, select OK on the Preferences screen as well.

Configure Your Default Picture Size

Your Treo is capable of taking two different sizes of digital photos: large—640×480 pixels, and small—120×160 pixels. The default size for newly captured photos is the larger format of 640×480 pixels, but there may be times when you prefer to use the smaller format—for example, if you want to conserve the amount of Treo memory that's used to store your Treo photos or if you want to send your photos using wireless connectivity applications like e-mail, MMS, or Sprint Picture Mail. The smaller format creates smaller file sizes that are easier to transmit over relatively slow wireless networks. Smaller files sizes also mean that the recipient of a message containing a photo will be able to download and view it faster than if it were a larger image file.

Be aware that the smaller image size results in a smaller file size and also a lesser-quality image. So, you should choose the appropriate photo size depending on what you intend to do with it.

You can toggle between the larger and smaller photo sizes at any time by configuring your camera preferences. The steps are listed here:

1. Launch the Camera application (as described in the earlier section "Take a Quick Series of Photos").

2. From any Camera view, press MENU on the keyboard.

3. From the Options menu, choose Preferences.

4. Select the Picture Size drop-down menu, shown in Figure 7-5, and choose the size you want and select OK.

FIGURE 7-5	Change the picture size

Turn the Camera Sound Off

When you take a photo with your Treo, you will hear a noise that sounds similar to the shutter sound of a film camera—assuming that the sliding switch on the top of your Treo that turns the sounds on and off is switched to On. The camera sound signals that the image has been successfully captured and also gives your Treo more of a camera aura. You have the ability to disable the camera sound if you wish. The steps for doing so are listed next:

1. Launch the Camera application (as described in the earlier section "Take a Quick Series of Photos").

2. From any Camera view, press MENU on the keyboard.

3. From the Options menu, choose Preferences.

4. Uncheck the Play Capture Sound check box and select OK.

When Capture Sound is disabled, you won't hear a sound to tell you that you have just taken a photo. Remember that you can turn off all of your Treo sounds by sliding the ringer switch on the top of your Treo to the right.

Other Configurable Camera Settings—Confirm Before Deleting or Saving a Photo

Your Treo camera also lets you decide if you want to be asked whether or not you want to continue with deleting or saving a photo. The confirmation process is an extra step that you may want to turn off to make using the camera faster and easier, but the trade-off is that if you delete an image by accident, you won't get a second chance to prevent it from being deleted. To change these settings, follow these steps.

1. Launch the Camera application (as described in the earlier section "Take a Quick Series of Photos").

2. From any Camera view, press MENU on the keyboard.

3. From the Options menu, choose Preferences.

4. On the Preferences screen, you will see check boxes for Confirm Before Deleting and Confirm Before Saving. To turn the confirmation off, uncheck the appropriate check box or boxes and select OK.

Define Your Backup Settings

Your Treo picture backup setting is very straightforward: you either want your pictures copied from your Treo to your PC during HotSync, or you don't. The trade-off is that if you do back up your pictures to your PC every time you perform a HotSync, the process will take longer. This is more important if you are performing a HotSync remotely instead of through a HotSync cable connected directly to your PC. But if you don't back up your pictures to your PC and you lose your Treo or have to perform a hard reset, your pictures will be unrecoverable. This warning is also written on the Backup Settings screen, which is shown in Figure 7-6.

To change your backup setting (the default setting is to back up your pictures during HotSync) follow these steps:

1. Launch the Camera application (as described in the earlier section "Take a Quick Series of Photos").

2. From any Camera view, press MENU on the keyboard.

FIGURE 7-6   Backup settings

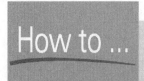 **A Word to the Wise: Back Up Your Photos**

Many of us have unexpectedly lost documents and other information that we had on our PCs and handhelds. This can happen for a variety of reasons, such as hardware or software failure or "pilot error," as they say, and if we are not in the habit of backing up our PCs and handhelds, we can end up permanently losing our files. This can be a painful experience, since we begrudgingly have to re-create those documents from memory. Since it is slightly more difficult—translation: virtually impossible—to re-create photos from memory, it makes it all that more imperative that we back up our photos. Backing up your photos can be done many ways, but the most common backup measure is to copy or move them to a writeable CD or DVD, a Zip drive, or a tape drive. Another way is to copy your photos to a few different computers or network hard drives so that if one fails, you have a backup. There are even online services that allow you to back up your files using the Internet. There are too many out there to recommend just one or two, but if you use an online search engine and enter a phrase like "online backup service," you will likely find something that suits your needs.

7

3. From the Options menu, choose Preferences.

4. On the Preferences screen, select the Backup Settings button.

5. If the Backup Pictures During HotSync Process check box is checked, it is set to back up automatically during HotSync. Check or uncheck the box according to how you want HotSync to deal with pictures.

6. Select OK on the Backup Settings screen, and then select OK on the Preferences screen.

Obviously, you can change this setting at any time depending on your circumstances—for example, you may want to perform a HotSync operation using the wireless network because you are traveling and are away from your office PC. If you are interested in synchronizing the new contacts you have made but are less worried about the hundreds of photos you have taken, you may want to turn off the Backup Pictures During HotSync Process setting to ensure that the HotSync takes significantly less time—and if you pay a user fee on the amount of wireless data you send, you will save money by not backing up your pictures until you are back in the office and can synchronize locally to your PC.

View Your Treo Photos on Your PC

Photos you take with your Treo will be copied to your Treo Pictures folder on your PC the next time you HotSync, provided your Treo is set to back up your pictures, which the default setting. Treo picture backup settings are covered in the preceding section "Define Your Backup Settings," while synchronizing your Treo with your PC is discussed in Chapter 3.

When you HotSync your Treo with your PC, your photos will be copied to your PC. To locate your Treo photos on your PC, you can browse to your pictures on your computer using the Palm Desktop. (After HotSyncing, Treo Pictures will be listed as an application on the desktop.) You can also use your PC file explorer to find your photos. Their most likely location is C:\Program Files\Handspring\Treo Pictures\ *username*. Or, if you upgraded to your Treo 600 from another Palm-powered device, your photos likely can be found at C:\Program Files\Palm\Treo Pictures*username*.

Once you've found your Treo photos, you can view them in your PC's default JPEG viewer by double-clicking a photo or by selecting Open from the Properties menu.

TIP   *If for any reason your Treo photos don't automatically launch an image-viewing application when you try to open them, you can always use your web browser to view them. JPEGs are supported in virtually every web browser. To view them, open your browser (Internet Explorer and Netscape Navigator are the most common), click the File menu, select Open, and then browse to the Treo photo you want to view. Select Open, and your photo should show up in your browser window.*

Transfer Your Treo Photos to Your Macintosh

If you use a Macintosh computer, the steps for moving your Treo photos from your Treo to your Mac are slightly different than they are for Windows users. There are three different methods for moving your photos from your Treo to your Mac: using an SD card, using e-mail, and using third-party software.

Move Photos from Your Treo to Your Mac Using an SD Card

Your Treo allows you to expand your memory using a Secure Digital (SD) card or MultiMediaCard (MMC). These memory expansion cards are fairly inexpensive, and you can use one to store all kinds of files, including games, music, and photos;

this greatly enhances the possibilities for what you can do with your Treo. Memory cards are available at many electronics stores as well as online at the palmOne web site (www.palmone.com). Once you have an SD or MMC memory expansion card, you'll need an SD card reader, which is also widely available and can be found for under $20. An SD or MMC card reader attaches directly to your PC and allows you to swap your SD or MMC card from your Treo to the card reader to quickly transfer photos, music files, applications, and other files to and from your Treo 600, without needing to HotSync. So, if you have an SD/MMC memory expansion card (or plan to get one), here is how you transfer your Treo photos from your Treo to your Mac:

1. Launch the Camera application (as described in the earlier section "Take a Quick Series of Photos").

2. Press the Pictures view (the second icon on the bottom of the screen that looks like a list).

3. Select the photo you want to send either by tapping the touchscreen or by using the five-way navigation control to highlight the photo.

4. Press MENU on the keyboard.

5. From the Picture menu, choose the Move option.

6. Choose either the category or expansion card that you want to move the photo to and select Move.

7. Remove the SD or MMC card from your Treo 600 and insert the card into your card reader.

8. If it isn't already plugged in, plug your SD or MMC card reader into your Mac.

9. The SD or MMC card will now show up as another hard drive on your Mac, allowing you to browse the card contents easily and copy your photos from the card to your Mac hard drive.

Move Photos from Your Treo to Your Mac Using E-Mail

Likely the easiest and least expensive way to get your Treo photos onto your Mac is to send them as e-mail attachments from your Treo to an e-mail account that you can access from your Mac. If you have not yet set up e-mail on your Treo, find out how to do so in Chapter 6. If your e-mail is already set up on your Treo, you can compose an e-mail, attach a photo, and send it to yourself using the wireless capabilities of your Treo 600. It is a good idea to only attach one image to each e-mail because of the file size of the photos. Then, on your Mac, check your e-mail and save the attached photo onto your hard drive. That's it. Pretty easy, right?

Move Photos from Your Treo to Your Mac Using Third-Party Software

Mac users have yet another option for moving photos from their Treos to their Macintosh PCs. There are third-party applications that allow your Mac to read your Treo 600 memory card as another hard drive when your Treo is connected to your Mac with the HotSync cable. One program that allows you to do this is Missing Sync 2.0 from Mark/Space (www.markspace.com).

Edit Your Treo Photos Using Third-Party Software

A significant difference between digital photography and film photography is that you don't have to be an expert or own thousands of dollars of film equipment to edit your digital photos. Your Treo produces photos and allows you to send them to others and copy them to your PC, so there isn't anything you *have* to do to your photos to enjoy them. But, if you wanted to edit and work with your photos, what would you use?

Imaging software has come a long way in the past few years, and this has lead to a proliferation of image-editing software on the market. While choice is rarely a bad thing, it can also present an overwhelming number of alternatives. Most software office suites that include word processing and spreadsheet applications also include some kind of image-editing program, so you may want to find out if you already have something you can use.

Find Out If Your PC Already Contains Image-Editing Software

If you're not sure whether you already have image-editing software, try to open one of your Treo photos. On your PC, Launch Treo Pictures in the Palm Desktop application. This will open the file directory where your Treo photos are copied when you HotSync. Double-click one of the JPEG files and see what application launches. You should have at least one image-viewing application. If you are not familiar with the one that opens, check its Help file to see what it's capable of and whether or not it will do what you want. A good thing to check first is whether it allows you to resize images.

Although many of the built-in tools may be fine for rudimentary image manipulation, you may want a different option. Your choices may be somewhat different depending on whether your computer runs a Windows or a Macintosh operating system; but either way, there are lots of choices available, including these:

- **Adobe Photoshop (www.adobe.com)**   A professional image-editing program for both Mac and Windows, Adobe Photoshop is the industry standard for graphic designers and professional photographers. It is fairly expensive, however (around $600), and because it's a powerful application, it can be challenging to learn.

- **Paint Shop Pro (www.jasc.com)**   Paint Shop Pro is a powerful image-editing application for Windows that offers a lot of functionality and is relatively inexpensive—around $80. You can download a trial version to see if it satisfies your needs. It is not the least-expensive alternative, however.

- **Microsoft Digital Image Pro (www.microsoft.com)**   Even Microsoft has gotten into the digital image-editing scene with its own product, which costs about $100.

- **Digital Image Viewer (www.proaxis.com/~rwi/imagevw.htm)**   With this free program, you can manage images from one location, performing operations such as viewing, resizing, deleting, renaming, creating slide shows, editing, and dragging a photo to a favorite program.

- **Artizen (www.supportingcomputers.com/)**   This is an image manipulation tool (about $40) that offers a large number of image effects and works with JPEG, GIF, BMP, and ICO formats.

- **Easypicture (www.virieu.com/easypicture/index.asp)**   This photo editor (about $40) offers the photo managing, editing, and JPEG compression tools you need to get photos from your camera to your web page.

Add Special Effects to Your Treo Photos

You can apply a ton of effects to your Treo photos. Some are just plain fun, and some add more of an artistic flavor. Of course, like anything, beauty is in the eye of the beholder. Most image-editing software packages have special effects or filtering options. Be sure to look through the users guide or help documentation of any software that you choose to make sure you're aware of all its functionalities. Even if you don't use the effects very often, they may still come in handy at critical times.

7

Use Fractal Effects

"So, what the heck is a *fractal*?" you ask. There are a lot of definitions on the Internet, and most are verbose mathematical descriptions. Let me say that fractal effects are less than subtle, so you may want to try them out to see they are useful to you.

Many high-end image-editing applications feature fractal effects, such as Fractal Explorer (www.eclectasy.com/Fractal-Explorer/index.html). This program allows you to generate polynomial and iteration sets such as Mandelbrot, Julia, and Newton fractals, as well as (just in case you have an aversion to Julia fractals) orbital fractals.

Make a Treo Photo Look Like an Oil Painting

Oil Painting Assistant (www.mxac.com.au/oilpaint.htm) is a software program that works with BMP format images to show you how your photos might look as oil paintings. Since your Treo produces JPEG files, you will need to use an image-editing application to convert your photos to BMP format first.

Sharpen Your Treo Photos

Though some great photos may be blurred beyond the point of no return, they may also be photos that can't be easily re-created—the fantastic back-flip Grandma did off the garage roof onto her BMX bike, for example—where you want to minimize the blur as much as possible. For such episodes, inexpensive software tools are available that allow you to sharpen your digital photos. The success rate of these products is reported to be good, but you may want to try them out yourself to ensure they meet your expectations.

Focus Magic

There is a product called Focus Magic (www.focusmagic.com) that allows you to improve the quality of photos. It is available for both Windows and Mac platforms, and you can try the software before you buy it. A brief explanation of the product, taken from the Focus Magic web site, describes the product:

> "Focus Magic has forensic strength technology to recover detail that is not visible to the naked eye. Unlike the Sharpen or Unsharp Mask filters, which increase the contrast at the edges of an image, Focus Magic reverses the formula by which the image got blurred. This forensic strength technology gives you as much of the original 'in focus' image as possible."

Unshake 1.4

Unshake (www.hamangia.freeserve.co.uk/Unshake/) is a freeware tool for Mac and Windows that is designed to improve blurred, and "shaken," photos by programmatically determining the form of the blurring and deducing what the photo would have looked like if it had not been blurred. The author of the software originally developed the software for his own use but now shares it for free with others (as long as they don't use it professionally). Isn't the Internet great? This Doctor doesn't even know us and he is willing to share his work. There is a scientific explanation on the web site that explains in detail how the software works. I always say "you don't have to study the roots of a tree to pick an apple." (If for some reason the web site link does not work, there is a good chance you will be able to find it by searching a web site search engine such as Google (www.google.com). To run this program, you will need to use software called the Java Runtime Environment, which can be downloaded from Sun Microsystems at http://java.sun.com/getjava.

Corel KnockOut

Corel KnockOut (www.corel.com) allows you to perform complex masking on your images. This allows you to preserve fine image details by improving blurred or out-of-focus edges, hair, smoke, water, glass, and shadows.

Harm's Tile 99 Graphics

Harm's Tile 99 Graphics (www.users.qwest.net/~sharman1/) is a freeware graphics application that allows you to create tiles and retouch your photos. It includes a set of filters and effects, and supports BMP, JPG, and GIF file formats.

Adjust the Color of Your Treo Photos

Most middle- to high-end image-editing applications allow you to adjust the color of your photos, while some are dedicated to image color manipulation. One example is Color Pilot (www.colorpilot.com), which describes itself on its web site as "Software for quick and easy color correction using the natural language of color. Correct digital camera or scanned photo images."

Reduce Photo Size

Your Treo produces image files in JPEG format, which is the most popular format for digital photographic images. This is why it's easy to find image-editing software that allows you to edit your Treo photos.

Did you know?

What Is Compression?

When a photo file is compressed, any data that is duplicated or is unnecessary is removed. This allows the file to be squished, or compressed, into a minimal file size. For example, if large areas of a photo are white—snow, for example—then the value of a single white pixel is saved along with the locations of the other pixels that share the same color. When the compressed image is opened for viewing or editing, the compression process is reversed. JPEG images are stored using a type of compression called lossy compression. The higher the compression settings, the more the quality and sharpness is reduced because similar colors are all changed to one color. For example, a highly compressed photo of a field covered in snow will show all of the snow as one color of white, whereas in reality that snow may be thousands of different shades of light gray, blue, yellow, and so on. However, because they are so light in color and therefore similar, high compression converts them all to white, losing visual subtleties of what the snow-covered field would really look like if seen through your own eyes. For most purposes, though, compression makes little difference, especially at lower resolutions.

Using an image-editing application, you can resize your photos from the larger Treo size of 640×480 pixels down to half that size (320×240 pixels). JPEG images do not scale up very well, however—that is, you will find that if you increase the size of a JPEG image using an image-editing application, you probably won't be happy with the results. But JPEG images *do* scale down well. One way to improve your images is to reduce the size using image-editing software.

TIP *Most image-editing applications have an option called Unsharp Mask. You should use this feature whenever you downsize a JPEG image. By applying this filter after you have reduced the size of an image, you will reduce some of the blur and sharpen the edges. You can usually find out if your image editor has this feature by looking in the application's Help files.*

Reduce the Treo's Default Compression

Though I'll talk about reducing your Treo default compression here (just so you're aware of it), there are currently no commercially available utilities to reduce the compression on your Treo. Having said that, I did find one such utility on the Treo

Central discussion board (http://discussion.treocentral.com/tcforum). Your Treo 600, by default, uses high-level compression on the photos you take. Compression is a process that reduces the file size of your images. It's very important that the files be small so you can easily send them to others using Multimedia Messaging Service, Sprint Picture Mail, or regular e-mail. In fact, it has been reported that the Treo compresses image files by about 65 percent. The result of this high level of compression is that the photo quality is reduced (depending on the content of the photo) in order to keep the file sizes small. Free utilities are available from enterprising independent developers that dial down the JPEG compression on your Treo camera, but there will likely also be commercial versions available soon that allow you to take better advantage of reduced compression.

Set Your Treo Wallpaper

Your Treo 600 has a default view that appears when you press the PHONE button. Many Treos are set to show the dial number pad when you press PHONE, but you can change the view to show an image instead. Your Treo background is called your wallpaper. There are two ways to change your wallpaper. The first method is as follows:

1. Launch the Camera application (as described in the earlier section "Take a Quick Series of Photos").

2. Select the Pictures view and choose the image you want to use as your wallpaper.

3. Press MENU on the keyboard.

4. From the Picture menu, choose the Set Wallpaper option.

5. A confirmation message will appear; select Yes.

The second method for changing your wallpaper is described here:

1. Press PHONE on the keyboard.

2. Press MENU on the keyboard.

3. From the Options menu, choose the Display Preferences screen.

4. Choose the menu at the top of the screen and select the Show Wallpaper option.

5. Choose the image you want to use and select OK.

Use Your Treo Pictures for Picture Caller ID

As long as your phone plan includes caller ID, you can use your Treo pictures, or any picture, to help you identify, at a glance, who's calling you.

1. Identify a picture you want to use to identify a contact when he or she calls.

2. Go to your Favorites by pressing the PHONE button and then selecting Favorites with the five-way navigation control.

3. Select an empty Favorite by tapping on the screen or select the CENTER button on the five-way navigation control.

4. In the Type menu, select Speed Dial.

5. Fill in a name in the Label field.

6. Type in the phone number of the person.

7. You can type in a Quick Key to speed up dialing this person, if you like.

8. Select the More button. This allows you to define advanced settings for this Favorite:

   ■ **Ringtone**   You can define a different ringtone sound that will be played when this person calls you on your Treo. To change from the default ringtone, select the menu and then select another ringtone.

   ■ **Image**   You can define a specific image to appear on the screen when this caller calls you. To do this, check the box beside the image text and press the Select Image button. After your picture list appears, browse to the image you want to use to identify this caller. (You can change the category to view by selecting the menu at the top right-hand corner of the screen and choosing the appropriate category.)

Other Software Available for Your Digital Photos

Although your Treo camera is primarily a tool for sharing fun photos with friends (and it does a fantastic job at this), it is also a great way to get into digital photography for very little money. In fact, the camera is really a free gift that palmOne threw into the deal when you bought your Treo 600. Digital photography is a booming business driven by both professionals and hobbyists alike. The digital nature of your Treo photographs means that the types of things that you can do to, and with, your photos on your PC is really only limited by your imagination. There is a wide variety of software and tools that let you do some very imaginative things to your photos, as well as practical tools that allow you to manage them. This section provides a list of some of the different types of software available that allow you to manage your Treo photos on your PC. Where appropriate, also included is whether or not the software works on Windows or Mac platforms.

CAUTION   *Digital photography can be addictive.*

Organize Your Treo Photos

When you get to the point where you've collected a large number of photos over a long period of time, you may discover that organizing your photos to quickly find what you want is a bit of a challenge. These same statistics state that families are taking over 1,000 digital photos per year. Organizing thousands of photos like this becomes unwieldy very quickly. Luckily, there are software applications that provide some help in this endeavor. These software applications allow you to view, track, and manage digital photos. Generally, the way they work is that they automatically scan your existing photo directories and create a database. Then you simply add information about the files in the program, select one or more images, and assign keywords such as "family," "reunion," and "vacation" to them. According to your key words, you can quickly search and locate the photos you want to view.

- **Photo Manager by ModTech (www.mt-ac.com)—Mac and Windows**
  This application allows you to create musical slide shows and add animated clips, effects, and captions. Once you have created your slide show, you can upload it for free (for 30 days) to www.photoshow.net, publish it as HTML for your web site, burn it to a CD, VCD, or DVD-ROM, or make a self-running executable file or a screen saver.

- **Adobe Photoshop Album (www.adobe.com)—Windows only**   Adobe has been the leader in digital imaging products for a very long time. This application allows you to see all of your photos, access your entire collection of photos (even your video and audio clips) in one place, no matter where they're stored, and locate photos by date. You can locate photos by the date they were taken using the sliding timeline or Calendar View, which lets you review your photos by day, month, week, or year. You can also use keyword tags and even touch up your photos.

7

Make a Digital Photo Album or Slide Show

The digital world, in some respects, does a fine job of emulating the nondigital world. We have been sharing, reminiscing, and embarrassing each other by showing off our family photo albums for decades. The idea of an old-fashioned photo slide show has been significantly updated. Even though the idea of sitting around watching Uncle Wally's holiday slides as he explains in stunning detail exactly what each slide is about is already pretty darned exciting, now you can combine sound and animation with your photo slides and run the whole thing on your PC.

There are two primary methods of putting your photos into a photo album or slide show format: doing so locally on your PC, or on the Web. (The online approach is discussed in more detail later in this chapter in the section "Publish Your Treo Photos on the Web Using an Online Picture-Hosting Web Site.") Here, however, I will discuss a couple of options that allow you to easily put your Treo photos together into a digital photo album on your personal computer.

Third-Party Software for Creating Digital Photo Albums and Slideshows

What would we do without software? (Besides spend more time outdoors.) There is some great software on the market that allows you to create digital slide shows easily to show off your digital photos.

- **Simple Star PhotoShow (www.simplestar.com)—Windows and Mac**   PhotoShow is an application that allows you to create and share multimedia shows using your own photos and music. You can choose photos, a soundtrack, transitions, and effects, and then drag and drop animated clip art and captions to create PhotoShows that can be shared online, burned to CD-ROM, used as a screen saver, or published to a web site.

- **SmoothShow Slide Shows (www.smoothshow.com)—Windows**   According to the product web site, "You'll have your first digital photo slide show running in less than two minutes after installing the software. Just choose your default transitions, start a new show, pick a bunch of images or an entire folder full, and you're ready to go!"

- **SWF 'n Slide by Vertical Moon (www.verticalmoon.com)—Windows and Mac**   SWF 'n Slide is a program that allows you to take both digital images and music and then create a slide show from them.

■ **Paint Shop Photo Album (www.jasc.com)—Windows**   Paint Shop Photo
Album makes it easy to enhance and edit your photos. You can even fix
photo imperfections, add a fancy frame or photo border or, for that antique
look, add a sepia tone, frames, photo edges, and borders. This next bit is also
kind of neat: "Give yourself or your friends a slim new look with Photo
Album's unique Thinify tool. You can make anyone look like they shed ten
pounds." You can also add captions and sound, and its one-click red eye tool
can help you get the red out.

Publish Your Treo Photos on the Internet

Yet another great thing about digital images, like your Treo photos, is that they are
easy to share with others by publishing them on a web page. This way, your friends
and family, and the general public, if you like, can view your Treo photos from any
PC or device using only a web browser. You can easily put your photos up on a web
page and then e-mail all of your friends the web site address, allowing them to
appreciate your photos with no more effort than clicking the site's link.

There are two primary ways to publish your digital photos on the Internet: using
a picture-hosting service and publishing your pictures on your own web site. The
easiest way is to use an online picture-hosting company, but that doesn't mean you
can't set up your own web site, if you don't already have one. Both options are
discussed next.

Publish Your Treo Photos on the Web Using an Online Picture-Hosting Web Site

Besides sending your photos by e-mail, MMS, or Sprint Picture Mail to friends and
family, another easy option is to post your photos on the Internet using an online
photo album service. This option is especially effective in that it allows you to share
a bunch of photos at one time with many people (after all, it's pretty inefficient to
e-mail the 439 photos you took at the Montreal Jazz Festival to 60 of your best friends
when you could simply send them a web link and let them browse through the photos
themselves). You can also show off your photos from anywhere you happen to be,
as long as you have access to a web browser. Some online picture-hosting sites are
listed here, but there are many others:

■ PictureTrail (www.picturetrail.com)

■ Photo Navy (http://pnavy.com)

Sharing My Walks with Family and Friends via the Internet

I walk about an hour every day around the neighborhood in downtown Seattle, WA. My Treo 600 documents these walks in pictures, even while entertaining me with tunes. As I walk, I snap the pictures, and after I snap each one, I e-mail it to my photo blog, where my friends and family who live all over the world can see what I see on my walks.

I use Buzznet (www.buzznet.com) for my photo blog. It's very simple to sign up for a free account, and you get your own e-mail address for posting the photos. Then you just snap a shot, hop over to e-mail, attach it to a note, and send the note to the Buzznet address. By the time I get home from my walk every day, my Buzznet blog is all up-to-date, and there is usually already a comment or two from my fans (okay, from my friends and family). Plus, I now have months of archives of my Treo 600's life that are fun to revisit. You can see photos from my Treo 600 on my blog at http://susandennis.buzznet.com.

—Susan Dennis, Seattle WA
www.susandennis.com

- PhotoIsland (http://pacific.photoisland.com)

- FotoTime (www.fototime.com)

 If you decide to create an online picture-hosting service, remember to only copy your photos to the web site—don't move them. You don't want to risk permanently losing your photos if anything should happen to the service company or their servers.

Publish Your Treo Photos on Your Own Web Site

This section is not intended to provide detailed instruction on how to set up your own web site. There are many, many resources that describe exactly how to publish images and content on the Web. You can find informative web sites to help get you up to speed, and most bookstores have web publishing guides and reference books.

Some great McGraw Hill/Osborne books about HTML and web publishing, whether you are just getting started or are more experienced with web pages, include the following:

■ *Web Design: A Beginner's Guide* by Wendy Willard (McGraw-Hill/Osborne, 2001) is available at book stores and online at Osborne's site (http://books. mcgraw-hill.com) or at Amazon (www.amazon.com).

■ *HTML & Web Design Tips & Techniques* by Kris A. Jamsa, Konrad King, and Andy Anderson (McGraw-Hill/Osborne, 2002) includes some advanced topics as well as the basics and is available at book stores and online at Osborne's site (http://books.mcgraw-hill.com) or at Amazon (www. amazon.com).

■ *Schaum's Easy Outline HTML* by David Mercer (McGraw-Hill, 2003) is available at book stores and online at Osborne's site (http://books.mcgraw-hill.com) or at Amazon (www.amazon.com).

The key point to understand about publishing your photos on the Internet is that it is *not* difficult. If you are willing to put some time into learning the basics, you can do it. The most important thing you need is a company to host your web site. Essentially, the web-hosting company provides a web server to load your photos and web pages onto so that others can view them on the Web. There are a lot of options, many of which are free or available at a low monthly cost. If you have a home Internet connection, chances are that the company that provides the service also provides web-hosting services.

Creating web pages has also become very easy if you have the right tools. Web page-editing tools have become so simple to use that you no longer have to learn HTML in order to publish pages and photos on the Web. There are a lot of choices when it comes to WYSIWYG (pronounced "whiz-e-wig"—What You See Is What You Get) HTML editors. In fact, most office document applications allow you to save a document as a web page (in HTML). Some examples of web page authoring tools include the following:

■ Virtual Mechanics SiteSpinner (www.virtualmechanics.com), about $50

■ Macromedia Dreamweaver (www.macromedia.com)—Windows and Macintosh, about $400

7

- Microsoft FrontPage (www.microsoft.com)—Windows, about $150

NOTE *Some versions of Microsoft Office include FrontPage, so you may already have it.*

- Evrsoft 1st Page 2000 (www.evrsoft.com), free

By no means are these the only options you have to create web pages easily. There are hundreds out there. If you are so inclined, you can even create web pages using pure HTML code by employing a simple text editor like Notepad—although this is not the easiest way to get going if you are just getting started with web technologies.

Use a Memory Card to Store Photos

Your Treo is equipped with a memory card slot that allows you to use removable Secure Digital (SD) or MultiMediaCard (MMC) memory cards. There are many memory card standards, so when you're looking to buy a memory card for your Treo, make sure you buy an SD or MMC card. Examples of memory cards that don't work with your Treo are Compact Flash and SmartMedia. Again, your Treo is designed for use with SD and MMC cards only.

Your Treo 600 has 24MB of available memory for files, applications, and pictures, so the ability to expand its memory is extremely useful. In fact, SD cards are commonly available in 256MB and 512MB versions. SanDisk even offers a 1GB version, which currently is an expensive option at $450, but expect this to drop steadily. This means that by adding a 512MB SD card, you effectively expand your Treo memory by over 21 times. Another advantage is that if you ever have to perform a hard-reset on your Treo, all of the memory will be wiped out, but anything stored on your SD memory card will remain intact. Memory cards are covered in more detail in Chapter 15.

TIP *You cannot store newly captured photos directly to your SD memory card. Initially when you take a photo with your Treo, the photo will be stored locally on your Treo. Once the photo is taken, you can move it to your SD card.*

Move Your Treo Photos to Your Memory Card

When you are ready to move your Treo photos from your Treo memory to an SD or MMC card, follow these steps. Note that if you have a Treo 600 from Sprint,

Did you know?

SD vs. MMC Cards

Your Treo has been carefully designed to allow you to use both SD and MMC cards. Each type of card has specific benefits that you should be aware of. The primary benefits of SD cards are speed (10MB/sec), input and output capabilities, security, and interoperability with other hardware. These features make it the most secure and flexible media type for expanding the Treo's capability to interoperate with other devices. The primary benefits of MMC cards are cost and Read-Only Memory (ROM) capability. Since ROM is less expensive than flash memory, MMC ROM cards tend to be the best choice for distribution of data, and they offer a significantly lower-cost alternative to SD cards and MMC flash cards.

7

the button names are slightly different, so both non-Sprint and Sprint versions are listed here.

1. If the Camera application isn't currently open, press HOME on the keyboard to open the Applications Launcher, and then find and select the Camera application.

2. If you are not already viewing your picture list, select the Picture List View icon on the bottom of the screen.

3. Find and select the photo you want to move to your expansion card.

4. Press MENU on the keyboard, and from the Picture menu select the Move option.

5. You will see a Category menu. Your expansion card will show up in the list; select it, and then select Move.

Wrap It Up

Ten years ago, not many of us would have imagined that mobile technology would have evolved as it has. Even fewer of us would have imagined that our cellular phones would be capable of taking digital photographs. As a matter of fact, I'm not sure I had even heard of digital photography ten years ago. The Treo 600 was not designed as a dedicated, high-quality digital camera, and hopefully not many Treo 600 owners based their purchasing decision solely on the camera functionality; however, it's a nice bonus to an already great device. This chapter covered a lot of ground, with discussions ranging from photographing dos and don'ts to digital editing and presentation software. One of the many things you can do with your Treo photos is create your own photo blog. Blogging is covered in the color section of this book, titled "Publish Your Own Photo Blog." Happy photographing!

Part II

Maximize the Capabilities of Your Treo

Chapter 8

Enjoy Music, Movies, and Games

How to…

- Listen to music
- Listen to the news and other radio programs
- Watch movies and videos
- Make music
- Play games

Turn Your Treo into an MP3 Music Player

In addition to being able to use your Treo 600 as a cell phone and an organizer, you can also use it for e-mail, the Internet, playing games, sending SMS (Short Message Service) or MMS (Multimedia Message Service) messages, and taking pictures. On top of this, you can play music on your Treo. Many of us have, or used to have, Sony Walkmans—or similar versions of portable radios, tape players, or CD players—and you can easily make your Treo into a music player as well. You are carrying around your Treo anyway, so why not use it to listen to your favorite music? One of the advantages of listening to MP3s as compared to listening to CDs or tapes on a portable device is that with MP3s there is virtually no skip or sound interruption if you are moving while you are listening to you music—for example, if you are listening to music on your Treo while jogging.

Learn about Sound File Formats

There are several types of files that can be played by electronic devices such as your Treo. Standards have evolved to help software and hardware manufacturers agree on formats that can be generated and played on a variety of different platforms. Many of the standards use similar technologies, and of course it is important to understand what file types your software can play so that you can convert files to other formats. The most common file types for digitally recorded and played music are MP3, Ogg Vorbis, WAV, and streaming audio/video. These technologies are discussed briefly here, and much more information is available on the Web if you want to find out more. Later in this chapter, there is brief discussion on converting your CDs to files that you can play on your Treo under the heading "Convert Music CDs to Files That You Can Listen to on Your Treo."

WAV Files

WAV files are noncompressed audio files that can be played by a computer like your Treo or PC. Most CD-burning software that allows you to convert your music CDs so that you can store and play them on your PC converts files to WAV format. WAV files are noncompressed, so the sound quality tends to be better than compressed audio files like MP3 and Ogg Vorbis. The drawback, though, is that WAV files can be very large—many megabytes—so storage space can be a problem on memory- and processor-restricted devices. That is why the MP3 and Ogg Vorbis files are more popular for devices such as your Treo.

MP3 Files

MP3 files are sound files that can be played by computer hardware running the necessary software to read and play the files. MP3 technology evolved primarily because of the need to reduce file sizes to make file transmission over the Internet faster and more efficient. This technology also minimizes how much memory is needed to store music files on your Treo. MP3s allow for smaller file sizes based on sophisticated file compression technologies. Music that you buy on CDs at your local music store is uncompressed and therefore requires a lot of memory, which is fine because the files are conveniently stored on a CD and are not taking up memory on your Treo or PC.

When uncompressed music from a CD is converted to an MP3 file, compression is applied that can reduce the file size to 10 percent of the original. How is this possible? The MP3 compression technology is mathematically complex, so we won't go into too much detail, but if you're interested, there are some great books and web sites devoted to the more technical aspects of MP3 technology. For the most part, most of us just want to listen to music and not worry about the technicalities.

Uncompressed files that are on your music CDs store more data than our brains can realistically process. For example, if two notes that are played simultaneously are very similar, our brains may hear only one note. Or if one note is much louder than another, our brains may only perceive the louder of the two. MP3 compression removes any data from the file that you are not likely to notice as missing. This allows for much smaller file sizes. There are different levels of compression, and obviously the more data that is removed from a sound file, the more the quality is reduced; so there is some trade-off.

One of the advantages of MP3 files is that additional information, such as the name of the artist, the track title, the album title, the recording year, the genre, and even personal comments, is stored at the beginning or end of an MP3 file. This is very useful for storing and tracking your MP3 collection.

8

Ogg Vorbis

Ogg Vorbis is a compressed audio format similar to MP3. (See the preceding section, "MP3 Files," for more information on audio compression; the same general principles apply to both Ogg Vorbis and MP3.) Ogg Vorbis is designed to provide better audio quality than MP3 while producing smaller file sizes. One of the advantages of Ogg Vorbis is that the technology used to create the audio files is not restricted by patents and therefore is royalty-free to users. More information about Ogg Vorbis can be found at the Vorbis web site (www.vorbis.com).

Audio/Video File Formats

There are many types of file formats. To make things more confusing, some of the file types are used for both music and video, but some of the formats you may see include MPEG/MPG, VCD, DIVX, and AVI files, among others. Some of these files are more common for video, which is covered in more detail later in this chapter.

Streaming Audio

Most music and audio files are stored in memory and played from memory. Even when you download music such as an MP3 file from the Internet, the entire file must be downloaded and saved before you can play it. Wouldn't it be great if we could begin to play the music before it is fully downloaded? Well, that is essentially what "streaming" media is all about. When you select a file to listen to, or watch in the case of streaming video, the file starts playing a few seconds after you begin downloading it, and as long as your Internet connection is steady, it will keep playing. If you have heard of Real Player or Macromedia Flash, these are examples of technologies that leverage streaming media.

So, the question is, how does streaming audio sound? Generally speaking, especially over relatively slow wireless connections, it tends to work better for talk radio than for streaming music. As connection speeds improve, however, streaming media will continue to improve. The best way to find out what streaming audio sounds like on your Treo is to try it out for yourself. Fortunately, you can use Pocket Tunes (www.pocket-tunes) to play streaming audio on your Treo using the SHOUTcast (www.shoutcast.com) service. See the section "Use Pocket Tunes to Play Music on Your Treo 600" later in this chapter for more information.

Listen to Music Files on Your Treo 600

Your Treo 600 doesn't come with a preinstalled audio player, so you will need to install a third-party music player before you can listen to music files on it.

Use a Stereo Headset to Listen to Music with Your Treo 600

If you have tried to connect a stereo headset jack to your Treo, you may already know that most stereo headset cords don't fit into the Treo jack. This is because your Treo earphone jack was designed primarily for hands-free phone usage with the included phone headset. The Treo jack is a 2.5 mm size, and most stereo headsets are 3.5 mm, so you will need a 2.5 to 3.5 mm adapter. Fortunately, palmOne sells an adapter to allow you to use a 3.5 mm stereo headset with your Treo. This is called the "Treo Stereo Headphone Adapter." Also, palmOne sells Treo stereo headphones that have a 2.5 mm connection so that you can use the stereo headset without an adapter.

Use Third-Party Applications to Play Music

There are several music players for your Treo. The most common applications are included in this list and are covered in more detail later in the chapter:

- **Pocket Tunes (www.pocket-tunes.com)**   In the U.S., NormSoft's Pocket Tunes is a gift when you register your Treo 600 with palmOne. With Pocket Tunes, you can play compressed audio files—MP3 or Ogg Vorbis—or uncompressed WAV files on your Treo 600.

- **RealPlayer for Palm (www.realnetworks.com)**   This application supports the local playback of MP3 and RealAudio content on your Treo that is played from a Secure Digital (SD) memory card or a MultiMediaCard (MMC).

- **AeroPlayer (www.aerodrome.us)**   AeroPlayer can be downloaded for free to try for 14 days. If you want to play MP3 files after the 14-day trial period has passed, you have to purchase a registration code; but if you only want to play Ogg Vorbis files, you can continue to use the software for free. AeroPlayer allows you to play both video and music files on your Treo.

- **MMPlayer (www.mmplayer.com)**   MMPlayer can play several types of files on your Treo 600. A notable difference between MMPlayer and many other video-capable players is that MMPlayer is able to play standard video formats, such as MPEG and AVI formats; some other video players require that videos be converted to a proprietary format that can only be played by that specific player.

8

TIP   *If you purchased your Treo 600 in the U.S., palmOne will give you Pocket Tunes MP3 player software for free just for registering your Treo on the palmOne web site (www.palmone.com).*

Pocket Tunes and RealPlayer are discussed in greater detail later in this chapter (see the sections "Use Pocket Tunes to Play Music on Your Treo 600" and "Use RealPlayer to Play Music and Other Audio on Your Treo 600").

Transfer Your Music onto Your Treo 600

Currently you must have a memory expansion card, either SD or MMC, to transfer music from your PC to your Treo. Expansion cards are covered in Chapter 15. There are two primary methods of transferring music from your PC to your Treo 600. The first method is to use the Palm Desktop and the Install tool. The second, and faster, way to transfer music files is to use a USB card reader to copy files onto your SD or MMC card.

Transfer Music to Your Treo Using the Palm Desktop

Chapter 3 discusses using the Palm Desktop and synchronizing your Treo 600 with your PC. Once your Treo and PC are set up to HotSync and your memory card is ready to go, follow these steps to transfer your music:

1. Open the Install Tool by selecting the Install button in the Palm Desktop application or by choosing the Install Tool (Start | Programs | Handspring | Palm Desktop). In newer versions of Palm Desktop, this tool is called Palm Quick Install.

2. Click and drag the files you wish to transfer into the Install Tool window. The files will appear in the Expansion Card area of the window.

3. Select Done.

4. If it is not already connected, connect your Treo to your PC using the HotSync cable and press the HotSync button on the cable, and the music files will be transferred to the correct location on your memory card.

Transfer Music to Your Treo Using a Card Reader

Once you have an SD or MMC memory expansion card, an invaluable tool is an SD/MMC card reader. Card readers are available in many places, and you can find them for less than $20 online or in specialty stores. (SanDisk is one of many manufacturers, and you can find it at www.sandisk.com.) The SD/MMC card reader attaches directly to your PC and allows you to swap your SD/MMC card from your Treo to the card reader to quickly transfer pictures, music files, applications, and other files to and from your Treo 600 without needing to HotSync. If you have an SD/MMC memory expansion card and a card reader, follow these steps to transfer your music from your PC to your Treo:

1. Once your card reader is connected to your PC, insert your SD/MMC memory card into the card reader.

2. On your PC, select Start | My Computer and double-click the drive that represents your memory card. This will vary depending on how many drives you have on your PC.

3. Open the AUDIO folder. If this is the first time you are using your memory card, you will have to create an AUDIO folder by choosing File | New | Folder on your PC.

4. Click and drag your music files (.ogg or .mp3 files) into your open AUDIO folder.

5. PalmOne suggests that you right-click the drive that represents your card reader and choose Eject before removing your card from the card reader. If you do not "eject" your memory card before removing it, the files on the card may be damaged.

6. Place the memory card into your Treo and select the files that you want to play on your Treo.

Use Pocket Tunes to Play Music on Your Treo 600

One of the most popular software applications for your Treo 600 is Pocket Tunes by NormSoft (www.pocket-tunes.com). In the U.S., you receive Pocket Tunes as a gift when you register your Treo 600 with palmOne. You must have an SD or MMC card to play MP3 or Ogg Vorbis files with Pocket Tunes. If you want to use stereo headphones with your Treo, you will also need a stereo headset adapter; for more information, see the section "Use a Stereo Headset to Listen to Music with Your Treo 600" in this chapter.

Pocket Tunes is available in two different versions. Of course the more expensive deluxe version (about $25) has more features than the basic version (about $13), but the basic version offers a significant number of features.

The basic version allows you to play MP3, Ogg Vorbis, and WAV files and also allows you to listen to streaming audio downloaded over your wireless Internet connection.

To use Pocket Tunes, you must have an SD or MMC card in order to play audio files such as MP3, Ogg Vorbis, and WAV. You do not need one if you only want to listen to streaming audio over the Internet.

The deluxe version of Pocket Tunes (www.pocket-tunes.com) includes more features than most of us need, including such things as crossfade, gapless playback, SHOUTcast streaming audio, and the ability to bookmark files. Following are some of those features:

- **MP3 and Ogg Vorbis decoding/playing**   You can play both MP3 and Ogg Vorbis file types.

- **Streaming MP3**   You can listen to SHOUTcast audio using your Treo and your wireless Internet connection.

- **Onscreen graphic equalizer**   You can adjust the music mix to suit your taste using the onscreen equalizer.

- **Background playback**   You can listen to music while running other applications.

- **Crossfade**   You can smoothly transition from one song to the next.

- **Bookmarks**   You can bookmark the music files you play most often.

- **Auto-bookmark**   You can create bookmarks automatically to easily find where you left off.

- **Pocket Tunes console**   You can control your audio playback from within other applications.

- **Screen blanking**   To help save power, you can have the screen turn off while playing music.

- **Full skin support**   You can choose from dozens of "skins" to personalize the interface.

- **High resolution**   With many of the skins, you can take full advantage of your Treo screen capability.

- **WAV file support**   You can play uncompressed WAV files in addition to MP3 and Ogg Vorbis files.

- **Five-way navigation control integration**   You can use the five-way navigation control to play, pause, and adjust the volume, skip to another song, and select a playlist so that you can use Pocket Tunes without ever touching your stylus.

- **Playlists**   You can create custom playlists to organize your music.

- **Shuffle and repeat**   You can toggle the Shuffle and Repeat buttons to change the order in which your songs are played.

- **Volume and balance**   You can adjust the volume and balance as the song is playing.

- **Seek bar**   You can seek to any position in a song by sliding the seek bar.

Create Pocket Tunes Playlists

You can create a custom playlist that includes what songs to play and the order in which to play the songs. To create a new playlist, follow these steps:

1. If Pocket Tunes isn't currently running, press HOME on the keyboard to open the Applications Launcher; then find and open Pocket Tunes.

2. Tap the Playlist button or double-click the CENTER button on the five-way navigation control to open the Select a Playlist screen shown in Figure 8-1.

3. Select the New button to open the New Playlist screen.

FIGURE 8-1   Choose New from the Select a Playlist screen to create a new playlist.

4. Type in the name of this playlist at the top of the screen and then select Add Song.

5. Select a song and continue adding songs until your list is complete.

6. You can use the Up and Down buttons to reorder the list.

7. When you are finished, select Save List.

Now you can select the playlist at any time, and the same songs will be played in exactly the same order. You can always create, delete, and edit your playlists at any time.

Play Songs in the Background with Pocket Tunes

Pocket Tunes will play music in the background even when you switch to another application, so you can listen to music while you work with other applications on your Treo. At any time, you can enable or disable background playback from the Background Preferences screen shown in Figure 8-2.

Adjust the Pocket Tunes Graphic Equalizer

Pocket Tunes includes a graphic equalizer that you can use to fine-tune the sound of your music. This is important, as different people prefer slightly different mixes— I like lots of bass. The ability to adjust the settings also enables you to adjust the sound for your headphones. You access the equalizer controls by selecting Graphic

FIGURE 8-2   You can enable and disable background playback in Background Preferences.

Equalizer from the Pocket Tunes Tools menu. You can select from three different equalizer modes:

- **Disabled**   When this setting is selected, the music will not be affected by Pocket Tunes.

- **Equalizer**   When this setting is selected, you can change the eight equalizer settings and customize your sound as you want. To change the equalizer settings:

  1. Select the name of the preset you wish to change.

  2. Select Rename to enter a name for your preset.

  3. Change the equalizer controls, based on your preference.

  4. Select OK to save your changes.

8

NOTE   *You can always press the reset button to restore the settings.*

- **Bass Boost**   More bass! When this setting is selected, the lower frequencies of the music are increased.

TIP   *The graphic equalizer uses more of your Treo processing power and can slow down performance, so if you notice any skipping or stuttering, try turning off the equalizer to see if the performance improves.*

Crossfade Your Songs with Pocket Tunes

Crossfade is a fancy word that means that you can seamlessly fade from one song to the next. It is only available in the deluxe version of Pocket Tunes. You can change your crossfade settings by following these steps:

1. Select the MENU button, and then select Crossfade Prefs.

2. To enable crossfading, select the Enable Crossfade check box, and set the desired crossfade duration by selecting a duration from the pop-up menu.

The duration setting in step 2 is the number of seconds that Pocket Tunes will overlap and fade from one song to the next. The gapless setting means that Pocket Tunes will seamlessly blend two song files together without leaving any gap.

According to Pocket Tunes, this feature requires a certain amount of additional memory on your Palm device in order to prepare the audio information for crossfading.

Longer crossfade durations require more memory. The Crossfade screen displays your available memory and the amount of memory required for crossfading; in addition, it displays a message indicating whether you have enough memory.

Create Bookmarks in Pocket Tunes

With Pocket Tunes, you can create a bookmark to save your place when you are part of the way through an audio file and want to return to the same place later on. This is particularly useful when you are listening to e-books or recorded radio broadcasts. Bookmarks are only available in the deluxe version of Pocket Tunes. Follow these steps to create a bookmark in Pocket Tunes:

1. In Pocket Tunes, press the MENU button and select the Add Bookmark option from the Tools menu.

2. In Bookmark Name dialog box, enter the name of your new bookmark and select OK. If you don't type in a new name, the default is that the title of the song will be used. If you want Pocket Tunes to always use the title of the song, then uncheck the Always Ask for Name check box.

Jump to a Bookmark in Pocket Tunes

Once you have defined a bookmark, you can jump back to the same place in the audio file by following these steps:

1. Select Bookmarks on the Tools menu in Pocket Tunes.

2. Select the bookmark you wish to go to, and then select the Go button.

You can also rename or delete a bookmark by selecting the bookmark and then selecting the Rename or Delete button, respectively.

Use the Pocket Tunes Auto-Bookmark Feature

Pocket Tunes has an auto-bookmark feature that allows you to automatically create bookmarks. When the auto-bookmark feature is enabled, Pocket Tunes will automatically create a new bookmark whenever you press the Pause option and then open a new audio file. This allows you to easily jump between different audio files without losing your place. You can enable the auto-bookmark feature by selecting the Auto-Bookmark option from the menu in Pocket Tunes.

Change Your Pocket Tunes Advanced Preferences

There are several settings that you can change to customize Pocket Tunes. You can access these settings by selecting the Advanced Preferences option from the

Prefs menu. There are several options that you can change, and some examples are listed here:

- **Stop Playing on Low Battery** By default, Pocket Tunes will pause music playback when you get a low-battery warning. This allows your Treo to go to sleep and prevents it from draining the battery.

- **Stop the Blinking** By default, Pocket Tunes will flash the LED indicator on your Treo while the screen is off so that you know that the Treo is doing something—in this case, playing audio. You can turn this off by deselecting the Flash LED While Screen Is Off option.

- **Automatic Startup** Pocket Tunes can be set to automatically start playing the last song you were listening to the next time you start up your Treo.

Change Your Pocket Tunes Skin

You can change the Pocket Tunes graphical interface so that is looks the way you think it should. You can even create your own interface if you are artistically inclined. To change the Pocket Tunes skin, you will need to download one that you like from the list of available skins on the Pocket Tunes web site (www.pocket-tunes.com/skins). You can also make your own skins, and more information and instruction about that is available on the web site.

If you find a skin that you like on the Pocket Tunes web site, follow these steps to download and use it:

1. Download the skin to your PC.

2. Double-click on the PDB file and perform a HotSync.

3. The next time you run Pocket Tunes, select the icon on the lower-left of the screen and select Choose Skin from the Tools menu.

4. You will see a list of available skins.

5. Select the skin name that you want to use and select OK.

Playing SHOUTcast Stations with Pocket Tunes

The easiest way to listen to SHOUTcast stations is to visit www.shoutcast.com on your Treo web browser, look for a station that you want to listen to, and select the Tune In button. If your Treo prompts you to open or save the file, choose Open. If your Treo prompts you as to whether or not you want to accept the file, select Yes. Pocket Tunes will then load the station and begin playing it.

8

You can also tune into a SHOUTcast station from the Choose Songs screen in Pocket Tunes. To do so, select the SHOUTcast option from the menu in the upper-right corner of the screen. On the screen, you will see a list of all the SHOUTcast stations you have listened to. You can add a new station manually by selecting the New button. Pocket Tunes will ask you for the SHOUTcast web site address or URL, and you can also enter the URL for a static (nonstreaming) MP3 or Ogg Vorbis file.

You can also use Pocket Tunes to play SHOUTcast stations from premium services such as Di.FM (www.di.fm). Many of the premium stations require a username and password. In order to access these stations, use the Pocket Tunes Choose Songs screen to add a SHOUTcast URL. The URL for the station should look something like this: http://*username:password*@10.10.10.10:8096.

 *Some SHOUTcast stations require a high-bandwidth connection. Look for the Kbps (kilobits per second) setting for these stations. If your current connection is 64 Kbps or lower, then you may have trouble playing these stations on your Treo wireless Internet.*

Use RealPlayer to Play Music and Other Audio on Your Treo 600

RealPlayer (www.realnetworks.com) allows you to play MP3 and RealAudio (.rm, .rmj) content from your SD or MMC memory expansion card. To transfer music files from your PC (Windows and Linux only) to your Treo 600, you will need to install the RealPlayer plug-in software on your PC. Like the other applications that allow you to play music files on your Treo, music files must be stored on the SD or MMC memory card—playing files from internal memory is not supported.

If you have ever used RealPlayer media player software on your PC, you know that PC-based RealAudio will play streaming audio. This is not the case on the Treo 600. Files must be downloaded or moved and stored locally on a memory expansion card; streaming audio is not yet supported on the Treo 600.

Play Files Using RealPlayer

The steps for playing music and other media files with RealPlayer are listed here:

1. Select the Real icon from the Applications Launcher screen.

2. Select Songs to bring up a list of available tracks.

3. Select the desired song to begin playback or use five-way navigation control to select a song.

4. Press the CENTER button to highlight the first track and use the UP and DOWN buttons to scroll.

5. Choose Select to play the song.

You will notice that information about the song is displayed in the light green status area, and you can tap the Information icon (shown in the upper right-hand corner of Figure 8-2) to view extra information about the song.

Create a New Playlist in RealPlayer

You can create a custom playlist that includes what songs to play and the order in which to play the songs. To create a new playlist, follow these steps:

1. If RealPlayer isn't currently running, press MENU on the keyboard to open the Applications Launcher.

2. Find and open RealPlayer, and then select Playlists.

3. Select New, name the playlist, and select Add.

4. From the list of available songs that appears, select the check boxes next to the songs you wish to add to your playlist.

5. Select Done to return to the Edit Playlist screen, select Done to return to the Playlist screen, and select Done to return to the list of available playlists.

6. Select Done again.

Use Your Playlist in RealPlayer

Once you have created your own custom playlists, you can play them at any time by following these steps:

1. If RealPlayer isn't currently running, press MENU on the keyboard to open the Applications Launcher.

2. Find and open RealPlayer, and then select Playlists.

3. Select the desired playlist.

4. Select the first song in the list to begin playback in the RealPlayer.

8

Download MP3 Files from the Internet to Your Treo

In addition to being able to copy and move files between your desktop PC and your Treo 600, you can download music directly from the Internet using the wireless Internet capabilities of your Treo.

 Some clever hackers have figured out ways to embed viruses into MP3 and movie files, so it is very important to use antivirus software on your Treo if you are going to be downloading media files directly to your Treo over the wireless Internet. More information about securing your Treo is covered in Chapter 13.

There are many web sites where you can download MP3 and Ogg Vorbis files. Just do a search on your favorite Internet search engine. Be aware that there are royalty and legal issues when downloading protected music.

Convert Music CDs to Files You Can Listen to on Your Treo

Recent technology makes it extremely easy to convert your CDs to MP3 files. Many third-party add-ons for Mac and Windows that are designed to play your CDs on your PC can also convert your CD music into MP3 files and/or Ogg Vorbis files. Examples are Cdex (http://cdexos.sourceforge.net) and dBpowerAMP (www.dbpoweramp.com). If you want to convert your CD files to MP3 files, you can search the Internet for software that allows you to do the conversion on your PC. Remember to look for software that converts WAV format to MP3 format because your CD music is WAV format.

Listen to Nonmusic Audio on Your Treo 600

Music is not the only type of audio that you can listen to using your Treo. There is a wide variety of audio that you can store and listen to on your Treo, such as the following:

- Audio books
- Audio magazines
- Audio newspapers
- Downloadable radio

There are some public radio programs that allow you to download segments or programs from web sites.

Audible.com (www.audible.com/palm2) is a service that allows you to download these types of audio content to your computer so you can transfer them to your Treo. An Audible.com membership allows you to download more than 18,000 audio books and programs to listen to on your Treo.

Some Great Ways to Use Your Treo 600 as a Music Player

As you have probably already figured out, your Treo 600 is an ultimately portable and useful device that is capable of many, many things. Well, now that you can use your Treo as a music and audio player by storing music on memory expansion cards, essentially what you have is a portable CD collection. Now, instead of hauling your CDs between your house, car, office, and weekend cottage, you can store all of your favorite music on SD or MMC memory cards and play it on your Treo wherever you happen to be.

Obviously, your Treo is a great personal entertainment center, but you can also use your Treo to play music through your car or home stereo.

Play MP3s Through Your Car Stereo

There are several ways to play your Treo music through your car stereo. Most of your options for your car stereo apply to your home stereo as well.

Use an RF Modulator (Radio Frequency Modulator)

This option likely has the highest "Cool!" factor. It allows you to wirelessly connect your Treo 600 to your car stereo using the FM capabilities of your car stereo, as well as a little device that you plug into the earphone output jack of your Treo 600. (Note that you will need a 2.5 mm to 3.5 mm adapter to plug the RF modulator into your Treo.) Once the RF modulator is hooked up to your Treo, you tune your car radio, or any FM radio, to one of the digitally tuned FM stations supported by your modulator. For example, the Arkon (www.arkon.com/sf.html) SoundFeeder FM Modulator allows you to use eight different FM frequencies: 88.1, 88.3, 88.5, 88.7, 107.1, 107.3, 107.5, and 107.7 MHz. So there is a very good chance that you will find a frequency that a radio station in your area is not using. Some users have reported great success

8

with this approach, but others have reported that it can be difficult to get static-free sound. An RF modulator solution is relatively inexpensive (about $30–40). Here are two vendors that manufacture and sell FM modulators:

- RadioShack (www.radioshack.com), product name iRock
- Arkon (www.arkon.com/sf.html), product name SoundFeeder

Replace Your Car Stereo

Obviously, replacing your car stereo is not always practical, but it is valuable to mention so you know it's an option. If your current stereo does not already have a 3.5 mm input jack, there are some models that do have the necessary input jack to allow you to plug your Treo directly into your car stereo using an inexpensive patch cable. You can buy this cable from a store such as RadioShack. Some of the manufacturers that offer car stereos with this capability include JVC, Aiwa, and Pioneer. Connecting your Treo to your home stereo may be more practical than connecting it to your car stereo since many home stereos have input jacks; however, you may need an adapter cable or two to make the connection.

Use a Cassette Adapter

If your car has a cassette tape player, then you can easily use a CD car adapter designed to allow your portable CD player to work via your tape deck. The adapter costs about $15–25, and here's how it works: The CD car adapter has a connector that fits into your car stereo tape deck and simulates a cassette tape. The adapter also has a cable that you plug into a portable CD player so that you can hear your CDs through your non-CD–equipped car stereo. You can plug the cable into your Treo 600 using a 2.5 mm to 3.5 mm adapter and hear music on your Treo through your car stereo. Adapters are generally available at electronics stores, and RadioShack is usually a good place to start.

Make Your Car Stereo into a Speakerphone

Being able to use a speakerphone while sitting in your car is useful and, perhaps more importantly, is a great way to impress your friends. There are no manufacturers that make products specifically for this purpose, but the same technology that allows you to use your Treo to play music and sound through your car stereo speakers also works great for converting your car stereo into a speakerphone. Basically, the way it works is that your Treo's hands-free microphone acts as the input for your voice, and your car stereo becomes the speaker half of the speakerphone.

If you have already read the "Play MP3s Through Your Car Stereo" section of this chapter, you are aware of RF modulator technology that allows you to wirelessly

Publish Your Own Photo Blog

This spotlight section is all about you. Specifically, it is about you publishing your own photo blog on the Internet. First, we will discuss blogging as a concept, then we will talk about your blogging options, and last we will talk about the steps for creating your blog and publishing your Treo photos on that blog.

The Blogging Revolution

A blog is basically a journal that is available for others to read on the Web. The term "blog" evolved by slightly modifying the word "weblog." Apparently, the term "weblog" was just too difficult to pronounce and took far too long to type, so *blog,* or *blogging,* was born. The term sounds far less thoughtful and intelligent than what it actually means. The activity of updating a blog is called "blogging," and someone who keeps a blog is called a "blogger." Blogs are typically updated every day using software that allows people with little or no technical background to update and maintain their very own blog. Postings on a blog are almost always arranged like a diary: in chronological order, with the most recent additions at the top of the list. Another feature of most blogs is that they include links to other web sites to help feed the discussion topic. These typically include other blogs, news sites, band web sites, bookstores, and whatever else the author finds interesting.

Seems pretty straightforward, right? Well, the concept is simple, but the fact is that blogging has become somewhat revolutionary in the world of publishing. Blogging helps level the literary playing field by making it tremendously easy to share thoughts, ideas, rants, opinions, and photos with the general public. Historically, in order to be "published," you first had to convince a publisher and printer that your writing was indeed worth publishing and that there was an audience that would pay money to read your words. But now, artfulness and monetary value are just icing on the cake. Now, anyone, even you and I, can publish our thoughts, ideas, rants, opinions, and photos on the Internet for the entire world to see— if we want.

Blogging Is Personal

The key characteristic of blogs is that they are personal. Bloggers rarely bite their tongues in order to avoid offending someone. Bloggers don't have to worry about doing the right things to maintain their employer's public persona like marketing writers and advertising copywriters do. Blogs accomplish two important things that web magazines (also known as "zines," such as Salon or Slate) can't. Because blogs are personal, they unabashedly reveal the temperaments, education, and beliefs of their writers. Many of us are increasingly doubtful of the authority and accuracy of *The Washington Post, Globe and Mail,* and *Newsweek* (thank goodness we can still trust the *National Inquirer*). We know that behind the professional layout and impressive vocabularies, their writers don't necessarily have a better or more valuable opinion than we do— we, the bloggers.

What we are talking about here is publishing your Treo digital pictures on your very own blog. The same restrictions that formerly constrained the written word used to apply to photographs as well. The essence of blogging means that no one has the right to tell you what is good or bad, artistic, or too self-involved in order to publish it. To show off your photos to anyone outside your immediate family used to involve convincing a magazine art director or art gallery curator that your photos had value and deserved to be shown. Well, now we can circumvent literally everyone and decide for ourselves what we want to show the world— and we don't have to ask permission to do it, either. Power to the people! Too melodramatic? Probably, but you get the picture.

Blogging Levels the Publishing Playing Field

In the days of the so-called Industrial Revolution, if your goal was to own the means of production, usually a factory and a workforce, this required a substantial amount of capital before you could begin to produce a product and call it your own. The Internet, as much as anything else it has done, has helped to level the playing field by allowing literally anyone that can get access to the Internet to voice his or her opinions. This is a powerful thing. Immediately after the terrorist attacks on the World Trade Center in Manhattan, the most powerful commentary and outpouring of emotions and opinions did not come from CNN, it came from online bloggers. The commentary arose from around the world and brought together people that didn't know each other but who shared a common experience. They talked about the calamity openly and without regard to what advertisers would think or what ratings they might get.

Be a Blogger—You Can Do It, Too

Well, you should now have a pretty good idea what blogging is about. While it can be an interesting concept for the techno-sociologists of the world, many of us are only interested in sharing details about our lives and experiences with our friends, and are generally less concerned about taking on the powers that be—whoever they are. The good news is that it has become extremely easy for you and me to publish our blogs on the Internet.

Create Your Treo Photo Blog

Once you have an idea of your blogging options and have decided on one, the next thing you will want to do (if you haven't already) is take some pictures with your Treo. The following are some common steps you may want to follow to get your photo blog on the Web. A common example would look something like this.

- **Arrange your pictures and thoughts**   An example would be to post photos from your holiday, school, or business trip, or maybe from a two-hour unicycle tour of your neighborhood back alleys wearing a Darth Vader mask in which you took pictures of graffiti and other urban artifacts.

- **Find and choose a blog hosting site**   A list of blogging sites appears at the end of this chapter, and a short list of options is discussed in the section "Blog Hosting Options—Where to Put Your Blog."

- **Learn how to post your blogs**   Learn the technology and learn how to publish your text

and images to the blogging server. This is largely dependent on understanding how your chosen blogging service works.

- **Post and update your blog**   Once your blogging account is set up and ready for your witty, charming, intelligent, and relevant content, you can update your blog as often as you like and will have earned the right to proclaim to all who will listen, "I am a blogger, and I am proud." Please note: the last step is not mandatory.

- **Invite your friends and family to look at your blog on the Internet**   When your blog is published on the Web, you can send the URL, or web site address (for example, http://*blogname.blogsite*.com), to your friends and family so that they can visit your blog on the Web.

These steps are covered in more detail in the next section.

Get Your Treo Pictures Ready for Your Blog

The first thing you'll need are some pictures to put on your blog. Chapter 7 discusses taking pictures with your Treo 600, including tips for getting the most out of the camera, viewing your Treo pictures on your PC, and using image-editing software to edit and improve your pictures.

Find and Choose a Blog Hosting Site

What is a blogging site? There are a few different twists on the blogging concept, but essentially a blog hosting site allows you to create your blog and update it as often as you want using only a web browser. This means that you don't need to install any software on your PC in order to update your blog.

TIP

Blogging software typically allows you to run your blog on your PC or on your own web server. These options tend to be much more technically involved, not to mention more expensive. If you are interested, some of these options are listed later in this segment in the section "Nonhosted Blogging Applications.

One of the other advantages of using a blogging web site to host your blog is that you can even manage your blog using the web browser and wireless Internet connection on your Treo 600. An example of a blog editing screen (from Blogger.com) that allows you to add a new posting to your blog is shown in the illustration. As you can see, the interface has just two text fields and a couple of buttons.

Things do get a little more complicated as soon as you want to add photos to your blog (something we'll cover a little later). Also, though the simplest blogging services don't offer much to intimidate you, if you're looking for something a little more complex, there are blogging services and applications that will challenge even the most seasoned blogging veteran.

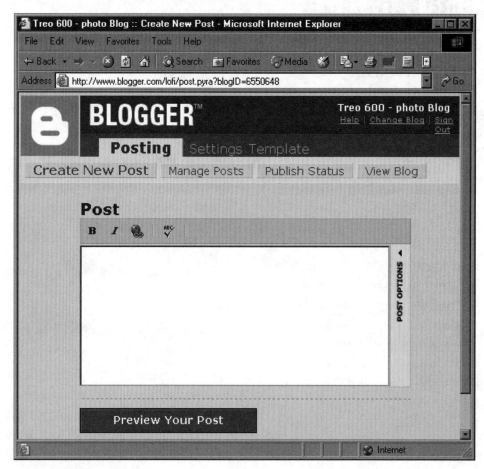

Blogger.com hs a new blog post screen.

4

Blog Hosting Options—Where to Put Your Blog

Like anything that can be accessed on the Internet—music, pictures, web pages, software, video, and so on—your blog needs to exist somewhere so that another Internet user can find and view your blog. There are several ways to do this.

- **Buy a blogging account from a blogging service provider.** The least expensive and easiest option is to buy a blog account from a blogging service provider. This is generally the easiest and most cost-effective option, and for most of us, even seasoned Internet professionals who are technically equipped to take one of the more challenging paths, it is a great way to post your blog on the Web while leaving most of the technical issues to someone else. For more information, see the sidebar "Hosted Blog Web Services."

- **Purchase web-hosting services from a web-hosting company.** A more expensive and more technically challenging option than using a blog hosting service is to purchase a web-hosting service from a web-hosting company. This means that you rent both disk space on a web server and an Internet connection *for* the web server from a web-hosting company. This allows you to publish and manage both your own web site and blog but is generally overkill for someone who just wants to post their ideas and photos on a blog.

- **Host and support your own web site.** The most expensive and technically challenging option is to host and support your own web site with your own web server and your own Internet connection. This option depends on having the necessary financial means (to acquire a web server, have a place to put it, pay for the Internet connection, and so on) and that you, or someone that you can rely on, has the necessary technical knowledge to set up and support your web site.

Of course, there are other options and combinations, but these are the major blogging alternatives, and for our purposes we will focus on the hosted blogging model—you pay an organization to allow you to use their web server to post your blog.

What a Paid Blog Account Offers over a Free Account

Most blogging sites that let you easily set up your blog offer both a free version and a paid version. So, what do you get if you upgrade to a paid account? Well, usually, quite a bit.

HOSTED BLOG WEB SERVICES

There are countless sites and services that allow you to easily post your blogs on the Web without needing to learn HTML, PHP, or any other web-authoring language. Most sites have more commonalities than differences, but you should still look at a few options to make sure you're getting what you need to be able to easily create and add to your blog. A comprehensive list of applications and services is listed at the end of this segment, but we will concentrate primarily on the hosted blog model, which means that your blog text and images are "hosted" on someone else's web server. If you already have your own web site, there are software options for adding a blog to your site. These are listed at the end of this segment as well.

Free Hosted Blog Accounts The basic free blogging sites—this is the general rule, though there are exceptions—allow you to set up and manage a mostly text-based blog. This is fantastic if all you want to do with your blog is add text and web site links, but this isn't enough if you also want to post your Treo pictures. If you already happen to have access to a web server where you can store your pictures, a text-only blogging solution may also work well because you can link your pictures across the Internet from the blog server to the web server where they are stored.

Paid Hosted Blog Accounts If you upgrade to a paid blogging account with a blog-hosting web site service, there can be many additional features to enrich your blogging experience. For example, with a paid blogging account, you have the ability to store pictures and other images on the blog server. The reason for this is simple: images quickly take up significant amounts of memory on the blog server, so you have to pay for using that extra hard disk space. Another difference between the free and paid blogging accounts is that often the free accounts tend to show more banner advertising and pop-up ads to the people viewing your blog. Obviously, these advertisers are helping to pay for your "free" account. When you upgrade to a paid account, less advertising is generally used (sometimes none, in fact), so the blogging experience is a little nicer for your blog readers.

Other features that you may not have access to with a free account include the following:

- XML feed publishing capabilities (ATOM/RSS)
- Sophisticated graphical design templates and layout options
- Commenting and user feedback systems
- The ability to support multiple blog authors

- Support for photo albums and picture galleries
- Support for book lists
- Support for discussion groups
- The ability to monitor your blog web traffic
- The ability to post to your blog using e-mail
- The ability to create online user polls
- An e-mail account to match your blog web address

N O T E

These features are highly dependent on your service provider, so it's important to be aware of your options before you sign up.

You can bet that more features will be added to the blogger sites as companies learn what is important to bloggers, and as they continue to compete for blogger business. Usually, the yearly cost of a paid blogging account is relatively low—currently about $15 to $35 dollars per year, depending on the site and the level of service you are buying. Of course, paying for the service helps ensure that the site hosting your blog will be around for a while. Some of your blogging service options are listed in an extensive list at the end of this segment (see "Blogging Sites, References, and Tools").

Learn How to Post Your Blog

Once you have decided on your blogging tool, it is important to understand how to use that tool. Each one is slightly different and therefore has its own idiosyncrasies that you will need to learn about and understand. Most of the blog hosting sites have online help and user manuals to help you get started. It may be a little tedious at first, but a little time spent learning what the tools can do will pay off in the end. The key point is to understand how to transfer your pictures over to the blog server so your blog users can view them. An example of how easy this can be is described in the next section on CamBlog.

Post Your Treo Photos to CamBlog with E-Mail

To see just how easy posting your Treo photos to your blog can be, check out CamBlog (www.camblog.com), which offers an incredibly simple way of doing it. On CamBlog, once you have registered your free account by simply filling out an online form, you simply e-mail your Treo photos to CamBlog (postcamblog.com) and your photos are posted to your blog immediately. When CamBlog receives the e-mail, it recognizes your e-mail address and posts the photo to your weblog. What could be easier than that? The really exciting and useful thing about this service is that it means you can take a picture with your Treo and immediately send it to your blog using your e-mail account and the wireless capabilities of your Treo 600. So you can post your photo on your blog within minutes of taking a photo and accomplish it all wirelessly from wherever you happen to be—provided you have wireless coverage.

Post and Update Your Blog

Once you have the pictures that you want to post on your blog, and you understand how to post your pictures and text to your blog, the rest is easy. Just decide what you want to say and upload your pictures to your blog. The essence of a blog is that it is updated regularly—but, of course, that part is up to you. Each blogging tool has a unique way of accomplishing this, the easiest and fastest of which we have yet to see is on CamBlog (www.camblog.com; described earlier in the section "Post Your Treo Photos to CamBlog with E-Mail").

Most of the hosted blogging sites allow you to post to your blog through a web-based form that allows you to select a picture located on your PC and then upload it to your blog.

Invite Your Friends and Family to Visit Your Blog on the Internet

Once your photo blog is up and running and looks roughly the way you want it to, you can send your blog web site address to your friends and family so they can see all of your hard work. When you sign up at a blogging site, you are assigned a URL that allows you and others to directly access your blog—for example, http://*blogname.blogsite*.com.

No one needs to know that you are not an experienced web designer or that you only put in a few hours of work to put the whole thing together.

Blogging Sites, References, and Tools

B logging has evolved into a subculture, and along with it software products and services have evolved to help you with your blogging needs. This section provides a short list of blogging tools, including both hosted blogging services and nonhosted solutions. There is also a list of blog directories to help you find other bloggers on the Internet and also to list your own blog so that others can read it.

Hosted Blog Sites Providing Free and/or Paid Accounts for Your Photo Blog

Following is a list of hosted blogging services. These are the easiest, and likely the cheapest, services available to bloggers because the sites take care of the hardware and technical support for you.

- **CamBlog (www.camblog.com)** A specialty hosting site specifically designed to allow you to create a photo blog using cell phone cameras like your Treo 600. CamBlog even allows you to post photos to your Blogger blog (www.blogger.com).

- **Fotopages (www.fotopages.com)** A site dedicated to letting you set up your photo blog.

- **M-Blog (http://m-blog.com)** A site with free photo blogs and hundreds of international blogs.

- **Big Blog Tool (www.bigblogtool.com)** A popular blog hosting site.

- **Blogger (www.blogger.com)** A popular blog hosting site.

- **Salon Blogs (www.salon.com/blogs)** A blog hosting site (requires you to install software on your PC).

- **Blog-City (www.blog-city.com)** A site providing support for blog photo albums.

There are many other blogging solutions that will show up in a quick web search.

Nonhosted Blogging Applications

The following is a list of software applications that you can use to set up your blog on your own web server. Some of these applications are open source (that is, free), but all of them require some technical knowledge.

- **Greymatter(www.noahgrey.com/greysoft)** Open source code featuring image handling.

- **Movable Type (www.movabletype.org)** Six Apart's publishing system, which runs locally on a web server and enables users to manage and update weblogs, journals, and other frequently updated web site content.

- **pMachine (www.pmachine.com)** Offers an easy way to get your blog going, as well as features for the more experienced user.

Blog Directories

The following web sites are directories that allow you to search for blogs with content on specific topics, such as the latest in designer kitchenware or recent trends in base jumping:

- **BlogSearchEngine.com (www.blogsearchengine.com)** This search tool has several categories to choose from, including Entertainment Blogs, News Blogs, Political Blogs and Government Blogs, Faith and Religious Blogs, Personal Blogs and Diary Blogs, Sports Blogs, Books and Literature Blogs, and more.

- **Eatonweb Portal (http://portal.eatonweb.com)** This portal was started back in early 1999 as a private blog list when there were less than 50 publicly known weblogs, and it has grown substantially over the years.

- **Weblogs.com (www.weblogs.com)** This site is a list of weblogs presented in descending time and date order, so the most recently updated blogs are listed at the top. This allows you to read someone's blog immediately after it is posted.

- **Globe of Blogs (www.globeofblogs.com)** Here you can browse blog authors by name and birthday, and search for weblogs by title, topic, and location.

- **Open Directory: Weblogs (http://dmoz.org/ computers/Internet/On_the_Web/Weblogs)** This search engine works in much the same way as a web search engine such as Google or AltaVista.

connect your Treo 600 to your car stereo using the FM capabilities of your car stereo and a little device that you plug into the earphone output jack of your Treo 600. (Note that you will need a 2.5 mm to 3.5 mm adapter to plug the RF modulator into your Treo.) Once the RF modulator is hooked up to your Treo, you tune your car radio, or any FM radio, to one of the digitally tuned FM stations that is supported by your modulator. An RF modulator solution is relatively inexpensive, about $30–40.

So once your RF modulator is hooked up to your Treo and you make or receive a phone call on your Treo 600, the voice of the person you are speaking to is played through your car stereo, and your voice is picked up by the phone microphone. (When you are using your Treo and car stereo as a speakerphone in this way, remember to use the speakerphone option, which is covered in Chapter 4.) There are some great car-mount kits that allow you to mount your Treo 600 to your dash for easy and accessible operation—and to keep your Treo near the stereo. These options are covered in Chapter 16.

Play Video on Your Treo

Your Treo 600 is capable of playing video files using third-party software. In fact several of the media players you can use to play music files also allow you to play video. A few of your video options are listed here:

- **AeroPlayer (www.aerodrome.us)**   AeroPlayer is a free download for you to try for 14 days. AeroPlayer is mentioned in the music section of this chapter, but it also allows you to play video files on your Treo.

- **MMPlayer (www.mmplayer.com)**   MMPlayer is one of your Treo music player options, and it can play several types of files on your Treo 600. A notable difference between MMPlayer and many other video-capable players is that MMPlayer is able to play standard video formats, such as MPEG and AVI formats, while some other video players require that videos be converted to a proprietary format that can only be played by those specific players.

- **Kinoma (www.kinoma.com)**   Kinoma is optimized specifically for the Treo 600 and includes support for the five-way navigation control.

Play Games on Your Treo

Like the drive-in movie and penny candy, the days of playing Pong on your TV and going to the video arcade to plug fistfuls of quarters into arcade games are long gone. Fortunately, your Treo 600 is equipped with a bright-color screen and stereo sound, which makes it an excellent choice for gamers. The Palm OS operating system also happens to be the platform of choice for many mobile game-development companies, which means that there is a huge selection of games available for your Treo. Many of the games that are available are shareware and freeware, so you can be a gamer without spending a fortune on new games as they come out.

This section provides only a short list of games to give you an idea of what is available on the market. To get a much better idea, many sites exist that you can search to find games designed for the Palm OS on your Treo 600. A few are listed here:

- PalmOne (www.palmone.com)

- Handango (www.handango.com)

- Handmark (www.handmark.com)

- Tucows (www.tucows.com)

Another great resource that will tell you what games are available and what other Treo 600 owners think of the games is the Treo 600 fan site discussion boards. A full list of sites is available in Appendix B, but here are a few examples:

- Treo600.com (www.treo600.com)

- Treo Central (www.treocentral.com)

- Everything Treo (www.everythingtreo.com)

Card Games

Your Treo allows you to play a game of cards without the cards—it ships with a version of Solitaire and other games. One of the standouts is CardSuite because it includes enough games to keep you from getting bored.

CardSuite

CardSuite by Glavark (www.glavarkcom), $20, is a collection of 10 card games and 70 Solitaire games, including the following:

- **Card games**   Euchre, Hearts, Cribbage, Spades, Gin Rummy, Rummy, Blackjack, Crazy Eights, Whist, and President

- **Solitaire games**   Klondike, FreeCell, Spider, Pyramid, and Memory

The game features include the following:

- Rules for all games

- Options for different game variations

- Games automatically saved on exit

- Undo feature in Solitaire games

- Statistics recorded for all Solitaire and card games

- Six card-back images

- Six background patterns

- 16-bit color, 256 colors, 16-level grayscale, and black-and-white support

Board Games

What could be better than a board game without the board? Good question. I don't know, but there are some great Treo games that are based on familiar traditional board games. A small cross section is listed here, but there are many others:

- **Backgammon 3.1, freeware**   Available on several web sites for download. Search on the full name in an Internet search engine. Even if you don't know how to play, you can learn to using your Treo by watching the Treo play against itself. Then play in the beginner mode, or challenge yourself with the advanced mode. This application lets you play backgammon with a friend or against the computer.

- **Chess Tiger (www.ChessTiger.com), $19**   If you are a chess player, this game has enough options to keep you entertained for a long time, including a training mode, different board sizes, and over 100 different skill levels.

- **Trivial Pursuit Handheld Edition for Palm OS (available from www. handmark.com), $30**   A digital version of the classic game, with more than 1,600 multiple choice and true/false questions. There are two modes of play, Classic play (the original game) and Flash mode (a quick-fix Trivial Pursuit game). There is multiplayer support of 2–6 players over Bluetooth and IR (infrared). A multiplayer lobby offers a meeting place for a networked game, including chat among players.

8

Puzzle Games

Games can be categorized differently depending on who is doing the categorizing. Generally speaking, puzzle games tend to be slower paced and involve problem solving and strategy.

- **Bejeweled (www.astraware.com), free trial; full version, $15**   This is a popular game that seems to be on the top of many Treo owners installed games lists. It offers the following features:

  - High-quality gray or color graphics and animation

  - Sound effects

  - Really addictive game play

  - Two modes: Easy (for relaxation) and Timed (for a frantic game)

  - Ability to export high scores to the Astraware Bejeweled Internet High Score Table

  - Instructions and tips to get you started

  - Automatic hints to help you play

- **Plumber Pete (www.palmstorm.com), free trial available at www.palmone. com; full version, $6**   This game offers a new twist on thinking against the clock. The objective of the game it so fix pipelines by rotating the pipe pieces into their correct positions, all while trying to keep water from leaking out of the pipes.

Action Games

This category is a little open to interpretation because one gamer's backgammon is another gamer's "action" game.

- **Sea Strike by Island Labs (www.islandlabs.com), shareware; full license, $15**   This game is based on a popular web-based game; and as you can tell by the title, it is based on the life and times of a military submarine. Along the way, you defeat enemy subs while avoiding depth charges, mines, and bombs. Also, in true-to-life fashion, you must catch fish in order to replenish your oxygen before you run out.

- **3D Master Thief FREE Demo Mission 1.3 by Cascata Games (www. cascatagames.com), freeware**   The Phoenix Gemstone worth a reputed $24 million has been stolen by the Russian Mafia, the Kombati. Your mission is to steal it back for a billionaire collector. Break into the Kombati Stronghold and find the hidden vault room, where you will find the gemstone protected by armed guards. You will be paid handsomely if you succeed.

- **Roids 1.2 by Flippinbits (www.flippinbits.com), shareware**   In case your life doesn't have enough stress already, your job in this game is to save the world. Hoards of aliens are heading this way with an even greater number of asteroids to block their way.

- **3D Air Hockey for Palm OS by Paul Ellams (available at www.handmark. com or www.handango.com), $8**   This game is slightly more portable than an air hockey table and almost as much fun.

Software to Help Your Game

Your Treo is also great for assisting you with nonvideo games. An example of software that can really help out—if you spend your time outdoors wearing plaid pants and spiked shoes—is software that you can use to improve and track your golf game.

IntelliGolf 7.0 for the Treo (Birdie edition) by Karrier Communications (www. intelligolf.com), $30, now includes support for GPS and Bluetooth and is the only golf software to include all seven Ss of golf. In case you, like me, don't know what those seven Ss are, here is a list of what they stand for:

- Scoring

- Shot tracking

- Satellite GPS

- Sidegame wagers (30+)

- Statistics and graphs (250+)

- Signature courses (18,500+)

- Sharing of information between handhelds

IntelliGolf for the Treo software comes complete with the software that resides on your Treo and PC synchronization software—everything you need to improve your game, except a new swing.

8

Wrap It Up

This chapter discussed some of the fun things you can do with your Treo 600. This is the kind of stuff that your boss doesn't need to know about. PalmOne has done a great job of designing the Treo in a small package that allows you to play music, watch video, and play games (whenever you aren't working on spreadsheets, swapping e-mail with the Chairman of the Board, or explaining the benefits of the United Nations, that is). After all, you work hard; you should have a little fun, too.

Chapter 9

Keep Your Treo Running at Its Best

How to...

- Back up your Treo
- Manage your battery life
- Charge your Treo on the road
- Use third-party application launchers
- Navigate faster
- Optimize text input
- Protect your Treo from damage

An important part of being a Treo owner is making sure that your device is set up to maximize its efficacy. This can involve many factors, including adjusting settings for the operating system, managing the battery, and acquiring third-party software and accessories to improve how the Treo works. There is no shortage of great ways to improve how your Treo works for you. In this chapter, we explore some of the ways that we optimize our Treos, and you can decide for yourself which of these will add value to you.

Back Up Your Treo

A very real hazard of integrating a mobile device like the Treo into your lifestyle is the risk that something could go wrong with your device and that you could lose all of your data. This could happen due to your battery running so low that memory integrity cannot be maintained, because of a bad piece of software you have loaded that forces you to hard-reset your device, or because of some other combination of bad luck.

NOTE   *Some people have begun talking about the risk of viruses getting onto your handheld device and not only damaging the data on your device, but potentially getting into your PC and perhaps your work or home environment through the device. We want to provide our opinion that although this is technically feasible, not a single incident of a virus on a mobile device has yet occurred, and the first ones are likely to be limited in scope and damage. Don't be talked into buying antivirus software for your handheld until such a risk actually shows up as a clear and present danger.*

To help protect yourself, it is essential to ensure that your Treo is backed up regularly. The Treo is equipped with some built-in backup capabilities, and there is third-party software that can help you perform more extensive and sophisticated backups, depending on what your needs are.

Perform a HotSync Backup

Every time you HotSync your Treo (as described in Chapter 3), the Treo performs a full backup of everything about your device. All installed applications are backed, up as well as preferences, favorites, and more. Your contact information, calendar, tasks, and notes will be synced with Palm Desktop, Outlook, or your third-party personal information manager (PIM). This synchronization will back up your PIM information. If you have a failure of your Treo and lose your data, you can restore it simply by performing a HotSync of your device.

Back Up Using Third-Party Software

The major drawback of HotSync-based backups is that they require you to be connected to your PC. If you are a traveler, don't HotSync frequently, or need to ensure you can recover your device while away from your PC, then you will require software that will back up your data to a storage card.

One such product is BackupMan from Bits 'n Bolts software (www.bitsnbolts. com) that we use to back up our Treo 600s to Secure Digital (SD) cards. BackupMan allows you to recover your entire device from a compact SD card in the event of failure while you are traveling.

With BackupMan, you can also schedule your Treo to back up its data automatically on a daily or hourly basis, as shown in Figure 9-1. There are many people who use Treo 600s in business environments where the data on their devices

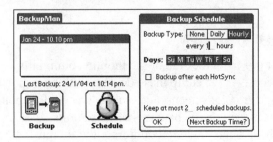

FIGURE 9-1   BackupMan allows you to back up your Treo on a scheduled basis to an external storage card.

changes frequently. Imagine you are a doctor and you use your Treo to keep patient notes and dispense prescriptions. As you go through the day, you can't keep running back to your PC to HotSync in order to protect your critical data. With BackupMan, you can schedule your Treo to back itself up to the storage card every hour throughout the day. That way, you are never in danger of losing more than the past hour's work.

With BackupMan, you need to make sure you have an SD card that is large enough in capacity to handle each backup set. You can also limit the number of backup sets to store on the card. We usually keep only two backup sets so that we have the most recent backup and the backup immediately before that.

BackupMan will also install itself onto the card so that in the event of a total hard reset of your Treo, you can load BackupMan directly from the card and then restore the backed up information from the card.

Another very useful feature of BackupMan is that you can restore only individual files. Let's say that you performed some action that ended up messing up the data inside one of your applications. A real world example of this is that when I first received my Treo, I inserted the SIM card that had previously been in my Sony Ericsson t68i. I had already HotSynced my Treo, and after inserting the SIM card I was prompted and asked if I wanted to copy the contacts of my SIM card into my Contacts application. When I answered yes, it copied the contacts from my SIM card in a format that was completely inconsistent with the way that I manage my contacts, creating many duplicate records and junk data in my Contacts application. Had I had BackupMan installed (and a recent backup set), I could simply have restored my Contacts-related files and returned to the state I was in before I ruined my data. Instead, I had to spend time cleaning the junk data manually—data that had now been HotSynced back to my Outlook folders, creating junk data in them as well.

The most recent version of BackupMan allows you to encrypt your backups (for data security purposes) and also to perform only partial backups of your Treo.

For a full listing of vendors that provide backup software for your Treo, refer to Chapter 16.

Maximize Your Battery

One of the biggest thorns in the side of the mobile community has been the battery life of mobile devices. As we equip these devices with more powerful processors, more memory, brighter-color screens, and embedded cellular phones, there are more and more demands placed on the batteries of these units.

Great strides have been made to counteract the increasing demand for power, but you still need to be very aware of your device usage and take appropriate steps

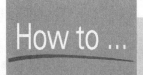 **Back Up an Orange Treo Wirelessly**

A unique feature of the Orange brand Treo 600 is the ability to backup your device over the air. You can initiate this service by selecting the Orange Backup application and selecting which of the databases on your device you want to back up.

9

When you initiate the backup, as shown in the following illustration, all of your critical data will be backed up wirelessly. If your Treo should ever be hard-reset, erasing all of your data, you can initiate a restore over the air to bring your Treo back to the same state it was in when you performed your last backup.

to get the most out of your battery. Although the Treo should, when the power gets low enough, switch into a "safe mode" that won't allow you to turn it on but will still protect your data, you shouldn't rely on this. If your battery gets low enough, you could find yourself having to reload all of your applications and data back on to your Treo.

Keep an Eye on Your Battery

On the main phone and application screens of your Treo, you will see an icon in the top-right corner that shows you the approximate strength of your battery:

If the battery is at or near full strength, the battery icon will appear solid. As the battery strength drops, the icon will show the battery as being less than full. How full the battery appears is roughly proportional to the battery strength left. If your Treo is plugged into a power source, the icon will show a bolt of electricity over the battery to show that it is charging, as you can see in the preceding illustration.

If you would like to see a reading of you your battery strength as a percentage of total battery strength, you can tap the battery icon to see the top bar replaced with a percentage number. If you would like to know more details about your battery, the BatteryGraph application discussed in the following section is available to help you with this.

You can also adjust some simple settings to help maximize your battery life. Select General in the Preferences application to see some options that you can configure, as shown in Figure 9-2.

The most important battery conservation setting is Auto-off After. This allows you to specify the time period after which you would like to have your Treo go to sleep when there is no activity from you. The options range from 30 Seconds to 3 Minutes. The longer the delay, the more battery power that will be consumed in an idle period. You will notice that there is no option to disable the Auto-off feature. This is because, inevitably, at some point we all forget to turn our devices off and

FIGURE 9-2   In the General Preferences, there are some settings that you can set to help reduce your battery consumption.

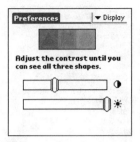

FIGURE 9-3   You can turn down the screen brightness to save battery strength.

then are upset because our battery is completely drained as a result. On the Treo 600, some reasonable Auto-off setting is mandatory.

Another place you can squeeze out some battery savings is in the Display Preferences, as shown in Figure 9-3. There are two slider bars that show—the top slider bar adjusts the contrast; the bottom slider bar adjusts the brightness. Turning down the brightness will consume less battery power if you find you are running through your battery too quickly.

Next we explore some third-party applications that will help you manage your battery most effectively.

BatteryGraph

The built-in software for telling you the status of your battery is very limited on the Treo. If you travel, or use your Treo intensively throughout the day, you may want to get more detail on your battery to help you gauge your usage pattern and know when you need to plan to recharge.

BatteryGraph is a free (for noncommercial use) application you can download for your Treo that will log your battery status in a database every time you turn your Treo on or off. This data can then be graphed so that you can see how your battery performs over time, as shown in Figure 9-4.

You can also set alarms to warn you when your battery drops below acceptable levels. Two different levels of alarms can be created. You can download your own copy of this utility from http://palm.jeroenwitteman.com/.

BatteryGraph will help educate you about your usage, but it doesn't directly reduce your battery consumption. For that, we look to some other third-party applications.

Sandman

If you make a lot of long phone calls while on your Treo, you will notice that your screen stays on during the call. This can consume a lot of battery power and

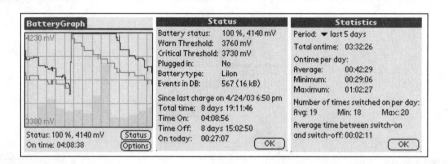

FIGURE 9-4   BatteryGraph is a free tool to help you gain more visibility into your power usage on your Treo.

reduce the operating time of our Treo. A free tool called Sandman, from Chatter (www.imchatter.com), allows you to turn off the screen when you are on a call to conserve battery strength. To activate Sandman, the best thing you can do is map it to one of your hard buttons so that when a call comes in you can push this button and blank the screen. Pushing any regular hard button will restore the screen to normal use.

If you use this application and find that it cuts out the sound, try adjusting the System Sound volume under General Preferences in the Preferences application.

Radio Control

The Treo 600 does not come equipped with a scheduler that allows you to turn the radio on and off at scheduled times. Many people don't receive phone calls at 2:30 in the morning! If you would like your Treo to automatically power the radio on or off at a certain time, you can download a free utility called Radio Control, shown in Figure 9-5. This battery-saving (and possibly sleep-saving) utility was written by a dedicated Treo user, Chris Hobbs. It can be downloaded at http://clanhobbs.org/treo.

With Radio Control, you can also set the Treo radio to automatically turn on after a soft reset. By default, when you soft-reset the Treo the radio will turn off. I have personally missed many calls when I have forgotten to turn my radio back on after a soft reset.

Recharge Your Battery

In addition to the standard charger that comes with your Treo, there are some other charging solutions worth considering, from car chargers to the solar panels.

| FIGURE 9-5 | Radio Control allows you to schedule when the radio of the Treo turns on and off. |

What PalmOne Offers

Many of the charging accessories you might be interested in can be purchased directly from palmOne. These include the following:

- **Combined charging and HotSync USB cable**   A cable that charges your Treo from the USB port on your laptop and syncs at the same time

- **Car charger**   A separate cable solely for charging your Treo from your car

- **Double charger**   A cable that serves double duty as both a car charger and a wall charger for your Treo

PalmOne also offers a new extended battery for the Treo 600. It is currently the only extended battery available for the Treo, and unfortunately it is not the most ergonomic unit, as you can see in Figure 9-6. It clamps onto the back and bottom of your Treo. If you really need the extra power, it will deliver 1,250 mAh (milliamp hours) of additional power, which equates to approximately an extra three hours of talk time or 180 hours of standby time.

iGo Juice

For the person traveling with a laptop and a Treo, the iGo Juice (www.igo.com) is a great accessory that allows you to charge your laptop and your Treo at the same time. With exchangeable tips, a wide range of laptops, phones, and PDAs can be charged. This one is a true must-have for the road warrior.

9

FIGURE 9-6   The Treo Extended Battery from palmOne will extend the life of your Treo by an additional three hours of talk time or 180 hours of standby time, even if it isn't the most attractive accessory.

Zip Linq

The ZIP-LINQ retractable sync cable (www.ziplinq.com) advertises the ability to both sync and charge your Treo from the USB port of your computer. After testing a number of these cables, we found that they did charge the Treo; but unfortunately, we were not successful in actually HotSyncing through the cables. These cables are also sold under different brands, including BoxWave (www.boxwave.com) and JAVOSync (www.javoedge.com), among others. An excellent small charger for travelers, but it appears not to live up to its full billing.

Instant Power

Electric Fuel has an interesting product called Instant Power, which is an emergency charger for your Treo 600. It comes sealed in an airtight bag, and when opened, causes a chemical reaction that gives off electricity that charges your Treo through the supplied cable. Each Instant Power charge pack is good for multiple charges of your device, as long as it is sealed back into its airtight bag when your Treo is charged. This product is available at www.instant-power.com.

SunCatcher Solar Charger

A very interesting offering for charging your Treo 600 is the SunCatcher Sport (www.powerqwest.com/powerline), which will charge your Treo 600 directly from the sun! This product is great for hikers, backpackers, pilots, and others who use their Treos for GPS navigation or may not be near a power outlet regularly.

Work More Efficiently

We carry a Treo for a number of reasons, one of which is that we want to be able to have access to information and communication at our fingertips. This means being able to get to what we need on the device efficiently. There are a number of tools that can improve the standard navigation of the Treo.

Launch Applications

The more applications you load on your Treo, the more challenging it can become to navigate quickly to what you need. There is a combination of built-in and third-party products that can speed your launching of applications.

Favorites

The Favorites screen was introduced in Chapter 4 as a way to create speed-dial shortcuts for your favorite phone numbers. The Favorites screen can also be used to create shortcuts to launch your favorite applications. To create an application shortcut, open the Favorites screen and select an empty favorite button to open the Add Favorite screen, as shown in Figure 9-7. (For a refresher on how to add speed-dial shortcuts, refer to Chapter 4.)

In the Type drop-down, select Application and then choose which application you want to launch in the Label field. You can also define a hard keyboard key that will launch this application when you press and hold the key.

FIGURE 9-7   You can add applications to your Favorites screen to make shortcuts to your favorite programs.

Hard Buttons

Another way to launch your favorite applications quickly is to link them to the four hard buttons on the front of your Treo to the left and right of the five-way navigation control. By default, the buttons will launch the Phone, Calendar, and Mail applications from left to right. The rightmost button will power the screen off. Pressing and holding the OPTION button and then pressing one of the hard buttons will launch a different application.

You can configure which applications are launched by the hard buttons in the Preferences application. Selecting Buttons from the drop-down will open the Buttons Preferences screen shown here:

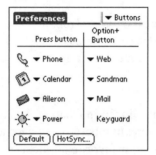

Every button is displayed with a drop-down arrow beside it. You can select the application you would like the button to launch by choosing it in the list. If you ever want to return to the default application associated with the button, just tap the Default button on the bottom.

The HotSync button, also on the bottom, allows you to change which application is launched when the button on the HotSync cable is pressed. By default, this launches HotSync, but there is rarely a reason why you would want to change this.

Hi-Launcher

For those of you who would like to navigate your Treo in the same way you do your desktop computer, Hi-Launcher from RaNo Software (www.hilauncher.com) will let you build a custom menu that pops up from the bottom, as in Figure 9-8.

You can choose any key to open the Hi-Launcher menu and then select the application or function that you would like to jump to. You can create your own entirely custom menu, including submenus, splitter bars, and links to applications or links to special functions such as screen brightness control. You can also set the colors for each menu background and font to help make it easy to read.

FIGURE 9-8	The Hi-Launcher menu provides an easy way to navigate among applications and functions on your Treo.

Today

The Today application is *the* product for people familiar with Microsoft's Pocket PC platform (and is great even for those of you who have been Palm users from the beginning). It gathers information from your other applications and presents it in a consolidated format on your screen using a style that is very familiar in the world of the Pocket PC.

You can see in an easy-to-read format the current date and time, any upcoming appointments you have, if you have unread e-mail, the number of active tasks you have to complete, and more, depending on how you have it configured. It also serves as a mini application launcher, allowing you to put icons for your most common applications on a bar at the bottom. Tapping the icon launches the program. In addition, the very top of the screen shows you a system summary of your battery strength and available memory.

This is another free Palm application developed by a dedicated Palm user. You can read more about the application and its author and download your own copy at http://nikman.k2.net/today/index.html.

Treo Butler

The Treo Butler is an application with a few tricks up its sleeve to help you use your Treo more efficiently. It offers the following functions and features:

- The ability to change the function of the Volume buttons to act as controls for scrolling the screen or switching between applications.

- The ability to disable the LED function or show if there is voicemail pending (on some carriers)

- The ability to launch your Favorites applications from anywhere, not just the Phone application.

- An alarm clock to wake you up or remind you of appointments.

This application is not free, but it isn't terribly expensive if you like what it does for you. You will need to pay $4.50 to register the application. You can try it out for free, though, to see if you like its functionality before paying for it. It can be downloaded from PalmGear at www.palmgear.com—in the Search area, select the Palm OS Software check box and search for Treo Butler.

Enter Text Faster

I find typing on the Treo 600 keyboard to be very easy even given its small size. The thing that I find tricky when I am typing away is pausing to hit the right key combination to get a capital letter or a special character. There is a free utility called KeyCaps600 that makes it extremely easy to type capital letters or special characters without having to use multiple keys to do it.

You can configure the application to give an uppercase instead of a lowercase letter by holding the key for a moment longer. Tapping the key twice will give you the special character on the key instead of the lowercase letter. You can customize what kinds of keystrokes trigger these reactions, as well as how long a delay you want before a different type of character is initiated.

This application is free and can be downloaded from www.geekandproud.net/
software/keycaps600.php. It is one of the applications that we highly recommend
as a productivity improver for the Treo 600.

Never Miss an Alert

One complaint of all-in-one mobile devices such as the Treo is that sometimes you
miss an important alert. You don't realize there is a voicemail waiting for you, or
an appointment reminder went off, but because you were going over a bump in
your car at the time you didn't feel the vibration, and the sound was lost because
the stereo was too loud. For just that reason, PDAapps (www.pdaapps.com) created
TreoAlertMgr, which will keep alerting and reminding you until you acknowledge
the alert. You can have your Treo play a sound, vibrate, and flash the screen (or any
combination thereof) when an alert comes in. Luckily, you can also schedule this
to occur only during certain hours so that if an SMS message arrives while you are
sleeping you don't have to deal with your Treo having a fit until you respond!

Protect Your Treo from Damage

Your Treo is a very hardy and well-built device, but that doesn't mean it is
indestructible. I am a true road warrior and am very hard on my devices. A common
joke in the office is "If you want to see how tough a device really is, give it to Derek
for a week. If it survives, it's a good unit." I haven't broken my Treo 600 yet, which
says a great deal about the quality of the engineering.

No matter how hard you try not to, someday you will drop your Treo, or it will
fall off your belt or face some other kind of trauma. There are a number of things
you can do to improve your odds of not damaging your device—from nonslip grips
to cases and screen protectors.

Use Better Grips

One unfortunate thing about the design of the Treo is that the sides of it are made
of the same polished metal that the whole case is formed out of. Other device

manufacturers have been learning that putting rubber grips on the sides of their devices makes them easier to hold and less likely to be dropped.

Since palmOne overlooked this detail, you do have the option of adding third-party grips that can be applied to the Treo to provide the same benefit. The leading provider of these grips is called Egrips (www.egrips.com).The Egrips product is applied to your Treo with a light adhesive. It provides you with a sure grip on your device and keeps it from sliding around on the dash of your car as well. These grips should be considered "consumables" because they wear out over a period of several months and need to be replaced. Without a doubt, these Egrips are one of the absolute "must-have" accessories for your Treo.

Use Better Cases

Treo owners are lucky that the case that ships with the product is of much higher quality than cases shipping with many competing products. However, a different case is another way of personalizing your Treo and serves the added benefit of providing extra protection in the case of a fall or bump.

You can choose from many different kinds of cases, and the number to choose from continues to grow on a daily basis as the Treo gains mass popularity. Different cases have different general features that may help you narrow your selection. Selecting a case is always a matter of personal preference, so you should consider what is most important to you from the following list:

- **Pouch/holster vs. always covered**   Some cases are pouch or holster types. This means that when you want to use your Treo, you take it out of the case and hold the "naked" Treo in your hands. The other kinds of cases always stay on the Treo, so they keep it covered at all times. The latter style usually offers more protection for the device. Most of the time when I drop my Treo, it is while I am fumbling to get it out of a case when a call is coming in. The drawback of an always-on case is that it does add to the bulk of the case.

- **Flip style versus nonflip style**   For the cases that are always on you, generally find two different fundamental styles. One type allows you to hold the Treo up to your head and take a call without having to open or flip up any cover. The other type has a flap that folds over the front of the Treo and must be opened before you can take a call. The flip style usually affords the most protection to the device; but for some people, having to open the cover to answer the phone is an annoyance that they do not want to deal with. One other bonus of the flip style is that pockets are often located in the flip cover to hold extras such as additional storage cards, credit cards, business cards, and so on.

- **Cutouts**   A case should have holes and openings cut in it to allow you to get at the controls you need while using the Treo. Missing holes can mean that you can't use the case in certain situations. For example, the case that comes with your Treo doesn't have a hole for the headphone jack. If you want to listen to music or talk on the phone while leaving the Treo clipped to your belt, you can't do it without resorting to a hole punch to make the necessary cut out. Some vendors have also completely forgotten that the Treo 600 has a camera in it and have failed to provide a cutout for the camera lens. If you want to snap a quick shot, you have to remove your Treo from the case first.

- **Belt clips**   Some cases come with belt clips; some do not. If you prefer to carry your Treo in your pocket, purse, briefcase, or portfolio, then having a belt clip isn't important to you. However, if you like to have your Treo clipped to your belt, then a good belt clip is essential. Most case vendors offer both clip and nonclip versions of their cases. Some vendors, such as Piel Frama, even offer a case with a removable belt clip so that you can use the case with a clip and then unscrew the knob from the case to keep it smooth when you don't.

9

- **Cradle compatibility**   If you use a cradle, some cases allow you to leave the case on the Treo and still plug the Treo directly into the cradle for charging and syncing. Others will only allow you to sync with a cord. If you like to use the cradle, you might find it a pain to take the case off every time you want to charge or sync. If you are a noncradle user, then this is a nonissue!

- **Storage**   If you like to carry extra storage cards for music, pictures, or for other reasons, look for a case with the ability to store the cards right in the case. Some cases can also carry paper money and a credit card so that you can leave your wallet at home!

- **Personalization**   A number of case vendors allow you to further personalize your case by choosing the material, color, and other features of the case. In addition, some will emboss your name, your company name, or your company's logo on your case.

A full listing and description of the cases that we are currently aware of is in Chapter 16, along with information on what key features they offer and our opinions of the overall quality and usability of the case.

Cover Up the Screen

One way to tell a new Treo from an old one is by how scratched the screen is. Inevitably, sometimes as you use the tool you won't bother to pull the stylus out of the back when you just want to tap something really quickly. Instead, you will use your fingernail, a pen with the lid on it, or some other object. There are other things that may come in contact with the screen as well. For example, if you wear earrings, you might accidentally scratch the screen while talking on the phone.

A popular product for protecting your screen is a clear adhesive screen protector that you can apply to the screen of your device. Once a screen protector is on, it is very hard to tell it's there. It forms an extra physical layer between you and the screen. The stylus works as easily as before, and the screen is just as bright. You lose nothing by applying a screen protector, and you gain a screen *saver,* so we highly recommend adding this accessory to your arsenal of Treo tools. There is a full list in Chapter 16 of providers of these protectors. Some work better than others as far as being truly invisible and for adhesiveness. The ones that we have been using on our Treo 600s are from BoxWave (www.boxwave.com) and are very reasonably priced.

These screen shields last a very long time; if you see that one has gotten scratched or dirty, you can simply peel it off and apply a new one.

Wrap It Up

Once you have begun using your Treo 600, you will continue to find more and more ways to improve your productivity and your fun with the device. The information in this chapter hopefully has empowered you to get the most out of these productivity and personal-life enhancements.

Chapter 10

Use Productivity Applications

How to...

■ Make appointments in your Calendar

■ Manage your Contacts

■ Take notes and memos

■ Convert measurements and weights with the Treo Calculator

■ Manage your shopping list

■ Track and protect your credit card numbers, frequent flyer numbers, and more

Depending on where you purchased your Treo 600, you may find that there are some slight variations in which productivity applications come preloaded on your device. This is because the Treo 600 is also your phone; and the carrier, or wireless service provider, that provides you with your mobile phone number and access might choose to configure the standard software on the Treo differently, due to marketing differentiation.

Generally you will not find any variance in the standard applications for managing your Calendar, Contacts, and Notes, but beyond that there will most certainly be differences. A number of the Treo 600s have been shipped with versions of the SplashData products, so we will cover those in this chapter. For applications that you may have custom loaded, you can refer to the manufacturers of those applications for additional information on how to use their software. Chapter 16 covers some of those vendors and tells you where to learn more.

Stay on Schedule with the Calendar

The built-in Calendar application that ships on the Treo is essentially the same calendar application that has been shipped with palmOne devices since the beginning of time (although Handspring modified it slightly). If you are familiar with using the Calendar on previous Palm or Handspring devices that you have owned, you might want to just skim this section and read about the features of this version of the Calendar that are unfamiliar to you. If the Treo is the first Palm OS device you have owned, this section we will show you how to create and edit appointments in your Calendar. The Treo Calendar has some unique and powerful features that you may not have seen before in other applications, such as the ability to have floating appointments and a built-in daily journal.

The Calendar application allows you to track your schedule, appointments, and activities.

Navigate Through Your Calendar

You can launch your Calendar application by pressing the button immediately to the left of the five-way navigation control. This button has an icon on it that looks like the pages of a calendar. This will open the Calendar to your default view. Unless you have changed it in your preferences, the default view is the current day view (the Day view), as shown in Figure 10-1.

The date you are viewing will appear on the top-left of the screen with the day of the week highlighted in the appropriate box on the top-right. You can move immediately to any day in the same week by tapping on the appropriate day box on the top-right of the screen. Tapping the arrows to the right or left of the day boxes will advance you forward or backward one week. You can also use the five-way navigation control to move ahead or back a day by tapping the RIGHT or LEFT button on the control, respectively. Tapping the UP or DOWN button on the control will scroll you up or down through your list of appointments, as will tapping the up or down arrows on the bottom-right of the screen with the stylus.

You can select any individual appointment or event in the Calendar by tapping it with the stylus or moving the cursor to it with the navigation control. Once you have selected an event, you can view its details, as shown here, by tapping the Details button at the bottom of the screen or by pressing the CENTER button on the navigation control twice:

This pop-up screen allows you to see all the details of the event and navigate to any notes that you have stored for the event, as shown in this example, by tapping the Note button:

The bottom-left corner of the Calendar screen contains six boxes (see in Figure 10-1, shown previously). Tapping a different box displays a different view of your Calendar. The leftmost box displays the Day view, which was as shown in Figure 10-1. The second box displays the Week view:

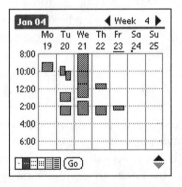

In the Week view, the gray boxes represent events in your Calendar. Tapping on an event will cause a pop-up window to appear, showing the event details, as shown in Figure 10-2. This pop-up window will stay visible for about two seconds.

In this view, you can also reschedule an event by dragging it with your stylus to a new date and time. You can navigate through weeks by tapping the arrows at the top-right of the screen or by using the navigation control to move left or right.

FIGURE 10-2   In the Week view, you can see an event's details simply by tapping on the event.

The third box at the bottom-left corner of the Calendar screen will take you to the Agenda view of the week:

This view gives you a little more detail on each appointment. Each box contains the day of the week and the date in the bottom right-hand corner. Tapping on this date will return you to the Day view for the current day. Tapping on any specific appointment will also return you to the Day view with that appointment selected.

At the very top of the screen, you will notice a small number 2 in a box. Tapping this number will show you two weeks in the Agenda view instead of one, as shown in the following illustration. Tapping the number 1 box at the top will return you to the Agenda view of the week.

10

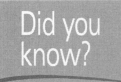

Keep Your Private Records from Being Displayed

When you see a gray box with a lock beside it anywhere on your Palm, this indicates that there is a private record there that is currently masked from view. To learn how to view these records or set up this security feature, refer to the "Secure Your Data" section later in this chapter.

Any time you view a multiday view, the current date will appear, flashing on and off or highlighted to help you to identify it.

The Week view also has some custom preferences that you can set to change how this view appears. From the menu, select Week Preferences to open the screen where you can edit these:

The preferences you can modify include

■ **Time Format** You can choose not to display the time or to display the time in different formats to conserve space.

■ **Display To Do** This allows you to choose to show To Do List items on the top or bottom of each day's box or hide them altogether so you can see more event information.

■ **Week Start** You can select the day of the week that you want your Agenda view of the week to begin with. You can have a fixed day of the week, or you can choose to have it use whatever the current day of the week is.

■ **Wordwrap Single Entry** If you have only one event in your Calendar for the day, the Calendar will wrap the event information onto multiple lines so you can view more information about the event. This is generally desirable unless you like to look for white space on the screen to find days that aren't as busy!

■ **Hide Untimed Floating Events** Floating events may distract you from your actually planned agenda for the day, and if so, you can choose to hide or show them here.

■ **Show Journal** By default, your daily Journal entries will not show up in the view, but if you would like to see them, select the check box beside this option.

■ **Include Week Numbers in Title** This shows you which week of the month you are viewing. The default is to not show this information.

The fourth box at the bottom-left of the Calendar screen will take you to the Month view, as shown in Figure 10-3.

This view is fairly self-explanatory except for the symbols that appear within a given date. The rectangles on the left of a date box are appointments in the morning. The bigger the rectangle is, the longer the appointment is. Rectangles on the right side of the date box represent events in the afternoon. A dot in the middle represents a task, a floating untimed event, or a journal entry for that date.

FIGURE 10-3 The Month view lets you see your entire month at a glance.

You can set what you would like to see on a date in the Month Preferences screen, which is accessed from the menu under the Options menu item:

On the Month Preferences screen, you can choose what you would like to be shown on your Month view. The options are Timed Events, Untimed Events, Daily Repeating Events, Week Number in the Title, and Zero Duration Events.

The fifth box on the bottom-left of the Calendar screen launches you into the Year view of your Calendar, where you can see the entire year at a glance:

Any date on which you have an event will show with a dark circle inside the date. The date you are looking at will flash on the screen, and the first event from that date will show up in the title area at the top of the screen. The arrows on the bottom-left will move you forward or backward within the current year one day at a time. The arrows at the top right will leap from year to year.

The Year view also allows provides a screen to let you to change what you see in the view by selecting Year Preferences under the Options menu or by tapping the Prefs button at the bottom of the screen:

The List view will generate a list of the events in your Calendar.

For the year preferences, you can choose to hide or show the following: floating and done items, untimed events, events with a duration of zero, events that are less than a duration you specify (the default is a half hour), and daily repeating events.

The sixth and final box in the bottom-left of the Calendar screen shows a view of your Calendar called the List view. It generates a list of all of your appointments from the current date you have selected and beyond, as shown in Figure 10-4.

The up and down arrows in the top-right of the screen allow you to move ahead or back in the list. If you tap the up arrow, you can select from a pop-up window to move one day, one week, one month, or to pick an item.

10

The icon on the right side of an event allows you to see if there is an alarm on the event, a note attached, or if the event is masked (a lock icon). You can select List View Preferences under the Options menu or tap the Prefs button to set your viewing and filtering preferences for this view:

The first section allows you to select to show or hide appointments, floating events, done items, alarms, and repeat events. In the middle section, you can choose how you want To Do items to appear (if you want them to appear at all), and if so, which ones (completed, uncompleted, dated, and undated). The third section allows you to specify a filer by tapping the check box beside Find. An entry field will appear allowing you to enter some text to filter by. For example, if you only wanted to see events related to Acme Company, you could enter **Acme** into the Find field. The final section allows you to choose to hide or show the day name and time.

Create a New Entry

There are four ways that you can create a new event in your Calendar. You can tap the New button at the bottom of the Day view, select one of the four New event menu items from the menu, tap on a blank space on your Day view for the time slot you want and begin entering details, or if you simply begin typing, a new event will be created as an untimed event.

With the first two techniques, you have to identify in advance what kind of event you are creating, either by selecting a menu item or choosing an option from a pop-up screen that appears when you press the New button. The event types you can choose from are Appointment, Floating Event, To Do, and Journal Entry.

New Appointment

When you choose to create a new appointment, you will be prompted to set a time for the appointment, as shown in Figure 10-5, unless you started your new appointment by tapping an empty time slot in your Day view, in which case you have already selected your time.

FIGURE 10-5   Setting a time for an appointment is the first step you must go through when creating a new Calendar entry.

You can select the Start Time or End Time field and type in the time using the keyboard or select the time using the selection boxes on the right of the screen.

Not every appointment will have a precise time, so you can also choose All Day or No Time using the buttons on the screen. Once you have entered your time, tap the OK button to continue.

You will be returned now to the Day view with an empty appointment line into which you can begin entering your appointment description. Once you have done this, you can tap the Details button to set the other information about the event:

On the details screen for this event, you can change the time and date by tapping on the respective fields. Tapping the Time field returns you to the time entry screen that was shown in Figure 10-5. Tapping the Date field takes you to the Set Date screen, where you can choose a date by tapping on it:

Months can be selected by tapping them, and the year can be changed by using the left and right arrows beside the year. You can immediately select the current date by tapping the Today button.

On the details screen, you can also move one day forward or backward by using the arrows to the immediate right of the Date field. Selecting the Alarm check box will cause an alarm time to be displayed. An alarm will be raised before the time

10

of this event to warn you that the event is near. You can set the alarm by putting in the number of minutes, hours, or days that you want to be alerted in advance. The unit (Minutes, Hours, or Days) is selected from the drop-down list to the right of the numeric field.

The next field, Repeat, allows you to specify if this event is recurring by defining when it repeats. By default, the Repeat field starts at None. Tapping this field opens a new screen, Change Repeat, where you specify how this event repeats:

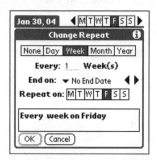

On this screen you select the repeat cycle (daily, weekly, monthly, or annually). For each repeat cycle, there is information that appears below that you must enter in order to complete the necessary information to schedule the recurring event. For example, if you had a meeting scheduled to meet with the Vice President of Sales, Judy Smith, every Friday at 9:30, you would select Week, specify every 1 week to recur, select No End Date for the recurrence, and select the *F* box for Friday in the Repeat On field. Once you have your schedule defined properly, you tap OK to return to the details screen.

Next, you can define the event as private by selecting the Private check box. This means that if you have security assigned to mask or hide private records, this event will show up as a gray box in your schedule.

Then you can change the type of event from an appointment to a floating event using the Appt and Float boxes at the bottom of the details screen. As described in the next section, a floating event can be complete or incomplete. If it is complete, you can select the Done box at the right to create a completed floating event.

To delete an appointment you simply select the Delete button from the details screen.

You can add a free-form note to the event by tapping the Note button and entering any text you would like to attach to the event. If you are meeting Judy, as in our example, in the note you might add a description as to where you are meeting and what you need to bring.

Tapping OK completes your work in the details screen and returns you back to the Day view of your Calendar.

New Floating Event

A floating event is very much like a To Do event. It is an appointment that you must mark as complete. If you don't mark it as complete, at midnight your Treo will move the appointment from the current day to the next day. It will keep doing this until you mark it as complete or delete the event. A floating event shows up with an empty circle, whereas a To Do item has an empty square. Once you complete the event, a check mark will be placed in the circle. If the event has no scheduled time, the circle will be on the left; if there is a time, the circle will appear on the right, as in Figure 10-6.

You can mark a floating event as complete by tapping on the circle with the stylus or by going into the event details by tapping the Details button and changing the Type field to Done.

CAUTION *If you synchronize with Outlook or another third-party desktop PIM tool, you will see that floating events synchronize with ##f as the first characters in the note field. Do not remove these characters, as this is how the Treo identifies these records as floating.*

10

New To Do

If you tap the New button in the Day view and elect to create a To Do from the pop-up window that appears, a new event will be created in your Calendar with an empty

| FIGURE 10-6 | A floating event is an appointment that must be marked as complete, or it will continue to flow to the current day on your Calendar until it is completed or deleted. |

check box and a number beside it. The number indicates the priority of the To Do item. Tapping on the number causes a small pop-up window to appear where you can select a new priority from 1 to 5.

Alternatively, you can tap the Details button, and you will be presented with the details screen for the To Do item, as shown in the following illustration. Here you can change the priority and assign a category for the To Do. For example, two categories I use are Personal and Business. That way, I can make separate views of my personal and work items in the To Do List application, discussed later in this chapter.

The Due Date field allows you to define a specific date by which this item must be done. If you tap this field, you will have options for setting the date to today, tomorrow, one week from now, a specific date, or no date.

Like the other records we have discussed, you can also choose to mark this record as private so that it cannot be viewed by others and you can attach a note to the record.

New Journal Entry

The built-in journal capabilities of your Treo are interesting and fun, if you like to keep a diary of your daily activities. When you select the New button and select Daily Journal from the pop-up list, a new free-for-text-entry field will be created. Your Treo will automatically insert the current time into the field, and you can type your journal entry immediately after it:

Create Templates for Calendar Events

If you have an event that occurs regularly in your Calendar and you would like to be able to create other events that are almost identical to it on a regular basis, you can make a template out of that event. To do this, simply create the first event with the details as you want them to appear next time. Then, from the Record menu, choose Create Template. To use the template, when you tap the New button in the Day view, choose Template from the pop-up window and choose the template from the list of templates, as shown here:

When you select the template, the event will be created in the current date being viewed in the Calendar. From there you can edit the event details. You can create templates for both regular appointments and floating events.

If you select a new daily journal but you already have a journal entry for the current date, your Treo will open the current journal entry and put a new line with the current time on it where you can add to your journal entry.

Journal entries in your Calendar show up with a diamond beside them on the left side and with an event name of Daily Journal:

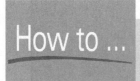 **Retrieve a Record You Deleted**

If you delete an entry in your Calendar and then change your mind, you can recover the record by selecting Undelete from Archive from the Options menu in the Calendar application. If you have deleted multiple items, this command will undelete the most recent item first; then, each successive time you select this menu item, it will delete the one before that until there are no more records in the undelete archive. Over time, this undelete archive can grow and take up memory. You can clear it at any time by selecting Purge Items from the Record menu.

Edit and Delete Entries

To delete an event from your Calendar, you open its details screen and tap the Delete button. When you do this, you will be presented with a pop-up screen that will ask you to confirm the delete and ask if you want to save a backup copy on your PC:

You can also designate whether or not you want to be prompted when you delete by changing the Confirm Each Deletion check box on this screen.

Jump to a Date

If you are at your dentist and are scheduling your six-month checkup, it is easier to jump to the future date than to use the regular navigation to try to get there. You can jump to the date by tapping the Go button on the bottom of the Day view. You can then use the Go to Date screen to select a year, month, and specific date to bring up:

If you are already looking at some date in the future or past, you can return quickly to the current date by tapping the Today button at the bottom of the Go to Date screen.

Send an Entry to Someone Else

Sometimes you want to share an entry in your Calendar with someone else. You might have a family get-together that you want your spouse to have in his or her Calendar. Perhaps you have just made an appointment to see someone, and you want to make sure you both have the details in your calendars.

You can send an appointment to someone by beaming it through the Infrared port of the Treo or by messaging it through e-mail.

NOTE *When you try to send appointments or other data to someone, in addition to the e-mail option you will see an option that says MMS for the Multimedia Messaging Service. This is a bug because you cannot actually send this type of data through the MMS service. If you try, you will see an error message. This isn't your fault, just the imperfect world of software!*

To beam the appointment to someone, you must be in close range so that the Infrared ports on both of your devices can see each other without obstructions. With the record you want to share selected in your Calendar view, select Beam Item from the Record menu.

A pop-up window will appear to show that your device is searching for another device with an Infrared port to receive the transmission. This can include any number of devices, including other Palm devices, Pocket PC devices, and some mobile phones.

Once a device is located, this screen will change to show the event that is being transmitted:

When the other device acknowledges receipt, the two devices disconnect from each other.

If the person you want to schedule the appointment with isn't standing right by you or doesn't have a handheld device, you can send the event through e-mail.

To send the contact by e-mail, you must select Send Item from the Record menu. When you do, you will see a small pop-up asking you which messaging system you want to use. The two standard choices you should see are Mail and MMS. Choose Mail, and you are prompted for whom to send it to using the Mail program; it will also ask if you want to attach a message. The recipient will get an e-mail with a .vcs file attachment. This is a standard format used by many calendaring programs, so it doesn't matter if people you are sending it to are receiving it on another Palm or in Microsoft Outlook. They can click on the attachment and accept the appointment into their calendars.

View Your To Do List

Although the Calendar application and the To Do application are shown as separate views in the database, as you can see from the preceding sections, the Palm OS really treats them both simply as events to be managed. Thus your To Do items will appear in your Calendar based on their due dates. This may not always be the easiest way to work with your To Do list, however, so there is a separate application called To Do List that you can launch from Applications Launcher. The main To Do List screen is shown in Figure 10-7.

By default, this view will show your To Do items sorted by priority and then due date. When you complete an item, you can select the check box with your stylus, and the item will be removed from the list. A page icon on the right side shows you if an item has an attached note. In the top-right of the screen, there is a drop-down

FIGURE 10-7   The To Do List can be a convenient way to work with your list of tasks.

selection box that allows you to choose to view all of your To Do List items or view them by category. As mentioned earlier, I find it beneficial to categorize my To Do List items by work and personal, so I set up these respective categories.

Tapping the Details button allows you to view and edit the settings for the currently selected To Do item, including its priority, category, due date, and if it is private:

From this pop-up, you can also choose to delete a To Do item. The Note button lets you view and edit any attached note on this item.

The Show button at the bottom of the To Do List view allows you to set your preferences for what you would like to view on your list. This button opens the To Do Preferences screen. Here you can define the order in which you want to see your items and what you want to show on the screen, including completed items, due items, record completion date, due dates, priorities, and categories:

10

Look Up a Contact in Your Phone Book

Sometimes when you are entering something in your Calendar you might want to look up a name and phone number in your phone book. For example, if I wanted to schedule a phone call with Dayton Foster, I could make an entry in my Calendar that says "Call Dayton Foster" and then highlight Foster in the title and select Phone Lookup from the Options menu. This would open the Lookup screen, and the Treo would locate any records whose last name matched what I entered, as shown in the illustration. If there are no records that match, the Treo continues searching, dropping the last letter of the name to try to find a match. It continues doing this until it exhausts letters.

From the match list, you can select the phone number that you want to paste back into your Calendar event and tap the Add button to return to the event. Dayton's phone number is now pasted into my event:

Set Your Preferences

First, let's look at how you can set the preferred font sizes for your productivity applications. Under the Options menu, you can select Font to open a pop-up window that lets you change the size and weight of your font from among four choices, as shown in the following illustration. The smaller and lighter the font, the more information you can get on the screen, but if you find yourself squinting, then the larger, darker fonts will be easier to read.

For the Calendar application specifically, you choose Preferences from the Options menu.

On the Preferences screen, shown in the following illustration, you can set the start and end times for your daily and weekly Calendar display. You can also set the default duration for a new event. By default, this is one hour, but if you generally have appointments that only last for 30 minutes, for example, you can change this by tapping the Event Duration field and changing this to 30 minutes.

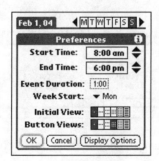

The Week Start field allows you to specify which day of the week you want to begin your weekly views of your Calendar events. The Initial View field lets you pick which of the six views you would like to have open by default when you run the Calendar application. By default this is the Day view, but your own choice might be something different.

The Button Views option allows you to specify which views you want the Calendar application to toggle through each time you press the CALENDAR button. You can select as many as you like by tapping them.

Tapping the Display Options button opens a screen where you can set options, as shown in Figure 10-8.

Secure Your Data

Overall security for your Treo is a topic that is handled in Chapter 13. Here we will look at security specifically as it pertains to the Calendar, To Do List, Memo Pad,

FIGURE 10-8   The Display Options screen allows you to specify what information you want to see in your Calendar views and how it should be presented.

and Contacts applications. When you select Security from the Options menu of any of these applications, you will see a pop-up allowing you to change your current Calendar privacy setting:

The three options you have to choose from are as follows:

■ **Show Records**   This means that anyone looking at your Treo will be able to see any records marked as private in your Calendar, Contacts, Memo Pad, and To Do List. If you are the only one who uses your Treo and if you have a password set for the whole device, then this is acceptable.

■ **Mask Records**   Your private records in these four applications will show as a gray bar with a lock icon beside them. Tapping the record will require the user to be prompted to enter the Treo password in order to view the record.

■ **Hide Records**   Any records you have defined as private will not show up in your screens. If you regularly pass your Treo off to others to use, this may be the setting you want to have.

If you do make a change in this field, and you have a device password set on your Treo, you will be prompted to enter the password to authorize the change:

In general, it can be rather a burden not to be able to see what is in your own schedule. Unless you have reason to be particularly paranoid, we would recommend that you implement some of the device-level security discussed in Chapter 13 but leave the Calendar and To Do List application security settings set to Show Records.

Synchronize Your Calendar with Your Desktop

All of your Calendar, Contacts, and other information are synchronized with either Outlook, Palm Desktop, or another third-party application, depending on how you have set up your Hot Sync settings. This topic is covered in Chapter 3.

Carry Your Contacts with You

In addition to your Calendar and To Do List information, your Treo will store all of your contact details in its phone book. There is no icon on the Applications Launcher to open the phone book Contacts application; instead you must navigate to your phone dialpad screen. From there, you can press down on the navigation control to open the Contacts main screen, as shown in Figure 10-9.

FIGURE 10-9   The Contacts application contains all of your phone numbers and addresses.

My Business Hangs from My Hip

Clint Eastwood carries a six shooter on his hip to take care of business; I carry a Treo 600 to take care of my business. I acquired the Treo 600 in early November of 2003, and it quickly exceeded my expectations. As an onsite computer consultant and trainer, I rarely stay in one place more than two hours. A cell phone connects me to my clients, colleagues, and family, and a PDA provides the organization and instant access to my important data that are invaluable for someone without a static office. Since 1996, I have carried a Palm-powered device and a cell phone. And it has been my dream to have to carry only one device instead of two. With the Treo 600, my dream couldn't get much better.

I started on that path in 2001 with the Sprint PCS Digital Link Springboard attachment for my Handspring Visor Platinum. This combination didn't provide the most elegant solution, but it was more than functional, and I found the nirvana of a converged device was indeed everything I hoped it would be. I used the Visor/Digital Link combo faithfully for well over a year before I bought and used the Treo 300. The more aesthetic look and size, along with even better integration, color screen, and the addition of a keyboard, quickly made me even more productive. But I knew that I wasn't quite satisfied with the overall performance or the form factor.

With the Treo 600, the ARM processor, increased memory, SD card expansion, and always-on network connection has proven to be another production booster. I now use the automatic e-mail delivery feature of SnapperMail (www.snappermail. com) daily and can keep in more timely contact with important clients and guests on my radio show. I use the built-in browser to look up technical information, to post and read messages on bulletin boards, and more.

My two most valuable Treo 600 business apps are Agendus 7.0 (www.iambic. com/agenduspro/palmos/) and HourzPro (www.zoskware.com). The tight and easy integration between my Palm/Outlook address book and the Calendar with Agendus makes scheduling clients and looking up their contact details unbelievably easy and fast. Agendus has made its software even more valuable for Treo users because of the ease with which you can dial a client from any view. You can dial from To Dos, Calendar, and, of course, the Address Book. The phone integration is nothing short of outstanding for me. I use the HourzPro to track my daily time and billing and to generate Excel spreadsheets at the end of each month.

Honorable mention goes to Mapopolis (www.mapopolis.com). Having a map of my entire county in my Treo 600 comes in very handy, and Mapopolis has become even more enhanced with its link to my Agendus address book.

Dataviz's Documents to Go (www.dataviz.com) gets some work on my Treo as well. When I combine this with my Treo foldable keyboard, I can compose articles and do e-mail from literally anywhere. For sheer ease of use and invaluable data in my day-to-day life, TopSecret (www.clicklite.com) keeps all of my important bank and credit card information securely at my side and ready for instant access. . . for my eyes only. For launcher capabilities, I used Launcher X (www.launcherx.com) and its predecessor with my Visor and Treo 300, but I find that the one-button hot keys in the phone pad of my Treo 600 are more convenient and powerful for the apps I use most often.

Of course, all work and no play make Johnny a dull boy. My favorite time killer is Yahdice (http://snipurl.com/yahdice), and like many other Treo and Palm users, I like Bejeweled as well. I also have a chess game, craps, and blackjack loaded. And I have fun posting to our radio show *moblog* (a mobile weblog) with my Treo 600 camera.

My little Treo 600 isn't loaded with tons of software or games or music. I use it to keep myself connected, informed, and productive. This Zen of Palm computing, in my opinion, is unequaled by any other handheld or computer device on the market today. Could the Treo 600 be improved upon for me? I would love for it to be a tad lighter and thinner, have a one- or two-megapixel camera, an internal antenna, and a high-resolution screen, but I'm splitting hairs now. The Treo 600 does its work admirably for me, and I am astounded at how organized and efficient it has kept my business.

—*Rick Castellini, MCP*
www.HelpMeRick.com

10

Navigate Your Contacts

By default, you will be viewing all your contacts when you first open the Contacts screen; but like other records, you can categorize your contacts to make them easier to sort through. Tapping the drop-down selection list in the top-right corner allows you to choose different categories to view or to edit your categories.

For each contact, you will see a phone number. Tapping on a phone number will open a pop-up window with the number displayed, and here you are asked if you would like to dial the number now. If you tap OK, you will be immediately connected to that phone number.

Tapping on the name line will open up the contact details:

If you want to edit the details for this contact, you can tap the Edit button to be switched to an editable screen.

You can navigate through your list of contacts by

- **Using your stylus**   You can scroll using the up and down arrows on the bottom-right of the screen and select any contact or phone number by tapping it.

- **Using the five-way navigation control**   You can scroll up and down using the control. Pressing the CENTER button on the control is the same as tapping a record. Pressing the LEFT or RIGHT buttons will switch from navigating the list to navigating the buttons on the bottom of the screen (in this screen there is only one button, New Contact).

- **Using the keyboard**   You can begin typing the name of the contact on your keyboard. The letters will appear on the top-left of the screen. With each keystroke, your Treo will search to find all the matches in your list and will display them on the screen. Keep typing more letters to narrow down your search. You can type the first name or last name because the Treo will attempt to match either one. Pressing the RETURN button produces the same effect as tapping the selected record.

Create a New Contact

Tapping on the New Contact button will open a blank contact screen in edit mode. You can type all of the details into the appropriate fields. The drop-down arrows beside the different types of contact points (phone numbers, e-mail, and so on) allow you to select different contact points for this specific contact.

Note that there is more information that can fit on one screen, so as you enter data you can scroll the screen down to enter the additional fields that are out of view.

Tapping the Details button allows you to specify a category for this contact, label it as private, and enter a free-text note relating to this contact. It is here that you can also delete a contact you no longer want to store by tapping the Delete button:

If you are creating a contact that is very similar to an existing contact in your list, you can save yourself some effort by duplicating the contact and then editing what is different. You do this by opening the details screen of the original contact and selecting Duplicate Contact from the Record menu. This will create a new contact with the word "copy" appended on the end of the first name. Now you can edit the new contact to change the fields that are different.

Send a Contact to Someone Else

Contact records are the most common information that people like to beam between two handheld devices. If you are sitting down having coffee with someone and your friend says, "I should really give Dayton a call. Do you have his number?" You can pull up Dayton in your contact list and beam Dayton's information to your friend's PDA. You do this by opening Dayton's record and selecting Beam Contact from the Record menu. Then you point your Treo Infrared port at your friend's PDA Infrared port, and the contact will be transferred to your friend's handheld. You can beam information between most handhelds, including Palm OS devices, Pocket PC devices such as the HP iPAQ, and even many mobile phones.

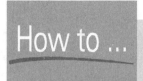 **Beam Your Business Card**

As you meet people at functions, you will notice more and more they exchange business cards by beaming their cards back and forth. To set this up on your Treo, you must first set up a contact in your list with your own personal information in it. This should include all the same information you would put on your business card, including phone numbers, your e-mail address, and so on. Then, while you have your own contact open, choose Select Business Card from the Record menu. You will be prompted to confirm that this contact is the one to be sent whenever you transfer your business card:

After confirming this, a small index card icon appears in the title bar whenever you view this contact detail. Now, from any contact in your list, if you choose Beam Business Card from the Record menu, it will send this record you have just specified.

Message a Contact

Sending an SMS to a contact is as easy as dialing. If you tap on a phone number for a contact that is designated as a mobile number, in addition to the option to dial the number, you will see a button allowing you to send an SMS:

Tapping this button will take you to the SMS application (discussed in detail in Chapter 5), where you can enter a short text message to be sent to the person's mobile phone.

Take Notes on the Go

Have you ever wanted to write down something that you just heard or saw, but after quickly tapping your pockets, you realized you didn't have a pen or paper? Now you don't have to get caught without a way to take a quick note. Your Treo can serve this function for you and can synchronize these notes to your Outlook or other desktop software for easy collection of these thoughts.

Navigate Your Notes

Launching the Memo Pad application from the Applications Launcher will open the main Memo screen, as shown in Figure 10-10.

As in other screens, you can categorize your notes and view only specific categories by selecting a category from the drop-down list at the top right-hand corner of this screen. Tapping any note or navigating to it with the navigation control and pressing the CENTER button will open the note. Every note opens in edit mode, allowing you to make changes to it right on the screen.

Create a New Note

If you start typing on the keyboard or you tap the New button, a new note will be started. The first line you type, in this case "My new note," will end up being the note title in the list in Figure 10-10:

The Details tab lets you pick a category as well as set the record as private. This is also where you delete notes if you no longer want them, or you can delete them with the Delete Memo menu option under the Record menu.

10

FIGURE 10-10   The Memo Pad application is great for taking notes on the fly.

Send a Note to Someone Else

You can send a note to someone else by beaming it if the recipient is within range. Simply select Beam Note from the Record menu to initiate the beaming from the Infrared port. You can also send a note by e-mail. If you do this, the note will be attached to your e-mail as a .txt file. Finally, notes can also be sent via Multimedia Message Service (MMS) if your carrier supports this. MMS is discussed in detail in Chapter 5.

Sort Your Notes

In the main Memo list, you can change the order of your notes by dragging them with the stylus within the list. If you would prefer to have them sorted alphabetically, you can change this under the Preferences menu item under the Options menu. This is the only preference that you can set for Memo Pad.

Convert Weights and Measures

The Treo, like many other PDAs, has a built-in calculator. What really sets the Treo calculator apart, though, is its advanced functions. It can function as a financial, statistical, logical, and advanced math calculator simply by selecting an option from the leftmost drop-down list below the display area, as shown in Figure 10-11.

In the drop-down list you will also find options for converting weight, temperature, length, area, and volume. For example, if you wanted to determine what 20 degrees Fahrenheit is in Celsius, you would enter the 20 using the keypad. Next, select Weight/Tmp from the drop-down list. Now select the units you are converting from,

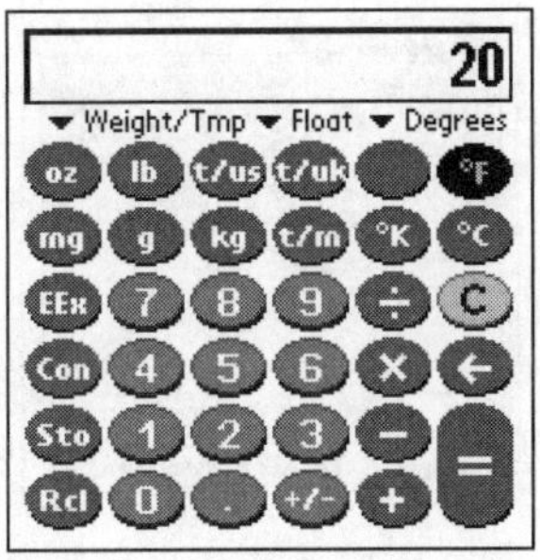

FIGURE 10-11 The Treo calculator provides advanced functions for finance, statistics, weight and measure conversion, and more.

in this case °F. Then select the units you are converting to, °C, and you get your answer: 20 °F = –6.67 °C.

TIP *If you have large fingers and would rather just have a simple calculator where you can tap on the screen with your fingers (remember to use a screen protector, as discussed in this chapter!), you can toggle between the advanced calculator and a simplified calculator using the Options menu.*

Organize Your Shopping Trips

Depending on where you bought your Treo, it may have come equipped with versions of productivity software from SplashData (www.splashdata.com). One of these applications is SplashShopper. This is a very useful application. I am sure everyone reading this has made a trip to the grocery store and then been unable to find the shopping list. Going from memory you do your best, but you always forget items you meant to pick up. Also, often you will be somewhere and think, "I need to remember to buy light bulbs," but since your shopping list isn't with you, you forget. With SplashShopper, you have your shopping list conveniently right on your mobile phone!

SplashShopper can track your shopping lists for a wide variety of goods, including groceries, books, clothes, take-out food, gifts, movies, music, wine, and any other category you might choose to create. For each category, you have a screen with two tabs, All and Need, as shown in Figure 10-12.

On the Need tab, you have what you currently are planning to purchase. As you cruise the aisles in the grocery store, you can check off each item as you place it in your cart. The All tab contains the list of all the foods that you normally buy,

SplashShopper lets you track your shopping lists for many different
categories of goods, from groceries to books.

so you can easily move them from the All tab to the Need tab when you need to.
Selecting an individual product in the list opens the details screen for that product:

You can see and edit details, such as which store to buy the product from, the
product description, which aisle it is in (if you have this level of information, you
won't be running back and forth through the store), and more. You can also put in
the price of the object. If everything on your list has a price defined, SplashShopper
will estimate the cost of your shopping excursion so you won't have sticker shock
when the clerk rings up your total.

Tapping the Home button on the bottom of the shopping list screen switches you
to the main SplashShopper screen, where you can switch among the different lists
and see how many of each item you have to purchase:

The piece of the SplashData family that you don't get with your Treo 600 is the companion desktop software. You can upgrade to this software at a 50 percent discount from the regular price at the SplashData web site at www.splashdata.com/treo. The desktop version of SplashShopper doesn't add a tremendous amount of functionality, but what it does do is allow you to enter all of your data with a nice large screen and a full keyboard, which alone is worth the nominal cost. The ability to enter all of your data on your PC and HotSync it over to your Treo makes the software much easier to use.

Store Your Credit Card, Passport, and Other Important Numbers

There are so many credit cards, ID cards, and other pieces of important information that we all receive that it becomes completely impractical to carry all of this information with us or memorize it. Yet it seems that just when we need a certain number or card, we don't have it handy. SplashID, shown in Figure 10-13, is a secure way to keep all of your personal information with you on your Treo. Your information is protected with a personal password and Blowfish encryption.

Like other software from SplashData, there is a desktop console you can purchase as an upgrade. This is handy for keeping a backup of your data and also for the ease of the initial data entry.

SplashID is a very simple program to begin to use and one that you will find extremely useful. It has thinned my wallet considerably!

FIGURE 10-13   SplashID lets you securely carry your personal information, such as passwords, credit card numbers, frequent flyer numbers, and more.

Stay on Time with CityTime

If you travel, or if your work or hobbies cause you to need to interact with people in multiple time zones, a very useful application that comes standard on the Treo 600 is CityTime:

With CityTime, you can see what time it is where you are and what time this translates to for other places in the world. You can default the display to show times for four other locations in the world. The world map updates to show you what parts of the world are in light and in darkness.

Another interesting feature is that you can see what time the sun will rise and set in your home location by selecting Sun Rise/Set from the Utilities menu:

Wrap It Up

Whether you are managing your time, To Do list, personal information, or something else, your Treo is your ideal personal assistant! In addition to the great personal productivity tools presented in this chapter, you can learn about others in Chapter 16. You may also want to refer to the references in Appendix B for where you can go to learn more about enhancing personal productivity with Treo.

Chapter 11

Work with Documents, Spreadsheets, and Slide Shows

How to...

- View and edit Microsoft Word documents

- Work with Excel spreadsheets

- Give PowerPoint presentations right from your Treo

- Read Adobe Acrobat files

- Open e-mail attachments

- Move files between your PC and your Treo

A truly powerful use of the Treo is to be a mobile office and PC replacement. You can read and edit Microsoft Office documents, spreadsheets, and presentations with the right software. When you receive e-mail with attachments on your Treo, you can open them right on your smartphone.

Your Treo comes with software onboard for reading Word and Excel files, but you will need to load additional software to get the full functionality of an office suite.

Work with Documents, Spreadsheets, and Presentations

With a converged smartphone like the Treo 600, it will be natural for you to receive e-mail from people with attachments you would like to read. You also may find that you want to have certain documents with you when you travel, and that are accessible on your device whenever you need them.

In order to do this, you can take advantage of software that comes preinstalled on your Treo. But if you want to do more than view files, you'll need to upgrade to a third-party software package like those discussed in this section. This chapter will focus on the Documents To Go package, but solid offerings from other vendors will be mentioned as well, a full list of which can be found in Chapter 16.

Start Documents To Go

Your Treo 600 comes equipped with a product called Documents To Go from DataViz (www.dataviz.com) that allows you to view Microsoft Word and Excel files on your Treo. It will be installed from the companion CD the first time you sync your Treo. This product is limited in that it doesn't allow you to actually edit or compose documents. However, you can upgrade to the Professional or Premium version of Documents To Go at their web site link, www.dataviz.com/t600. The enhanced versions allow you to not only view but also edit and create documents and spreadsheets. In addition, you can view and edit PowerPoint slide shows.

When you launch Documents To Go, it will open to the document that you were last working on, or if it is your first time running the program, you will see a list of documents currently on your Treo, as shown in Figure 11-1.

The list will show all the documents on your device, including Word files, PowerPoint presentations, image files, and spreadsheets. The icon on the left side will allow you to distinguish between the different types of files. If you tap on the icon with your stylus, a pop-up menu will appear that lets you choose from the following options:

- ■ **Details** Lets you view and edit information on the file, including the name, where it's located, the category, format, size, and time it was last modified.

- ■ **Delete** Allows you to remove the document from your Treo. You will need to either confirm or cancel the action before the file is permanently deleted.

- ■ **Beam** Transfers the file to another computer, smartphone, or handheld through the Infrared port.

- ■ **Send** Allows you to e-mail the file to another person using your mail program.

- ■ **Move to Card** Allows you to move the file from the built-in memory of your Treo to an external Secure Digital card or MultiMediaCard.

11

FIGURE 11-1   The documents that you can work on will be shown in the list view that appears when you open Documents To Go.

The name and size of the file will be shown, and on the right side of the screen you'll see a column with either a HotSync symbol or a dash. If there is a HotSync symbol, this indicates that the file will be synchronized with the file on your desktop using Documents To Go DocSync technology. This is a great feature that incorporates any changes you make on the Treo back into the original file on your PC. If you do not want your changes synced back to your PC file, tap on the HotSync icon to make it switch to a dash. The dash indicates that the file will not be synced.

The final column on the right will have an icon of a storage card if the file is located on the card. If the file is in the memory of your smartphone, the column will be blank.

You can filter the list to only show documents of a certain category using the category drop-down in the top right-hand corner of the screen. You can choose to filter for only a certain type of document using the Show drop-down at the bottom of the screen. Your filter options are to show all supported formats or any single format.

To open a document for reading or editing, simply tap the filename.

Compose Documents with Word To Go

When you move a file from your desktop to your Treo through the Documents To Go conduit, it will, by default, convert it to a lighter format called Word To Go—however, you *can* select the format you would like to work with, as explained later in this chapter. The primary advantage of the Word To Go format is that it takes less memory on your handheld to store. Just the same, you may want to keep documents in your native format if you plan to send them direct from your Treo using e-mail or beaming. Both formats show up in the document list with an icon depicting a page of paper with a small blue *w* on it. Tapping the icon will open the document in the Word To Go application, as shown in Figure 11-2.

FIGURE 11-2   Word To Go is the document-editing software where Microsoft Word files can be viewed and edited.

How to ...   Count the Words in Your Document

If you need to know how many words are in your document, this is easily accomplished using the Word Count menu option under the File menu. Before you choose the menu item, you should either select the text you want to get the word count for, or if you want the count for the whole document, make sure that no text is selected.

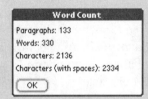

Word Count

Paragraphs: 133
Words: 330
Characters: 2136
Characters (with spaces): 2334

OK

The resulting pop-up window will tell you how many words, characters, and paragraphs are in your document.

The document will be formatted to make it as readable as possible on the small screen of your Treo, but you will notice that much of the desktop formatting has been removed or modified out of necessity.

Edit Your Document

When you have opened a document, you can edit the content using your stylus and keyboard. Unfortunately, the Word To Go application has only limited ability to take advantage of five-way navigation control on the Treo. You can highlight the text area and press the CENTER button. Then you can use the control to scroll up or down in the document, but you cannot control the cursor. This means you will need to use the stylus to move the cursor around the document and to do any fine scrolling.

If you want to make changes to a block of text such as deleting it, copying it, or changing its font, you must first select it. You select a block of text using the stylus. Place the stylus at the start of the text block, and then drag the stylus to the end position. This will cause the text to be highlighted in yellow. If you type anything, the highlighted text block will be deleted and the new text that you type will replace it.

11

You can also cut, copy, and paste text like you do on your desktop, using the appropriate options under the Edit menu. If you happen to make a mistake and want to return to the state you were in before, there are also Undo and Redo menu options under the Edit menu.

You can change the format of the selected text in two ways. First, you can use the formatting buttons on the top-right corner of the screen. The first three will toggle the text into (or out of) bold, italic, and underline, respectively. If the text is currently formatted with any of these properties, the buttons will appear with a blue background. If the text does not have that property, the button background will be white.

The next three buttons are used to change the justification of the text (to left, center, right, or full justified), toggle normal bullets, or toggle numbered bullets.

The second way to change the formatting of the selected text is to use the buttons at the bottom of the screen or the menu items under the Format menu to change the font, paragraph formatting, or bullet and numbering style.

The button with the capital *A* character will open the Font screen where you can set the properties for the font of the selected text.

In the Font drop-down list on this screen, you can choose from Arial, Courier, Courier New, Helvetica, Symbol, Times, and Times New Roman fonts. The Size selection will let you pick appropriate font sizes from 8 up to 72 points. The Underline option will let you select from none, single, double, dotted, wavy, and word only underlining of the selected text. You can also turn on bold, italic, strikethrough, superscript, subscript, and all capitals using the check boxes. Tapping the Color box will let you select the color for the text from a pop-up color tablet that fills your entire screen. The Highlight box performs a similar function, allowing you to choose a color for the highlighting of the selected text. When you are finished setting the properties for the font, you can select OK or Cancel to close the Font screen and return to the document editing.

The next button at the bottom of the screen shows the paragraph symbol plus some lines on a page. This button will open the Paragraph formatting screen.

On this screen, you can select the alignment (or justification) of the text. You can also set indenting (both left and right) as well as any "special" or "advanced" indenting (different settings for the first line or a hanging indent). Finally, on this screen you can set your line spacing options.

If you select Bullets & Numbering from the Format menu, you will be able to adjust the characteristics of how the current paragraph or selected text is numbered.

This works very much the same as it does in the desktop Microsoft Word software. You will select whether the text is to be bulleted or numbered. There are only two options under Bullets, On and Off. However, under Numbers, you have several options as to the style of the numbering, which you can select on the screen using

 **Spell Check Your Document**

You might think that you have to give up spell checking on a smaller platform like the Treo. Not so! Word To Go contains its own mini–spell checking utility to help you out.

To launch the spell checker you select the Check Spelling menu item under the File menu. It will search any text you have selected, and then prompt you to see if you want to search the rest of the document.

If it finds a word it doesn't know, it will open up a section at the bottom of the screen with the unknown word highlighted. You can correct it right on the line, or you can ask the spell checker to make recommendations. This is different from desktop word processors which will automatically make recommendations. On the Treo, searching the dictionary can be a little slow, so it won't search for recommendations until you ask it to. Recommendations will appear in the box below and can be selected with your stylus.

After you have either made changes (or chosen not to), you can use the buttons at the bottom to change this word once, or throughout the entire document. You can also choose to add the word to your standard dictionary. You can also ignore this instance of the word or all instances of this word in the document.

Tapping the left arrow on the bottom-left of the screen will exit the spell checker and return you to editing the document.

the appropriate button. You can also choose if you want to restart the numbering, or continue the numbering from the numbered paragraphs previous to the current text.

Although there may have been images in your document when it was put onto your Treo, you can't use Word To Go to insert images into the document. You can, however, insert a page break or table from the Insert menu:

- ■ **Page Break**   Inserts a manual page break into the document.

- ■ **Insert Table**   Opens a pop-up window allowing you to define the number of columns and rows for the table that you want to insert into the current document.

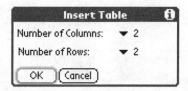

The table will be inserted where the cursor is in the document. You can then enter the information into the table. When you have finished entering information into the table, you can tap the left arrow at the bottom of the screen to return to editing the document. From that point on, you will see the words "Edit Table" above any tables in the document. Tapping the Edit Table label will open up the table so you can change the information in it.

11

- ■ **Insert Bookmark**   Allows you to define a name for the current position of the cursor. Then at any future point if you tap the Bookmark icon (on the bottom-right of the screen), you will see a list of defined bookmarks. Selecting a specific bookmark will scroll you immediately to that point in the document. This can be very handy for moving around quickly within large documents.

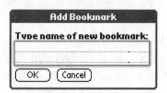

Bookmarks can also be added right from the Bookmark icon's pop-up list. If you want to rename or remove a bookmark you have defined, you can choose Edit Bookmarks from the pop-up list.

■ **Insert Hyperlink**   Allows you to insert a *hyperlink,* which is a line of text that appears underlined, and when the reader clicks or taps it, it links the user to another file or resource. These resources are usually on the Internet.

For example, you could define a link for the name of a company you are referencing in your document. You could have the text show "Sonic Mobility," and create a link that says www.sonicmobility.com. The text Sonic Mobility will show up in the document underlined in blue (by default). When the user taps on "Sonic Mobility" or selects it with the navigation control, it will open up the web browser with the home page of Sonic Mobility showing.

Start a New Document

To begin creating a new Word To Go document, you must return to the Documents To Go list by closing the current document you are in. This is accomplished by tapping the Done button in the lower-left corner. If you have unsaved changes, you will be prompted to save the document as discussed in the next section.

In the document list screen, you can select the New Selection button on the bottom-left. Notice that this button has an arrow on it. This is because the button will open a pop-up window where you must define what kind of new document you are going to create.

Under the Format drop-down list, you will choose either a Word To Go, Sheet To Go, Slideshow To Go, or native Microsoft Word or Excel file format. You can also define a category for this document, but this isn't a required field. The Location field will let you choose between storing the document in the memory of your Treo, and saving it onto an external storage card. Finally, you will enter a name for your document. Tapping the OK button will take you to the appropriate Documents To Go application to begin editing your new document.

Save Your Document

When you are working in a document, you can save that document either from the menu options (Save or Save As) or by tapping the Done button on the bottom-left of the screen. If the document is a new document, you will see three options in a pop-up window after pressing the Done button:

The three options are Save Document, Return To Document, or Delete Document. If the document is an existing document, you will have four options: Save Changes, Save As (a new file), Don't Save Changes, or Return To Document:

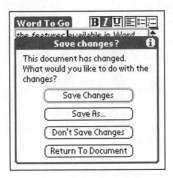

Change Preferences

You can tweak the behavior of Word To Go so that it better fits the way you work. This is accomplished by opening the Preferences screen from the File menu.

There are five check boxes on the top of the screen that you can toggle on and off. These check boxes include the following:

- **Include Word To Go in Global Find** This option will search any documents on your Treo for text entered using the find/search function on the Treo. It allows you to search for text in documents, but does make the find process take slightly longer.

- **Enable Font Viewing** Allows the text in the document to be displayed in the Word To Go font that you have specified for it. If unchecked, then all text will be displayed in the standard system fonts.

- **Hide "Edit Table" Controls** This causes the Edit Table box above any embedded tables to not be displayed. It also means that you cannot edit the tables unless you uncheck this box.

- **Enable Active Text Field** Allows text entry utilities like word completers, spell checkers, and others to work. For example, the KeyCaps600 utility mentioned earlier is enabled by checking this box.

- **Omit Graphics in Native Files** Will not display graphics in any native Word or Excel files.

On the bottom of the screen you can select your preferred save mode. The default option is Confirm Changes. In this mode, you will be presented with the options discussed in the "Save Your Document" section earlier. In the AutoSave Changes mode, you will not see these options. Instead, any changes to the document will be automatically saved when you tap the Done button, similar to the way the Memo Pad application functions.

Work the Numbers with Sheet To Go

Being able to open and work with spreadsheets on your Treo is extremely valuable. Whether you are scoring your golf handicap while on the course, converting exchange rates, tracking expenses while traveling, or marking off an inspection checklist, spreadsheets are something that virtually all of us can put to use.

Spreadsheets and workbooks show up in the Documents To Go list with an icon of a sheet that has a small green *X*. You can tap the document, or select it with the navigation control (highlight the list, press the CENTER button, scroll to select your spreadsheet, and then press the CENTER button again) to open the spreadsheet.

Navigate a Workbook

Once you've opened the worksheet, you will see the first page of the workbook displayed, as shown in Figure 11-3.

If your workbook has multiple sheets, each sheet will be shown as a drop-down option in the top-right corner. In Figure 11-3, the sheet that is currently being viewed is titled Golf Stats. You can move between sheets by selecting the sheet you want from this drop-down.

You can navigate around the current sheet by tapping the arrows at the bottom center of the screen. You can use the navigation control to move one screen in any direction (one screen being the number of columns currently displayed).

11

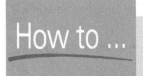 **Use the Global Find Feature**

One invaluable feature of the Treo is the ability to search all applications, contacts, and more for a particular block of text. To launch this feature, press the OPTION button on your keyboard plus the SHIFT/FIND button (which has a small magnifying glass icon on it to symbolize the Find function). This will open the Find pop-up window.

Enter the text you are searching for and tap the OK button. Your Treo will now search through everything in its memory looking for the text you entered. If it finds it, the display will show you the application the information was found in. You can tap on the line or select it with the navigation control to be taken to the information. It will only show one page of results at a time. Once the first page is full, it will wait for you to select one of the matches, or you can tap Find More to search for more matches.

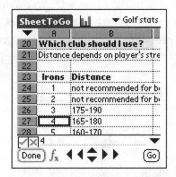

FIGURE 11-3   Sheet To Go lets you work with your Excel spreadsheets right on your Treo.

The Go button in the bottom right-hand corner will allow you to jump to a specific location in your sheet. Tapping this button opens the Go pop-up window.

You can enter a specific cell address in the Go To Cell field, or you can jump to any cell that has a bookmark or comment by selecting it from the list and tapping Go.

Editing

To edit the contents of a cell, you must first select it. This is best accomplished with the stylus by tapping it or using the navigation arrows on the bottom of the screen to move to the right cell. The selected cell shows up with a dark outline around it. The contents of the currently selected cell are shown on the dotted line immediately below the cell display area. Tapping the line will allow you to use the keyboard to enter text and numbers on the line. If you need more space to enter your value for the cell, you can tap the down arrow to the right of the entry line. This will open a pop-up window that expands the entry line to a full screen.

You can also enter formulas in the same way you would in Microsoft Excel on your desktop. If you haven't memorized all the formulas that you can use, there is a convenient way you can enter them. If you tap the f_x icon on the bottom-left (right beside the Done button), the navigation arrows will be replaced by a formula bar:

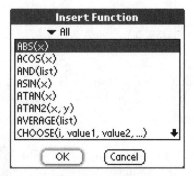

The button bar contains the symbols for addition, subtraction, multiplication, and division. There are also parenthesis buttons for creating order of operations within mathematical equations. The button on the far right is for creating a Sum function, likely the most commonly used function in spreadsheets. The button to the left of the Sum button is the holy grail of function buttons. It opens up a list of all of the functions you can use in your formula. The list will also show you how the arguments need to be entered into the formula.

By default, all formulas are shown; however, you can select a subgroup of functions from the drop-down list at the top of the screen. After selecting the function that you want, tap the OK button to paste the function back into the cell value line.

How to ...   Set a Column Width

By default, columns are created with a standard width. If the standard isn't appropriate for what you are entering, you can use the stylus to change the width of the column. Tap and hold the stylus on the line on the right of the column whose side you want to adjust in the column header. The normal dotted line in the sheet will be replaced by a solid vertical bar. Now drag your stylus left or right to make the column the size you would like.

You can use the two buttons to the immediate left of the entry line to accept your entry (the green arrow icon) or cancel (the red *X* icon).

An important part of editing spreadsheets is the ability to insert new rows, columns, and sheets. You can do all of this from the Insert menu by selecting the type of object you want to insert. If you select Row or Column, you will be prompted to enter the number of rows or columns you would like to insert.

If you select Sheet, you'll need to specify where you want to insert the new sheet. You can place the new sheet at the end of your workbook, before the current sheet, or after the current sheet.

Under the Edit menu, you'll find standard options for cut, copy, and paste, as well as menu items for clearing a cell, or deleting cells, rows, columns, or sheets.

11

Another key editing feature is the ability to change the formatting of your cell or sheet. This is done through the Format menu. The Cell menu item will open a pop-up screen where you can change the alignment of the cell, as well as change the font to bold or normal. The Locked check box allows you to set the cell so that someone looking at the workbook is unable to edit that cell. Finally, you can set the color for both the cell and the text in the cell using the two color buttons. The currently selected colors are shown to the right of the button.

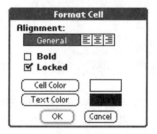

You can also control the formatting of numbers in a cell or range of cells. To change the formatting, select the cell, or cells, that you want to modify. Then select Number from the Format menu. The current format for the cell will show up in the Format pop-up screen that appears. If the format you select has additional options you can define, they will appear in the pop-up screen. For example, for some formats you can choose how many decimal places of precision you would like, and how you want the number to appear if it is negative. By default, negative numbers will be shown with a minus (–) sign in front of them, but you can change this to show negative numbers with parentheses such as "(1.25)," which is a standard for financial information. You can also choose to have negative numbers show up in red.

The default format is General; however, you can change the format to

- **Fixed**   With this option you can define how many decimal places you want to display, how you want negative numbers to be shown, and if you want a separator for numbers greater than 1,000.

- **Scientific**   Displays the number in a standard scientific format with a specified number of digits of precision. For example, a value of 125.35 in scientific notation to four digits of precision would show as 1.2535e+02. This format is normally used for displaying very large or very small numbers.

- **Currency**   This is for handling financial numbers. In addition to the standard formatting, you can also select the currency type, including the U.S. Dollar, Canadian Dollar, Euro, Japanese Yen, British Pound, and many others—from the Australian Dollar to the Thai Bhat. Selecting a currency changes the symbol that appears next to the number to the correct symbol for the currency.

- **Percent**   Shows decimal numbers as a percentage with the percent sign (%) beside it. For example, 0.12 would show up as "12%".

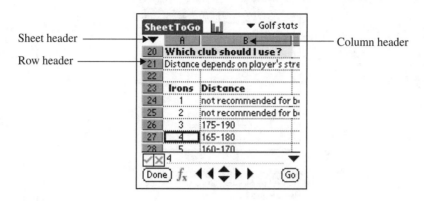

FIGURE 11-4 Tapping on the row, column, or sheet headers will open a menu for actions you can take that will affect the relevant item you have selected.

- **Text** Shows the number as a text label instead of a general number.

- **Date** Displays the number as a date field. You can further define the format of how you would like the date to appear.

- **Time** Displays the number as a time value. You can also define the format that you like your time to be displayed in.

Column, Row, and Sheet Menus

When you want to take an action that is to affect an entire row, column, or the whole worksheet, you can take advantage of the row, column, and sheet menus. These menus appear when you tap either a row number, column letter, or the small arrow that appears on the top-left corner where the row number and column letters meet, as shown in Figure 11-4.

The Column Header pop-up menu has eight options you can select from, as shown here:

- **Freeze (or Unfreeze)**   Allows you to fix the current column plus all columns to the left of it in place. When you scroll the spreadsheet, the frozen columns will stay displayed. This is very handy when the left column of your spreadsheet contains labels that you want to be able to see as you scroll to the right. If you already have this column frozen, then the menu will show an Unfreeze option instead of Freeze. Selecting Unfreeze will remove the current column freeze.

- **Fit**   Causes the column width to resize to fit the widest text in the column.

- **Home**   Returns you immediately to column A, regardless of what column you are currently viewing.

- **Select**   Causes the entire column to be selected. This is so you can perform an operation on the entire column, such as cut, copy, or format.

- **Insert**   Allows you to insert columns before the column whose header you tapped. You will see a pop-up screen prompting you for how many columns you want to insert.

- **Delete**   Allows you to select the current column (or more). A pop-up screen will allow you to confirm that you want to delete the column and will also allow you to delete multiple columns if you choose.

- **Hide**   Hide allows you to make the column invisible. Once a column has been hidden, it can be made visible with the Unhide menu item that appears in the column to the immediate right of the hidden column. Selecting this will make the hidden column visible. Alternatively, the sheet header pop-up menu contains an Unhide All option which will make all hidden columns and rows visible.

- **Sort**   Allows you to re-sort all the selected columns by specific criteria. Note that you must select the columns in advance of pressing the Sort button. Any data outside the selected area will not be shuffled with the sort.

11

The Row Header pop-up menu contains a subset of the items from the Column Header pop-up menu. The two excluded functions are Fit and Sort, which aren't relevant to rows. The difference, of course, is that when you select any of the actions on the row header pop-up menu, it will affect the row, not the column. For example, selecting Home returns you to Row 1 but doesn't change your column.

The Sheet menu contains some different options that impact the current worksheet you are working with:

■ **Find**   Allows you to enter text that you want to find in the current workbook or sheet. You can limit the search to only the current sheet if desired.

- ■ **Find Next**   Allows you to search to the next instance of the text you entered in the Find pop-up screen.

- ■ **Home**   Returns you immediately to column A and row 1 of the current worksheet.

- ■ **Unhide All**   Makes all hidden rows and sheets visible.

- ■ **Reset View**   Returns all column widths to their default setting. This isn't something you should do often, so if you hit this by accident, remember that there is an Undo menu item in the Edit menu. If you select Undo, you can return all your column widths to their previous settings.

- ■ **Format Sheet**   Allows you to change the name of the current sheet and also to protect the sheet. Protected sheets can be viewed but not changed.

Create a Chart

11

A picture can be worth a thousand words, particularly when you are looking for a summary of information such as financial results, polls, or other numerical data where comparing multiple fields is important.

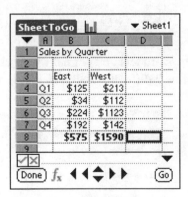

You can create charts on the fly in Sheet To Go using the Chart button, which is the small bar chart icon at the top center of the screen. Before tapping this button, select the data in your spreadsheet that you want to make a graph out of.

After tapping the Chart button you will be taken to the Chart Wizard, which is a series of screens that will define the properties of your chart.

First, you must define the type of chart you want to create. There are many varieties to choose from, including pie charts, columns, stacked columns, lines, bar charts, and more. The data range field is the set of cells that you want to include in the chart. If you selected a range before tapping the chart icon, this will already be populated for you. Tap the Next button to move to the next screen, or the Finish button at any time to jump right to viewing the chart.

The next screen in the wizard lets you define if your chart series is in rows or columns. You can also define a different label for each series in the chart.

The final screen lets you define titles for the chart and the chart axis. You can also choose not to display the axis titles if you prefer.

The Finish button will cause your finished graph to be displayed. You can tap the Details button to return to the wizard and change information. The Legend button will open up a legend showing you each of the graph series labels. You can also tap any data point on the graph to see its precise value and details.

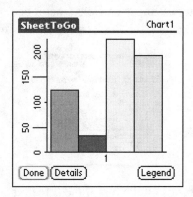

Tapping the Done button will prompt you to either save the chart, or not. If you decide to save it, the chart will be saved as a new sheet in your workbook. Afterward, you can open it using the sheet selection drop-down in the top-right corner of the Sheet To Go main view.

Start a New Spreadsheet

To begin creating a new Sheet To Go workbook, you must return to the Documents To Go list by closing the current document you are in. This is accomplished by tapping the Done button in the lower-left corner. If you have unsaved changes, you will be prompted to save the document as discussed in the next section.

In the document list screen, you can choose the New selection button at the bottom left. You'll notice that this button has a drop-down arrow in it. This is because the button will open a pop-up window where you must define what kind of new document you are going to create.

For a new spreadsheet, you will select either Sheet To Go or Excel as the document type.

Save Your Spreadsheet

As with documents, when you're working in a spreadsheet, you can save that document either from the menu options (Save or Save As) or by tapping the Done button on the bottom-left of the screen. If the spreadsheet is a new document, you will see three options in a pop-up window after pressing the Done button.

11

The three options that appear are save the document, return to the document, or delete the document. If the spreadsheet is an existing document, you will have four options: Save the Document, Save as a New Filename, Don't Save Changes, and Return to Document.

Change Your Preferences

You can tweak the behavior of Sheet To Go so that it better fits the way you work. This is accomplished by opening the Preferences screen from the File menu.

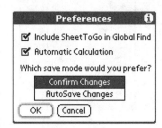

There are two check boxes on the top of the screen that you can toggle on and off. These check boxes include the following:

■ **Include Sheet To Go in Global Find**   This option will search every Sheet To Go file on your Treo for text entered using the find/search function on the Treo. This allows you to search for text in spreadsheets, but does make the find process take slightly longer.

■ **Automatic Calculation**   This option causes Sheet To Go to recalculate any formulas in your workbook dynamically as you are working. If you are working with a spreadsheet that makes extensive use of formulas, this option could make it very difficult to actually get any work done since the slow recalculations are performed with every value you enter. If you turn this option off, you can manually recalculate the fields in the workbook using the Recalculate menu item under the File menu.

On the bottom of the screen, you can select your preferred save mode. The default option is Confirm Changes. In this mode, you will be presented with the options discussed in the Save Your Spreadsheet section earlier. In the AutoSave Changes mode, you will not see these options. Instead, any changes to the spreadsheet will be automatically saved when you tap the Done button.

Present Like a Pro with Slideshow To Go

A lot of business people give presentations while on the road, and this has generally required hauling around a bulky laptop with you when you travel. Now you can carry, edit, and present your PowerPoint slide shows right on your Treo! In order to accomplish this, you will have to use a combination of third-party software and hardware. You can load, edit, and view PowerPoint files right on your handheld with just software, but to connect to a projector or monitor, additional hardware is needed.

Presenter To Go is the third component of the Documents To Go suite. It is only included in the higher-end versions. With it, you can view, edit, and compose slide shows right on your Treo.

A Presenter To Go file is opened right from the main Documents To Go screen. It appears with an icon next to it that looks like a page with a red box on it.

Navigate a Presentation

Once you've opened the presentation, what you will see next depends on how you last exited the application. By default, the Slideshow view will be used and you will see one of the pages of the slide show displayed, as shown in Figure 11-5.

If you were in Outline view or Notes view when you exited Slideshow To Go last, it will open back up in that mode. The three buttons on the top-right will let you switch between Outline, Slideshow, and Notes view, respectively. The drop-down arrow in the top-right corner will let you jump to any slide in your slide show. The up and down arrows in the bottom-right corner will let you page through your slides one at a time. In Slideshow view, there is a button on the bottom-left with a plus (+) sign on it. This button will zoom in on the slide to make it easier to read any small

11

FIGURE 11-5   Slideshow To Go lets you view and edit PowerPoint slide shows on your Treo.

details. While zoomed in, this button changes to a minus (–) sign, which will return you to a normal view when tapped.

To begin displaying a slide show, choose the View Show menu item from the Slide Show menu. This will let you move through the slides in a presentation mode and advance the slides by tapping the slide with your stylus. You can time your presentation by tapping the Start Timer button on the bottom-right. This lets you rehearse your slide show and see how long you are spending on each slide. While timing, a stopwatch with appropriate controls will appear at the bottom of the screen.

Editing

To edit the contents of a slide show, you must be in Outline mode, as shown in Figure 11-6. In Outline mode, you can put the cursor right into the text with the stylus and add, modify, and delete any of the text information on the slide. You cannot change

FIGURE 11-6   All slide show editing is done in Outline mode, where you will find the most functionality.

any graphical information such as background, colors, or images on the slides. To do these advanced functions, you will need to sync the slide show to your desktop and modify it with the full version of PowerPoint.

The arrows on the bottom next to the Done button only appear when you are working on bullets in the slide. With these arrows, you can promote or demote any bullet.

From the Edit menu, you can perform standard cut, copy, and paste functions with the text. You can also delete the slide from this menu, or launch the slide sorter where you can reorder your slides by dragging them with the stylus.

To create new bullets for your slide, select New Bullet Item from the Insert menu. On the Insert menu, you can also insert a new slide into your show or create a duplicate of the current slide.

The Notes view is specifically for viewing the written notes associated with a slide in the slide show.

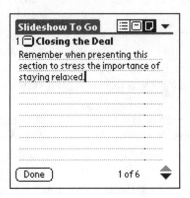

11

Start a New Slide Show

To begin creating a new Slideshow To Go presentation, you must return to the Documents To Go list by closing the current document you are in. This is accomplished by tapping the Done button in the lower-left corner. If you have unsaved changes, you will be prompted to save the document, as discussed in the next section.

In the document list screen, you can select the New Selection button on the bottom-left. You will notice that this button has a drop-down arrow in it. This is because the button will open a pop-up window where you must define what kind of new document you are going to create.

For a new slide show, you will select Slideshow To Go. When you start from scratch on a new slide show right on the Treo, it will be the very basic black text on a white background with very little formatting. If you want to create slide shows with more pizzazz on your Treo, try loading a few base template shows with some initial formatting on your Treo, and then doing Save As to save the file with a new name.

Save Your Slide Show

As with documents, when you are working in a slide show, you can save it either from the menu options (Save or Save As) or by tapping the Done button on the bottom-left of the screen. If you are working in a new slide show, you will see three options in a pop-up window after pressing the Done button.

The three options are save the document, return to the document, or delete the document. If the slide show is an existing document, you will have four options: Save Document, Save as a New File Name, Don't Save Changes, or Return To Document.

Change Your Preferences

You can tweak the behavior of Presenter To Go only slightly. To make changes, open the Preferences screen from the File menu.

There is only one check box on the top of the screen that you can toggle on and off. This check box is Include Slideshow To Go in Global Find. This option will search any Slideshow To Go files on your Treo for text entered using the find/search function on the Treo. This allows you to search for text in slide shows, but does make the find process take slightly longer.

On the bottom of the screen, you can select your preferred save mode. The default option is Confirm Changes. In this mode, you will be presented with the options discussed in the "Save Your Slideshow" section earlier. In the AutoSave Changes mode, you will not see these options. Instead, any changes to the slide show will be automatically saved when you tap the Done button.

Hook Up Your Treo to a Projector or Monitor

To use your Treo to drive presentations, you will need add-on hardware. Two vendors that produce this hardware are iGo, with its Pitch Solo and Pitch Duo products, and Margi with its Presenter To Go.

iGo Pitch Solo

The Pitch Solo from iGo (www.iGo.com) is an incredible device and an absolute must-have for the business traveler who has to frequently give presentations while traveling. It is a stand-alone piece of hardware, shown in Figure 11-7, which connects directly to the monitor or projector being used for the presentation.

The Pitch device connects directly to the monitor. Your Treo sync cable then plugs into both the Pitch device and the sync port of your Treo. Then, from the Treo, you run the supplied iPresent software to select a preloaded PowerPoint presentation. One of the great features of the Pitch product is that it runs through the sync cable (or Bluetooth, if you have the Pitch Duo product) instead of having to plug into the SD slot. This means that your SD slot is free for storing your presentations. As part of my work, I give many graphic-intensive PowerPoint presentations. To store them all in the internal memory of the Palm would be impossible, so the ability to load the presentations onto an SD card is absolutely critical.

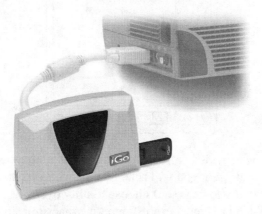

11

FIGURE 11-7   The iGo Pitch Solo allows you to run high-quality PowerPoint presentations on a projector or monitor, right from your Treo.

Once you have opened the presentation you want to give, you can view the outline or notes views, but to get right to the most important function, you can tap on the presentation icon on the bottom and your presentation will now begin on the monitor you are plugged into! Using the up and down arrows on the bottom-right of the screen will advance you from slide to slide, or you can pick a specific slide from the list and jump right to it. You can also use the navigation control to move through the slides by tapping up or down.

When you use the provided software on your desktop to move your PowerPoint presentations onto your Treo, you will select the resolution that you would like to use and the format that allows you to choose quality over file size, or vice versa. Unfortunately, the Pitch product doesn't support the fancy transitions and animations that PowerPoint is capable of, so keep this in mind with some of your sophisticated slide shows.

Another fantastic feature of the Pitch product is the capability to display the screen of your Treo live through an external monitor or projector. To give you a real-world example, my company develops software that runs on the Treo. We can give live demonstrations of the software to groups by using the Pitch Solo to display those screens on a large monitor. This is a much better way to give demonstrations than asking people to try to gather around our Treo and look at the tiny screen while we try to show our software!

To transmit your screens through the Pitch device, you simply run the iPitch software on your Treo, and then press the Start button. Now, use your Treo as normal and the screens will show up on the monitor as you go. Unfortunately, the iPitch software displays a Palm-style interface with a Graffiti input area, which isn't what your Treo really looks like. Hopefully, in a future release, you will be able to pick the "skin" you want to put around your display so it can reflect your Treo 600.

Margi Presenter To Go

Another hardware solution for giving slide shows directly from your Treo is the Margi Presenter To Go (www.margi.com). It offers comparable functionality to the Pitch solution with the capability to present high-quality slide shows, display your Treo screen in real time, and more. There are also some unique and interesting features such as the ability to view your slide notes on your Treo while the slides are displayed on your monitor or projector—a handy tool for any dynamic presenter!

The drawback to the Presenter To Go solution is its reliance on running through your SD slot. This is somewhat awkward since the cable running out of the top of your Treo feels odd compared to a cable coming out of the sync port at the bottom. Also, because this device is hooked into your SD slot, it means that you cannot use external storage cards to store your presentations.

Read Acrobat Files

Another very popular format for files is the Adobe Acrobat standard. Though these files have the .pdf extension, you can view them on your Treo using third-party

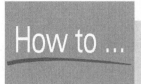

How to ... Run a Presentation Without Wires

The iGo Pitch Solo device has a brother called the Pitch Duo. The Pitch Duo is the same as the Solo except for one feature: the ability to connect with a device and run a presentation through Bluetooth, a short-range personal area networking wireless standard. A Bluetooth connection acts much like your sync cable and would allow you to make your presentation wirelessly as long as your Treo and the Pitch device are within 30 feet of each other.

The caveat to this is that presently, this would require two things that are issues. The Treo doesn't yet feature built-in Bluetooth, so you must plug in an external Bluetooth SD card to get the wireless connectivity. (This means that you cannot keep your presentations stored on an SD card since you can't have two cards in the slot at once!) The second problem is that, as of this writing, the Bluetooth SD cards on the market do not yet have drivers to support the Treo. (Even the Bluetooth SD card available from palmOne doesn't support the Treo yet.) Most vendors have announced drivers for the Treo, but they are not yet on the market. By the time you read this, hopefully this will have been resolved and you will be able to get Bluetooth connectivity on your Treo.

software that will convert the files to a readable format for your handheld. For example, the Documents To Go software that we have been profiling in this chapter allows you to sync PDF files to your Treo through their standard interface. When it moves the file, it is converted to Word To Go format. All images are stripped out and what you receive is a reformatted version of the text of the document.

Unfortunately, the need to convert the file before syncing it to your Treo means that PDF files that arrive as an e-mail attachment on your Treo are still not readable. Watch for improvements in third-party mail products to enable this feature in the near future.

Read E-Mail Attachments

One of the powerful and compelling features of the Treo 600 is its capability to keep you connected not only to your important e-mail, but also to the attachments within an e-mail. Most common e-mail attachment formats can be opened and viewed right on your Treo, including Microsoft Word and Excel files, images (JPEG), and more. For detail on this capability, refer to Chapter 6.

Move Files Between Your PC and Treo

To read and work with documents on your Treo, you must get them onto the device either by receiving them as an e-mail attachment, or by syncing them over from your PC. This latter task is accomplished with the desktop companion software for the productivity tool that you have chosen to use with your Treo. With Documents To Go, this is accomplished by using your mouse to click the Documents To Go icon on your computer desktop. This opens the window shown in Figure 11-8.

You can drag and drop files from your desktop into either the Handheld or Expansion Card pane. Files dropped in the Handheld pane will be converted and synchronized into your Treo's internal memory. Files dropped in the Expansion Card pane will be synced to the SD or MMC card in your Treo.

Each pane will tell you the details and status of the file. First you will see the filename and an icon indicating the desktop file format. The Type column will tell you what the file format will be on the handheld device when the file is synchronized, while the Size column displays the size of the file after it is converted. The software

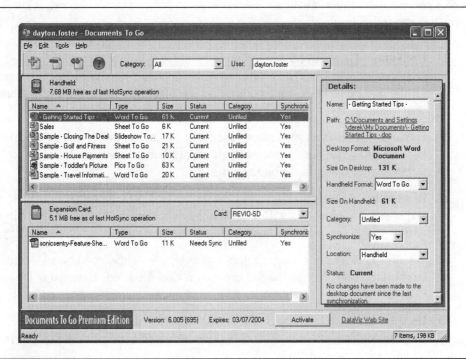

FIGURE 11-8   The Documents To Go desktop application manages the synchronization of your documents between your PC and your Treo.

will attempt to make the file as small as possible given the limited storage capabilities of mobile devices in general. The Status column will tell you if the files on the handheld and the desktop are current, or in need of synchronization to bring the handheld up-to-date.

When you select any particular file, the details of that file will appear in the box on the right. Here you can change some of the characteristics of the file to control how it is synced to the Treo, its format, and so on.

Syncing your Treo will bring any new files over to your smartphone and will also update any desktop files with changes you have made on your Treo. This last feature is a great tool since it allows you to ensure that both your desktop and smartphone files are always in sync.

Print from Your Palm

It is only natural that once you start carrying and working with documents on your Treo, at some point you will want to be able to print a document out. In order to do this, you will need third-party software that will function as a print driver and allow you to connect to a printer. There are various ways to connect your Treo to a printer, including the following:

- **HotSync**   Files can be queued up to print from your desktop-connected printer when you HotSync your handheld. This has a somewhat limited value for the mobile traveler since you could then just print any synced files from your desktop.

- **Infrared**   This is a much more functional model for the Treo user since it allows you to use the Treo's Infrared port to beam a printed document to a printer with a similar infrared port.

- **Bluetooth**   Although not yet available on the Treo 600, support is imminent, and when available, this will prove a handy wireless technique for allowing you to print from your Treo within 30 feet of the printer.

- **Wi-Fi**   This longer-range wireless technology will also soon be supported on the Treo 600 through the SD expansion slot. This will allow your Treo to connect to your office network and print to any network-connected printer.

- **Data connection**   Through the data connection discussed in Chapter 5, you can connect to your office network with a VPN and print to any printer on your office network.

Once you know which form of connectivity you will be using to print, you will need the software to support your printing in that format. A full listing of Treo 600–compatible software is provided in Chapter 16; one type of software that is fully compatible with the Documents To Go software discussed in this chapter is PrintBoy from Bachmann Software (www.bachmannsoftware.com). It supports printing to most of the major printers on the market today through all of the techniques just mentioned. It also conveniently allows you to print using the Send function in many of the built-in Treo applications.

Wrap It Up

The software solutions discussed in this chapter are an absolutely essential component of turning your Treo 600 into a fully functional mobile office. The ability to work with the same kinds of files that you work with every day at your desk will greatly enhance your mobile productivity. Although we focused on one primary software product in this chapter, there are many excellent products you might consider for your needs, including QuickOffice, WordSmith, and others. Please refer to Chapter 16 for more details on these alternatives.

11

Chapter 12

Manage Your Finances with Your Treo 600

How to…

- Download and install mobile financial management software
- Manage your accounts
- Work with the account register
- Manage your investments
- Categorize your financial information
- Manage your payees
- Protect your information with passwords
- Synchronize with desktop Quicken

This chapter will focus specifically on what you can do on your Treo with financial management software such as LandWare's Pocket Quicken software and SplashData's SplashQuicken. It is not our intention to teach you how to use products like Quicken, but rather to show you how your Treo can factor into your personal financial management.

Chances are that you use either Quicken or an alternative financial package on your desktop. To make it easier, we've divided this chapter into two parts. The first part focuses on mobile software for Quicken users, while the second section looks at other financial software.

Before you install Pocket Quicken, you must have already installed Quicken on your desktop PC; otherwise the two programs will not synchronize properly. Once you have successfully installed and synchronized them, you are ready to go.

Account List

The primary window of Pocket Quicken is the Account List, as shown in Figure 12-1. In the Account List screen is a list all of your accounts with their current or ending balances showing. (You can choose between Current and Ending Balance using the drop-down selection box in the column header.) The net balance of these accounts is displayed at the bottom of the window, which, if you have every account entered, will be your approximate net worth. Tapping on a checking, savings, or credit card account will highlight that account. Then tapping the Register button at the bottom of the screen will take you to the Register for that account (see the next section, "Account

```
┌─────────────────────────────┐
│ Account List      ▼ All Types│
│ Name        Type    ▼ Ending ≙│
│ Checking    Bank    $3,389.24│
│ Savings     Bank    $1,357.00│
│ Visa        CCard    $-382.00│
│ Investment  Invst  $14,660.00│
│                              │
│                              │
│ Balance Total      $19,024.24│
│ (Details) [Accounts] Register│
└─────────────────────────────┘
```

FIGURE 12-1   The Account List window lists all your accounts and the current balance.

Register"). If you tap the Register button without selecting a specific account, you will see the consolidated Register for all the accounts. Tapping the Accounts button at the bottom will allow you to toggle back to the Account List screen.

If you wish, you can select in the drop-down account type filter at the top-right of the screen to view in the list only a subset of accounts. You can choose among Bank Accounts, Credit Cards, Cash Accounts, Assets, Liabilities, and Investments. This can be very helpful if you have a large number of different accounts and complex personal finances.

At the far right of the screen, you will notice a striped arrow pointing upward. Tapping this arrow will open a pop-up window, shown next, allowing you to change the sorting of the Account List screen to sort by name, type, or preferred; or you can choose Display Preferences to open the Preferences screen (discussed later in this section).

```
┌─────────────────────────────┐
│ Account List      ▼ All Types│
│ Name     ┌───────────────────┤
│ Checking │Sort List by Name  │
│ Savings  │Sort List by Type  │
│ Visa     │Sort List by Preferred│
│ Investment│Display Preferences│
│          └───────────────────┤
│                              │
│ Balance Total      $19,024.24│
│ (Details) [Accounts] Register│
└─────────────────────────────┘
```

Tapping the Details button at the bottom of the screen will open the Account Details screen, shown next, where you can see more information about the account in general, such as the account number and the contact information for your banking representative. You can also select the Preferred check box to set an account as being preferred, a category that can be used to sort the accounts in the Account List screen.

In the Account Details screen, you can view a summary of the account balances by tapping the Balances box at the top of the screen. In the Account Balances screen, shown next, you can view the ending, current, and minimum balances of the account. You can also see what currency this account is in. If your desktop version of Quicken is not set for multicurrency support, this field will show as None Selected.

Tapping the HotSync box will open the Account HotSync Settings screen, where you will be able to view and adjust how this specific account is handled during the synchronization process. By default, the account will be set to the Send & Receive option to send and receive transactions, which means that it will be kept in sync with the account in your desktop Quicken. In some situations, you may not want an account on your handheld to sync at all, or you may only want to put transactions you enter on the handheld into your desktop Quicken, without pulling new transactions down. You can do this by changing the Transactions drop-down to No Transfer or Send Only, respectively.

You can toggle between any of these three views using the boxes at the top of the screen and can tap the OK or Cancel button to return to the Account List screen. This is also the screen where you can delete an account by tapping the Delete button.

New accounts can be set up by selecting Add Account from the Activities menu. Though this is possible to do, it is generally discouraged; and LandWare recommends you set up all new accounts on your desktop. The Add Account option will take you to a blank version of the Account Details screen, from which you can also select the Balances and HotSync boxes to open blank versions of the Account Balances and Account HotSync Settings screens. On these three blank screens, you can define all the properties of the new account.

Account Register

The Register screen, shown in Figure 12-2, can be accessed by tapping any account in the Account List screen and then tapping the Register button at the bottom of the Account List screen. Every transaction in Quicken has an associated Register entry. The default view of the Register will show the date of the transaction, the reference number and payee, and the amount of the transaction.

You can change the center column to display different information as suits your particular preferences. Following are the items you can choose to view:

- Account

- Payee

- Account and payee

- Year and payee

- Reference number and payee

- Memo

FIGURE 12-2   Manage individual transactions in the Register screen.

■ Category

■ Class

The top-right drop-down behaves a little differently from what you might be used to. It allows you to change which transactions you are viewing in the Register screen. When you tap it, a new pop-up screen will appear, as shown here:

In this screen, you can pick All Accounts or a specific account from the list to view. There are also tabs on the left side of the pop-up to allow you to see subsets of all the accounts by account type. This can be very handy if you have a large number of accounts in your Quicken file.

The bottom of the Register screen shows, by default, the ending balance in your account. If you prefer, you can use the drop-down selection box on this line to change the view to the current balance or the available credit.

Enter a New Transaction

Tapping the New button at the bottom of the Register screen will open a pop-up screen containing three options to specify what kind of new transaction you wish to create: Payment, Deposit, or Transfer.

If you choose Payment, you will be taken to a blank Edit New Transaction screen to enter the details of your new transaction, as shown here:

Being able to enter new transactions on your Treo is extremely handy. You can record transactions while you are at the checkout, gas bar, movie theatre, or wherever, instead of trying to remember them all later! The details you need to fill in including the following:

■ **Ref**   This is the reference number or text. This might be the check number, or it could be text that will remind you of how it was paid. For example, EFT stands for electronic funds transfer. If you tap the drop-down selection arrow, you will be presented with a list of predefined references you can use. If you don't remember what your next check number is, you can choose Next Check Num and it will fill in the number for you!

■ **Pay**   This is the payee, or who you are making the payment to. You can fill in the name of the payee; or if you have memorized transactions with them, you can access the transactions by tapping the drop-down selection arrow. The curved arrow on the right of the entry field will cause Pocket Quicken to attempt to fill in the rest of the blanks based on the payee name you entered and the entries in your memorized transactions list. (See the section "Memorized Transactions," later in this chapter.)

12

■ **Payment** This is the amount of the transaction.

■ **Memo** Any notes you want to record about the transaction go in this field.

■ **Cat** This is the category for the transaction. Quicken uses categories to help you track where you spend your money for budgeting and planning purposes. If you tap the drop-down selection arrow, you can find the category in your category list.

Tapping the Split button allows you to define multiple categories for the payment. For example, imagine that your cable TV provider is also your Internet provider. You can then break down the amount of the bill that is related to your cable TV charge and the amount that is related to your Internet service.

Edit Split Transaction	
Category	**Amount**
▼ Utilities:Cable TV ▤	16.95
▼ Utilities:Internet ▤	16.30
▼ ▤	
▼ ▤	
▼ ▤	
Split Total:	33.25
Remainder:	0.00
Total:	**33.25**
(OK) (Cancel) (Edit...) (Adjust) ◆	

■ **Class** This field allows you to specify a class for the transaction. For example, you may have classes defined to track how you spend (essential, discretionary, emergency), or perhaps to differentiate between personal and business expenditures.

The Details button at the bottom of the screen opens a Transaction Details pop-up screen, as shown here, that shows you the status of this transaction—whether it has been cleared, when it was created, and if it has been synced to the desktop yet.

Even if the transaction you are entering is not a payment, but a deposit, the screen will look very similar to a payment screen. The only difference is that in the Payee field you will enter who the money being deposited came from.

If the new transaction is a transfer, you will need to enter the Category field as a "transfer" category. Transfer categories are indicated by the prefix Txfr: and are followed by the name of the account you are transferring funds into. For example, to transfer an amount from your checking account to your savings account, you would create a new transaction in your checking account as a Transfer. You would fill in the amount of the transfer, and under Category you would select Txfr:[Savings] to complete the deposit into your savings account.

Categories

Categories are an important part of Quicken and therefore have been fully implemented in Pocket Quicken. Categories are used in new transactions, as discussed earlier; and when transposed back to your desktop Quicken, they allow you to better manage your finances through budgeting and planning.

The Category & Transfer List screen can be opened from the Lists menu. On this screen, you can see all of your categories and subcategories, as shown in Figure 12-3.

FIGURE 12-3   Display all the categories and subcategories available to you in the Category & Transfer List window.

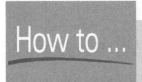 **Edit Your Reference Field List**

The list of options that come up for the Ref field in a transaction can be customized to use the values that you use most often. This is accomplished by selecting the Reference Field option from the Lists menu. This will open the Edit Reference Field List screen, where you can create new list items (select New), delete ones you don't use (select Delete), and rename any that just aren't quite right (select Rename).

 *Categories cannot be created or edited in Pocket Quicken. This activity is reserved for the full desktop version of Quicken.*

The Transfers button scrolls the list to the end of the categories and the beginning of the transfers.

Investments

Unfortunately, Pocket Quicken features only very limited support for your investment accounts. If you invest or trade regularly in the stock market, the ability to manage your portfolio from your Treo would be invaluable. Until LandWare adds this feature to the product, you must content yourself with checking your portfolio on your Treo using your broker's online interface.

Investment accounts in Pocket Quicken only show you their current market value as per your last synchronization.

Memorized Transactions

Pocket Quicken keeps track of historical transactions (transactions you've made previously). You can reference this historical list and reuse the transactions as you need them. You access this list by choosing the Memorized Transaction option from the Lists menu. This opens the Memorized Transaction List screen shown in Figure 12-4.

In this list, you can see the names of your payees and also the amount and category of a transaction. You can select any individual transaction from the list and tap the Use button to create a new transaction using the same information. You can then edit the information before saving the new transaction. For example, I could reuse my Shaw Cable memorized transaction, but perhaps this month my bill is slightly more or less. All I have to do is edit the payment amount and save it as a new transaction.

Tapping the Delete button after selecting a memorized transaction will delete the transaction from the list.

The Built-In Calculator

Even though your Treo has its own built-in calculator, if you want to use it you have to exit Pocket Quicken, make your calculation, and then get back into Pocket Quicken to enter your calculated value. To save you from this frustrating process, Pocket

FIGURE 12-4   Memorized transactions are historical transactions that you have entered in Quicken.

Quicken has its own built-in calculator that can be accessed at any time with the Use
Calculator option on the Activities menu:

Work Your Budgets

Budgets are a core feature of Quicken, but Quicken users don't often use them.
Because of this, the budget functionality of Pocket Quicken is hidden until you enable
it in the general preferences, as described in the following section, "Quicken Options."

Once enabled, you will have a Budget button on the bottom of your Account
List and Register screens. Tapping this button will open the Budget screen, where
you can see for each expense and income category the amount of your monthly
budget and the amount remaining in your budget. If you like to consult this
before making purchases, it is very handy to have this in your Treo when you need
to decide if you should buy that new pair of jeans or not!

Quicken Options

There are many places in Pocket Quicken where you can make adjustments to the
default behavior of the program to make it better match how you like to work.

General Preferences

When you choose Preferences from the Options menu, you will be taken to the
Preferences screen, where you can toggle between General, Notify, Display, and
QuickFill preferences using the boxes at the top of the screen.

In General Preferences, shown in this illustration, you have the ability to define which screen you want to open first each time you start Pocket Quicken. You can choose between Account List, Register, Budgets, or whatever you were looking at last when you exited.

You can also define a default account. This means that as you move between the Account List and the Register, by default Pocket Quicken will select the specific account you specify instead of showing all of your transactions in the Register.

You can also set a home currency, but LandWare recommends you let this be set by your desktop version of Quicken to help prevent any accidental conflicts of information.

If you like to use budgets in your desktop Quicken and you want to be able to consult those budgets using your Treo, you can check the Track Budgets check box to synchronize those budgets with your smartphone.

If you select the Global Find check box, the information in Pocket Quicken will be searched when you use the global find function in the Treo applications.

Display Preferences

The Display Preferences screen is where you can adjust what you want to show on the screen and how. You can choose to show historical transactions, hidden accounts, cleared status, and currency symbols (or not to show them), as shown here:

To help make the Register easier to use, you can also define row shading. This is an option we highly recommend. It will cause every other row in the Register to appear with the background color you specify. This makes reading the Register much easier. Note that not only must you check the Use Row Shading check box, you must also pick a color by tapping on the Pick Color box; otherwise, you won't see the rows being shaded any differently because the default color is white!

12

Notify Preferences

The Notify Preferences screen, shown in the following illustration, is where you can specify occasions when you want Pocket Quicken to prompt you with warnings. You can elect to be notified when a transaction is uncategorized, when a synchronization attempt is unsuccessful, or when the register exceeds a specified number of items. You can set the number of entries before the notification occurs by tapping on the number in the appropriate preferences line (the default is 100).

You can also elect to have Pocket Quicken confirm with you when you delete an item as well as confirm the exchange rate when different currencies are used.

QuickFill Preferences

The QuickFill Preferences screen is where you can change how Pocket Quicken attempts to speed your data entry by completing some fields for you.

In the Data Entry section, you can choose whether to have Pocket Quicken attempt to complete the field into which you are currently entering data by looking up what you have typed and comparing it with previous entries you have made. For example, if I enter **Sh** in the Payee field, Pocket Quicken will see that I have previously made payments to Shaw Cable and will fill in the rest of the field for me. If I keep typing, it will continue to try to match up previous entries for me. If I like what it has recommended, I need only tap the next field and continue. This can speed data entry in Pocket Quicken considerably.

If you select the second check box in the Data Entry section, Pocket Quicken will automatically enter the Pocket Quicken tag into the Memo field of all new transactions. This means that it will insert "PQ:" at the start of the Memo field of each new transaction, which can make it easier to identify transactions entered from Pocket Quicken later when you are looking at your desktop Quicken register.

Selecting the third check box on this screen causes Pocket Quicken automatically to add all new transactions you enter into the historical list.

HotSync Preferences

On any of the General Preferences screens, you can tap the HotSync Preferences button on the bottom of the screen to be taken to the HotSync Options screen, shown in Figure 12-5. This screen can also be opened by choosing HotSync Preferences from the Options menu.

You can toggle between the Receive and Send option settings using the two boxes at the top of the screen. In the Receive options, you can choose what you want to pull down from Quicken on the next sync. This includes the Account, Currency, Category, and Class lists. If, for any reason, you don't want one of these lists, you can deselect corresponding relevant check box.

The next two options are designed to limit how much historical data you cache on your Treo. Memory space is always at a premium, and your Quicken files can quickly grow very large. In order to keep the data on your handheld optimized, you can limit how far back transactions are synchronized by setting the historical time period of transactions you want to receive.

12

FIGURE 12-5   You can control what is synchronized with the desktop version of Quicken on the HotSync Preferences screen.

The Send options, shown next, are very brief. The only thing you can elect to do here is to send your new transactions or not, but I have yet to determine why you wouldn't want to send the transaction you enter!

Manage Data Volume

As mentioned in the previous section, it is important to make sure you don't let your Pocket Quicken data grow too large, lest it impair the functioning of your Treo. Another tool for monitoring this is the Quicken Data Summary screen, shown here, which you can open by selecting Data Summary from the Options menu:

At the bottom of the screen, you can see the total amount of data Pocket Quicken has loaded on your Treo, along with the amount of free memory currently available on your Treo. You can see a breakdown of these records in the information at the top of the screen.

Tapping the Trim Transactions button takes you to a screen where you can remove historical records from Pocket Quicken. These records will remain on your desktop version of Quicken; you just won't be carrying them around in your Treo any longer.

You can specify to remove records from all accounts or from specific accounts. You can then specify which records you want to eliminate by indicating any record before a specific date or the oldest *x* number of records (where you define *x* by tapping the box beside The Oldest). Alternatively, you can elect to remove records with any date but with a specific status. You can choose statuses of Uncleared, Cleared, Reconciled, Cleared or Reconciled, or Any Status. These two options can be combined to eliminate only records before a specified date and with a specific status or only the oldest *x* number of records and with a specific status.

Set a Quicken Password

Your financial information is private and sensitive information. If you have not already secured your Treo from unauthorized use by employing a device password or one of the other techniques described in Chapter 13, you can add a password specifically to the Quicken application to prevent unauthorized access. (Or if you are particularly paranoid, you can use all of the above for extra levels of security!)

To set a password for Pocket Quicken, select Security from the Options menu. The Pocket Quicken Security pop-up screen will appear, in which you can set and confirm the launch PIN you want to use. From this point on, you will be asked to enter the PIN whenever you start Pocket Quicken. You can reset this number by tapping the Delete PIN button.

12

On this screen, you can also set an option to hide account numbers in your records so that in the event that someone gets into your financial information, it will be impossible to extract your account numbers.

In the desktop version of Quicken, you can also specify a password to open the file on your desktop. If you have this option set on your desktop, you must set a matching password in Pocket Quicken in the Quicken File Password field or Pocket Quicken will not be able to synchronize the financial data. Furthermore, I have found a bug in Pocket Quicken where both the desktop Quicken and Pocket Quicken must have a password entered or the synchronization will fail. This means that having your desktop Quicken with no password, which is the default for most users, will not work. This may be corrected by the time you read this. If you have trouble synchronizing and you don't have a password, check your HotSync log for an error from Pocket Quicken indicating that the passwords do not match.

Other Mobile Financial Software

There are literally hundreds of other mobile financial software packages that you can load on your Treo. They range in cost from free to expensive. You can find many of them by referring to the Palm OS software sites mentioned in Appendix B. Here are a few that you might want to take a look at:

- **SplashMoney from SplashData (www.splashdata.com)**   A full-featured financial application with many of the same functions that are addressed in this chapter. It has the ability to track all of your accounts, enter transactions, and work with budgets. It can also upload transactions into Quicken or Microsoft Money; however, this is not a smooth and seamless process as it is with LandWare's Pocket Quicken. A trial version of SplashMoney comes with your Treo on the companion CD.

- **Ultrasoft Money by Ultrasoft Limited (www.ultrasoft.com)**   A great fit for people who prefer to use Microsoft Money. It synchronizes fully with Microsoft Money and allows you to perform virtually all of the same functions that Pocket Quicken does, except with Microsoft Money instead. If you don't use Quicken or Money, then Ultrasoft's CheckBook product may be just what you're looking for.

- **Expense-n-Go by Solid Rock Software (www.budgetprogram.com)**
  A handy tool for tracking the expenses for your business.

There are hundreds of other software programs for managing personal finances on your Treo. Check out the sources in Appendix B to find the product that meets your specific need!

Wrap It Up

The bottom line for managing your finances on your Treo is that there are solid solutions available for both Intuit Quicken and Microsoft Money users, with the restriction that we haven't yet found one that will update stock prices in your portfolio through the Treo's Internet connection. However, given the rapid growth of the Treo platform, we anticipate you will see this feature appearing in these products in the very near future.

In closing this chapter on mobile financial software, we would like to add that it would be nice if Intuit, the manufacturer of Quicken, would provide Treo-compatible Quicken software to all Quicken users for no additional cost, but this seems unlikely in the immediate future.

12

Chapter 13

Secure Your Treo

How to…

- Identify security risks
- Take precautions to minimize security risks
- Use third-party software to secure your Treo data and connections

This chapter discusses both personal and corporate security. You will notice that some topics in this chapter are directed toward individual users, while others are directed toward the individuals responsible for corporate data and network security. It is a good idea to understand both the risks and the steps that you can take to reduce the risks.

Why Worry About Security?

Portable mobile wireless devices like your Treo continue to be hot topics in the press, and not all of the press is positive. Interestingly enough, the primary qualities that make mobile devices like your Treo so useful and convenient are the same attributes that make them open to security risks. For example, mobile devices such as your Treo 600 are small and portable, meaning that they are also easy to misplace. Your Treo is capable of storing large amounts of personal and corporate information, meaning that the consequences of losing it can be significant if it gets into the wrong hands. The tremendously useful wireless connectivity that allows you to send and receive e-mail, browse the Web, play games, and perform countless other tasks also means that there is a relatively unguarded path for malicious programming code to get onto your Treo, and possibly onto your PC. There are two general categories of security risks:

- Damage caused by viruses
- Damage caused by personal or corporate information falling into the wrong hands

The Risk of Data Falling into the Wrong Hands

Your Treo is a compact, powerful device with enough memory to store at least 24MB of data; it can store much more than that if it contains a Secure Digital memory card.

This is a significant leap ahead in mobile computing, but it also means that if your Treo is lost or stolen, your e-mails, documents, and pictures are in grave danger of being misused.

Your Treo has the powerful ability to transmit messages and data using wireless networks. Wireless connectivity is an extremely useful feature that allows you to stay connected and stay mobile. But this also means that there are many ways a virus can be transmitted to your Treo—through the voice phone channel, the GPRS data channel, the Infrared port, and even infected memory expansion cards. Wireless data is easy to intercept, and your information may be scanned right out of the air.

So what's the big deal? Most of us feel that our personal data would not be very useful to anyone else or damaging to ourselves, but personal information can be very damaging if it gets into the hands of people who know how to use it for their benefit. If you use your Treo for work as well as for personal data, the security risk can be many times higher than the risk for someone who uses the Treo strictly for personal data; the level of risk depends on the nature of your work.

The risks involved with losing your Treo or having it stolen are listed later in this chapter in the section "Risks of Your Treo Being Lost or Stolen."

The security risks are much greater for companies, and these risks, as well as preventive measures that should be taken, are presented later in this chapter under the heading "Corporate Security."

The Risk of Damage Resulting from Malicious Code

You are likely familiar with viruses that spread through the Internet. Examples of well-known viruses include "Mydoom," "Chernobyl," and "Anna Kornakova," but new viruses are released many times a day. If you have ever had the misfortune of having your PC infected by a virus, you can identify with the amount of inconvenience that can be caused. For example, I was sitting in an office with a coworker who had his entire hard drive erased by a version of the "Chernobyl" virus. It is an understatement to say that it was not a fun day for him. In fact, he permanently lost a significant amount of data, not to mention the lost time it took him to rebuild his laptop. In addition to the inconvenience factor, viruses can be very expensive for the organizations that fall victim to them. This topic is covered in much more detail under the heading "Corporate Security," and your antivirus options are listed later in this chapter.

Risks of Your Treo Being Lost or Stolen

As stated earlier, the two primary qualities that make mobile devices like your Treo so useful and convenient are the same attributes that make these devices possible

13

Wireless Mobile Device Sold on eBay for $15.50 Reveals Bank's Secrets

A former vice president from the financial services firm Morgan Stanley decided that he no longer needed his wireless mobile device. He had bought the device with his own money and had been using it to send and receive e-mail messages through his Morgan Stanley e-mail account. The person who won the eBay auction paid $15.50—plus shipping—and received not only a wireless device but also more than 200 Morgan Stanley internal e-mails. These e-mails included guarded financial secrets and a database of more than 1,000 names, job titles (from vice presidents to managing directors), e-mail addresses, and phone numbers (some of them home numbers) for Morgan Stanley executives worldwide. Morgan Stanley was understandably unhappy, but who was really at fault?

security risks. Unless you attach your Treo to your hand with duct tape, which is not recommended, by the way, there is always a risk of losing it or having someone pick it up when you are not looking.

Research information collected by David Melnick, Mark Dinman, and Alexander Muratov for the book *PDA Security: Incorporating Handhelds into the Enterprise,* (McGraw-Hill, 2003) reveals the types of information that are commonly stored on wireless mobile devices. Based on feedback from executives around the U.S., those types of information are the following:

- **Network passwords** Obviously, your Treo is a very convenient place to store those hard-to-remember usernames and passwords. The risk is that if the wrong person gets ahold of this information, there can be a gateway into your entire network, critical data, and systems to which you have access.

- **Customer information** According to many executives, customer information getting into the wrong hands is a public relations nightmare and possibly a lawsuit waiting to happen. In the financial services sector, if customer data leaks, the company is legally obligated to contact every customer to inform them that their personal information may have been compromised. Or wouldn't it be less than ideal if a competitor somehow got your customer list and contact information?

■ **Press releases**   If your organization routinely shares prepress release information via e-mail, or if an employee works on public relations documents on his or her Treo, there is the risk that private information is released to the public long before it is intended to be released. Having this happen is especially risky if your company is publicly traded. In the U.S., the Securities and Exchange Commission (SEC) has very strict rules about releasing information before public distribution. Remember Enron and Martha Stewart?

■ **Bank account numbers and credit card information**   This type of information is commonly stored on mobile devices, even though many of us know better. But it is just so darned convenient. A user is even more likely to store this information as Internet purchasing and banking transactions become more common. The risks here are relatively obvious; if an unscrupulous person gets your credit card number, there is a good chance that you may be financing something like a world-class collection of a rare Beanie Babies for someone you don't know.

■ **Corporate financial information**   E-mail is generally the way most organizations share information. Users routinely exchange spreadsheets and other documents as attachments. You may be surprised at just how much inside information you keep in your e-mail Inbox. Whether it's an in-progress annual report or the internal projections for next quarter's sales, the inadvertent leak of financial data may have a serious and long-lasting impact on your organization.

■ **E-mail**   Again, there is no telling what kind of information mobile device users have conveniently stored in their e-mail. When most of us stop to consider it, there is likely a significant amount of information that we would prefer to keep private.

■ **Intranet access**   Are you familiar with the term "The keys to the castle?" Users who work for companies that have corporate intranets—web sites not meant for use by anyone outside the company—often store username and password information on their mobile devices. This risk is relatively obvious, but the other risk is that many web browsers allow cache login information. So a person who picks up a Treo may be able to access a corporate intranet by simply choosing a shortcut or web favorite and clicking "log in." This provides an ultra-convenient way for someone to gain a lot of insider knowledge about an organization.

13

- **Price lists**   Consider this scenario. Your best salesperson just finished a meeting with a valued long-time customer, and when she left, she forgot her Treo on the boardroom table. The customer picks up the Treo to return it and notices some interesting information on the screen: the prices that a major competitor has been paying your company for products. "My largest competitor is getting a better deal!" This situation may cause irreparable damage to the relationship and cost the organization dearly.

- **Employee information**   Privacy legislation does not look favorably on an organization publicly sharing employee information, whether it was intended disclosure or not. If employee information is publicized, the potential costs include litigation and the significant negative impact of bad publicity.

- **Medical (HIPAA) information**   This point is aimed directly at organizations that are involved in health care. The U.S. Health Insurance Portability and Accountability Act of 1996 (HIPAA) deals with the privacy of patient records and other health care information. Palm-powered devices are very popular for doctors and health care workers, because there are many applications designed specifically for medical information uses. If a mobile device containing patient information is lost or stolen and HIPAA rules are violated, the fines can be upwards of $50,000. The negative backlash that could occur because of a security breach could be devastating for a health care organization. After all, if you can't trust your doctors and nurses, who can you trust with your private information? More information about HIPAA is available at www.cms.hhs.gov.

See the heading "Treo 600 Authentication and Encryption Solutions" for solutions to help minimize these risks.

Precautionary Steps for Minimizing Security Risks

If your Treo is misplaced or stolen, you and your employer will be relieved that you took some important precautionary measures. Some of these precautions are included in the following list and should not be taken lightly.

- **Password-protect your Treo.** The steps to set your Treo security settings include setting your Treo to autolock after a defined amount of time has passed. After that amount of time passes and your Treo autolocks, a user must enter a password in order to access your Treo. Defining your Auto Lock settings is covered in Chapter 2.

■ **Regularly back up your Treo.** By regularly backing up your Treo data to your PC through routine HotSync operations, you will minimize how much data you will permanently lose if you lose your Treo.

■ **Encrypt sensitive data.** Data encryption is very important for data in your Treo memory, as well as data stored on expansion cards and sent over the network. Software options to help you encrypt your data are mentioned later in this chapter.

> TIP   *Some applications developers have taken the initiative to help you protect your Treo from prying eyes by including password protection and data encryption. Some of your options are mentioned later in this chapter under the heading "Treo 600 Authentication and Encryption Solutions."*

Corporate Security

You are likely aware of some of the technical security risks that too often are topics in the press. This section provides an overview of the potential security risks of your Treo 600—and wireless handhelds in general—for companies.

Much of the talk about corporate security risks and what should be done to defend against attacks amounts to nothing more than technical fear mongering. Despite the attempts to guess dollar values for security attacks that have not yet occurred, the fact is that the actual cost of a security breach cannot be known until after it has already happened. This fact does not mean that precautions are not warranted; in fact, ideally, you don't want to ever find out how much an attack costs your organization. The best way to avoid incurring costs is to understand the risks and protect yourself and your organization.

"Inoculating the Network," a survey that was published in *The Economist* on June 22, 2002, stated that, out of 503 companies surveyed by the Computer Security Institute of San Francisco and the Federal Bureau of Investigation (FBI), 90 percent reported security attacks during 2001. The estimated average loss was $1.9 million per company. This obviously does not take into account companies that don't publicly admit to being attacked or companies that either don't know how much the attacks cost or won't say. It is clear that security breaches can be extremely costly.

In addition to the financial costs, there are some costs that are more difficult to value in monetary terms. For many companies, the costs associated with destroying the confidence of customers and business partners is devastating. The larger an organization is, the more a negative public impression will cost the company in the long run. Many organizations work hard to create positive public perception, and even a small security problem that becomes public can erase years of effort and negatively impact a company's bottom line.

13

The security risks associated with wirelessly connected mobile devices can be divided into a few general categories: theft or loss of a device, interception of wireless data, and the threat of damage caused by viruses and malicious code.

Minimize the Risk Involved with Using Wireless Mobile Devices

There are specific precautionary steps that should be followed by every organization with employees using mobile devices. This section is directed at the corporate IT or security person responsible for network access and data, but the information is valuable for any mobile device user, as it can help avoid unnecessarily risking company assets.

1. **Research and understand the risks.** The first step is to understand how employees are using their Treos and other wireless mobile devices. Answering these questions will allow you to understand some of the risks and the scope of any potential issues.

   ■ How many employees use wireless mobile devices?

   ■ What devices are being used?

   ■ Do the users synchronize their devices with network computers?

   ■ What type of data do users store on their devices?

   ■ What applications do users use on their devices?

2. **Create or modify security policies.** Create or modify your organization's security policies to ensure that wireless handheld devices are within the control of the organization and clearly convey the policies to staff.

   ■ Often, many of the devices in an organization are personally owned, rather than supplied by the company. It is crucial that you define policies that effectively define how these personal devices interact with corporate data and systems. The policies should include sections that cover situations in which employees have their own mobile devices. Issues like whether or not the organization will allow employees to synchronize devices with work computers should be included. Another item that should be included is a detailed list of specific security concerns regarding particular devices or software.

■ Convey the very important point to users that they must use the password protection that is built into their devices. Often, users turn off this protection for the convenience of being able to use their Treos without having to log on, but the cost to the organization could be significant if a device is lost or stolen. Some of the software options to help enforce this security policy are listed later in this chapter under the heading "Treo 600 Authentication and Encryption Solutions."

3. **Track mobile devices, also known as *asset management*.** Most organizations take time and effort to ensure that they have an up-to-date inventory record of each server and workstation being used by the company. Usually this information includes hardware and software configurations, as well as network addresses and which users are assigned to specific hardware. Doesn't it make sense to do the same thing for mobile devices? Gartner Group estimates that companies with more than 5,000 employees could save between $300,000 and $500,000 per year by tracking, tagging, and storing contact information about their wireless mobile devices.

4. **Dictate standard security software that mobile users must use.** Requiring mobile device users to use antivirus and virtual private network (VPN) software can go a long way toward protecting your network assets. It is also important to ban any software that may be a security risk. For example, some organizations ban certain document applications because of the security vulnerabilities they cause.

Third-Party Software

13

The Treo 600 has some valuable built-in security features, such as Auto Lock and password protection, but some enterprising software developers are also sensitive to the unique security requirements of mobile devices. The software listed in this section allows you to enforce passwords and encrypt data on your Treo; it also facilitates secure network connections through authentication and network data encryption.

Software for Enterprise Device Support and Security

As mobile devices like your Treo 600 are adopted by organizations and corporations, it has become increasingly clear that supporting, managing, and securing these devices can be a significant challenge. There are some software vendors that are meeting that challenge head on.

sonicsentry (www.sonicmobility.com)

Sonic Mobility has been providing software that allows systems administrators and IT professionals to manage back-end computer systems and network infrastructure using wireless mobile devices. Sonic Mobility is leveraging its experience with wireless technologies to help organizations effectively manage their mobile devices. The company's product is called sonicsentry, and it is designed to help enterprises and wireless service providers support, manage, and secure their wireless mobile devices. The key functionality is listed here:

- **Device monitoring**   Information about specific devices is sent back to the central server, including connection status, battery levels, location, and other asset management and user statistics.

- **Alerting**   Based on device feedback and configured alert thresholds, alerts are generated to ensure that the correct people are made aware of changes requiring attention.

- **Real-time visual monitoring**   The server console features a graphical interface that allows a support person to see the status of a device at a glance.

- **Real-time control**   The challenges associated with supporting mobile devices are similar to the challenges of remotely managing any network node (that is, server, workstation, router, and so on): you need to ensure that the device is working properly and that it is connected, secured, and running the correct software and patches. Real-time control of mobile devices generally falls into two broad categories:

  - **Support**   An example might be a user experiencing difficulty receiving e-mail, so a support person accesses the device from the sonicsentry server to diagnose the problem and change settings to get the user up and running again.

  - **Security**   An example might be when a device has been lost or stolen and a support person wipes the data to prevent unauthorized access.

- **Autonomic self-healing**   The sonicsentry agent software resides on each mobile device and contains logic that allows it to take independent action based on changes that occur on the device, such as network connectivity changes or hardware and software changes.

- **Security** The mobile agent may be configured to enforce security standards—for example, that each device must be password enabled, meaning that the user cannot disable the password lock functionality.

- **Asset management** The application maintains up-to-date records of each mobile device, including ownership, owner contact information, physical location (using GPS), installed software and hardware configurations, and so on.

- **Reporting** A vast amount of information is collected from the organization's mobile devices and archived for reporting purposes. This data may be used to report such information as hardware and software inventory, usage patterns (amount of data sent, time spent using the phone, and so on), and any other important metrics.

PDA Defense (www.pdadefense.com)

PDA Defense by Asynchrony Solutions, also discussed under the heading "Treo 600 Authentication and Encryption Solutions," is mentioned here because of its specific value to companies. This type of software helps defend your Treo data against unauthorized access by enforcing password protection, encrypting data, and managing connection types, such as the ability to disable the Infrared port on a Treo. Some of the features of PDA Defense are given in the following list. This software is a cost-effective way—about $20 for a single-user license—to help ensure that your data is protected in the event that you lose or misplace your Treo.

- 128–512-bit encryption

- Card encryption support

- Encryption of databases

- Password encryption

- Bitwiping (deletion of data based on defined rules)

- Admin IrDA disabling

- Password history tracking

- Password masking

13

■ Temporary unlock password

■ Application launch protection

■ Admin application lockout

■ Custom splash screens to display your corporate identity

■ User-specific policy settings

■ Enterprisewide policy settings

Antivirus Software to Protect Your Treo, Your PC, and Your Network

The Internet is an extremely effective way to distribute software viruses that are aimed at disrupting services, causing user frustration, and inflicting financial pain on people and organizations all over the world. This fact is great if you are a hacker or virus programmer but not so great if your organization is vulnerable. The Internet is a public network and therefore results in inherent security and privacy concerns. Computer viruses have unfortunately become commonplace. Most viruses target specific application weaknesses in places like operating systems, databases, web servers, and e-mail servers. For the most part, mobile devices have not been popular targets yet. But you can bet that this will change as mobile devices become more popular and hackers and virus programmers become motivated to attack devices such as your Treo 600. After all, your Treo is connected to the Internet just like any home PC or corporate web server.

Fortunately, there are companies that offer software to help protect your Treo from malicious virus attacks. Antivirus software that you can use falls into one of two main categories:

■ Software that runs on your desktop PC and protects your PC and network by scanning files for viruses during and after a HotSync operation

■ Software that runs natively on your Treo 600 and operates in the background to scan for viruses and malicious programs.

Each type of software offers protection and, if you can, it is a good idea to run antivirus software on both your PC and your Treo. All of the major software

Did you know?

E-Mail Viruses

The most common types of viruses are distributed via e-mail, and destructive commands are generally stored within e-mail attachments. Most viruses cannot infect your Treo unless you open the attachment. While most viruses are not designed to target your Treo 600 directly, the most significant risk may be to your PC and your network. A virus can be easily transferred from your Treo to your PC and network when you HotSync with your PC. This is one reason why antivirus scanning is extremely important even if your Treo is not the intended target of a specific virus.

companies that offer antivirus virus protection for PCs will detect known viruses if they are found in your Treo HotSync files.

Antivirus Software for Your PC

The first type of antivirus protection is the most common: software that runs on your PC to prevent viruses from infecting your computer and the network and to prevent viruses from spreading to others through your computer. When you synchronize data from your Treo to your PC, the files will be scanned to prevent malicious programs (programs you may have picked up from e-mail or Internet activity on your Treo) from infecting your PC or network.

Antivirus Vendors for Windows PCs

Following is a cross-section of antivirus vendors, but there are many more to choose from, and some, like AVG Control Center, offer free versions to noncommercial users.

- McAfee, a Network Associates Company (www.mcafeeb2b.com)

- Symantec (www.symantec.com)

- Aladdin Knowledge Systems (www.ealaddin.com)

- FRISK Software International (www.f-prot.com)

- F-Secure Corp. (www.f-secure.com)

13

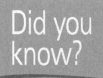

How Antivirus Software Works

Antivirus software generally refers to single-purpose applications that scan your Treo or PC for any pattern that may indicate a malicious computer program. The patterns that the software looks for when it scans your device or PC can be very complex. When malicious code is identified, the code is quarantined to prevent damage, and if the software "knows" how to patch damage, it will do so. Antivirus vendors are constantly working on ways to identify and fix viruses as soon as they are known, and program update files are loaded to your PC or Treo on a regular basis over the Internet to ensure that you always have the latest virus protection.

- GFI Software Ltd (www.gfi.com)
- Panda Software (www.pandasoftware.com)
- Symantec (www.symantec.com)
- Trend Micro, Inc. (www.trendmicro.com)
- AVG (www.grisoft.com)

Antivirus Vendors for Macintosh PCs

A cross-section of vendors that provide antivirus software for Macintosh personal computers is listed here, and there are also others.

- Norton AntiVirus 9.0 (www.symantec.com)
- Sophos (www.sophos.com)
- Intego (www.intego.com)

Antivirus Vendors for Linux PCs

While Linux is not a common platform for desktop computers, it is worth mentioning that companies such as AVG (www.grisoft.com) and Alwil Software (www.avast.com) offer antivirus software for Linux systems.

Antivirus Software That Runs on Your Treo 600

As mobile devices like your Treo 600 are becoming more popular, more software vendors are offering virus-scanning and other security products designed for them. The two largest companies in the antivirus protection market are Symantec and McAfee, and both offer antivirus software that runs on your Treo to scan for viruses and other malicious programs.

The products listed here run natively on your Treo 600 and run in the background to scan your Treo files, looking for signatures of viruses and Trojan horses and worms; they also prompt the user if malicious code is detected. Depending on the product, updated virus definition files are either loaded to your Treo during synchronization with your PC or sent over the air directly to your Treo using the wireless Internet connection. Some of the following vendors offer software for earlier versions of the Palm operating system (version 4.2 and earlier) and are in the process of releasing more recent versions for your Treo 600, which runs Palm OS 5. By the time this book is published, all of the vendors should be supporting Palm OS 5 and therefore your Treo 600.

- Symantec AntiVirus for Palm OS (www.symantec.com)

- McAfee Anti-Virus Resident Scanner (www.mcafee.com)

- McAfee VirusScan Wireless (www.mcafee.com)

- F-Secure Anti-Virus™ for Palm OS (www.f-secure.com)

- Trend Micro PC-cillin for Wireless Version 2.0 for Palm OS (www.trendmicro.com)

- Computer Associates InoculateIT (http://ca.com/)

Treo 600 Authentication and Encryption Solutions

Authentication and encryption have been mentioned several times in this chapter because they are so important. There are software products in the marketplace that allow you to protect the data on your Treo by enforcing password authentication and encrypting the data stored on the device. Both of these are extremely important for protecting your personal and corporate information. *Authentication* simply means that a user needs to enter login credentials to access the Treo applications and data, while *encryption* means that even if a person steals your Treo and is able to move the data off of the device, the data will be encrypted and therefore unreadable.

A cross-section of the products that are available for your Treo is listed here. Expect many other products to enter the market as the Treo 600 becomes even more popular. Some of the following vendors offer software for earlier versions of the Palm operating system (version 4.2 and earlier) and are in the process of releasing updated versions for your Treo 600. By the time this book is published, all of the vendors will likely be supporting Palm OS 5.

- SplashID (www.splashdata.com)

- Chapura Cloak (www.chapura.com)

- Certicom movianCrypt (www.certicom.com)

- Asynchrony PDA Defense Enterprise (www.pdadefense.com)

- Credant Technologies Mobile Guardian (www.credant.com)

- TealPoint Software Corporate TealLock (www.tealpoint.com)

- Trust Digital PDASecure (www.trustdigital.com)

- Kasten Chase Assurency SecureData for Palm OS (www.kastenchase.com)

> **TIP** *Your Treo 600 ships with a trial version of SplashID already installed. SplashID is a great application that is designed to store your passwords, bank account numbers, and other private information in an encrypted format. If you like the trial version, you can easily upgrade to the full version over the wireless Web.*

VPN Solutions

Virtual private networks (VPNs) are valuable tools, especially for wireless use, because they allow you to securely connect to a remote network and encrypt all of the data that is passed between your Treo and your network. This is extremely important when you are connecting over the public wireless networks because data is easily scanned out of the air. If the information is encrypted by a VPN solution, the data packet will appear as a bunch of scrambled random characters that are useless to the would-be hacker. Some examples of vendors that provide VPN solutions for the Palm platforms are listed here, but expect more to enter the marketplace as devices such as your Treo become more popular and the market grows.

- Certicom movianVPN (www.certicom.com)

- V-ONE Corp. SmartPass for Palm (www.v-one.com)

- SafeNet SoftRemotePDA (www.safenet-inc.com)

- Mergic VPN for Palm OS (www.mergic.com)

NOTE
Some of these vendors offer software for earlier versions of the Palm operating system (version 4.2 and earlier) and are in the process of releasing more recent versions for your Treo 600 that run Palm OS 5, so by the time this book is published, all of the vendors should be supporting Palm OS 5.

Enterprise Network Authentication

Many organizations are understandably concerned about the risks associated with allowing a wireless mobile device to connect to the corporate network over a wireless network. Some of the solutions that address these risks are mentioned in the preceding section on VPNs and in other parts of this chapter. One of the ways to help ensure that users who are attempting to remotely connect to the corporate network are really who they claim to be is by using one of the sophisticated user authentication solutions. These products use more than just a username and password to authenticate a user, which makes unauthorized access very difficult even if someone has stolen your Treo. A cross-section of some of the products that are available for your Treo 600 is presented here:

- **RSA Security SecurID (www.rsa.com)**   SecurID on your Treo is used in conjunction with a RSA ACE Server, and it works by using a one-time-use SecurID access code that automatically changes every 60 seconds.

- **Trio Security Trio VAULT (www.triosecurity.com)**   Trio VAULT combines three-factor user authentication, a single-sign-on solution, and access management.

NOTE
Some vendors of this type of software offer software for earlier versions of Palm OS (version 4.2 and earlier) and are in the process of releasing more recent versions for your Treo 600 that run Palm OS 5. By the time this book is published, all of the vendors should be supporting Palm OS 5.

13

Wrap It Up

This chapter was not designed to scare you but to make you aware of any possible risks and the best ways to minimize those risks. Of course, any risks are generally more significant for some groups of users than others and are dependent on how you use your Treo and who you work for. Clearly the FBI is more concerned about security than many of us need to be, so it is only necessary to take precautions where appropriate.

Chapter 14   Navigate with GPS

How to...

- Use GPS to determine your location

- Navigate to anyone in your Contacts list

- Find a restaurant, gas station, bank, or other site in any city

- Play team sports with GPS

Have you ever wished someone were beside you in the passenger seat, guiding you to an unfamiliar address? Or perhaps you've been in a strange city and were trying to find the nearest restaurant or gas station?

Figuring out where we are and where we are going has always been cumbersome and often inaccurate. You can buy a map for a city, but as time passes and things about the city change, it gets less and less accurate. Well, navigational tools have been greatly improved courtesy of Global Positioning System (GPS) technology.

What Is GPS?

GPS is a network of 24 satellites around the globe that broadcast radio navigation information you can use to determine your exact position anywhere. These satellites act as reference points to determine any position within meters. Actually, these satellites can be used to determine location down to centimeters, but that level of accuracy is only accessible to the U.S. military, who designed and created the system (at a cost of over $12 billion).

Initially, GPS devices were expensive and only practical for large businesses and the government. However, continued advancements have reduced a complete GPS system to a few miniaturized integrated circuits, dramatically shrinking its cost and size. GPS has become available to just about everyone and has found its way into cars, boats, planes, construction equipment, and farm machinery. It can even be attached to your Treo. (Who knows? Maybe future Treo versions will fully integrate GPS.)

How Does GPS Work?

GPS works by comparing the signals from multiple GPS satellites (at least four are required for this process to work). A GPS receiver accurately measures the distance from four or more satellites whose positions are known, and then uses this information to compute its precise location.

Sprint Treo 600s Have Integrated Support for GPS

The Sprint version of the Treo 600 has integrated support for Assisted GPS (A-GPS) through the gpsOne technology. Unfortunately, the application programming interfaces (APIs) are not yet available for this, making it impossible for GPS software vendors to tie into this technology. A program is planned to help developers do this soon, so watch for news on this.

You can learn more about the A-GPS technology at http://www.cdmatech.com/solutions/products/gpsone_cdma.jsp. A-GPS uses a combination of satellite and terrestrial signals to locate the precise position of the handset.

NOTE *The explanation of GPS used here is simplified. For a more technical understanding of how GPS works, refer to www.trible.com/gps for an excellent tutorial.*

What Do We Use GPS For?

GPS can be used in a wide variety of ways. The possible uses fall into one of five general categories:

- **Location-based services** To determine where you are. If you are a hiker, you could use GPS with your Treo to find your current position. GPS could also be used with a wireless service to deliver *location-based services,* services that combine your current location with other information and software you load into your Treo, which can then feed you information relevant to you for your current location. For example, suppose you are looking for a particular type of shoe. You could use shopping software loaded on your Treo to indicate you are in the market for these shoes. Then, when you walk past a shoe store, your Treo's location-based services software could determine if that store has your shoes on sale, in stock, and in your size.

- **Navigation** To get from one location to another. This is why you find GPS systems (such as the Hertz Neverlost system) in more and more rental cars and available as options on many new vehicles. Now you can have this functionality in your pocket everywhere you go. If you like to fish, you can use your GPS to locate and easily return to your best fishing holes!

14

■ **Tracking** To monitor the movement of people or things. Many trucking companies have adopted GPS to help their central dispatching keep track of where all their vehicles are. This has also been used effectively in the fields of law enforcement and security.

■ **Mapping** For cartography. Almost all modern maps are created using GPS technology for precision.

■ **Timing** To accurately determine the time, GPS satellites can be used as a form of atomic clock, allowing you to get very precise time on your GPS receiver. Every GPS satellite has its own atomic clock on board.

GPS on Your Treo

Your Treo will not come installed with a GPS solution. If you want to perform GPS functions with your device, you will need to acquire both a GPS receiver and software. Some sources for this equipment are listed at the end of this chapter in the section "GPS Hardware and Software." For the purposes of this chapter, we will use the iTrek Mouse GPS receiver from Semsons and Co (www.semsons.com) as an example. This device connects to your Treo through the serial port at the bottom of your smartphone. It is extremely compact, easy to use, and comes with a vehicle power adaptor for powering both the receiver and your Treo while you are in your car. Other vendors produce hardware that connects to your Treo through Bluetooth wireless technology, although we are unable to test these devices until the Bluetooth SD drivers are released for the Treo 600. For software, we will use Navigator for Palm OS 5 from Mapopolis (www.mapopolis.com) as an example in this chapter. You can use any vendor's hardware (check to make sure it conforms to the NMEA standard) or software you like; the techniques discussed in this chapter can be applied to most GPS software packages.

We will not be teaching you every function of Mapopolis, but rather focusing on the most common GPS navigation activities that a Treo user might want to accomplish.

 *If you are driving a car, never attempt to interact with a GPS navigation system while the car is in motion. If you need to change an address, you should pull over or allow a passenger to update the information for you. Most GPS software packages will give you audible instructions through your Treo's speaker when you need to turn or perform some other action.*

The main interface of your GPS software will likely contain a large map-viewing area, along with a menu or control buttons on one edge, as in Figure 14-1. In Mapopolis, you have some other common interface elements:

- **Compass**   The lower-right corner contains a compass that shows you which direction is north. North isn't always up, and the map will rotate to face the direction you are going if you have it set to Auto Rotate. If the top of the map is indeed north, then the compass box will disappear.

- **Scale indicator**   The lower-left of the map area contains a box with a line in it that indicates the scale. The size of the line represents the distance indicated by the number to the right (in Figure 14-1, it is 1 kilometer).

- **Menu buttons**   The menu buttons are used to interact with the Mapopolis map, open the menu, zoom in and out, and more.

Note that touching the Menu button on the far right of the button set will open the main Mapopolis menu, shown in Figure 14-2, which will get you into the other parts of the software discussed in this chapter.

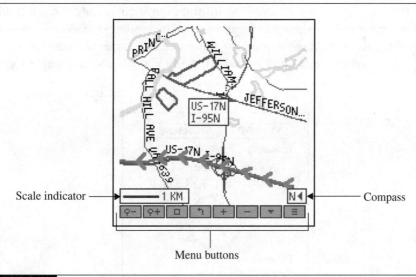

FIGURE 14-1   The Mapopolis interface contains a large map-viewing window with additional controls at the bottom for changing the view and other options.

FIGURE 14-2   The main Mapopolis menu is where you go to enter destinations and manage your navigation.

Check GPS Status

Before you can use your GPS, you need to make sure it is working properly. To ensure that the GPS is indeed communicating, select the GPS button from the menu shown in Figure 14-2. This is where you can configure your GPS settings, start and stop your GPS, and find out GPS-provided information such as longitude, latitude, elevation, and speed, as shown in Figure 14-3. The graphical readout at the very bottom of the screen will show you how many satellite connections the GPS unit currently has, and the strength of the signal. A full bar indicates a stronger signal

FIGURE 14-3   The GPS status screen will tell you the details of your connection with the GPS satellites.

than a half bar. You must have at least four full bars for the GPS receiver to be able to relay accurate information. Incidentally, the GPS transmissions are "line-of-sight," so there cannot be obstacles between you and the satellites. Because of this, your GPS generally doesn't function indoors, in parking garages, or in other such locations.

In this example, we are currently connected to four satellites (the minimum). The lines connecting to each satellite indicate the strength of the satellite signal. You can also see your current latitude, longitude, altitude, and velocity (if you are moving!). With some GPS software, you can also see the date and time. This is an extremely accurate date and time because it is based on the atomic clocks aboard each of the GPS satellites you are communicating with. If your software shows a number beside each satellite readout, this is the unique identification number of that particular satellite vehicle (SV).

If you are running your GPS with software and hardware from different vendors, you will need to tell them how to talk to each other. To do this, press the GPS Settings button on the top-right of the GPS status screen. This will open the configuration information, as shown in Figure 14-4.

On this screen, you can specify the type of connection that your GPS receiver will is going to have. This is done with the drop-down selection box at the top of the screen, where you can choose between serial ports, infrared, or Bluetooth connections. After connecting to a new GPS unit, you may need to return to the main GPS screen and manually start the GPS. Now that you have the hardware and software talking, you are ready to start using your GPS!

14

FIGURE 14-4   The configuration screen allows you to set up how your software communicates with your GPS receiver.

Other options that you can configure on your GPS Settings screen are

■ **Auto-Scroll Map**   This setting will cause Mapopolis to scroll the map as you drive so that you are always viewing your current position in the center of the screen. This should be turned on for GPS-based navigation.

■ **Auto-Rotate Map**   This will cause the software to automatically change the direction of the screen to match the direction you are driving. Forward is up. This can cause north to be in different positions, but it is generally the preferable option for GPS navigation.

■ **Keep Device Power on for 1 Hr**   This is an essential option for GPS navigation. The natural Treo tendency to turn itself off after a few minutes of inactivity to conserve battery power is very counterproductive when trying to navigate with GPS!

■ **Display GPS Data on Map**   This will cause GPS bearing, range, heading, and speed to be shown in the upper-left corner of your map view.

■ **Restart GPS at Program Start**   This will cause Mapopolis to reset its communication with the GPS receiver each time Mapopolis is started, which is recommended.

Find Your Current Location

Finding out exactly where you are can be useful if you get lost, if you are hiking in the backcountry, or if you work in a situation where your physical location is important to coordinating your work activity, such as is the case for bicycle couriers in large metropolitan areas, for example. Most GPS software will provide you an option for finding your current location, often with the precise street address. Mapopolis will show your current location on the map as soon as you start your GPS receiver. The GPS screen will also give you your precise location in longitude and latitude.

Navigate to a Destination

The most common use for GPS capability on a Treo is to help you find your way from one place to another. We find this particularly useful when we are traveling and have appointments all over town in a city we are unfamiliar with. To navigate to a destination, you must tell your GPS software where you wish to go. You can do this by providing an address, specifying an intersection, or selecting a specific

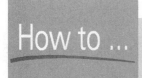 **Use Your GPS When You Are Away from Civilization**

The ability to find your current location is very valuable for hikers, surveyors, marine enthusiasts, and many others. Software like Mapopolis is useful for navigating cities and streets, but not so useful if you are on the water or hiking in the backcountry. For these uses, you will need different software, such as that offered by MapTech (www.maptech.com). MapTech's Outdoor Navigator product will allow you to load U.S. Geological Survey maps onto your Treo and navigate with them.

Of course, if you do plan to use your Treo in these rugged conditions, you will need to give special consideration to battery life and rugged conditions. The battery life of your Treo won't last you through a multiday hike unless you use the GPS very sparingly. Consider carrying spare batteries, an *electric fuel* battery recharger (a chemical battery that can be used to recharge your Treo on the fly), or a solar-powered recharger like the iSun unit from ICP (www.icpglobal.com). You will also need a GPS receiver that isn't dependent on being plugged into a vehicle power supply.

If you are traveling in conditions where your Treo is going to be exposed to a lot of moisture or dust, you should consider some kind of a protective or "ruggedized" case, or an alternative case to help protect your device when you need it most. MapTech also sells a generic environmental protection sleeve that will fit your Treo.

point on a map. In addition, you may have a set of favorite addresses for places that you go to often, or you can look up a particular contact in your address book. Mapopolis also features a powerful Points of Interest feature that allows you to get a list of the closest restaurants, banks, gas stations, and many other useful destinations. If you find yourself in an unfamiliar location and want to see all the restaurants within three miles, you can find that with the Points of Interest feature.

Specific Address

One of the most common ways to navigate is to enter the address of the location you are going to. Mapopolis offers a variety of ways to do this, all of which give the same result. Each method simply starts with a different piece of information—the

14

FIGURE 14-5   You can enter a specific address to navigate to with your GPS.

address, the street, the city, a place, or an address from your Contacts. For example, if you wanted to search for an address, you would check the Address check box and then begin entering the address information on the line below the check boxes. As you enter the data, Mapopolis matches what you are typing against its database of addresses for the map you have loaded. Matching results will be displayed in the box, as shown in Figure 14-5.

If you change the drop-down selection list at the top of the screen to Street Intersection, you can navigate to a specific intersection of two roads. You enter the name (or a part of the name) of the first street in the first line. Then you can enter the name (or part of the name) of the cross street on the second line. Tapping the Find button will cause the software to find any streets in its currently loaded map that match your 1st Street selection. They will appear in the first box. When you tap the street you want in the first box, it will then match your 2nd Street entry and populate the second box with streets that match and intersect with your 1st Street selection.

After using any of the preceding methods, you can press the Go To button to calculate the best route from where you are to where you want to go. Your next turn or instruction will appear in the box at the bottom of the map area as shown in the following illustration, and your path will be outlined on the map with a green line and arrows indicating the direction of travel. As you begin to drive, the maneuvers you need to complete will be displayed one by one at the bottom of the map-viewing area (see the following illustration) until you arrive at your destination. If you have your Treo sound turned on, you will also receive verbal instructions on when to turn and what maneuvers to make.

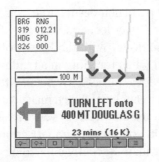

Get There by Pointing

You don't always have to enter specific street information to get to where you want to go. If you can visually locate where you would like to end up on the map, you can simply point to your destination using the stylus and the software will determine where that is. You access this functionality by choosing the Navigation button from the Mapopolis menu. This will open the Navigation screen, shown in Figure 14-6.

14

FIGURE 14-6   Using the map to point at a destination on the map is another way to tell Mapopolis where you want to go.

On this screen, you can set the start and end points for your navigation. For either point, you can use the On Map button to open the map and select a specific point with your stylus.

You can use the zoom controls (magnifying glasses with plus and minus signs) to move around the map and also use the navigation control to scroll around. Once you identify where you would like to go, simply tap the location with the stylus to begin navigation.

Favorites

You might find that there are particular destinations you need to get to often, such as your home, office, day care, or other location. You can set the software to remember a group of "favorite" destinations. With the Mapopolis software, this is called a Geomark. I find this useful when traveling in an unfamiliar city, and I often drive between a variety of meeting locations and my hotel. After picking up my rental car, I instruct the GPS to navigate to my hotel. I then make the hotel a "favorite" destination so that I do not have to reenter the information every time I want to return to the hotel.

To create a new Geomark, you select Geomark from the Mapopolis menu, and then tap the location on your map. Recently entered destinations are automatically added as Geomarks. To begin navigating to a Geomark, you select the button with the down arrow on the lower-right of your map view.

Contacts

Many of the destinations to which you might want to navigate are contained within your contacts on your Treo's Contacts application, discussed in Part I of this book. You can select from your list of contacts by choosing Find from the Mapopolis menu, and then using the Address Book check box. As you enter a part of a name in the entry field, Mapopolis looks up the matching people from your contacts. You will then see a list of your matching contacts, as shown in Figure 14-7.

Place By Category

The Place By Category feature of Mapopolis is a wonderful, extremely useful feature. It allows you to find the nearest destination from a given category. Imagine you are in an unfamiliar city, and you need to find a gas station or a bank machine. When you select Place By Category in the Find menu, Mapopolis will populate categories of points of interest in the upper box; and when you select any of the categories, the matching destinations appear in the lower box (see Figure 14-8). This makes it easy to find your way to common destinations.

FIGURE 14-7   You can navigate to the address of any of the contacts stored in your Treo's Contacts application.

FIGURE 14-8   It is easy to find the nearest gas station, bank, restaurant, and other key locations with the Place By Category feature.

Load and Switch Maps

Your Treo has a limited amount of memory, and GPS maps are very detailed, meaning that they require a lot of storage space. If you plan to do a lot of traveling and need to have a number of maps with you, buying a 64MB or larger (Secure Digital) SD card is highly recommended. If you travel to only one destination at a time, always returning home in between, you can load and unload the maps you want as you need them.

Mapopolis has a complete application for loading and unloading maps. You simply have to download the map you require from the Mapopolis web site, and then sync the .pdb file to your Treo. The map selection screen shown in Figure 14-9 lets you select the map you want to begin working with by tapping it with your stylus.

You can load multiple maps onto your Treo and also your expansion card. To see which maps are on your card, you will need to tap the Go To Card button at the upper-right of the window.

FIGURE 14-9   The map selection screen allows you to choose which map you want to work with.

GPS Hardware and Software

In addition to the Semsons GPS receiver and Mapopolis software used in the preceding examples, you should consider many other vendors and configurations of hardware and software for your Treo GPS needs. The GPS units come in one of four formats:

- **Serial cable**   These GPS units connect into the Treo via the serial port. Power is usually not drawn directly from the Treo to power the unit, so an external power source such as a vehicle cigarette lighter is usually required.

- **SDIO card**   SDIO GPS receivers use the SD slot on the top of the Treo 600 to connect to your smartphone. These units usually draw their power directly from the Treo or through an external adapter.

- **Bluetooth**   This is one of the newest types of GPS. It is essentially the same as a serial port unit; however, it makes its serial connection with the Treo via a Bluetooth connection and thus is wirelessly connected instead of needing cables.

- **Stand-alone**   Stand-alone GPS receivers are units that can function with or without the Treo (although the Treo usually extends the receiver's functionality and usability). These receivers tend to connect to the Treo through the bottom serial port. One nice feature about this type of receiver is that you can use it alone, with a Treo, or with a laptop.

More detail on alternative GPS hardware and software is contained in Chapter 16 of this book.

Other Software

In addition to the GPS vendors listed earlier, you can consider a few other pieces of software for personal navigation.

MapQuest

If you aren't in the market for a full-fledged GPS solution, you can take advantage of offerings from MapQuest (www.mapquest.com). At MapQuest's web site, you can look up maps and create driving directions prior to leaving on your trip. You can then download those maps to your Treo through an AvantGo (www.avantgo.com) sync conduit. Now when you are traveling around, you can pull up these maps on demand to help you navigate.

TomTom CityMaps

One concern about GPS systems is the lack of maps available if you are traveling outside North America. A few software companies support maps for non–North American cities. TomTom (www.tomtom.com) has a database of more than 100,000 cities across Europe that ships on a CD-ROM. (Some of the larger cities are available in electronic downloads from the TomTom web site.) This software is well designed and very user-friendly.

Wrap It Up

In this chapter, we wanted to introduce you to the world of personal navigation with GPS on your Treo. It isn't possible to give you a detailed analysis of all the features, software, and hardware products in this space. The vendors listed in this chapter can provide a great deal more detail on their products and features.

In addition to basic personal or business navigation, GPS is rapidly catching on for location-based services. An example of a location-based service might be a vendor providing you with information when you are near its facilities or an airport telling you, when you arrive in the airport parking lot late for a flight, that it can automatically rebook you on the next flight or possibly hold the airplane. A popular new recreational sport has even popped up around personal GPS navigation. It is called *geocaching*. It involves groups of people hiding or "caching" something in a location and then identifying where these caches are with their GPS coordinates. For more details on this sport, check out www.geocaching.com.

If you would like to dive a little deeper into the technology underlying GPS, we recommend an online tutorial put together by Trimble, one of the major GPS vendors. You can find it at www.trimble.com/gps.

14

Part III

Select Essential Hardware Accessories and Software for Your Treo

Chapter 15

Store Information and Go Further with Secure Digital and MultiMediaCards

How to...

- Add storage memory to your Treo 600

- Format a storage card

- Use storage cards to swap files between your Treo and your PC

- Use SDIO cards to add capabilities to your Treo

There is a saying in the high-tech world, "You can never be too rich, too good looking, or have too much storage space." This cavalier, off-the-cuff comment is particularly true when it comes to mobile devices. Rarely do the devices have sufficient on-board memory to accommodate all of your needs. This is one of the reasons why your Treo 600 comes equipped with a slot for external memory and hardware expansion. As you begin to use your Treo for more advanced functions like GPS, photo albums, and MP3 and video entertainment, external expansion cards will be an absolute necessity.

What Are SD and MMC Cards?

The Treo 600 can use both Secure Digital (SD) and MultiMediaCard (MMC) formats for storing information externally. These storage cards are extremely small, about the size of a postage stamp, and currently have the ability to store up to 1GB of information. This is about 40 times the memory currently available to you on your Treo 600. That represents a lot of music, documents, and other files you can carry with you. A Secure Digital card is shown in Figure 15-1.

These memory cards are *nonvolatile*. This means that they do not require any power to maintain the memory they contain. You can remove the card from your Treo, and it will keep the information stored on it ready for you when you need it next. This type of storage is also called *solid state*. This means that it has no moving parts to skip or break down. It transfers data very fast, which makes it an ideal storage medium for your smartphone.

Although SD and MMC cards are very similar, there are differences you should be aware of when selecting one or the other to store your information:

- **Size**   The MMC card is marginally smaller than the SD card, but both will work just fine in your Treo 600 expansion card slot.

- **Speed**   SD cards transfer data faster than MMC cards, which is important when loading large files such as GPS maps from the card into the Treo memory.

FIGURE 15-1   The Secure Digital card allows you to store a tremendous amount of extra information on your Treo 600.

- **Durability**   The extra thickness of the SD card makes it somewhat more durable than MMC.

- **Write protection**   SD cards have a small switch on the side of them so you can make them read-only. MMC cards do not have this. This is useful if you want to prevent accidental overwriting of important information on a storage card.

- **Copyright protection**   The SD card has additional capability for enhanced copyright security, although this may not be relevant for the average consumer.

- **Cost**   MMC cards are usually a little less expensive than the comparable SD card.

So which card you pick will depend on what you need it for, but it is safe to say that Secure Digital is becoming a much more common standard than MMC.

15

Use the Treo Card Slot

The Treo 600 contains a slot on the top of the unit for inserting SD and MMC cards. When your Treo 600 shipped from the factory, there was a fake SD card inserted in the slot to keep out dust and other foreign objects. When your expansion slot isn't in use, you should reinsert this dummy card to protect the slot from damage. The dummy card serves no other purpose.

To remove cards from the slot, you simply push down on the card that is in the slot and it will eject with a spring-loaded push. A new card should be inserted far enough

Watch Out for Counterfeit SD Cards

Did you know you can void your warranty by using cheap expansion cards? In our modern era of cheap, knock-off products, it is possible to purchase noncompliant SD cards if you're not careful. These cards can actually damage your Treo 600, so when buying them, ensure that they contain the SD logo, have a notch on the card opposite the write-protect switch, and only have the angle notch on one side. (Some fake cards are angled on both sides.)

until you feel it lock into place. The card is inserted into the slot with the card label facing the rear of the Treo 600, which is slightly counterintuitive, so you will need to pay close attention. This means that the angle notch on the card is pointed away from the antenna.

When you insert a storage card into your Treo, it will open up the card's contents with the Applications Launcher, showing you any applications installed onto the card, as shown in the following illustration. Your card can also contain other nonapplication files. Unlike your desktop PC, you cannot simply browse the files on the SD card; you must use applications to move to the files stored on the card.

You can find out all about the card by running the Card Info application, shown here, when a storage card is inserted:

This will show you the type of card, its size, how much memory has been used, and more. This is also where you can use the Card menu to rename or format the card. Renaming the card, as shown here, simply changes the name that appears in the drop-down list of categories when the card is inserted into the Treo:

Formatting a card is rather more severe because it will erase all of the data on the card. This can be a quick way to prepare an old card when you no longer care about the contents of the card. Although most computing devices format SD cards the same way, there are some devices that format SD cards in a nonstandard format, requiring them to be reformatted before they can be used in your Treo. For example, my MP3 player can use expansion cards to store extra songs, but the cards are formatted in such a way that they cannot be read by my home computer or my Treo.

Storage Capacity and Cost

Storage cards represent a very low-cost way to store more information on your smartphone. The price scales up along with the storage capacity, but you will find that the storage capacity gets larger and the price per megabyte gets lower every day. Currently, SD and MMC storage cards start around $40 for a 64MB card (about 63 cents per MB), and run up to $389 for a 1GB card (about 40 cents per MB). This means that for about $50, your Treo can have more on-board memory than the Spirit and Opportunity rovers that NASA put on Mars!

You can buy these cards at virtually any computer or photo store (many digital cameras use the same kind of cards for storing digital pictures), or you can find them online. The online sources include the manufacturers themselves, as well as online retail stores:

■ SanDisk (www.sandisk.com)

■ Kingston Technology (www.kingston.com)

■ Lexar Media (www.lexarmedia.com)

■ SimpleTech (www.simpletech.com)

■ Delkin eFilm (www.delkin.com)

■ Mobile Planet (www.mobileplanet.com)

■ Amazon (www.amazon.com)

TIP   *Prices for storage cards are falling all the time. If you are buying online, you can check some of the large price comparison sites to find the best deal. Sites such as PriceGrabber (www.pricegrabber.com) and CNET Shopper (http://shopper.cnet.com/) can be good sources. At these sites, you can select the specific product you are looking for, and they will search dozens of online vendors to find the best price. These sites also provide information about the reliability of the vendors in the list.*

Move and Launch Applications from the Expansion Card

After you insert a new storage card into your Treo, if there are any applications loaded on the card they will appear in the Applications Launcher. You can launch any of the applications on the card by tapping the application's icon on the screen with your stylus or highlighting it and pressing the center of your navigation control. You will notice that the name of the card appears in the drop-down selections at the top-right of the screen. These selections allow you to switch between viewing applications on the card and applications installed directly on your Treo.

As you load more applications on your Treo, you may want to conserve some of your precious internal memory by moving some of your less-used applications to a memory card. If you do this, be careful to make sure that the applications support Palm OS 5.2; otherwise they may not execute properly when moved to a storage card. To move an application to the storage card, you must be in the Applications Launcher. From the App menu, choose Copy. This will open up the Copy screen, as shown in Figure 15-2.

FIGURE 15-2   You can use the Copy function in the Applications Launcher to move applications onto storage cards.

After you have moved the application to the expansion card and confirmed that it works properly, you can delete the application from your Treo by selecting Delete from the App menu.

This will open the Delete screen, from which you can select and delete any applications that are loaded, as shown in the following illustration. You must first specify if you are deleting the applications from the Treo or the storage card. If you are deleting from the Treo, you set the Delete From field to Phone. To delete from the storage card, you select the name of the storage card in the drop-down list in the Delete From field.

Note that applications that are loaded on an external storage card must be copied to the local memory in your Treo before they can run. This means that you must leave sufficient memory empty on your Treo to allow programs stored on a card to be loaded locally as needed.

Use Storage Cards to Swap Files

The ability to move files quickly from your PC to your Treo can be very handy. Perhaps you want to move a collection of your favorite MP3s from your hard drive to your Treo so you can listen on the go (or use them for ringtones, as discussed in Chapter 4!). Maybe you have a number of Microsoft Word documents that you want to take with you in case you need to reference them on a business trip.

You could sync these files to your handheld using your appropriate desktop application, but it is often faster and easier to move them directly onto your storage card. In order to accomplish this, you must have a storage card reader attached to your PC. Many laptops and printers today have storage card slots built right in, but if yours don't, you can buy storage card readers as external accessories. My Fujitsu laptop has a convenient SD slot where I can insert the cards from my Treo directly into my laptop. My HP 7350 PhotoSmart printer also has a card reader built into it. When I insert a card into either of these slots, the SD card appears as a new drive letter on my system, allowing me to read and write files to the card.

15

You need to be careful when moving files onto your storage card. Your Treo will expect your files to conform to a specific format; if they don't, you run the risk that the files you copy over will be ignored. In Figure 15-3, you can see the file structure for a sample SD card from the card reader in my laptop. Your Treo will expect to see a folder in the root of the card called Palm. Inside that folder, it will expect to find two subfolders, Launcher and Programs. The Launcher folder is for applications that are loaded on the card and that appear in the Applications Launcher on the Treo. The Programs folder contains data for specific programs that use card storage. In Figure 15-3, you will notice subfolders for the applications BackupMan and Documents To Go, which are discussed in Chapters 9 and 11, respectively.

The SD card listed in Figure 15-3 is called Revio SD and has been given the drive letter F: on my laptop. In the root directory of the card, you will see two folders called DCIM and PALM. The first one, DCIM, is from my digital camera. It contains all the photos from my camera. The second folder, PALM, contains all the information relevant to my Treo. This shows how the same card can be used in two different devices without the information conflicting.

In the PALM directory, there are two subfolders. The Launcher folder contains any applications that have been loaded on the card. The Programs folder contains any program-related information. The BackupMan subfolder contains the actual .prc file for the BackupMan application, which allows me to restore my backed-up files from the card, even if my Treo has been wiped out. (Refer to Chapter 9 for more information on this important use of a storage card.) The Programs folder also contains a subfolder called DXTG. This is my Documents To Go folder. If I want to copy a group of documents or spreadsheets onto my card, I can copy them directly into this folder. Then, when the card is inserted in my Treo, the Documents To Go application can find them using its Search For Files feature.

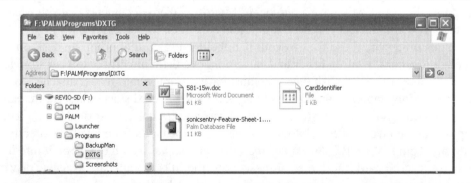

FIGURE 15-3   Storage cards used in the Treo conform to a specific file structure you should adhere to.

Use SDIO Cards to Add Hardware Features to Your Treo

Your Treo 600 expansion slot is capable of delivering much more than just extra memory for your smartphone. It also supports the Secure Digital Input/Output (SDIO) spec, which means that it can be used to drive actual external hardware. We have already discussed some of this hardware throughout the book, but we will reference it here for your convenience.

 The Treo 600 is a very new device, and some of the accessories mentioned in this section do not yet have Treo 600–compatible drivers available. All vendors mentioned here have announced Treo 600 support, but check the relevant vendor's web site to confirm that Treo 600 support has been released.

Go Wireless

There are products that allow you to turn your Treo into a multiprotocol wireless device. Your Treo already supports either GSM (Global System for Mobile Communications)/GPRS (General Packet Radio Service) or CDMA (Code Division Multiple Access), depending on which carrier you purchased your Treo from, but it can also be equipped to connect to your office wireless local area network (WLAN) with the SanDisk Connect Wi-Fi SD card. This card will stick slightly out of the top of your Treo, but it will allow you to surf the Web, send e-mail, and run connected applications at speeds many times that offered by your mobile carrier. Wi-Fi connects at speeds up to 11 Mbps, which is over 200 times faster than a standard GPRS connection!

Note that, although SanDisk has announced formal support for Palm OS 5.2, the drivers were not available at the time this book was written. Check SanDisk's web site at www.sandisk.com to confirm driver availability.

You can also expand your Treo with Bluetooth SD cards that are available from many vendors. (Note that drivers for the Treo 600 are still in development but should be out by the time you read this.) With Bluetooth, you can connect your Treo to many accessories, including GPS receivers, wireless phone headsets, presentation devices, printers, and much more!

Make Presentations

There are SDIO cards that will allow you to connect your Treo to a PC monitor or projector to display screens or PowerPoint slideshows on a large screen. The Margi Presenter-to-Go product already has all the necessary Treo 600 drivers available.

15

Presenting from your Treo is covered in more detail in Chapter 11, and you can learn more about this specific product at www.margi.com.

Biometric Security

To further enhance security, biometric fingerprint scanners are being released now that adhere to the SDIO standard. As these products become available, you can further enhance the security of your Treo by requiring it to recognize a fingerprint or thumbprint that you swipe across the top of the expansion card slot. Without the appropriate recognition, biometric security will prevent access to your Treo files.

Better Cameras

The Treo 600 has a built-in 0.3-megapixel camera, but if you are a photo buff, you might find yourself wanting a higher-quality camera for your Treo. There are 1.3-megapixel SD cameras coming onto the market. For example, Veo (www.veo.com) has been working with palmOne to make its 1.3-megapixel SD camera compatible with the entire palmOne line. Other innovators are also now developing SD cameras with built-in flashes (an absolute necessity for indoor photos) and the ability to take full-motion video.

Wrap It Up

The ability to insert storage cards and expansion cards into the top expansion slot of your Treo 600 opens up whole new worlds of what you can do with your smartphone. For example, you now can carry a street-by-street map of the world with you everywhere you go or keep an extensive music collection for your entertainment. Libraries of important documents are at the ready.

In addition, the future is unlimited when you consider what kinds of hardware expansions might soon be developed for this flexible tool. Watch for more exciting innovations that you will be able to leverage with your Treo in the near future!

Chapter 16

Explore the Peripheral and Software Jungle

How to...

■ Expand your Treo with new hardware

■ Choose software that adds value

The Treo 600 by itself is a powerful and useful tool, but it was also designed to be adaptable and expandable. Many companies are creating products to enable you to get even more out of your Treo, and new items are appearing on the market all the time. In this chapter we examine some of the products that are available and give you our impressions of their value to you, the Treo user.

In each section we have tried to set up a standard format to help you compare the products and select the one that might best fit your needs best. We have not tested all of the products listed. If it is a product with which we have direct personal experience, we review the product and share our opinions.

Hardware Accessories

As the Treo 600 is still quite a new device, there aren't many hardware accessories available for it; but many companies are developing accessories specifically for the Treo 600.

Headsets and Car Kits

In this section we look specifically at audio accessories and related equipment for your Treo. This includes telephone headsets, in-car kits, and mounting brackets.

When looking for a new headset to use with your Treo 600, you have a very wide selection from which to choose. You will need to decide which style of headset you prefer. The standard headset styles include

■ **Over-the-head**   These headsets usually cover one ear and use a plastic "headband" to go over the top of your head.

■ **On-the-ear**   These headsets have hooks or loops to hang on the ear, and these hooks and loops position the speaker to cover the ear.

■ **In-the-ear**   This style is often referred to as an "earbud," and the speaker goes right in your ear. One advantage of this style is that it blocks out more of the ambient noise, usually making it easier for you to hear the caller. This is a very popular style due to its small size and low cost.

■ **Behind-the-neck**   These headsets rest on the back of your neck, much like popular headphone styles with portable music players. One of the prime attractions of this headset style is that it doesn't interfere with hats, helmets, or fancy hairdos!

■ **Binaural**   These headsets cover both ears, allowing you to focus more on the caller but not allowing you to hear any of the other sounds in your immediate vicinity.

A good source for the hundreds of different headset combinations is www.headsets. com. You can generally use any headset with a standard 2.5 mm headset plug.

> **TIP**
>
> *If you plan to use your Treo and headset in a noisy environment or in a car with the windows open, you might want to consider investing in a noise-canceling headset, which can help to filter out background noise so your caller doesn't hear it.*

Handspring High-Performance Headset

An improvement over the standard headset that ships with your Treo is the Handspring High-Performance Headset.

Product	High-Performance Headset
Manufacturer	palmOne (www.palmOne.com)
Web link	www.handspring.com/products/Product.jhtml?id=410005&cat=310005
Description	A mono earbud-style headset for use with your Treo 600. It includes a button on the in-line microphone for answering an incoming call and disconnecting a current call. The microphone has a noise-canceling feature that makes this an upgrade from the earbud headset you receive with your Treo 600.
Price	$14.99

Handspring Stereo Headphones

Of course, the standard headset that comes with the Treo doesn't let you listen to music or other sounds in stereo because it only has one earbud. Handspring's solution for this is its Stereo Headphones.

16

Product	Stereo Headphones
Manufacturer	palmOne (www.palmOne.com)
Web link	www.handspring.com/products/Product.jhtml?id=410007&cat=310005
Description	Classic earbud-style stereo headset that plugs directly into the 2.5 mm jack of your Treo 600. Allows you to listen to music, streaming audio, and other sounds from your Treo. This set doesn't have a microphone, so it is not appropriate as a hands-free communication headset.
Price	$19.99

Handspring Stereo Headphone Adapter

If you would like to use your standard stereo headphones with your Treo, you will find that the plug will not fit into the smartphone, but Handspring offers this adapter from its web site.

Product	Stereo Headphone Adapter
Manufacturer	palmOne (www.palmOne.com)
Web link	www.handspring.com/products/Product.jhtml?id=410006&cat=310005
Description	This adapter plugs into the 2.5 mm headset jack of your Treo 600 and allows you to use any standard set of 3.5 mm headphones to listen to the sounds from your Treo. Similar adapters are available from a variety of sources such as RadioShack (www.radioshack.com), so check around for your best price.
Price	$5.99

Seido Hands-Free Stereo Headphones

Handspring doesn't have the market cornered on stereo headphones. Luckily, the Treo has a standard size and style of headphone port (conforming to the 2.5mm standard) that allows you to use products like ones from Seido.

Product	Hands-Free Stereo Headphones
Manufacturer	Seido (www.seidoonline.com)
Web link	www.seidioonline.com/ProductDetails.asp?ProductCode=HMESVOT-SL
Description	This handy headset is great because it allows you to use it as a hands-free kit for making calls from your Treo 600, and it can be used as full stereo headphones for listening to MP3 and other sounds. Seido also has many other headset products that are compatible with the Treo 600.
Price	$27.95

ZipLinq Retractable Earbud Headset

For the road warrior who hates cables, ZipLinq offers a retractable headset.

Product	Hands-Free Headset With Universal Jack
Manufacturer	ZipLinq (www.ziplinq.com)
Web link	www.ziplinq.com/retractable-cable-hands-free.html
Description	An earbud-style headset with an answer/disconnect button mounted on the microphone. This headset is unique in that the cable retracts on a small spool; this makes for very easy storage and long life.
Price	Not priced
Review	This product is very handy for people like me who tend to snag their headset cords on every object within three feet. In fact, I usually ruin two or three corded headsets a year, just walking around with them. I also find that the cords are always tangled up in something, making it awkward to pull out and use when you want to. The retracting feature is a wonderful option. The only drawback to this unit is a merely mediocre microphone. This product would work much better with a higher-quality microphone, preferably with noise-canceling features.

Cases

In Chapter 9, you were introduced to some of the important aspects of cases to protect and personalize your Treo 600. Some case vendors you can look to are listed in this section.

Bellagio (www.bellagiodesigns.com)

Bellagio features two styles of cases for the Treo 600. Both of the cases are made of Italian leather, are available with or without a spring-loaded swivel belt clip, and provide all the right cutouts for accessing your Treo 600 controls. Both cases can also be personalized with your name, company logo, or other information. The first model is a one-piece, always-on case, and the second is an always-on case with a flip-top cover.

Product	Treo 600 Cell Phone Leather PDA Case
Manufacturer	Bellagio Designs (www.bellagiodesigns.com)
Web link	www.bellagiodesigns.com/showcategory3.php?cod_category3=28&cod_category1=1#1
Description	A one-piece case that stays on your phone all the time, offering continuous protection.

Product	Treo 600 Cell Phone Leather PDA Case, *continued*
Price	$24.95
Review	This is a well-made case that offers solid protection. It features all the appropriate cutouts for the camera, speakers, headphone jack, microphone, reset button, and sync cable. Our only concern with this case is that the top snap obstructs the belt clip, causing the phone not to swivel properly when the belt clip is being used.

Product	Treo 600 Flip-Style MOD "B" Leather PDA Case
Manufacturer	Bellagio Designs (www.bellagiodesigns.com)
Web link	www.bellagiodesigns.com/showcategory3.php?cod_category3=28&cod_category1=1#1
Description	A flip-style case with a cover that flips over the front of the Treo 600 to protect the keyboard and screen. This cover also provides a convenient storage space for credit cards, as well as two holders for SD/MMC cards. One very unique feature of this case is the flip-out stand at the bottom that allows you to stand your Treo up so you can see the screen. This is an interesting feature if you use the speaker phone and want to stand your Treo in the middle of the table.
Price	$39.99
Review	This case features the same high-quality features of the Bellagio case in the previous listing with the addition of the interesting flip-out stand. Generally, we feel that flip-style cases for the Treo are impractical because the Treo is by its nature a telephone, and the flip case is something that you have to scramble to open when your phone rings. Then, when you are talking on the phone, the top flap flips up over the top of your head and looks rather silly.

Brando WorkShop Case (www.brando.com.hk)

Brando is based out of Hong Kong and features a deluxe leather case in both a pouch and flip-top style.

Product	Treo 600 Deluxe Leather Case
Manufacturer	Brando WorkShop (www.brando.com.hk)
Web link	http://shop.brando.com.hk/bwtreo600case.php
Description	A basic and functional design. The pouch case works in a very similar fashion to the nylon pouch case that came with your Treo 600. The flip-top case has a leather tail to keep the top cover in place and features a single slot for holding an SD/MMC card.
Price	$32.00 (HK $220.00)

Covertec Cases (www.covertec.com)

Covertec has a reputation for being one of the highest-quality PDA case manufacturers in the market. Having had first-hand experience with their top-end product, we can personally vouch for the fine workmanship, quality stitching, and practical functionality of their cases.

Product	Treo 600 Pouch and One-Piece Case
Manufacturer	Covertec (www.covertec.com)
Web link	www.mobileplanet.com/private/covertec/listing.asp?unit=H.T600
Description	Horizontal pouch-style cases and one-piece, always-on cases. Both styles are available in two-tone black, red, and tan leather. Overstitching is beige, which adds style and class to the case. The pouch has a built-in belt clasp, while the one-piece model has a removable swivel belt clip.
Price	$29.95
Review	The Covertec case is my current case of choice for my Treo 600. It is without question one of the highest-quality cases that I have seen on the market. It is a distinctive and classy case that looks good in both business and casual environments.

EB Slipper Case (www.ebcases.com)

E&B Company is another popular case vendor that makes a product for the Treo 600.

Product	Slipper Treo 600 Case
Manufacturer	E&B Company (www.ebcases.com)
Web link	www.ebcases.com/Detail.bok?no=3200
Description	Form-fitting, one-piece case with a removable cover and Velcro closure.
Price	$46.95 (additional $3.00 for the belt clip option)

Handspring Form-Fit Case (www.palmOne.com)

Handspring offers a one-piece case that keeps your Treo protected all the time.

Product	Form-Fit Case
Manufacturer	Handspring (www.palmOne.com)
Web link	www.handspring.com/products/Product.jhtml?id=410010&cat=310003
Description	Form-fitting, one-piece case with a clear front panel that protects the screen and keyboard from scratches and dirt. A unique feature of this case is a fold-down flap that protects the camera lens. However, this same flap must be held down with a finger when you are taking a picture.
Price	$29.99

Handspring Side Case (www.palmOne.com)

A slight upgrade to the case that comes with your Treo is the Handspring Side Case.

Product	Leather Side Case
Manufacturer	Handspring (www.palmOne.com)
Web link	www.handspring.com/products/Product.jhtml?id=410011&cat=310003
Description	A standard pouch case with the same design as the nylon case that came with your Treo 600, except that this case is leather.
Price	$29.99

Krusell Cases (www.krusell.se)

Krusell is a world-class case manufacturer that has a great deal of experience making high-quality cases for a variety of handheld devices.

Product	Classic Multidapt and Handit Multidapt Case for Treo 600
Manufacturer	Krussell (www.krusell.se)
Web link	www.krusell.se/product.php?s=2&prodGrp=4&product=932
Description	Krussell, a popular worldwide case manufacturer in Sweden, has delivered cases of both one-piece and flip-top styles. These cases are generally available though online retailers, such as Incipio (www.incipiodirect.com).
Price	$29.99
Review	One of the fantastic features of the Krussel cases is their Multidapt clip style. This is unique among all the cases we've reviewed. It allows you to easily adapt your Krussell case to attach to a variety of surfaces. The clips can attach as a simple miniclip, a spring-loaded clip, or a twist-on clip. There are also full-swivel clips in four different formats that you can try out to find the one that fits your preference. The same Multidapt clip can also be used with a Krussell car mount, or one of my favorites, a bike holder that attaches your Treo to the handlebars of your bike. This is handy if you like to use GPS with your Treo and also for bike commuters.

Nutshell Cases (www.tuff-as-nuts.com)

Nutshell has a reputation for cases that are simple and functional.

Product	Treo 600 Natural Leather Case
Manufacturer	Nutshell (www.tuff-as-nuts.com)
Web link	www.tuff-as-nuts.com/Treo-600_203.html
Description	Nutshell makes a vertical, pouch-style case with options that include belt loop style (leather or stainless steel), a choice of colors, and storage slots.
Price	$39.99

Piel Frama Cases (www.pielframa.com)

Piel Frama's cases are considered to be some of the higher-end cases in the marketplace.

Product	Treo 600 Luxurious PDA Case
Manufacturer	Piel Frama (www.pielframa.com)
Web link	www.pielframa.net/prodi.asp?ID=504
Description	Piel Frama makes an extremely high-quality, executive-style case. The Treo 600 models are all flip-top models. The leathers are patterned and come in either a cowskin-crocodile (black) or cowskin-ostrich (brown) style. The magnetic closure strap is a nice feature. The case also includes a money pocket and two slots for SD/MMC cards. An ABS plastic insert also protects the front screen from impact.
Price	90€ (approximately $112.00 U.S.)—includes courier shipping from Spain

Proporta Side Case (www.proporta.com)

Proporta's cases feature a soft leather construction in a flip-top style.

Product	Leather Case
Manufacturer	Proporta (www.proporta.com)
Web link	www.proporta.com/detail.asp?id=593
Description	The Proporta case is made in Brazil out of soft leather. It is a flip-top style case with storage for credit cards, business cards, and SD/MMC cards.
Price	$31.95

Seido (www.seidoonline.com)

Seido has two different styles of cases for your Treo 600, an executive pouch-style case and a swivel holster.

Product	Swivel Clip Holster
Manufacturer	Seido (www.seidoonline.com)
Web link	www.seidioonline.com/ProductDetails.asp?ProductCode=SHLHSTR600
Description	The swivel clip holster is a very useful product that allows for quick and easy access to a ringing Treo. The face of the Treo faces in to protect it from scratches while it is in the holster. This case is made out of high-impact plastic.
Price	$29.95

16

Product	Classic Pouch Leather Case for Treo 600
Manufacturer	Seido (www.seidoonline.com)
Web link	www.seidioonline.com/ProductDetails.asp?ProductCode=OCAPHSTR600-BK
Description	A high-quality, vegetable-tanned Arizona cowhide exterior with lamb-suede interior. This custom-designed case will securely fit your Treo 600. Accented with stylish nylon bonded thread.
Price	$39.95

Sena Cases (www.senacases.com)

Sena Cases has quickly become a dominant case vendor in the mobile device market. Although its product for Treo 600 is very new, it appears it will also have a significant impact in the Treo 600 space.

Product	Treo 600 Flip-Top Case
Manufacturer	Sena Cases (www.senacases.com)
Web link	www.senacases.com/
Description	A flip-top leather case for the Treo 600. This is a new case, and the final version is not yet available.
Price	Unknown
Review	We reviewed an early prototype of the Sena case for the Treo 600. The Sena cases have long been some of our favorites because of their high-quality leather, fine stitching, and stylish looks. The prototype case we were able to review was not in final form and did not yet exhibit these classic Sena case characteristics. The prototype also did not have a cutout for the camera lens, which means you must remove the Treo from the case every time you want to take a picture. Given Sena's long history of quality, I think these issues will be rectified by the time the final version of the case ships. I also have high hopes that Sena will produce a one-piece case for the Treo 600, as I think that this is a much more functional case design for the Treo 600 than a flip-top.

Suntek (www.suntekstore.com)

Suntek makes a leather flip-style case that has a unique design.

Product	Leather Case for Handspring Treo 600 (Flip-Over)
Manufacturer	Suntek (www.suntekstore.com)
Web link	www.suntekstore.com/pm-cs-treo600.html
Description	A black leather flip-style case. This case is different from others in that it flips from the bottom rather than the top.
Price	$21.95

Leather International (www.leatherintl.com)

Leather International manufactures a Treo 600 case that uses the "holster" style.

Product	Horizontal or Vertical Holster for Treo 600
Manufacturer	Leather International (www.leatherintl.com)
Web link	www.leatherintl.com/products/products.asp?id=106
Description	A very stylish leather holster (pouch style) in both a horizontal and vertical format. You can customize the product with your own logo or image.
Price	Not published

Vaja Cases (www.vajacases.com)

Vaja is the Cadillac of case manufacturers for PDAs and mobile devices. Its Treo 600 cases are great examples of its artistic work. Vaja offers two styles, the one-piece iVolution and the flip-top Classic.

Product	iVolution T6 for Treo 600
Manufacturer	Vaja Cases (www.vajacases.com)
Web link	www.vajacases.com/images/smartphones/handspring/treo_600/treo_600.html
Description	The iVolution T6 is a one-piece leather case with a swivel belt clip.
Price	From $84.90
Review	The iVolution T6 is a unique case offering for the Treo 600. It is a semi-rigid, one-piece design that is extremely durable and that acts like an extra layer of armor for your smartphone. It features all the appropriate cutouts to ensure that you can charge and sync your device, as well as use the headphone jack, volume controls, camera, and SD slot.

Product	Classic 797 for Treo 600
Manufacturer	Vaja Cases (www.vajacases.com)
Web link	www.vajacases.com/images/smartphones/handspring/treo_600/treo_600.html
Description	The Classic 797 is a flip-top case made of fine-quality leather.
Price	From $54.90
Review	The Classic 797 is another example of fine Vaja craftsmanship. The leather is of the highest quality, as is the stitching. The case fits the Treo 600 extremely well and can be customized with embossing and other personal features.

Chargers, Cradles, and Cables

Every mobile device faces challenges with power consumption. If you are a traveler or a heavy user of your Treo, you will need to think about how, where, and when you will recharge your device. In this section we will look at some options for powering and syncing your Treo 600.

Small Sync/Charge Cables

There is a host of very small cables on the market that will charge your Treo from the USB port on your computer. Many of these are actually manufactured by a single company and are just resold under different labels. With every sample mini-sync cable that we tried, we were able to charge our Treos but never successfully initiated a HotSync with one of them.

One of the primary vendors of these mini-sync cables is ZipLinq (www.ziplinq. com). The cable retracts to a very small size and is highly portable. This is a great way to recharge while on the road. The size makes it easy to carry in a pocket.

Another mini-sync vendor is BoxWave (www.boxwave.com). BoxWave also offers a car adapter and wall adapter that can be used to charge your Treo with the mini-sync cable. You may think the tiny cable would break easily, but we found it to be very durable and strong. The cable measures 35 inches when fully extended.

Pocket PC Techs (www.pocketpctechs.com), a vendor that you will see referenced a few times in this chapter, also offers a version of this sync cable called the Lil-Sync.

You can generally get the mini-sync cables from any of these vendors, and your local computer store also probably stocks the cables.

Of course, there is a multitude of power and sync accessories available right from palmOne (www.palmOne.com). These include

- **Treo Double Charge** A power adapter that can plug into the wall or your vehicle power port to charge your Treo (6-foot cord).

- **Treo Laptop Travel Cable** USB charging and syncing from your laptop or computer (two-foot cable). This cable has a physical HotSync button, which seems to be necessary for initiating synchronization with the Treo 600.

- **Treo Serial HotSync Cable** This cable replaces the USB sync cable that came with your Treo. If you have an older computer without a USB port, you will need this cable to plug into your serial port to synchronize your Treo.

- **Treo Vehicle Power Charger** A dedicated cable that plugs into your vehicle power port to charge your Treo in your car.

- **Treo USB Docking Cradle**   This handy accessory sits permanently on your desk, and when you want to charge and sync your Treo, you can simply drop it into the cradle. It also holds the Treo screen at a readable angle, affording you the opportunity to interact with your Treo easily. I have often been in the middle of working on something on my desktop computer, and when I want to quickly check my calendar, I check on my Treo because it's faster that starting Outlook to check my calendar.

- **Treo External Battery**   If you are a "power user" of your Treo and find that the built-in battery simply doesn't last long enough, you can attach this external battery to your Treo to get more talk time. This battery is 1250 mAh, which equates to approximately 3 additional hours of talk time and 180 hours of standby time.

We are very big fans of the iGo Juice product from Mobility Electronics (www.igo.com). The Juice is a universal adapter for charging all the devices that you carry. It allows you to charge your laptop, Treo, and other accessories. You can charge them from an outlet, auto power adapter, or airline power port. We travel frequently and tend to carry many different devices due to our line of work, and with the iGo Juice we significantly lighten our travel load.

External Keyboards

There are many vendors that make external keyboards for mobile devices; however, given how new the Treo 600 is to the market, your best option for the moment is from palmOne directly. The palmOne folding external keyboard is well constructed and is provided by a major manufacturer that also builds external keyboards for other vendors, such as Dell. It collapses to a size that easily fits into a jacket pocket. The web link to learn about this product is www.handspring.com/products/Product.jhtml?id=410009.

You can also get a keyboard that will work through the infrared (IR) port on the top of your Treo. This keyboard comes from ENR Tech, and you can order it at www.pocketirkeyboard.com.

Also watch for keyboards from popular vendors, including Targus (www.targus.com) and Logitech (www.logitech.com).

GPS Systems

We found two GPS systems that you can connect directly to the serial port of your Treo 600. The first is the iTrek Mouse, which is used in the GPS section of this book. The iTrek Mouse is manufactured by Semson's & Co. (www.semsons.com). This GPS functioned flawlessly in our trials. It was quick to acquire the GPS satellite

16

signals and maintained a strong lock throughout our tests. This unit ships with software from Mapopolis.

A second GPS option is available directly from Mapopolis (www.mapopolis.com). This is a similar hardware option that will connect to your Treo 600 through the serial port and will plug into the power outlet in your vehicle.

Once Bluetooth connectivity is available on your Treo 600, you will have many more options for GPS with powerful wireless GPS modules from Pharos (www.pharos.com), Socket (www.socketcom.com), and others.

Memory Cards

You can purchase SD and MMC memory cards from a variety of vendors; however, you will see some quality differences. One of our preferred memory card vendors is Kingston (www.kingston.com). We have found this company's cards to be well built and durable, and we have never experienced any issues with them. Cards from SanDisk (www.sandisk.com) have also held up very well to our abuse.

We strongly recommend buying name brand–quality memory cards, and imitation cards run the risk of not only losing your data, but damaging your Treo and voiding your warranty.

Screen Protectors

Screen protectors are simple, transparent semi-adhesive pieces of plastic that stick right to the touchscreen of your Treo 600. They allow you to use your Treo 600 as normal but protect the screen from scratches and dirt. These are highly recommended and inexpensive accessories that no Treo owner should be without. A single protector can last for a very long time and is disposable; if it becomes scratched, you can simply peel it off and apply a new one. Some users have expressed concern about these protectors potentially reducing the sensitivity of the touchscreen, but we can tell you from experience that with the higher-quality screen protectors, this is not an issue.

There are many vendors offering screen protectors that fit the Treo 600, and you can likely find the protectors in your local computer store. Some of the vendors are listed here:

- **Boxwave Clear Touch (www.boxwave.com/products/cleartouch/index.htm)**   Adhesive screen protector.

- **Brando WorkShop Screen Protector (http://shop.brando.com.hk/screenprotector.php)**   Vendor based in Hong Kong.

- **G2 Screen Protectors (www.pdascreenprotectors.com/)**   Adhesive screen protector.

- **Javo Screen Protectors (www.javoedge.com/)** Adhesive screen protector.

- **Martin Fields Screen Protectors (www.overlayplus.com/product.asp?id= 1082&model=treo600)** High-quality, adhesive protectors; very clear and durable.

- **NuShield Screen Protectors (www.nushield.com/products_main_ treo.htm)** This protector is nonadhesive, so it slips under the edges of your screen border, instead of relying on mild glue to hold the protector to the screen, as other models do. If you are leery of putting anything adhesive on your screen, then this is the screen protector for you!

- **PalmOne (www.palmone.com/us/products/accessories/styli/)** Of course, palmOne offers its own version of this product.

- **Pocket PC Techs (www.pocketpctechs.com/ws.asp)** Its WriteShield product comes in two kits, standard and deluxe. WriteShields are also nonadhesive. The protectors in both kits are the same; the difference is the accessories you get with each kit. The standard kit comes with three screen protectors, four cleaning cloths, six applicator/remover picks, and a high-quality microfiber cloth for cleaning your screen. The deluxe kit comes with everything the standard kit does, plus it comes with a two-ounce pump bottle of screen cleaning fluid.

- **PurpleMoo Screen It (www.purplemoo.com/)** Adhesive screen protectors.

In-Car Accessories

The hands-free audio equipment mentioned earlier in this chapter could follow as part of the in-car accessories group, but there are some other products that you should be aware of as well.

Please note that you should never operate your Treo while driving a car, and attempting to do so could be extremely dangerous. Only operate your Treo if your vehicle is stopped, or have a passenger work your Treo for you.

One of the products that you can consider if you use your Treo in your car is the Treo Installation Car Kit from palmOne (www.palmOne.com), as shown in Figure 16-1.

This kit includes a cradle for securely holding your Treo, a microphone, an external antenna, and a wiring kit and charging adapter for keeping your Treo charged in the vehicle. The audio components include built-in echo and noise cancellation to make your Treo more usable for voice calls while in your car.

There are also other vendors who provide general car mounts for holding your Treo 600 in your vehicle. These types of kits are not full hand-free kits but will provide

16

FIGURE 16-1   The Treo Installation Car Kit allows for complete hands-free operation
of your Treo in your vehicle.

a stable platform for operating or viewing your Treo 600. The advantage to these kits
is that they can be used with external GPS solutions that plug into the serial port. The
vehicle mount kits that we use are from ProClips (www.proclipusa.com). They have
mounting kits for most vehicles, the majority of which are very easy to install and
make no permanent attachment to your car (meaning that you don't have to screw
plates into your dashboard or other parts of your vehicle to make them stable). The
ProClip Treo 600 Swivel Mount has been very useful for working with GPS in our
vehicles.

You can also find mounts that will attach to your windshield with a suction
cup like the Slim Line Universal Mount Kit for Treo 600 found at Seido (www.
seidoonline.com). However, we have had limited success with the windshield mount
versions, because they never seem to stay adhered to the window, no matter what
we try.

Styli

If you need to replace your stylus for your Treo 600, you can do that directly through
palmOne, or you can look to third-party providers for some interesting stylus upgrades.

Pocket PC Techs has a great addition for your Treo 600 stylus. Their custom
stylus includes a built-in pen. No longer do you have to search for a pen to write with,
because there is always one tucked conveniently inside your Treo 600 stylus. This
product can be purchased directly from Pocket PC Techs (www.pocketpctechs.com)
for $12.99. You can also order pen refills at this site.

Stylus Central (www.styluscentral.com/treo600.html) also has a stylus with
a built-in pen for your Treo.

Software

Throughout the book we have referenced various software programs that can add value to your Treo 600. Here we will provide a quick summary of some of the software products we covered, as well as some others that are recommended by Treo 600 users. This section also tells you where to learn more about the products. Remember that there are more than 10,000 commercial software applications available for the Treo 600, and this is just a set of the software that we use, as well as software that has been recommended by other Treo 600 users.

Communications

You will find a wide range of communications software products for your Treo, including the following:

Product	Description
PhoneGuard from Geakware (www.geakware.com)	PhoneGuard is a utility for Treo 600 smartphones that can prevent the SPACEBAR and RETURN buttons from answering phone calls. It also has a feature that allows you to turn off the screen when a call is answered, thus saving valuable battery life. ($8.99)
Chatopus (www.chatopus.com)	Chatopus is a Palm OS instant messaging (IM) client for the Treo 600 that allows you to instantly communicate with other people via instant messaging. Chatopus allows users to communicate with Jabber contacts. What's more, it also supports the transport aspects of Jabber, allowing users to establish links to other IM solutions, including MSN Messenger, ICQ, AIM, Yahoo! Messenger, and others. ($14.95)
Chatter (www.imchatter.com)	Chatter is an IM and communication tool for the Treo 600 that seamlessly integrates IM programs (Yahoo, ICQ, Microsoft, and AOL) with e-mail ("push" e-mail via IMAP and e-mail sending via SMTP). All network communication in Chatter is done asynchronously, meaning that instant messages and e-mail are being received and sent "in the background," so there's no waiting for connections to be made or messages to be delivered. Chatter works while you're actually in Chatter or in other Treo applications, while your Treo is "awake" and while it is "sleeping." ($20.00)
GoodLink from Good Technologies (www.good.com)	A high-end enterprise, real-time push e-mail delivery product that enables real-time e-mail delivery, as well as wireless calendar and contact synchronization with your enterprise. (Price is negotiated based on enterprise deployment.)

16

Product	Description
Hand RSS News Reader from Stand Alone Inc. (www.standalone.com)	RSS News feeds are the newest way to download and read news stories on a variety of subjects, from all over the Internet. Handheld Headlines/RSS for Palm OS allows you to download these news feeds to your Treo 600 via HotSync or wirelessly; you can then read them later. Use it to keep updated with the latest news, sports, and financial updates and to read your favorite web sites! Hand/RSS for Palm OS is preconfigured for a variety of news feeds, including BBC News, Boing Boing, CNet News, Fark.com, MSNBC, Salon.com, SlashDot, The Register, Wired, and more. Additionally, you can add any new feeds quickly and easily from other RSS sources. ($14.95)
Handmark Express from Handmark (www.handmark.com)	This useful product will wirelessly download useful information to your Treo 600 on a scheduled basis or on demand. You can keep on your handheld the latest news, sports scores, weather forecasts for multiple cities, and much more. In addition, this product gives you the ability to look up phone numbers (including reverse lookup) and to locate addresses on maps and download them in real time to your Treo 600. This is a tool that no Treo 600 should be without! ($69.99/year or $6.99/month)
Mergic VPN from Mergic (www.mergic.com)	Allows you to establish a virtual private network (VPN) or secure connection to a corporate network for the purposes of e-mail access, systems management, intranet access, and more. ($29.99)
Mobile TS from DDH Software (www.ddhsoftware.com)	Mobile TS allows you to use your Treo 600 to make a Microsoft Terminal Services or Remote Desktop connection to another computer and see the screen of that computer right on your Treo; it also allows you to have your keyboard commands and mouse commands (screen taps) sent back to the remote system. ($39.99)
PDANet Modem from June Fabrics (www.junefabrics.com)	This handy program allows you to use your Treo 600 as a wireless modem for your laptop. By connecting your Treo 600 to your laptop with a HotSync cable, you can now wirelessly connect to the Internet to download e-mail and surf web sites. Remember that this is a wireless connection and will not run at the speed of the broadband connection you are likely accustomed to! ($34.00)
Radio Control from Chris Hobbes (www.clanhobbs.com/treo)	A useful utility for automatically turning the radio of your Treo 600 on and off at predetermined times (like when you are sleeping). This helps to prevent interruptions and also conserves battery power. (Free)

Product	Description
SnapperMail from SnapperFish (www.snappermail.com)	One of the most popular e-mail programs for the Palm platform. It includes attachment support and automatic mail fetching. ($29.95 to $49.95)
TAKEphONE by ShSh (www.shsh.com)	TAKEphONE is an add-on utility for improving the usability and integration between the Treo 600 contacts application and the phone. It helps you find phone numbers and create and edit contacts. ($19.95)
TreoAlertMgr from PDAApps (www.pdaapps.com)	If you want to use your Treo 600 as a replacement for a pager, you may miss the "nag" ability of most pagers that do not just alert you once about an incoming page, but repeatedly nag you (if you want) until you acknowledge the page. We have often been surprised when we turned on the display of the Treo and discovered that we had a missed call, unheard voicemail, or an unread message that we missed because the unit went on standby before we saw the alert. TreoAlertMgr allows you to completely control how and when your phone alerts you about missed calls, unheard voicemail, and unread text messages and pages. You can have the system play a sound and vibrate and/or flash the screen periodically when you have unheard voicemail or unread pages/text messages. ($14.95)
VeriChat from PDAApps (www.pdaapps.com)	An instant messaging (IM) client for your Treo 600 that allows you to have online chats with Yahoo, MSN Messenger, ICQ, and AOL Instant Messenger users. ($24.95 plus an annual subscription fee of $19.95 after the first year)

Multimedia

The Treo is growing in capability as a multimedia device thanks to some of the following software packages:

Product	Description
Kinoma Player/Producer from Kinoma (www.kinoma.com)	Kinoma Player 2 delivers full-screen, full-motion, full-color, high-resolution video on your Treo 600. The Player only plays back files that have been encoded with the Kinoma Producer software, which can convert your DivX, MPEG, AVI, and other file types. (Player is free; Producer is $29.99)
MM Player (www.mmplayer.com)	MM Player (short for Multimedia Player) allows you to play back a variety of audio and video file types on your Treo 600, including MPEG, MP3, WAV, and AVI, among others. ($14.95)

16

Product	Description
Pocket Tunes from NormSoft (www.pocket-tunes.com)	Pocket Tunes turns your Treo 600 into a portable audio player. You can play compressed audio files (.mp3 or Ogg Vorbis) or uncompressed .wav files from a flash memory card, or you can stream .mp3 files live over your wireless Internet connection. This is one of the most popular audio players available for the Treo 600. ($12.95 to $24.95)

Productivity

A key goal of most Treo 600 users is to increase their productivity. The software featured here can help.

Product	Description
Documents To Go from DataViz (www.dataviz.com)	Treo 600 version of popular Microsoft Office programs for working with documents, spreadsheets, and presentations. ($29.95 to $69.95)
QuickOffice from Mobility Electronics (www.mobl.com/software)	Allows you to create and open native Microsoft Office documents on your Treo 600. ($39.95)
WordSmith from BlueNomad (www.bluenomad.com)	A full-featured word processor for the Treo 600. ($29.95)

Security

Mobile device security is a very significant problem, and Treo 600 users, particularly in a corporate environment, should understand how they are protecting (or should be protecting) their devices.

Product	Description
sonicsentry from Sonic Mobility (www.sonicmobility.com)	An enterprise application for monitoring all of your company's Treo 600 and other mobile devices. You can also interact with the devices in real time over the air to provide remote support and security functions. (Enterprise pricing)
PDA Defense from Asynchrony (www.asynchrony.com)	Encrypts and protects data on your Treo 600 from being accessed by unauthorized people. ($19.95)
SplashID from SplashData (www.splashdata.com)	Allows you to encrypt and store important numbers in one place, such as credit card numbers, membership numbers, bank accounts, and more. ($29.95)
3nity Password Keeper from Smart Mobile Applications (www.smart-mobile.net)	Also allows for encrypting and storing your important numbers. ($17.00)

Utilities

These are valuable software products that can help you make your Treo function even better.

Product	Description
Backup Buddy from BlueNomad (www.bluenomad.com)	A backup utility for backing up and restoring data from your Treo 600, right to your SD or MMC memory card. ($16.95)
BackupMan from Bits & Bolts (www.bitsnbolts.com)	This is the backup software covered in the Backup and Recovery section of this book. It allows for full backup and restore to and from your SD or MMC cards on an ad-hoc or scheduled basis. ($10.00)
TimeSync from Blue Nomad (www.bluenomad.com)	Allows you to synchronize your Treo 600 clock to your desktop clock at HotSync time. ($4.95)
BatteryGraph from Jeroen Witteman (www.jeroenwitteman.com)	Allows you to monitor and graph your battery strength and usage. If you want to see how various applications and actions impact your battery, this is a very useful tool. (Free)
HandZipper from HandWatch (www.handwatch.com)	Most Palm applications on the Internet are stored in a WinZip (.zip) file. With this utility, you can easily unzip and zip files right on your Treo without having to use the HotSync application to load them. It also works for attachments you may receive that are in a .zip format. ($9.95)
HiLauncher from RaNo Software (www.hilauncher.com)	Creates a Windows-like Start menu for your Treo 600. An easy and useful way to launch your most popular applications. ($14.95)
KeyCaps600 (www.geekandproud.com/software)	A utility that makes text entry easier. By holding or double-tapping a key, you can select uppercase, lowercase, or special characters. This is must-have software for the Treo 600 user. (Free, but a $10 donation is appreciated)
mCamLock from MotionApps (www.motionapps.com)	Allows you to disable the camera on your Treo 600. This is a concern for many organizations where privacy could be compromised with a camera-equipped device, such as at a hospital. ($19.99, and enterprise licensing is available)
mLights from MotionApps (www.motionapps.com	Gives you control over backlight settings to better conserve your battery power. ($7.99)
Skinner from 79b Media (www.79bmedia.com)	Allows you to change the appearance of your Treo 600 with downloadable "skins." ($8.99)
Today from Jonas Lindstedt (nikman.k2.net/today/)	Gives you a Pocket PC–like Today screen upon startup of your Treo 600. (Free)
TreoButler by Hobbyist (available from PalmGear www.palmgear.com)	A utility for managing alarms, alerts, navigation, application launching, LED control, Keyguard, and more. ($6.00)

16

Wrap It Up

The Treo 600 may be a relatively new device to the marketplace, but already there are a host of third-party accessories and options that can help you to expand the capabilities of your Treo. Being able to personalize your Treo to your own tastes with a case and other accessories helps when integrating your smartphone into your mobile lifestyle!

New products are being announced every day, so watch the web sites referenced in Appendix B to find out about new product announcements for useful accessories and software for your smartphone.

Part IV

Appendixes

Appendix A

Troubleshoot Treo Problems

How to…

- ■ Overcome the most common Treo user problems
- ■ Overcome the most common technical issues

PalmOne has designed and engineered your Treo 600 with the utmost attention to detail to ensure that your experience with your Treo is as painless and trouble-free as possible. That said, there are a few user and technical scenarios that may cause problems for you, your Treo applications, or the Treo 600 itself. This chapter serves to help you overcome the most common known issues that you may encounter. The chapter is divided into functional categories to help you quickly locate answers to the most common questions.

Error Messages and Troubleshooting

Many computers and applications log "events" to make the task of finding out what happened a little easier. Event logs create paper trails so that when a computer or application misbehaves, you can track down the problem. Your Treo has the same type of log. When your Treo crashes, it resets itself and stores the reason for the crash in an error log. Often, when your Treo crashes and resets itself, the issue is automatically resolved; however, if your Treo is resetting itself more often than you would like, you can access the error log to help you find out what is causing the crashes. The steps to get to the error log are a little different depending on what flavor of Treo you have, GSM or Sprint. The steps you should take to find the error log are listed in this section.

GSM/GPRS Treo 600

If you have a GSM/GPRS Treo 600 (in the U.S. any non-Sprint Treo 600 and in Europe any Treo 600 on the Orange network), follow these steps to find the error log:

1. Press the PHONE button on the keyboard.

2. Dial **#*377** on the dial pad on the screen, or type **#*377** on the keyboard; then select Dial.

A dialog box appears, displaying the date of the last crash, the application running at the time of that crash, and if appropriate, the error message that resulted from the crash.

Sprint CDMA Treo 600

If you have a Sprint CDMA Treo 600, follow these steps to find the error log:

1. Press the PHONE button on the keyboard.

2. Dial **##377** on the dial pad, or type **##377** on the keyboard; then select Dial.

A dialog box appears, displaying the date of the last crash, the application running at the time of that crash, and if appropriate, the error message that resulted from the crash.

There are many types of possible errors. There is an extensive list of these error messages and the most likely cause of each one on the palmOne support site (www.palmone.com).

It is also worth mentioning that the palmOne support web site lists general desktop errors, Windows errors, Macintosh errors, and HotSync log errors.

Third-party applications are commonly the cause of errors. If a particular application name shows up in the error log, you may want to consider deleting that application. The steps for deleting an application from your Treo are covered in Chapter 3.

Treo 600 Battery

Your Treo has a built-in, state-of-the-art lithium ion battery that generally doesn't require maintenance; but just in case, a few tips can help you troubleshoot battery challenges. This section lists some potential battery problems and their solutions.

My Treo battery doesn't seem to charge.

Is the power adapter plugged in correctly? Make sure that it's hooked up to an active power outlet and that all connections are tight. If the connection to your Treo seems a little loose, try disconnecting it and reconnecting it again. To check to see if your device is charging, open the Applications Launcher screen by pressing MENU on the keyboard. Then look at the battery meter at the top of the screen. You will see a lightning bolt symbol over the battery when it is charging properly.

Sometimes the charging light can malfunction, in which case you will need to perform a reset to bring your Treo back to normal functioning.

A

■ **In-cradle reset**   This may be necessary to "reboot" the charging circuitry. The steps for performing an in-cradle reset are covered later in this chapter under the heading "Perform an In-Cradle Reset."

■ **Soft reset**   Steps for performing a soft reset on your Treo are covered later in this chapter under the heading "Perform a Soft Reset."

My battery loses its charge very quickly.

Your Treo has a lithium ion battery that will eventually wear out and that you will have to replace, but there are a few things that you can do to maximize your battery life:

■ Recharge your Treo battery before it drains completely.

■ If you can, charge the battery often, even before it gets low.

Treo Sound and Speaker

Your Treo has a built-in speaker on the back of the device. It also has a jack for an earbud or headphones to allow you to listen to music and the sounds of games, video, and so on.

Why does my Treo 600 speaker buzz when I play music loudly?

The Treo speaker is designed to play system sounds such as ringtones and applications "beeps." It is not designed to play loud music, and if it is buzzing, you likely have the volume too high. Like any other speaker, it can be damaged if too much volume is being pushed through it. Here are some steps to help you avoid damaging the built-in speaker:

■ **Use headphones.**   Using headphones with your Treo 600 is covered under the next heading, "My stereo headphone cable doesn't fit into the earphone jack on my Treo."

■ **Don't use MP3 volume boost.**   Some MP3 encoders allow you to boost the volume of a song by as much as 15 dB. If you are encoding MP3s for use with your Treo 600, don't boost the volume when encoding. More information should be available from the company that developed your MP3 or in the documentation.

My stereo headphone cable doesn't fit into the earphone jack on my Treo.

The headphone jack is designed to be used with the headphone cable. This cable is a mono headset with a call-control button and microphone meant for telephone use. It allows you to talk on your Treo phone in a hands-free mode. You can use a stereo headset to listen to music and other sounds, but the Treo only works with a 2.5 mm stereo headset plug or a standard 3.5 mm stereo plug with a 2.5 mm to 3.5 mm adapter. This type of adapter is sold by palmOne and other Treo accessory vendors, and most consumer electronics stores will likely have an adapter that will work.

The Treo Screen

Your Treo has a 160×160–pixel bright VGA color screen, and a few tips for troubleshooting Treo screen issues are covered in this section.

Why does my handheld screen flicker or shimmer?

You may have noticed faint white lines that appear diagonally when you are scrolling quickly in an application. This is normal behavior for your Treo, but there are some known application conflicts that increase screen flickering. The most common applications that may cause flickering are some games, launchers, and theme applications, because they tend to change the display settings to suit their needs. If this flickering problem just began happening, consider if you recently installed an application. If you think you know which application may be causing the flickering, uninstall it to see if the problem is resolved.

There are also some types of third-party applications that are more likely to cause flickering. These include applications that were initially designed for previous versions of Palm OS and were later updated to run on OS 5 or later.

My Treo is looping, flashing, or frozen on the Palm Computing Platform logo.

If your Treo 600 encounters a system extension that is corrupted or isn't working properly after a device reset, it will automatically reset and try to load the corrupted extension again, which causes it to reset again. This creates an infinite loop situation that your Treo can't break out of.

A

TIP   *A system extension is a software program that is loaded the first time your device starts after a reset. System extensions add to the functionality of your device. An example of a system extension is the software that allows your device to send data through the Infrared (IR) port.*

The Treo Screen Is Slightly Asymmetrical

You may have noticed that your Treo 600 screen is just a little off to one side. According to palmOne, that is intentional. In order to design the Treo 600 as one of the most compact smartphones, palmOne had to squeeze the screen and the other components into a space of 4.4×2.4×0.9 inches. So rather than make the device symmetrical, and larger, palmOne nudged the screen less than a quarter of an inch off-center to accommodate the other components in a minimal amount of space.

If your Treo is stuck in an infinite loop, try performing a soft reset on your Treo, which is described later in this appendix under the heading "Perform a Soft Reset". If this doesn't help, you may have to perform a hard reset, as described under the later heading "Perform a Hard Reset." Note, however, that performing a hard reset means that you will lose all of your data, so use it as a last resort.

Synchronization with HotSync

Your Treo is best used in conjunction with a PC to allow you to synchronize data between the two. Synchronization is covered in Chapter 3. Before you can synchronize your Treo with your PC, you need to install the HotSync software on your PC. This software is included on the CD-ROM that came with your Treo.

I keep seeing the error "Unable to Hotsync due to system error" when I try to Hotsync.

This error may occur when you try to perform a HotSync operation at the same time your Treo is on an active call of any type. Possibilities include making a voice call, sending or receiving e-mail, browsing the Internet, or downloading files from the Internet. There are a few options for overcoming this error:

- **Ensure no active Web operations are occurring.** Ensure that you are not making a voice call, browsing the Web, or downloading files from the Web, and then try to HotSync again.

■ **Disable automatic e-mail checking.** Another reason this may happen is that some e-mail applications check your e-mail in the background. This means that you may not always know when your Treo is checking for e-mail. If this error seems to happen irregularly, this may be the problem. You can disable automatic e-mail checking in your e-mail application, perform the HotSync operation, and then turn automatic e-mail checking back on. You may have to check the documentation of your e-mail application to find out where to change this setting.

■ **Turn off Wireless Mode.** If the two previous suggestions don't work, turn your Treo Wireless Mode off, perform the HotSync operation, and then turn it back on again. With the Wireless Mode off, there is no chance that an application is performing Internet functions without you knowing about it.

Treo Phone

Mobile phone technology has been mainstream for many years, and the technology is relatively mature; however, problems can still arise.

I am having trouble dialing phone numbers with the keyboard.

Your Treo 600 is likely set up to start a Contacts search when you type rather than dial a phone number. One or the other of the settings must be active, but not both. The steps for toggling to the option for typing a phone number are listed here:

1. Press the PHONE and then the MENU button on the keyboard.

2. From the Options menu, select Display Preferences.

3. In the menu that appears, select the second of the following two options:

■ **Typing Starts Contacts Search**   When this option is selected, any typing you do in the Phone application will cause the Treo to try to find the contact that matches the letters you type. So if you are trying to type a phone number, your Treo will behave strangely.

■ **Typing Dials Phone Number**   When this option is selected, the number pad on the keyboard is active and you can type a phone number.

I'm not happy with the sound quality on my phone.

There are many factors that can cause problems with the sound quality you hear, or that the person you are speaking to hears, when you are talking on your Treo phone.

A

These factors include

- The phone of the person you are talking to
- The signal strength and the quality of the connection between the phones
- The environment: weather, background noise, solar flares, and so on
- Wireless network problems

Some things you can do to maximize the sound quality of your phone conversations are listed here:

- **Hold your Treo correctly.** Position the Treo handset closer to your ear to prevent sound from leaking back to the microphone. Be sure you're holding the Treo so that your hand is not near the microphone hole on the back. Your hand, or any other reflecting surface, tends to conduct the speaker sound down to the microphone and cause echo on the recipient's end.

- **Turn down the phone volume.** Try decreasing your Treo volume to avoid *coupling,* or feedback, on the receiver's end. (Coupling occurs when the receiver hears his or her voice as it goes through your speaker, is picked up by your microphone, and gets sent back with a slight delay as it travels through the network.) This applies to both the speakerphone and the built-in ear speaker.

- **Turn your Treo over.** If you are using the speakerphone functionality, try turning the Treo over so that the screen is facing down.

When talking on my Treo, I hear echo, echo, echo!

If you are hearing your own voice echo when you are talking, the echo is originating from the other person's phone, not yours. You can ask the other person to either turn down the phone volume or to hold the speaker closer to the ear to minimize feedback.

I hear static when I talk on my Treo phone.

Static is generally caused by a barrier between your Treo and the cellular tower to which your Treo is connected. For example, a barrier exists when you get into an elevator while talking on your phone. There is not too much you can do except to be aware of barriers and avoid talking on your phone when you are in an elevator or driving though a tunnel, for example.

Wireless Connectivity

Your Treo 600, as you know, is equipped with wireless radio components to allow you to make wireless phone calls and send and receive wireless application data. Due to the complexity of this feature, and depending on whether or not your Treo arrived perfectly configured, you may need to do a little troubleshooting to ensure that your Treo is set up correctly.

Why does my GPRS or PCS Vision service disconnect periodically?

You may have already experienced intermittent service as you move around within your city, state, or province. Wireless networks do not yet cover every square mile of surface area, and many areas have better connectivity than others. So if you are disconnected, it may be because you are in an area without wireless coverage.

Some mobile service providers log wireless users off after a given period of time—from hours to days, depending on the carrier. This is another explanation for unexpected disconnections. You may be automatically disconnected regardless of whether you have been using your connection during the defined time period.

How do I reestablish my wireless connection?

Provided you are in an area with GPRS or PCS Vision coverage, launch an application that requires a data connection, such as a web browser or an e-mail application. Your connection should be established automatically, but you may have to approve the connection when prompted.

What should I do if I can't connect to the Internet at all with my GPRS Treo?

If wireless applications such as e-mail and the Web will not work, here are some things to try to help get you going:

- ■ **Check your wireless service contract.** If you have never been able to use e-mail or have never had access to the Web on your Treo, check to see whether your wireless service contract includes GPRS data services. Not all service contracts include data services by default, and it is possible that you are only covered for voice data and not other forms of data. To make sure your GPRS service is enabled, contact the company that holds your contract. Contact information for major carriers that host Treo 600 service is listed at the end of this chapter. If you have your service contract handy, the contact information should be provided there as well.

A

■ **Find out if GPRS is provided in your area.** GPRS networks do not offer coverage everywhere, and it is possible that GPRS is not provided in your area. This may not seem like a particularly useful point, but sometimes a user buys a device from a source other than from the local service provider. For example, I bought my Treo 600 on eBay because the carriers in my area are not selling them yet. Obviously, you can't use GPRS if it is not supported in your area.

■ **Be sure that your username and password are correct.** Some wireless service providers require that you enter a username and password to allow you to connect to their wireless network. This information is stored in your Network Preferences settings, and your Treo should have been preconfigured with this information. If it wasn't, your Treo will not be able to authenticate with the wireless network.

■ **Turn your Wireless mode off and on again.** When you do this, your Treo will try to reauthenticate with the network and will often fix a broken connection.

■ **Contact your WSP for assistance.** If none of these steps helped, contact your wireless service provider directly for assistance. Remember, GPRS is a relatively new technology, and the support and configuration kinks are still being worked out in many areas. Therefore, problems often originate with the carrier rather than directly with you or your Treo.

Browse the Internet

The ability to browse the Web is one of the most interesting features of the Treo. Even if you are a seasoned Internet veteran and are already familiar with PC-based web browsers, there are some differences between PC and smartphone web browsers that you should be aware of when browsing the Web on your Treo.

I'm having trouble downloading a specific file with the Blazer Web Browser.

Your Treo will not download any file type that is not supported on your Treo. That is, unless an application on your Treo can read or use the file, it is unsupported. The types of files that can be downloaded by default include the following:

■ **PRC files (** *filename***.prc)**   Palm application files

■ **PDB files (** *filename***.pdb)**   Palm database files

- ■ **MIDI files** (*filename*.**mid**)   Sound files commonly used for ringtones

- ■ **JPEG files** (*filename*.**jpg**)   Image files, the same format the Treo saves files in

If a file cannot be downloaded, you may see one of the following error messages:

```
Download Error: The file type you are attempting to download is not
supported on your device.
```

```
Data Timeout: The page download could not be completed. Please try
again later.
```

If the file you are trying to download is one of the supported file types, the following are some of the other reasons why you may be having trouble downloading the file.

Did You Lose Network Coverage?   If you lose wireless network coverage at any point during the download, the download will not be completed. This is more likely to occur with large files that may take several minutes to download. Also, if you are moving in a vehicle while downloading a file, you may lose your connection to a cell tower as the signal is handed off to another tower. Staying in one area with good wireless coverage while a file is downloading tends to offer the best results.

Did the Connection Time Out?   Your Treo web browser may time out while waiting to hear back from the Web or another server along the way. If this happens, you may see this error:

```
Data Timeout: The page download could not be completed. Please try
again later.
```

The timeout could be due to web congestion or a slow connection. Try again later.

Do You Have Enough Free Memory on Your Treo?   Your Treo must have enough space to store the file that you trying to download. If there is not enough space to store the file, you will see this error message:

```
There is not enough memory available on your device to download
this file.
```

If you see this message, then you are running out of memory and will need to remove some files. This topic is covered in this chapter under the heading "What can I do if my handheld is running out of memory?"

A

I can't connect to the Internet at all.

See this topic under the heading "What should I do if I can't connect to the Internet at all with my GPRS Treo?"

Why does my Treo Web Browser crash when I try to enter a URL?

If the Blazer web browser is consistently crashing or resetting whenever you try to enter a web site address, you may see an error message similar to this:

```
A reset was caused on 05/19/2004 at 11:13 while running "Web":
Fatal Exception, Datamgr.c, line:6341 invalid unique ID passed.
```

This type of error is known to occur if the "predictive text database" in the Blazer browser becomes corrupted and is therefore unusable. To resolve this issue, follow these steps:

1. On your desktop PC, go to the web site http://nosleepsoftware.sourceforge.net and download a file utility called "FileZ." This utility allows you to delete the database on your Treo that is normally a hidden and undeletable file. There are other utilities that allow similar functionality, but FileZ is sanctioned by palmOne, so we know it works.

2. Once you have downloaded FileZ to your PC, install it on your Treo using HotSync. Chapter 2 details the steps for installing applications.

3. Once FileZ is installed, open the Applications Launcher screen by pressing HOME on the keyboard. Find and launch FileZ.

4. In FileZ, choose the View and Edit Files option.

5. Locate and select the file named Web Find AutoFill.

6. Press MENU on the keyboard and select the Delete option from the menu.

7. Select Yes when the file delete confirmation screen appears.

8. Now, locate and select the file named Web URL AutoFill.

9. Press MENU on the keyboard and select the Delete option from the menu.

10. Select Yes when the file delete confirmation screen appears.

Now you should be able to enter URLs into the browser to view web pages without experiencing any problems.

E-Mail

A few tips for troubleshooting Palm Mail are included in this section. Many other e-mail software options for your Treo 600 are available, however, and they are covered in Chapter 6. If you have trouble with one of those e-mail applications, you can find answers by consulting the vendor's product documentation or by contacting the software company directly.

I am having memory issues with e-mail.

Many of us tend to use e-mail more than even the phone, and we get many messages per week. It is important to be conscious of how many e-mail messages you are storing on your Treo. E-mail messages can eat up a lot of memory and can affect other applications. Storing too many e-mails can cause a painfully slow HotSync process as well.

Refer to your e-mail documentation to learn how to archive or delete older e-mails (not applicable to web-based e-mail). PalmOne provides technical support for Treo Mail and Palm Mail on the palmOne web site (www.palmone.com).

MMS

Chapter 5 discusses Multimedia Message Service (MMS), and provides some tips for troubleshooting MMS problems, but here are some additional tips. Note that the Treo 600 sold by Sprint in the U.S. does not support MMS but offers similar functionality with its Picture Mail application. Sprint Picture Mail is covered in Chapter 5.

I can't send an MMS message.

Are you talking on the phone when you are trying to send the MMS message? Your Treo 600 doesn't allow you to send an MMS message and talk on the Treo phone at the same time, so you will need to wait until you are finished talking on the phone to send the message.

MMS freezes my Treo, and then I can't turn it off.

If this happens when you are trying to send an MMS message, this is a sure sign that you don't have MMS activated on your mobile account or your manually entered MMS settings are wrong.

The first step toward working through this problem is to perform a soft reset on your Treo; see the section titled "Perform a Soft Reset," later in this chapter, for tips on how to perform a soft reset. Then you should contact your wireless service provider

A

to ensure that you have MMS capability active on your account and that your MMS settings are correct.

SMS

This section provides tips for troubleshooting some common Short Message Service (SMS) issues. (The Treo 600's SMS application is discussed in Chapter 5.)

My SMS application crashes when I import messages.

If you haven't used the SMS application before, you may find that when you first launch the SMS application your Treo resets itself. If this is happening, check the error log to find out if a fatal error occurred. Error logs were covered at the beginning of this chapter under the heading "Error Messages and Troubleshooting."

If a fatal error occurred, a likely cause is that you upgraded to your Treo 600 from a previous Treo smartphone and didn't install the Treo software from the CD included with your Treo 600. When you install the desktop software on your PC, it filters out incompatible applications that won't work on your new Treo smartphone. If you don't install the desktop software, the incompatible applications will not be filtered out and the incompatible applications may cause your Treo to crash or cause other unexpected behavior.

What should I do if my SMS application crashes when I am importing messages?

Install the software from the CD that came with your Treo smartphone. When asked if you want to quarantine (filter) incompatible content, choose Yes. Perform the HotSync operation as directed, and let the installer finish its job. Then launch the SMS application on your Treo smartphone. This should return it to normal.

Camera

Your Treo camera is very easy to use but, like anything technical, you may experience challenges.

Why won't an image transfer from my desktop to my Treo with HotSync?

The first step is to make sure you are following the correct steps for HotSyncing. Consult the Treo 600 user guide for the steps. If you are sure you are doing everything correctly, the most likely reason the picture is not being transferred correctly to your Treo is that the picture is too big.

If the picture you are trying to transfer is larger than 2048×2048 pixels, HotSync will not transfer it to your Treo. Before transferring it, you will need to reduce its size with an image-editing software package. Digital photo editing, including resizing images, is covered in Chapter 7.

I am having display problems caused by third-party software.

Some third-party software can cause interference when displaying pictures on the Treo screen. Essentially, the problem stems from software that changes the screen color settings for the application's own purposes. The result of the modifications is that some images won't display correctly. Butterfly and Psycho Path are applications known to have this effect.

I did a Hotsync, but I can't find my Treo pictures on my PC.

When you perform a HotSync operation on a Windows PC, your images are transferred to the following file location:

C:\Program Files\Handspring\Treo Pictures*username*

All images will be in JPEG format, which is one of the most common formats for images on the Web.

If you have a Macintosh, there are three ways you can transfer pictures taken with your Treo camera to your Mac:

- **Using an SD card**   To do this, you need a Secure Digital memory expansion card and an SD card reader. This is covered in more detail in Chapter 7.

- **By e-mail**   To do this, e-mail the picture as an attachment to yourself, and open it when you check your e-mail on your Mac. Then save the picture to your hard drive.

- **With Missing Sync**   You can also use third-party software called The Missing Sync from Mark/Space (www.markspace.com) to transfer the pictures to your Mac.

Why does the Treo camera preview image look funny?

Your Treo camera was designed to allow you to take quick, easy-to-use digital snapshots. On its web site, palmOne says "We'll be the first to admit that while it's a great little camera that most people are happy with, it's not the same as a professional-grade 4-megapixel digital SLR. The pictures taken with a Treo are

A

more like those taken with a 110 instamatic camera: consumer-level quality in a small, accessible format." See the picture-taking tips for using your Treo camera in Chapter 7.

Why do my Treo pictures have blue spots on them?

If you have light blue dots on your images when viewing them on your Treo screen (the dots are likely more obvious in the darker areas of the image), it is usually an indication that the picture was taken under poor lighting conditions. Chapter 7 provides steps for getting the most out of your Treo camera, including tips for improving the quality of your pictures and image editing.

Music

Your Treo does not play music right out of the box, unless you count MIDI ringtones as music. The good news is that there are many third-party applications that allow you to listen to music or watch video with sound. If your Treo seems to be functioning properly except that it can't play music, contact the vendor that produces the software you are using to find solutions to problems specific to that software. See also "Reset Your Treo 600," later in this appendix, for a possible solution.

 *If you purchased your Treo in the U.S., palmOne offers NormSoft's Pocket Tunes software as a gift when you register your Treo 600. You can register your Treo on the palmOne web site at www.palmone.com.*

Movies

Your Treo does not play movies by default, but there are applications that allow you to watch video on your Treo. If your Treo seems to be functioning except that it can't play videos and movies, you should contact the vendor that makes the software you are using to find out about problems specific to that software. See also "Reset Your Treo 600," later in this chapter for a possible solution.

Third-Party Applications

One of the many great things about the Treo is that a lot of new applications, games, and utilities are being developed for this popular platform. Yet while software seems plentiful, many of these applications are not much more than hacks. (A *hack* generally refers to software written by an individual for a specific purpose that may do what it is designed to do but is not thoroughly tested.) Use software hacks at your own risk.

If your Treo or your data is damaged as a result of using a hack, you don't have any recourse.) In fact, many developers honestly call their own programs hacks. Some of these less-tested freeware and shareware applications may cause problems with your Treo hardware or software or may interfere with other applications.

How do I figure out whether a third-party application is causing trouble on my device?

Since there are so many applications available for your Treo 600, it is best to get support from the author or vendor of the third-party software that you installed on your device. There are a few of steps you can try to do to troubleshoot a problem with a third-party application on your Treo:

1. If your Treo is resetting, look in the error log to see if the log names a specific application. Viewing the error log is covered earlier in this chapter under the heading "Error Messages and Troubleshooting."

2. Next, try a soft reset, which is covered in this chapter under the heading "Perform a Soft Reset."

3. If the problem continues after a soft reset, continue to step 4.

4. Try a system reset, which is covered in this chapter under the heading "Perform a System Reset." A system reset can be very helpful if a third-party hack is causing the problem.

5. If you have tried a system reset and are still encountering the problem, you can try disabling all hacks in any third-party extensions manager you may have installed (HackMaster, X-Master, TealMaster, and so on). You may have to look at the extensions manager's documentation to find out what you have to do.

6. If none of these steps has solved the problem, you may need to try a hard reset, which erases all data and returns your device to its factory state. This is covered later in this chapter under the heading "Perform a Hard Reset." The good news is that if a hard reset fixes the problem, it indicates that the problem was caused by a third-party application or a corrupted file.

A

If you now know which third-party application is causing the problem, it is a good idea to delete that application. Chapter 3 gives instructions on deleting applications from your Treo.

Security

If you are experiencing problems with third-party security software, contact the software vendor or use the vendor's online support services. The item listed here is related to the built-in security features of your Treo.

My Treo used to auto-lock but doesn't anymore.

If you have recently performed a hard reset on your Treo, that is likely the problem. Performing a hard reset erases your password, and without a defined password your Treo won't lock. This is because, of course, you wouldn't be able to log in without a password. To reenable the auto-lock functionality, you will have to go back to the Security Preferences screen to reenter the password you want to use to log in to your Treo when it auto-locks.

Expansion Cards

Your Treo 600 supports SD (Secure Digital) cards and MMCs (MultiMediaCards) only. So when you decide to buy an expansion card, be sure that it is an SD or MMC card. There are many types of cards for specific purposes, such as extra memory, applications, games, Bluetooth cards, 802.11 Wi-Fi cards, and so on. If you are sure that you have the correct type of card for your Treo but are having difficulty, contact the card vendor directly.

Memory

Your Treo 600 has 24MB of user-accessible memory. This may sound like a lot of memory, but you may be surprised how quickly you will fill it up as you add applications, digital pictures, and receive e-mail. To keep your Treo running at its best, you need to be conscious of how much memory is available.

What can I do if my handheld is running out of memory?

There are several things that you can do to reduce the amount of memory you are using. These are explained next.

Purge and Archive Old Records   The built-in Treo 600 applications, such as the Calendar and Contacts, To Do List, and Memo Pad, retain data until you delete it. One way to minimize the amount of unused data on your Treo is to purge and archive the application data.

You can archive your application data on your Treo by simply moving unused data to your PC during a HotSync operation so that you retain a copy of it on your PC and delete it from your Treo. This frees up precious memory.

Purge or Archive Your Old Mail Items   To purge or archive your old Mail items, follow these steps:

1. Launch the Palm Mail application.

2. Press MENU on the keyboard and select the Purge Items menu option.

3. In the Purge screen which appears next, select the parameters for which data you want to purge, including the Before date, which allows you to define the calendar day that splits your mail into what you will keep and what you will purge. In other words, any mail older that this date will be deleted.

NOTE   *If you want the data to be backed up to your PC when it is deleted, make sure the Save Archive Copy on PC option is checked.*

4. When you have defined the parameters you want, press OK. The next time you HotSync, old items will be purged from your Treo memory.

Purge or Archive Your Old Calendar Items   To purge or archive your old Calendar items, follow these steps:

1. Launch the Calendar application, ensuring that it is in Day View—the screen should show only one day at a time.

2. Press MENU on the keyboard and select the Purge Items menu option.

3. In the Purge screen, which appears next, select the parameters for which data you want to purge, including the Before date, which allows you to define the calendar day that splits your Calendar items into what you will keep and what you will purge. In other words, any Calendar items older that this date will be deleted.

NOTE   *If you want the data to be backed up to your PC when it is deleted, make sure that the Save Archive Copy on PC option is checked.*

4. When you have defined the parameters you want, select the OK button on the screen. The next time you HotSync, old items will be purged from your Treo memory.

Clear Your Blazer Web Browser Cache or Memory   To make your web browsing experience faster when you return to previously viewed web pages, the Blazer browser stores web page information and images in a memory location known as the *cache*.

A

This memory can get large, so it's a good idea to delete the cache regularly and set a lower limit for it. To clear the Blazer cache, follow these steps:

1. If Blazer is not currently running, press HOME on the keyboard to open the Applications Launcher screen. Find the web icon and launch Blazer.

2. Press MENU on the keyboard, select Blazer Preferences on the screen, and then select Advanced.

3. Change the Cache Size to a lower setting. (If you change your mind later, you can change the setting at any time.)

4. Tap the Clear button to delete the Blazer cache, and then select OK.

Move Files to an SD/IO Card   If you have a memory expansion card for your Treo 600, it is a great place to store data without slowing down your Treo. You can even run applications right off of the card; and cards, like any technology, are coming down in price all the time. Be sure you get a Secure Digital card or a MultiMediaCard (MMC) because these are the only formats your Treo 600 supports.

Reset Your Treo 600

A Treo reset will fix many problems you may be experiencing with both software and hardware. A reset is conceptually similar to rebooting a PC. There are a few different types of reset actions that you can perform, and these are explained in this section.

 *Be aware that a "hard reset" will erase all data on your Treo, including your auto-lock password and network and connection settings, so use it only as a last resort.*

Perform a System Reset

Why would you do a system reset? A system reset bypasses any third-party extensions that may be causing problems and bypasses the Palm OS system extensions that enable your handheld to beam and perform other functions. Once you have identified and removed the software that is causing the problem, remember to perform a soft reset (see the upcoming section "Perform a Soft Reset") to restore these functions.

A system reset tells your Treo to stop what it is doing and start over again. No records or entries stored in your device are deleted when you properly perform a system reset. You can perform a system reset by following these steps:

1. Press the UP button on the five-way navigation control.

2. Locate the reset button on the lower-right side of the back of your Treo 600. Don't mistake the microphone hole on the bottom of the Treo for the reset button. (Don't laugh—I've seen it done by a well-known author!)

3. Unscrew the point of the stylus or get a paper clip and straighten it.

4. While pressing the UP button on the five-way navigation control, gently press the reset button with the built-in reset tool in the stylus or with the straightened paper clip.

5. The Palm Computing Platform screen appears. Release the UP button when you see this screen.

6. Once you've tested that the system reset worked, be sure to perform a soft reset. Otherwise, some functions, such as Beaming (covered in Chapter 2), will not work properly.

Perform a Soft Reset

A soft reset can fix a variety of problems and is similar to rebooting a desktop computer or server.

NOTE   *Performing a soft reset does not usually affect the personal data on your Treo, but it is a good idea to perform a HotSync operation before you perform any reset to your Treo. This will help to ensure that if you do lose any data during the reset process, it will be easy to restore that data from your PC.*

CAUTION   *Do not perform a soft reset if you are receiving warnings that your battery is low.*

Follow these steps to perform a soft reset:

1. Locate the reset button on the lower-right side on the back of your Treo 600. (See Figure 2-4 in Chapter 2 for the location of this button.)

2. Unscrew the point of the stylus, or straighten a paper clip.

3. To perform a soft reset, use the straightened paper clip or the built-in reset tool in the stylus to gently press the reset button.

A

A soft reset tells your device to stop what it is doing and start over again. All records and entries stored in your handheld are retained with a soft reset.

What if a soft reset deleted my data?

If this happens, then your Treo may have a more serious hardware issue. Contact the company from which you bought your Treo or contact palmOne to find out where to take your Treo to have someone look at it.

Perform an In-Cradle Reset

The major reason you would need to do an in-cradle reset on your Treo is to help your battery recharge correctly if you find that your Treo turns off as soon as you turn it on and won't charge in the cradle. The reset will reboot the recharge circuitry. Here's how to perform an in-cradle reset:

1. Connect your Treo to its charger. If you are using a powered cradle, make sure the power adapter is attached to the cradle or cable and plugged into a live power outlet.

2. Without lifting the Treo off the cradle or cable, perform a soft reset, as explained in the preceding section.

Perform a Hard Reset

The explanation for performing a hard reset is provided in this section; however, please read the following Caution before you do this.

 *A hard reset will erase everything on your Treo, including configuration settings. All your personal data and third-party applications will be deleted. Do not perform a hard reset unless you have backed up your data to your PC or you are willing to lose all of your data.*

Follow these steps to perform a hard reset:

1. Hold down, and keep holding, the power button, also known as the Wireless Mode button, on the top of your Treo. (This button is to the right of the antenna if you are looking at the top of your Treo from the front of the device.)

2. Locate the reset button on the lower-right side of the back of the Treo. (See Figure 2-4 in Chapter 2 for the location of this button.)

3. Unscrew the point of the stylus or straighten a paper clip.

4. While continuing to hold down the power button, turn your device over so that you can see the back of it. Use the straightened paper clip or the built-in reset tool in the stylus to gently press the reset button.

5. When the Palm Computing Platform logo is displayed on the Treo screen, release the power button.

> A warning appears on the screen to advise you that you are about to erase all of your Treo data.

6. Press the UP button on the five-way navigation control to complete the hard reset or press any other button to perform a soft reset and leave your data alone.

Your device then takes you through a series of screens to walk you through initial setup.

Recover Your Data After a Hard Reset

The good news is that even if you perform a hard reset and later regret doing so, your data and applications will be loaded from your PC the next time you perform a HotSync. This is one of the reasons why regularly HotSyncing your Treo with your PC is a good thing to do, that is, it allows you to keep up-to-date data backups for your Treo.

Traveling Outside Your Country of Residence

By design, wireless connectivity means mobility, but, that doesn't mean you won't experience some challenges if you move around a lot. A few tips for troubleshooting connectivity issues if you are traveling outside your home country are listed in this section.

Can I use a GSM Treo in countries other than my own?

Your GSM Treo is a quad-band device and is capable of running on 850/900/1800/1900Mhz networks, so provided that you have a roaming contract that covers the countries in which you are traveling, you can use your Treo.

Can I make calls with my Treo from outside my country?

To make calls outside of your country with your Treo, you will need to activate international calling and roaming with your mobile service provider. Talk to your carrier if you need additional information about international roaming.

A

What countries have GSM coverage?

GSM is a well-defined and supported standard for communications. You can confirm coverage for GSM networks in a specific country by using the official GSMWorld web site (www.gsmworld.com/gsminfo/index.htm). In many cases, several GSM carriers are located in an area. To be sure there is GSM coverage in the area in which you will be traveling, contact your wireless service provider.

Find More Information about Troubleshooting

There are many places where you can find information about troubleshooting Treo hardware and software problems. If you are having trouble with a particular software application, search the program's help files or contact the application vendor directly.

- **PalmOne**   The support site at palmOne (www.palmone.com) is a great place to search for troubleshooting tips.

- **Treo 600 user groups**   Appendix B provides sources for more information on resolving user and technical problems. Many of the Treo 600 fan web sites, such as www.treo600.com and www.treocentral.com, have user groups where you search for topics and answers or post questions to other users. Often, you can get answers to your questions within a short time.

- **Ask your wireless service provider**   Contact your wireless service provider's support department for assistance. Following is contact information for the largest providers:

  - AT&T Wireless (www.attws.com), 1-800-888-7600

  - Cingular Wireless (www.cingular.com), 1-866-246-4852

  - Sprint PCS (www.sprintpcs.com), 1-800-974-2221

  - T-Mobile (www.tmobile.com), 1-800-937-8997

  - Orange (www.orange.com), +44 (0) 207 984 1600

Appendix B

Find More Information

How to...

■ Locate web sites about the Treo 600 and mobile computing

■ Find magazines for Palm OS users

■ Get up-to-date information on mobile computing at conferences

You can explore many sources of interesting information about your Treo, and the amazing (and not so amazing) things you can do with it. Given the relatively long history of the Palm operating system (Palm OS), you will find many web sites containing large databases of software and information, although much of that is not specifically focused on the Treo 600. In the references provided in this appendix, you will find information ranging from the practical, such as troubleshooting tips for when your Treo 600 won't power on, to the zany, with some bizarre and unusual uses for your smartphone.

We have categorized the information sources by type and given a brief description of what you can expect to find at each of these sources. The number of potential information sources is growing so fast that we cannot possibly list them all here, but we will take as thorough a cut at the Treo 600 space as possible.

Web Sites

In this section, we focus on Treo 600–specific web sites first, and then follow with some general Palm OS–related web sites that have useful information for the Treo 600 owner.

Treo 600–Specific Web Sites

The following sites are primary sources of information on the Treo 600:

■ **PalmOne (www.palmOne.com)**   PalmOne will always be a great source for information on your Treo. Here you can expect to find information on accessories for your Treo 600, special offers from the carriers, news about the Treo, and tips and tricks. You can even sign up for the Treo newsletter.

- **Treo 600 Essentials (http://treo.tc/info.html)**   This site is associated with Treo Central (see the next listing) and is a mobile, browser-accessible version of Treo Central. Some sections are still labeled with the original Treo 600 Essentials branding, and some have the Treo Central branding. This site is formatted to fit the browser on your Treo 600 and is lightweight and easy to use while on the go. You will find the latest news relevant to Treo 600 owners, product reviews, software lists, discussion forums, FAQ information, and more.

- **Treo Central (www.treocentral.com)**   Treo Central is one of the main Internet sites for Treo owners. It addresses issues of owners of all Treo models, not just the Treo 600, so you will find software and other information that doesn't necessarily apply to your smartphone. The site does include Treo 600–specific sections, however, where you will find forums and plenty of information on accessories, software, news stories, and more.

- **treo1.com (www.treo1.com)**   This site is very similar in structure to the Treo 600 Essentials web site mentioned previously in this list. It is formatted for your mobile screen and is easy to browse. It contains information on mobile accessories, software, news, ringtones, weather reports, and more.

- **Treo 600 (www.treo600.com)**   This web URL will redirect you to the Treo 600–specific portion of the www.pdaphonehome.com web site. You can purchase Treo 600 accessories and also access Treo 600 discussion forums.

- **PalmSource (www.palmsource.com)**   Just prior to Palm's merging with Handspring, it spun off its Operating System Group as a new company called PalmSource. PalmSource produces and markets Palm OS, the operating system used in your Treo 600. There is a great deal of useful information on this web site, both for developers of Palm OS applications and for people who use the devices for personal and business purposes.

- **TreoMB (www.treomb.com)**   A new web site with news, reviews, and user discussion forums for the Treo 600.

Treo 600 Users

There are a number of dedicated Treo 600 users who post their experiences, their favorite software, and more on the Internet. You can learn from these users by visiting their sites or weblogs:

B

- **The Shifted Librarian**   Jenny is a technically savvy librarian who uses her Treo 600 to the max. Learn how she puts it to use by reading her weblog at **www.theshiftedlibrarian.com/stories/2003/12/04/whatsOnMyTreo600. html.**

- **The Connected PDA** The user who runs this site keeps a number of documents up-to-date on what software he runs on his Treo 600, as well as other interesting mobile information for the Treo user at **http://radio. weblogs.com/0124865/stories/2003/10/17/whatsOnMyTreo600.html.**

- **The Connected PDA Treo 600 Moblog (http://mconnick.textamerica. com)** The owner of the preceding site also runs a mobile weblog, which he updates and maintains exclusively from his Treo 600.

- **Shades of Grey (http://piquant.us/shades)** A user weblog with interesting thoughts on many topics, as well as information on how he uses his Treo 600.

- **Vikrampant (www.vikrampant.com/treo600)** This user has assembled an excellent collection of information on how he uses his Treo 600. He also provides some useful advice and interesting stories.

Other Web Sites

A large number of other sites we wanted to list have relevant information for the Treo owner, and more such sites seem to appear daily. These sites may be more general than the ones previously listed—related more to Palm or mobile computing than specifically to the Treo 600—but nonetheless may have useful information for the Treo owner.

General, News, and Reviews

These web sites focus on general information, news, and product reviews relevant to either the Palm world or to the world of mobile computing in general:

- **Brighthand (www.brighthand.com)** Probably one of the most active and popular mobile discussion forums. Information on new devices, rumors, and other assorted news often appears here long before it does anywhere else.

- **Palm Blvd (www.palmblvd.com)** A very active collection of news and discussion forums, and a vast library of downloadable software for your Palm device. Be sure to check compatibility to make sure that software you download will run on your Treo 600.

- **Palm Infocenter (www.palminfocenter.com)** A chat board with active news threads and discussion forums.

- **SmartPhones (www.smartphones.com)** News on smartphones with downloadable screen savers and ringtones.

■ **BargainPDA.com (www.bargainpda.com)**   Shopping, discussion forums, and a summary with links to used handheld device sales on eBay.

■ **PalmStation (www.palmstation.com)**   A Palm news and ramblings site.

■ **The Gadgeteer (www.the-gadgeteer.com)**   A massive set of reviews of just about every high-tech gadget that Julie and Judie, the site authors, can get their hands on. Material useful for the mobile enthusiast often shows up here.

■ **PalmLoyal.com (www.palmloyal.com)**   Software, links, and Palm discussion.

■ **HappyPalm (www.happypalm.com)**   A Palm fan's thread of news and ramblings about Palm devices.

■ **EuroCool (www.eurocool.com)**   A Palm news and discussion forum with a European flavor.

Software

The following sites are focused solely on software. Some are for Palm only; others offer software for a variety of handhelds and mobile devices. Most of the sites advertise a mixture of freeware, shareware, and trial software. Sites like Handango actually sell the software, and CNET has free downloads.

■ **Handango (www.handango.com)**   One of the most popular mobile software sites.

■ **FreewarePalm (www.freewarepalm.com)**   A host of free applications for your Treo.

■ **VersionTracker (www.versiontracker.com/palmos)**   The latest Palm software with optional e-mail updates.

■ **PalmGear (www.palmgear.com)**   Palm software, accessories, and more. At last check, over 21,000 software titles were available for downloading. At PalmGear, you'll also find active discussion forums and knowledge bases for learning more about your devices.

■ **CNET Download.com (www.download.com)**   Downloads of all shapes and sizes, but if you select Palm OS applications specifically, it will filter for you.

B

- ■ **Tucows (pda.tucows.com/palm.html)**   Many shareware applications for your Palm OS device.

- ■ **PDA Buyer's Guide (www.pdabuyersguide.com)**   An online review and product resource for PDA buyers. This site covers all PDA types, not just devices that run Palm OS.

Magazines

There are a variety of both print and electronic publications for the Palm OS, although, so far, no magazines have surfaced that are dedicated to just the Treo 600! A couple of the more popular publications are listed here:

- ■ *Palmtop User* **(www.palmtop.co.uk/palmuser)**   A bimonthly print magazine with lots of useful information for all Palm OS users.

- ■ *Palm Tipsheet* **(www.palmtipsheet.com)**   A free monthly electronic newsletter with useful information on the Palm platform and tips for how to use it better.

Conferences

Conferences are always an interesting place to get up-to-date information on the mobile computing world and meet other enthusiasts who use Treo and Palm devices. Conferences can be a little expensive, but if you learn of a conference in your area, the exhibit halls are usually free.

PalmSource Developer Conference

The PalmSource Developer Conference is an annual conference geared primarily toward developers of Palm OS accessories and software. However, this is often the place where new leading-edge products that may be useful to you on your Treo are announced. Full information can be found on the PalmSource web site at www.palmsource.com.

COMDEX

The main COMDEX conference is held annually in Las Vegas. It is a huge conference, related to everything in the high-tech industry. Its coverage is very broad, but mobile computing, Treos, and Palm devices are an important part of the show every year.

Smaller, regional versions of this show are held in Vancouver, Toronto, Chicago, and Atlanta. The organizers of this conference have now gone global and hold COMDEX shows in Greece, Scandinavia, Australia, Saudi Arabia, China, Egypt, Mexico, Japan, Korea, Switzerland, France, and more. More information can be found at www.comdex.com.

Mobile & Wireless World

Owned and produced by *Computerworld* magazine, this conference focuses specifically on how wireless and mobile technologies are affecting, or in the future may affect, the enterprise workspace. More information is available at www.mwwusa.com.

CES

For a more consumer-oriented look at the mobile space, you will find there is a lot to see at the Consumer Electronics Show (CES) held each year in Las Vegas. This is an extremely large show with over 100,000 attendees annually and over 2,000 exhibitors. It focuses on all aspects of computer electronics, but Palm OS applications and hardware are part of the action. For more information, visit www.cesweb.org.

3GSM World Congress

The 3GSM World Congress conference in Cannes, France is one of the main forums where new mobility products and technologies are discussed and introduced. Not only the Treo, but certainly the Treo 600 and related products, will be there. With over 26,000 attendees from 154 countries and almost 600 exhibitors, this is a very large event. More information can be found at www.3gsmworldcongress.com/congress.

B

Index

Numbers

3COM, 6
3D Air Hockey, 235
3D Master Thief FREE Demo Mission 1.3, 235
3GSM World Congress, 447
802.11 expansions cards, 145–146

A

About screen, Palm Mail, 173
AC charger cable, 20
access point name (APN), 116
accessibility, web-based e-mail accounts, 159
accidental calls, preventing with Keyguard, 101–102
account balances, Pocket Quicken, 330
Account List screen, Pocket Quicken, 328–331
accounts, e-mail
finding your, 158
setting up, 158–160
types of, 157–158
action games, 234–235
adapters
cassette adapter for car stereo, 230
headset jack, 24
stereo headphone, 217
add-ins, Palm Desktop, 76
Address Book
Contacts, 51, 76
defined, 59
using, 65–66
Adobe Acrobat, 321–322
Adobe Photoshop, 197, 203
AeroPlayer, 217, 231
Agenda view, Calendar, 259
Agendus 7.0, 278

A-GPS (Assisted GPS), 367
alarm clock, 250
alarms
event-related, 263
setting for Date Book event, 65
alerts
not missing, 251
Palm Mail preferences, 172
SMS messages and, 143
antenna, 22
antivirus applications, 358–361
for Linux PCs, 360
for Mac PCs, 360
third-party suppliers, 359–361
for Treo 600, 361
for Windows PCs, 359–360
AnyWho, 86
APN (access point name), 116
Apple
Macintosh. *See* Macintosh
Newton, 6
applications, 43–50
beaming, 53–54
Blazer Web Browser, 49
Calc, 44–45
Calendar, 45–46
CityTime, 46
To Do List, 49
Documents To Go, 47
downloading/installing, 144–145
games, 49–50
installing with Palm Desktop, 67–68
launching, 39–40
Mail, 47
Memo Pad, 47
MMS, 48

INTERNATIONAL CONTACT INFORMATION

AUSTRALIA
McGraw-Hill Book Company
Australia Pty. Ltd.
TEL +61-2-9900-1800
FAX +61-2-9878-8881
http://www.mcgraw-hill.com.au
books-it_sydney@mcgraw-hill.com

CANADA
McGraw-Hill Ryerson Ltd.
TEL +905-430-5000
FAX +905-430-5020
http://www.mcgraw-hill.ca

**GREECE, MIDDLE EAST, & AFRICA
(Excluding South Africa)**
McGraw-Hill Hellas
TEL +30-210-6560-990
TEL +30-210-6560-993
TEL +30-210-6560-994
FAX +30-210-6545-525

MEXICO (Also serving Latin America)
McGraw-Hill Interamericana Editores
S.A. de C.V.
TEL +525-1500-5108
FAX +525-117-1589
http://www.mcgraw-hill.com.mx
carlos_ruiz@mcgraw-hill.com

SINGAPORE (Serving Asia)
McGraw-Hill Book Company
TEL +65-6863-1580
FAX +65-6862-3354
http://www.mcgraw-hill.com.sg
mghasia@mcgraw-hill.com

SOUTH AFRICA
McGraw-Hill South Africa
TEL +27-11-622-7512
FAX +27-11-622-9045
robyn_swanepoel@mcgraw-hill.com

SPAIN
McGraw-Hill/
Interamericana de España, S.A.U.
TEL +34-91-180-3000
FAX +34-91-372-8513
http://www.mcgraw-hill.es
professional@mcgraw-hill.es

**UNITED KINGDOM, NORTHERN,
EASTERN, & CENTRAL EUROPE**
McGraw-Hill Education Europe
TEL +44-1-628-502500
FAX +44-1-628-770224
http://www.mcgraw-hill.co.uk
emea_queries@mcgraw-hill.com

ALL OTHER INQUIRIES Contact:
McGraw-Hill/Osborne
TEL +1-510-420-7700
FAX +1-510-420-7703
http://www.osborne.com
omg_international@mcgraw-hill.com

Sound Off!

Visit us at **www.osborne.com/bookregistration** and let us know what you thought of this book. While you're online you'll have the opportunity to register for newsletters and special offers from McGraw-Hill/Osborne.

We want to hear from you!

Sneak Peek

Visit us today at **www.betabooks.com** and see what's coming from McGraw-Hill/Osborne tomorrow!

Based on the successful software paradigm, Bet@Books™ allows computing professionals to view partial and sometimes complete text versions of selected titles online. Bet@Books™ viewing is free, invites comments and feedback, and allows you to "test drive" books in progress on the subjects that interest you the most.